MW01273503

Two Years in the Klondike and Alaskan Gold-Fields

1896–1898

Two Years in the Klondike and Alaskan Gold-Fields

1896–1898

A Thrilling Narrative of Life in the Gold Mines and Camps

BY

William B. Haskell

(A Returned Gold Miner and Prospector)

WITH PREFACE BY

Terrence Cole

UNIVERSITY OF ALASKA PRESS

FAIRBANKS, ALASKA

Library of Congress Cataloging-in-Publication Data

Haskell, William B.
    [Two years in the Klondike and Alaskan gold-fields]
    Two years in the Klondike and Alaskan gold-fields, 1896-1898 : a thrilling narrative of life in the gold mines and camps / by William B. Haskell ; with preface by Terrence Cole.
        p. cm. — (Classic reprint series ; no. 5)
    Originally published: Two years in the Klondike and Alaskan gold-fields. Hartford, Conn. : Hartford Pub. Co., 1898.
    Includes index.
    ISBN 1-889963-01-1 (cloth : acid-free paper). ISBN 1-88963-00-3 (pbk. : acid-free paper)
    1. Klondike River Valley (Yukon)—Gold discoveries. 2. Alaska-Gold discoveries. 3. Haskell, William B.—Journeys. 4. Klondike River Valley (Yukon)—Description and travel. 5. Alaska—Description and travel. 6. Yukon River Valley (Yukon and Alaska)—Description and travel. I. Title. II. Series: Classic reprint series (Fairbanks, Alaska) ; no. 5.
F1095.K5H37 1997
971.9'1—dc21   97-39397
                                                                 CIP

Originally published 1898 as *Two Years in the Klondike and Alaskan Gold-Fields* by Hartford Publishing Company, Hartford, Conn.

Preface by Terrence Cole © 1998 University of Alaska Press

International Standard Book Number: cloth 1-889963-01-1
                                              paper 1-889963-00-3

Library of Congress Catalog Number: 97-39397

Printed in the United States by Thomson-Shore, Inc.

This publication was printed on acid-free paper that meets the minimum requirements of American National Standard for Information Sciences-Permanence of Paper for Printed Library Materials, ANSI Z39.48-1984.

Publication coordination by Deborah Van Stone, University of Alaska Press
Cover design by Dixon Jones, Rasmuson Library Graphics, University of Alaska Fairbanks.
Index prepared by Kish Indexing Service, Mendocino, CA

Cover illustration: "Bound for Klondyke: A Prospectors' Camp on the Road to the Mines, Dinner in the Snow," drawn by J. Gulich. From the front page of *The Graphic. An Illustrated Weekly*, October 2, 1897, No. 1453-Vol. LVL.

This facsimile reproduction made possible by the Alaska and Polar Regions Department of the Elmer E. Rasmuson Library, who provided the University of Alaska Press with a copy of the original publication.

Two Years in the Klondike and Alaskan Gold Fields 1896–1898 is volume No. 5 of the University of Alaska Press's Classic Reprint Series. This series brings back into print highly regarded, classic works of enduring excellence. For more information contact the University of Alaska Press, P.O. Box 756240, University of Alaska Fairbanks, Fairbanks, Alaska, 99775-6240.

CONTENTS.

List of Illustrations.

From Special Photographs made expressly for this Work,
and not Published Elsewhere

PREFACE

BEFORE reading any memoir of the Klondike gold rush, it is wise to remember the warning that appeared in the *Seattle Times* in August 1897. "They now say there are more liars to the square inch in Alaska than any place in the world."[1]

Gold fever and gullibility naturally go hand in hand, but the Klondike craze of 1897–1898 stretched the limits of irrationality to new heights. As one reporter said, the discovery of gold in the Klondike unleashed such a barrage of crazy schemes for instant riches, it seemed as if some gigantic "insane asylum had been thrown open, and the inmates turned loose."

"The magic word 'Klondike' seems to be ample indorsement [*sic*] in the estimation of the public for any kind of an Alaskan proposition," the *Chicago Tribune* stated in the summer of 1897, "no matter how wild or ridiculous its scope.... If some crazy man should propose the sawing of the flinty Alaskan ice into railway ties and telegraph poles...it would cause no more than a passing spasm of surprise. Everything is possible in Alaska, according to the promoters."[2]

---

1. *Seattle Daily Times*, August 17, 1897.
2. *Chicago Daily Tribune*, August 8, 1897, p. 26.

A San Diego woman who followed the occult pleaded
for money to fund a Klondike expedition in January 1898.
"Now, you need not smile," she wrote, "but I know a man,
with great psychic powers, who has studied occult science in
Egypt, and this man has the power of leaving his body....
He recently left his body and went up to the Klondike
region, and there he discovered a wonderful amount of gold."
She and her far-ranging psychic traveler pledged to go back
to the Klondike, and promised to bring home "TONS and
TONS" of gold for whoever would provide them with a
grubstake to feed their mortal shells.[3]

William B. Haskell never claimed to have traveled on
the astral plane, never tried to leave home without his body,
but he returned from the Klondike in 1898 with his own
remarkable story. Haskell's *Two Years in the Klondike and
Alaskan Gold-Fields* (1898) is a literary and historical gem,
far superior in both style and substance to any other Klondike
memoir, and deserves a place on the shelf of classic western
literature. In the tradition of Richard Henry Dana's *Two Years
Before the Mast*, William B. Haskell's *Two Years in the
Klondike* tells the hard reality of a young man's quest for
adventure. Well crafted and rich with humor and authentic
detail, Haskell's book gives a vivid portrait of mining camp
life and death that rivals the work of Bret Harte, Mark Twain
or Jack London.[4] Though what became of Haskell after 1898
is not clear—apparently he never wrote another book—he
left an enduring legacy.

Haskell's autobiography has been a major source for
every thorough history of the gold rush era in the past

3. *Seattle Daily Times*, January 18, 1898, p. 5.

4. Another authoritative contemporary account of the Klondike gold rush
was *The Klondike Stampede* (1899) by Tappen Adney, a correspondent for
Harper's Weekly.

century, even though his book has actually been out of print for nearly a hundred years. This new edition of his memoir, published in commemoration of the gold rush centennial, brings back his remarkable eyewitness account of the Klondike stampede.[5]

Most of the Klondike books that swamped the market during and after the 1897–1898 gold rush were as useless as the multitude of Klondike scams pawned off on unwary gold seekers, like food pills, magic gold separators, gold mining gophers, ice locomotives, homing pigeons, and Arctic underwear. Publishers eager to cash in on the rush churned out a library-load of Klondike memoirs and Klondike travel guides, instant books by instant experts, usually comprised of material lifted from government reports, newspaper accounts, and other guidebooks.

"The east is being flooded with worthless publications about the Klondike," the *San Francisco Chronicle* complained in August 1897, "most of which are filled with revamped stuff about gold mining in California and other countries."[6]

In September 1897 the *Seattle Post-Intelligencer*, about to unveil its own Klondike Special Edition, blasted the trashy Klondike books which lacked both truth and literary merit. "During the past summer," the Seattle editor stated, "several books containing alleged 'Facts About Klondike' have been published and circulated, but in none of them has there been any reality. They have contained a mass of jumbled up matter, disconnected, incomplete and often unreliable."[7]

---

5. The editor thanks Alaska history buff Dan Perkins of Halibut Cove for initially recommending a reprint of Haskell's classic account.

6. *San Francisco Chronicle*, August 26, 1897, p. 6.

7. *Seattle Post-Intelligencer*, September 29, 1897, p. 4.

Generally Klondike books varied in price anywhere from twenty-five cents to as much as two dollars. High pressure salesmen peddling A. C. Harris' *Alaska and the Klondike Gold Fields* (1897) door to door were urged to "work eight to twelve hours every day. Visit every house, and try to sell a book to every voter in your territory." Equipped with a special large pocket inside their coats, to keep the prospectus hidden until just the right moment, the agent approached each home with a memorized spiel.

"Good morning, Mr.———. My name is ———, and I am introducing a work in which everybody is interested. I say everybody, for I have found such to be the case. A great deal is said...about the wonderful discoveries of gold in Alaska, and people want to know all about it. They want reliable information, not mere newspaper stories that one can place little dependence upon. Now here is a work that is reliable; and it is comprehensive, telling you all about Alaska and the Gold-fields."

"[*Now show your canvassing-book, and call attention to its size, the style of binding, the excellent quality of the paper, and read the title-page in a clear distinct voice, having previously practiced it until you can read it fluently....*]"

After listing the many topics covered in the book, the agents were told to "read over the names of your influential subscribers," and mesmerize the customers with the "array of signatures" on the order form. "Men often subscribe because their neighbors have."[8]

Every volume on the market claimed to be the indispensable Klondike Bible for gold seekers, the only true word on what was needed in the north, and warned of the dangers

---

8. A. C. Harris, *Alaska and the Klondike Gold Fields* (J. R. Jones, 1897); *Chicago Tribune*, August 9, 1897, p. 3.

of rival publications. "Beware of the *worthless catch-penny* books that are being issued," stated one Klondike publisher, "prepared by *newspaper* men with *paste and scissors* out of clippings from newspapers—*wholly untrustworthy*."[9] The so-called *Official Guide to the Klondyke Country and the Gold Fields of Alaska* (1897) from the W. B. Conkey Co. of Chicago—official only because it was mostly stolen from official-looking articles and documents—claimed to include all the "useful and trustworthy" information about the Klondike. "There is living and reliable authority at the back of almost every statement," it claimed.[10]

Charles Frederick Stansbury, author of *Klondike: The Land of Gold* (1897), honestly admitted he knew nothing about the Klondike when he started his book, and only wrote it because he wanted practical information in "a non-hysterical and concrete form…. Not being able to find it, he compiled this volume from the best sources of information for the benefit of himself and the public."[11]

Ghostwritten accounts by men who had returned from the Klondike, personal stories of the trail from rags to riches, appealed to a wide audience. William Stanley, the Seattle newsdealer who returned home with $112,000 in gold dust, hired a secretary to help write *A Mile of Gold*. He professed to have no interest in whether his autobiographical account earned a profit. "If it entertains or instructs my readers, I will be well satisfied," Stanley claimed, "even though it does

---

9. Ernest Ingersoll, *In Richest Alaska and the Gold Fields of the Klondike*, (Chicago: The Dominion Co., 1897), advertising broadside.

10. *The Official Guide to the Klondyke Country and the Gold Fields of Alaska*, (Chicago: W. B. Conkey, 1897), p. 15.

11. Charles Frederick Stansbury, *Klondike: The Land of Gold* (New York: F. Tennyson Neely, 1897), p. 1.

not result in a financial success, for of gold I have enough and to spare."[12]

J. I. Clements, one of the discoverers of Eldorado Creek, said he wrote *The Klondyke* because after he returned from the Yukon he was "besieged daily by hosts of friends, acquaintances and strangers, and deluged with letters from all parts of the American Continent" asking about the gold fields. "Unlike most of the books published on the Klondyke," his editor said, "this book is not full of wild, crazy statements made by irresponsible persons...."[13]

The vast wasteland of fake gold rush literature could have papered the trail all the way to the Klondike and back. In this literary wilderness William Haskell's 1898 "thrilling narrative" of *Two Years in the Klondike and Alaskan Gold-Fields* is unique. In a charming, witty and poetic style, Haskell writes of his trek to Fortymile and Circle City in the spring of 1896 preceding the Klondike discovery, and recounts his adventures in the gold fields before and after the stampede of 1897–1898. This gritty and realistic account of life in the north on the eve of the Klondike rush also details the enormous changes that took place once the flood of stampeders arrived.

Few biographical facts are known about Haskell other than what appears in this book.[14] Born on a farm in Vermont just after the Civil War, he was sent at age fifteen by his parents to boarding school in Massachusetts. "Anything like

12. William Stanley, *A Mile of Gold* (Chicago: Laird and Lee, 1898), p. 151. See also *Seattle Times*, September 10, 1897.

13. J. I. Clements, *The Klondyke* (Los Angeles: B. R. Baumgardt and Co., 1897), p. 7.

14. Haskell is listed in the 1901 census records for Dawson City, available at the Dawson City Museum in the Yukon Territory.

hard study was out of my line," Haskell wrote, "and I seldom engaged in it. I would sit for hours and hear the city boys tell stories, would read tales of wonderful adventure, forgetting entirely to go to bed.... I wandered about aimlessly in the fields of literature, not neglecting the great masters. But I never studied the lessons staked out by the teachers like so many narrow garden plats."[15]

After leaving school Haskell found himself at age twenty-two behind the counter of a Boston mercantile store. "It took very little time," he admitted, "for me to discover that there was no romance in the life of a dry-goods clerk."[16] His quest for "aimless adventure" took him west to Colorado and eventually Alaska in March 1896 following "rumors of gold." At that time, nearly a year and a half before the start of the great stampede, he joined a slow but steady stream of prospectors crossing the passes into the Yukon basin.

Haskell was a keen observer of human nature and his insightful, witty comments on conditions in the Yukon Valley in 1896–1897 are delightful reading. These are among the finest pages in all of Alaskan literature, with choice sentences and paragraphs worth savoring slowly in every chapter. Whatever the topic, his comments have a ring of originality and authenticity, and a list of his witticisms could fill an encyclopedia of Alaskan life.

On traveling conditions: "The man who travels in Alaska only when the weather is good will make about a mile a month, on an average. And it is a country of magnificent distances."[17]

---

15. See page 35.

16. See page 37.

17. See pages 101-102.

On the regularity of mail: "If any one is looking for a strong illustration of the uncertainties of existence in this world, he can find nothing better than the mail service on the Yukon."[18]

On the quality of Alaskan bread: "It was a question whether the gold dust or some of the bread made in that camp had the greater specific gravity. It is fortunate that in such a climate the digestive organs are equal to almost anything."[19]

On the lack of reading material: "If one wishes to realize how interesting (labels on boxes of food) can be, let him camp in a gulch somewhere in latitude sixty-four, North America. A trademark on a pick handle becomes fairly eloquent in that solitude."[20]

On hunger: "Many a time that winter I would often have gladly given one hundred dollars in nuggets for a slice of beefsteak. It did seem at times as if all the riches we were taking out were not to be compared with even the lowliest home in civilization."[21]

On the weather: "'Does it always rain here?' I once heard a traveler ask of an Indian. 'Snow sometimes,' replied the native in the most matter-of-fact manner."[22]

On the aurora: "The more I reflect on this life and the hereafter, the more I am in doubt as to whether the gold in the frozen placers of Alaska is in itself worth going after. But the aurora of Alaska is worth seeing, even if you have to live on short rations of bacon and beans for three months and find no gold."[23]

---

18. See page 443.

19. See page 297.

20. See page 295.

21. See page 296.

22. See page 73.

23. See page 316.

On the White Horse Rapids: "Terrible as is the experience, there are few places more sublime to the view. Standing on the bank in safety, the eye is charmed by the waters that leap and foam around the highly-colored rocks. You may watch it for hours and turn away with regret.... Everything is on a grand scale, and one acquires a faint realization of what this planet must have been in those un-trimmed, uncut, glacial times when the earth was dotted with raging waters like these, and mammoths stalked or crawled about the gloomy hillsides."[24]

On the lure of the dance hall: "After long seasons of hard work in the mines up the creeks...even the rasping music of a dance hall sounds sweet. The rough miner delights in a bit of a square dance, or the enlivement of a reel, or, possibly, if his early education has not been neglected, of a waltz or polka. He knows that he is in a society which cares nothing about the cut of his clothes, and is not critical about the grace of his steps."[25]

On growing a beard in winter: "...It becomes a solid mass of ice, and cannot be thrown off like a parka when entering a warm room. The only thing to do is to sit over the fire and let the glacier on your chin melt. In view of this inconvenience, the majority of miners keep their whiskers trimmed very short in winter, and allow them to grow in the summer as a protection against mosquitoes. Then they are a real blessing, and many times a man will wish himself as hairy as a baboon."[26]

Readers may pick and choose from the literary treasures in this book, but among my favorites are Haskell's reflections on mosquitoes, which he called "thorns in the flesh and destroyers of the soul. For he is a pretty good

24. See pages 129-130.

25. See page 164.

26. See page 312.

missionary in Alaska who will not swear once in a while in the mosquito season." Everyone who has ever been to Alaska in the summertime can tell stories about the horrific mosquitoes, but no one has ever matched Haskell's poetic depiction of walking through a swarm, like Moses trying to part the Red Sea. "One may hurl a blanket through a cloud of them, but ranks are closed up and the cloud is again intact before the blanket has hit the ground. All day long, and of course in July that means for about twenty-four hours, they are on the alert, always after anything that has blood in its veins. Any one who reads the Bible in this region in the summer must wonder at the weak nature of Pharaoh. There surely never could be a plague like this."[27]

Today's reader can not help but be struck by Haskell's generally insulting references to Native peoples. His blindness to the charms of Indian cultures is all too obvious. In contrast his perceptive analysis of the place of women in northern society seems strikingly modern, as if the words were penned in the 1990s rather than the 1890s. Unlike many other gold rush participants, he took the women who went north seriously, instead of simply dismissing them as foolish females trying to do men's work.

Along the trail to Chilkoot Pass, Haskell observed women unlike any he had ever seen in his life. "One could not fail to notice many instances...in which the women seemed to show a fortitude superior to the men. It was a revelation, almost a mystery. But after a while I began to account for it as the natural result of an escape from the multitude of social customs and restraints which in civilized society hedge about a woman's life.... She steps out of her dress into trousers in a region where nobody cares. Her nature

27. See page 156.

suddenly becomes aware of a freedom which is in a way exhilarating. She has, as it were, thrown off the fetters which civilized society imposes...."[28]

Haskell's partner drowned in an accident on the trail as they were leaving the gold fields, and the tragedy left him numb with grief. Consumed with the bitter memory of his friend's death, he could barely comprehend the Klondike craze he found sweeping the country upon his return to the West Coast in early 1898. "To one who has just returned from a two-years experience in the gold regions of the Yukon, who has seen death and suffering as an incident of everyday life, who knows what mining in Alaska or in the Klondike means...and who has seen his dearest friend swept away under the ice by a raging river which can count its victims by the score, these preparations for rushing for fortunes into those frozen mountains appeared like madness."[29]

His advice for those planning to head North was simple: Don't Go! But the constant cry of the Klondike chorus drowned out sane discussion. "Wherever I went I heard little but 'Klondike' talked about on the cars, in the hotels, in the saloons, and even on Sundays at church. Whenever you observed a knot of men in the street, in a rural highway, or in any public place in California, you were pretty sure to find that the latest news of new strikes in the Klondike diggings was under discussion.... 'Yes, I'm going this spring,' was a popular button worn."[30]

Demand for information about the Klondike, he said, "amounted almost to hunger. The public libraries all had constant calls for literature relating to Alaska. All the returned Klondikers were run after and appealed to by crowds

28. See page 81.
29. See page 528.
30. See page 521.

of men and a few women for Klondike information. The more successful Klondikers were driven to exasperation by unaccountable questions from droves of people."[31]

The insatiable public desire for knowledge of the Klondike inspired Haskell to write his blunt account of the real conditions which he knew awaited potential gold seekers. No matter what the public wanted to believe, he wrote, "gold does not grow upon the bushes of the Yukon hills."[32] Despite his conviction that anyone planning a trip north in 1898 was making a horrible mistake, he nevertheless included an entire chapter of practical suggestions for those who insisted on going anyway.

"Take no trunks. They are about as difficult to get over the passes as six-story buildings."

"It is constructive suicide for one to go to the Klondike with less than one year's supply of food."

"Fur coats might seem valuable, and some will say that they are. They are most usually worn when people are having their pictures taken to send home to their friends."

"Revolvers will get you into trouble, and there is no use of taking them with you...."[33]

Despite Haskell's hard-won knowledge, his readers were no more likely to find gold than anyone else. In the end so few individuals found gold that historian Pierre Berton called the Klondike gold rush "one of the most useless mass movements in history."[34] Certainly the stampeders of 1898

---

31. See page 523.

32. See page 531.

33. See pages 553-555.

34. Pierre Berton, Klondike Fever (New York: Alfred A. Knopf, 1974), p. 433.

would have never dreamed that after a hundred years one of the most lasting treasures from the gold rush would be a book some carried with them, a book about one man's adventures in the Klondike.

−Terrence Cole
History Department
University of Alaska Fairbanks

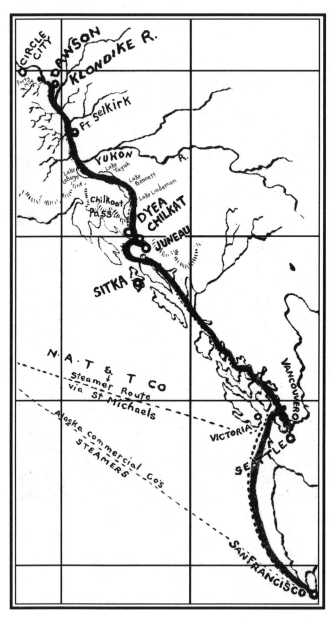

ALASKA AND THE KLONDIKE
WITH DETAIL OF ROUTES ABOVE.

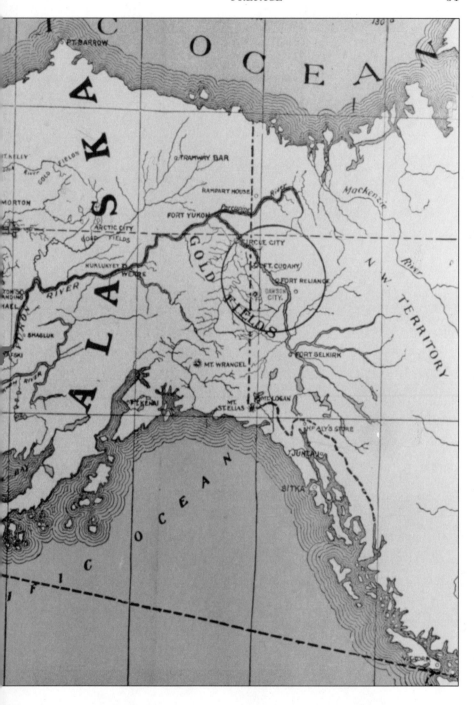

TWO YEARS

IN

THE KLONDIKE AND ALASKAN

GOLD FIELDS

CHAPTER I

MY BOYHOOD AND EARLY LIFE — WHAT LED ME TO
ADOPT THE LIFE OF A GOLD-SEEKER — WHY MY
EYES WERE TURNED TOWARDS ALASKA.

Boyhood on a Vermont Farm — Scanty Rewards of Toil — Forgetting
the Cows — My Father Has Ambitions for Me — I Am Sent to School
but Am Negligent in Study — The Mystery of Inheritance — Book
Knowledge — I Choose a Business Career in the City — Behind a
Counter in a Dry-goods Store — My Unhappy Lot — Sighing for
the Great West — Temptation to Break Away — It Finally Over-
comes Me — News of Wonderful Finds of Gold — I Take My Little
Belongings and Arrive in Chicago — Life as a Brakeman — Falling
in with Gold Miners — Something about Nuggets — A Tramp's
Luck — The Creede Rush — Cripple Creek — Two Irish Boys and
Their Mountain Patch — Meeting Joe — Alaska for the Gold-Seeker.

THIS is the plain story of one who began life in a little
township of Vermont about thirty-two years ago,
and who, several times during the past two years,
has been dangerously near losing it in a search for gold
along the glacier-bound coasts of Alaska, in the frozen
regions of the Yukon, and in the rich gulches of the Klondike.

It is of the observations, adventures, and experiences of
the last two years that this story is written. That of the
first thirty may be briefly told, for it is commonplace —
the story of a country boy upon whose future career his

(33)

struggling parents built great expectations only to be cruelly
disappointed.   That is usual enough, for parental fondness
always indulges extravagant hopes in a youth whose own
more moderate expectations are seldom realized, even after
his hardest struggles.   If at last there comes a time when,
in some measure, their fond anticipations are realized, they
may be sleeping in their narrow graves.   My parents were
industrious and poor, a combination of circumstances of
which life affords many instances, especially upon remote
and somewhat stubborn New England farms.   A boy growing up in such surroundings could not fail to be impressed
with the scanty rewards of the most unremitting toil.

But any boy finds sources of delight in his surroundings,
be they never so poor and unpromising, and, though early
enlisted in some of the necessary work of the farm, such as
replenishing the wood-pile and churning the cream, my
inclinations were always to wander in the woods or over the
meadows, chasing the squirrels, or endeavoring to drive
the woodchucks from their holes; so that many times when
sent off on the mountainside after the cows, I often entirely
forgot my errand in the pursuit of some chance game or
childish fancy.   The admonitions of my father on such occasions never seemed to do any good.   Seldom was I able
to enter with persistence and interest into any useful piece
of work.

But for one thing, however, I should probably have remained there on the farm like so many others, who, not
having looked beyond their own narrow horizons, settle
down to think their little world is like all the rest.   Though
very poor, my father entertained high ambitions for me,
and he determined, at whatever sacrifice, to provide me with
an education.   He never ceased to regret what he himself

lacked in this respect, and fondly hoped that, if I were blessed with a little learning, I would fill a place in the world of which he would be proud, and that his declining years would be years of happiness and contentment.

So at the age of fifteen I was sent away to an academy in Massachusetts, and immediately my ideas began to undergo a marvelous change. I became possessed by a desire to break away from the limitations of a routine life and rush into the great world of which I thought I saw a glimpse. But I had no definite purpose. I had not the least idea of what I should do if I entered the world which my imagination so brilliantly pictured. My disposition remained the same. It was simply let loose in a wider field, like an unbroken mustang. Anything like hard study was out of my line, and I seldom engaged in it. I would sit for hours and hear the city boys tell stories, would read tales of wonderful adventure, forgetting entirely to go to bed. Little by little my taste in reading improved, and I wandered about aimlessly in the fields of literature, not neglecting the great masters. But I never studied the lessons staked out by the teachers like so many narrow garden plats. I knew that my low marks were a severe trial to my parents, and it was painful to me, when I came to think of it and realize what a sacrifice they were making in my behalf. At times I would resolve to do better, and would try to study hard, but it was no use. My mind quickly fled away into more congenial fields.

It seems to me that it is unkind to hold a man too rigidly responsible for the mixture he finds in his nature. We are largely controlled by inherent qualities of which it is difficult to rid ourselves. These innate characteristics make us what we are, and I suppose that is why we are oblivious to our own faults. I know now that my disposition has always been that of a wanderer, though I cannot understand why I should have inherited such a nature from my parents. Possibly it may be explained upon the principle that the chemical union of substances results in combinations surprisingly different from the originals. It may be that a person can inherit a nature widely different from that of either parent, and still be the natural combination of their natures.

Notwithstanding my neglect of prescribed studies, I managed somehow to squeeze through the curriculum, and I was declared to be fitted for college, but really I was fit for nothing which had any definite aim in it. I had extracted from the books I had so diligently read a certain amount of information which, for the right person, would doubtless have been more useful than all that the hardest students had extracted from their text-books and teachers, but it was apparently of little use to me. My father had hoped that I would develop a determination to enter the ministry. He sat in his pew every Sunday, looked up to the minister and imagined me in the pulpit, eloquently holding forth upon decrees and judgments, while the people hung breathlessly upon my words. But I had no more taste for theology than for politics, which I entirely ignored. From my reading I had formed the opinion that a wise Providence would control the world in its own way, without regard to systems of theology, and that our civil government would somehow " run itself," no matter which party was in power. I was quite willing to let others expound theology, or struggle for political prizes. My nature was different, and my purpose, or lack of it, might be summed up, as nearly as it could be summed up at all, in the words " aimless adventure."

So I adroitly begged off from going to college, explaining to my father that, even if I had any inclination in that direction, I knew that he could not afford it, and that it would be better for me to go into business. I had no ambition in that direction either, but I had the unpleasant realization that I must do something for a living.

Thus it happened that at twenty-two I was behind a counter in a big dry-good store in Boston. It took very little time for me to discover that there was no romance in the life of a dry-goods clerk. The requirements were altogether too definite to suit my nature. All my inclinations were to drift about, to find adventure, to see life in its various phases, and there I was day after day for long hours in a crowded corner of a great store, answering myriads of questions, some of which I thought the women who asked them knew better how to answer than I, and calling for a cash boy who loitered until my customers had become impatient and upbraided me. Variety, there was none. I made my board, and a little more, because I paid very little for my board and received accordingly.

My Sunday respites brought me little consolation, for though they afforded me temporary delight in wandering off into the country, they only served to sharpen my appetite for greater freedom. I used to wish that a war would break out so that I could enlist and give my nature vent in an atmosphere of gunpowder. Often I thought of joining the recruits to the regular army, but upon investigation I concluded that there was little for a soldier to do except to waste his time in a dull routine.

To a spirit like mine the possibilities of the great West naturally appealed. I had very little idea what any part of it was like, and that is doubtless one of the reasons why I

longed to see it for myself.   It made no particular difference
to what part of it I went, nor was it essential that I should go
for any well-defined purpose.   That would take care of
itself; indeed, I disliked to be hampered by certainties.   I
knew I was not in my right place.   What business had I, a
big six-footer, built on Vermont lines, broad, muscular, and
tough, dallying behind a dry-goods counter! stuck up in a
corner like a house plant when I sighed for the free open air,
the winds, and the storm.

I clung resignedly to my unpleasant work, however,
saving all I could at many a bitter sacrifice of my inclinations, for I had sufficient wisdom to realize the risks of rushing empty-handed into regions of which I knew little, and
where no one knew me.   I was sick and discouraged at
times over the monotonous routine of my daily duties.

In such papers as I allowed myself to buy I always read
with great interest and care every scrap of information or
news about the Great West, and like many others, even with
a disposition less restless than mine, I was deeply impressed
with the stories of rich strikes in the mining regions and the
fortunes made in what seemed an incredibly short time.   I
began to read all I could lay my hands on relating to mines
and mining, and to study, with a zeal which I had never
shown before, the science of that great industry; thus acquiring a store of information that would be very valuable if
ever a time should come when it could be brought into connection with practical experience, but worth little without it.

In the spring of 1889 came the stories of the excitement caused along the Pacific coast by the discoveries
in Lower California.   During March an average of six hundred men a day rushed to the mines in the Santa Clara district, about one hundred and twenty miles south of San

Diego. One of the first workers, so the stories ran, washed out four thousand dollars' worth of gold in four hours, and a Mexican digger took out one thousand five hundred dollars in two days in a space eight feet square.

As I read these and similar tales, the temptation became too great for me to resist. I had as yet saved only a small amount of money, but I had enough to take me a part of the way, and then, I thought, I might secure employment further west, and a little nearer the region of the Pacific Coast. So, after one of my hardest, most exasperating days behind the counter, I resigned my position, and for the first time in many months walked to my boarding place with a light heart. After receiving what was due me at the store, and buying a ticket for Chicago, I packed my small belongings in a valise, and with my accumulated capital, about thirty dollars, in my pocket, westward I took my undetermined way.

Considerable time was lost in an unsuccessful search for employment at Chicago, and gradually my small capital became greatly reduced. I avoided the dry-goods stores and of course knew little about any other line of business. My eyes were still turned westward, and quite naturally I haunted the railway depots and offices until destitution finally compelled me to engage as a brakeman on a freight train on one of the leading lines running West from Chicago. It was a hard life, and yet I enjoyed some features of it. Even my imagination had not portrayed the Great West as I found it, with its broad stretches of prairie, its busy cities and towns, its teeming harvests, and thrifty homes.

Gradually I worked my way westward, constantly shifting from one division of the railroad to another, each tend-ing still farther west than the last, till one evening I found myself in Colorado Springs. Seeking out a moderate-priced hotel, I entered and found myself in an eating-room where a number of men were drinking and smoking, most of them engaged in earnest conversation. Seating myself at a vacant table, I ordered as good a meal as I thought was warranted by my rather scanty funds.

"Yes, thar's some mighty big stories 'bout fellers as struck it rich," I heard the old man who sat at the next table say to his companions, who were all considerably younger, "but I'm only tellin' what I've seen to be true. One day, when I was in Shasta county, 'bout fifteen years back, three fellers that looked like Frenchmen druv into town, and droppin' into a hardware store to get somethin' or other, asked the proprietor whar was a likely place to mine. They looked tenderfoot like, and I guess they was. The proprietor kinder careless like, ye know, p'inted north, and said ' Go over to Spring Creek.' Wal, sir, they went, and after prospecting around they located a claim a little ways up the stream, an' in a few days one o' them durn'd Frenchmen picked up a nugget wuth over six thousand.

"You don't find sech nuggets as them in these days," chimed in one of the younger men as he took out a roll of bills and beckoned to the waiter. He had a swaggering manner, and it was easy to see that the others regarded him with a degree of deference.

"How big d' ye say yourn was, Sandy?" asked the old man.

"Only forty-eight ounces, but it was enough, so I sold the claim for big money to the Denver parties."

"Wal, ye say, Sandy," resumed the old man, "that big strikes ain't made these days, but it ain't so long ago when

I was down on the Gila that I heard of a lucky find a little way off the Southern Pacific in Californy. Two fellers trampin' up the coast got put off a freight train at Calliente, and they started to hoof it to Bakersville. In two days, back they came to Calliente with a lump of gold and quartz. The boys thought they might have robbed a camp, and p'raps killed the miner to get it. But they told how they was goin' 'bout in the dry bed of an old stream not far from the Bealeville placer camp, in search of wood for a fire, and stumbled on the gold. They had offered to sell it to a railroad man before they came back to Calliente, but he suspected the strangers, and wouldn't bargain. Wal, sir that lump was sold afterwards in Los Angeles for two thousand seven hundred and fifty dollars. It weighed 116 ounces. The boys rushed into that old stream but they never found any more big nuggets."

I forgot my supper, hungry as I was. The effect of such conversation upon a tenderfoot with but a little silver in his pocket, and who was impatient to send comforting news to his far-away home in Vermont, may be imagined. " Roughing it," and "striking it rich," was just my ideal then. I had tried roughing it somewhat, and all I needed was to strike it rich.

" Excuse me, gentlemen," I said, slowly turning my chair, and somewhat nervously facing the group, " but I am down this way to see what I can do in a mining country, and I am interested in your talk. Is there any chance anywhere around here for a fellow like me to strike in? "

They looked at me critically for a moment, and the young fellow who seemed to be spending the money, said: " Stranger, you look all right, and I guess you are. Say, stranger, where you from? "

I told them that I came from New England, and they glanced at my clothes, which, notwithstanding the rough wear of the past few weeks, were not at all bad. At this the man whom they called " Sandy " informed me that he had just sold one of his claims, but he had another that could be bought for fair money, and his companions also began to expatiate upon the value of claims they would dispose of. I had to confess, sorely against my inclination, that my capital did not permit me to buy claims, but I would like to get work in a mining region, and trust to my luck.

It seems that Sandy had recently come in from the wild regions about Willow Creek, and a rush was then just beginning toward the place where Creede made his discovery. I listened eagerly to the stories of fabulous fortunes and sudden wealth narrated by these prospectors. To my overwrought imagination it seemed easy to become rich where gold was so abundant. The result was that the next day I started with a party of a dozen others on my first rush to gold fields. Thus it was that I began to supplement my store of book information about mining with the details of practical experience. These details were not unlike those of others in the mining districts of the Rockies, and the story has often been told. I worked in the mines till I secured a good understanding of mining as it was there conducted. I was grub-staked and spent much of my time wandering over the mountains, along creeks and streams, and through gulches. It was on the whole an agreeable life, but I failed to make a strike. That is also a story which has often been told.

Not long afterwards came the rush to Cripple Creek, where a cowboy had found in Poverty Gulch ore which, when taken to Colorado Springs, was found to yield two hundred and forty dollars to the ton. Those going in early found ore of even higher value. After the Buena Vista mine was sold, the attention of the entire country was attracted to Cripple Creek, and the great rush to that now famous district began. They poured in over the mountain tops and through the gulches, and claims were staked in all directions, regardless of the character of the rock. Many hardships were endured in the early days of the opening of this district, but a rough life proved not at all distasteful to me, though I met with no marked success. Still, there was always the chance, and, in some notable cases, men, after prospecting and suffering many hardships without success, had, when on the point of packing their traps and returning to their former employments, stumbled upon ore that made them rich within a few months.

One of the notable discoveries coming some little time after the rush was that of the Portland mine. Two Irish boys from Portland, Me., owned a small patch of poor land which they did not know exactly what to do with. One day a miner of some experience came along and asked what they would give if he found pay-rock for them. They offered a third. The miner found it that afternoon, and in time that third interest became worth millions.

I kept on prospecting, always buoyed up by the hope of making a great discovery that would eclipse all others and yield me a princely fortune.

In the fall of 1895 I fell in with another prospector about my age, named Joseph Meeker. There was a certain compatibility in our dispositions and tastes, and we soon became fast friends. Joe had originally come from North Carolina, but he had spent a year in Alaska, and had been mining for several years in Colorado, but with no better suc-

cess than had attended my efforts.   He never grew tired of
talking about Alaska.   It had a strange fascination for him,
and he would return to the subject again and again.   We
were sitting close to the fire in the cabin one night when Joe
suddenly inquired how much money I had.

"I've saved about eight hundred dollars," I replied,
wonderingly.   "Why?"

"I've got 'bout seven hundred dollars," he said, "and
I'll tell you why I ask.   You are strong and hearty.   You
ought to stand it, and I know I can.   The only place to
hunt for gold now is in Alaska.   I was up there two years
ago, worked in the Treadwell mills awhile, and in the summer crossed over to the upper Yukon.   There's gold there
in river banks, but the ground's frozen twenty feet deep,
and the climate is beastly in the winter.   I got caught on
the Yukon late in the fall, and had a hard time getting back.
I didn't have any outfit, and when I came out I was as near
dead as I could be.   But I believe that's the place for us,
and if we put our money together it will be enough to buy
a good outfit and pay our way to Alaska, and next spring we
can go in all right.   How does it strike you?"

The proposition startled me.   Alaska was a long way
off, and it was comparatively an unknown country.   I was
already far from home and kindred.   Besides I was not so
sanguine of success as my companion appeared to be, and
mining in a country where the ground was "frozen twenty
feet deep" did not at first impress me as a particularly attractive scheme.   I hesitated, but only for a few moments;
for, impelled by my restless and unsatisfied love of adventure, and the alluring possibilities in a new land from
whence rumors of gold had already come, I said, "I'll go."

CHAPTER II

ALASKA was about the only country of the world into
which my venturesome imagination had not taken
me. I knew that the United States bought it of
Russia in 1867 for less than half a cent an acre, but I had
never figured from the total purchase price how many acres
it made. It was something of a revelation to me, therefore, when Joe, who was an exceedingly well-informed man
in many ways, and particularly upon Alaska, convinced me
that this territory was nine times the size of New England,
twice the size of Texas, and three times that of California;
that it had a coast line of over eighteen thousand miles,

greater than that of all the rest of the United States, and
that, measuring from the most eastern point of Maine to
the most western point of the Aleutian Islands, which extend over into the eastern hemisphere, the half-way point
of the United States would be a little west of San Francisco.

Joe had a fund of general information concerning the
country. While I had been dreaming vaguely of the Great
West, he had been looking with quiet determination towards that land from which he had with so much difficulty
only recently escaped, and in spite of that severe experience
he had been working hard to save money enough to enable
him to return and prospect with safety on the Yukon.
While it was generally known that the first lease of two
tiny islands returned to the United States Treasury a sum
equal to the purchase money, and that the salmon industry
had yielded a like sum for the first six years of its establishment, the outside world had as yet heard very little about
its gold resources. Summer pleasure-seekers had turned
back at the Muir Glacier, which is over a thousand miles
south of Point Barrow, and had rarely ventured as far as
the Aleutian Islands, which stretch to a point two thousand
miles west of Sitka. A few explorers had wandered over
some of the rough Indian trails, and had nearly lost their
lives in climbing the snow-capped mountain peaks. For
several years poorly maintained trading posts had been collecting furs from the Indians, and here and there over the
vast region were mission stations which had produced little
effect on the dull and dirty natives. Dogs and Indians
were the beasts of burden, the dogs being far superior, for,
though born thieves, they would work under the lash; but
the Indians were lazy, and, after exacting the most extravagant prices for packing over the trails, were quite likely

to throw down their packs and return home, leaving the explorer helpless in the desolate regions. As all contracts with these Indians included their keeping, and as no one had had ever discovered a limit to their appetites when others provided the food, the poor explorer usually found that the Indian packers would eat up all they could carry before going far into the interior. At home they would live frugally on nothing but fish, some of it very ancient, for most of them were too lazy to catch any till driven to it by gnawing hunger. When carrying a pack for a white man they were rarely able to lift an ounce till they had eaten two or three pounds. Then they would trot along with a pack that no white man could stagger under.

What means of navigation existed on the Yukon were exceedingly primitive. Running two thousand miles across Alaska and into the Northwest Territory, into which the head tributaries stretched five hundred miles further, navigation could hardly be attempted before July, and towards the last of September the river generally began to freeze. The quickest way to reach the headwaters of the Yukon was overland from the coast, but one could do little more than take his life in his hands, to say nothing of provisions, if he ventured from the trails, which were full of dangers, while in the summer the mosquitoes, Joe emphatically said, had been known to "kill bears." In five months the country receives as much sunshine, or rather daylight, as California receives in eight, and in seven months as much night as California receives in nearly a year and a half.

"But there's gold there," said Joe. "And I know it."

It was the gold that he was thinking of, and though I was not unmindful of it either, I could not help but weave

fanciful pictures of life in a little-known country reputed
to be full of dangers, and hence attractive to one of my disposition. To me it was a pleasant picture to contemplate.
I knew nothing about the reality. What little was known
of the mineral possibilities of the country in the fall of 1895
was fairly well known by my partner, who had industri-
ously sought information from every possible source.

It is a curious fact, though an experienced miner will
not recognize it as such, that the Yukon and the streams
which flow into it have been prospected for years. The
reader must not suppose that all one has to do is to come to
the right spot to find gold staring him in the face. Experienced prospectors traveled many times over some of the
richest rocks in Colorado before their treasures were discovered, and the conditions along the frozen banks of the Yukon
are even more misleading, as will be seen later. But
as early as thirty years ago, even before the seventies, gold
was known to exist in the beds of the streams which empty
into the Yukon. Only a few prospectors ventured into
these forbidding regions and they found small returns for
their hardships and drudgery. It appears that the first real
prospecting was done by George Holt, who crossed either the
Chilkoot or the White Pass in 1878 and found coarse gold in
the Hootalinkwa river. In 1880 a party of twenty-five,
headed by Edward Bean, found bars yielding $2.50 a day on
a small tributary of the Lewis. In subsequent years gold
was found on the Big Salmon, Pelly, Hootalinkwa, Lewis,
and Stewart rivers. When Lieutenant Schwatka made his
trip down the Yukon in 1883 he made the acquaintance of
Joseph Ladue, who was years after to become famous as
the founder of Dawson. Ladue was digging about persistently, but he found little in the holes which he sunk with

the greatest difficulty. Schwatka also heard of others who had been prospecting many seasons with poor results. Still there were traces of gold almost everywhere, and a miner knows that where there are traces of the precious metal a source of supply must exist somewhere.

Early in the seventies there were miners working at the headwaters of the Pelly River, near the Cassiar Mountains, and, as will be seen by the map, near where some of the feeders of the Pelly and the Mackenzie approach each other. Some of them had learned of the existence of a large lake beyond the Cassiar and made an effort to reach it, but failed and returned disgusted. In 1872, two Irishmen named Harper and Hart; Fitch, a Canadian; Kanselar, a German; and Wilkinson, an Englishman, believing that gold existed on the Mackenzie because it had been found in some quantities on some of the principal streams, started on a prospecting trip. At Laird River they fell in with two men named McQuesten and Mayo, who were also prospecting. Wilkinson determined to try his luck there, but the others continued, and finally by way of Bell's River and the Porcupine came to Fort Yukon, an old supply point at the junction of the Porcupine and Yukon and close to the Arctic Circle. There they found an Indian who had some native copper which he said had come from White River, 400 miles up the Yukon.

They determined to work their way up there, and did eventually, but were stopped near the White River in September by ice. They built a cabin and during the winter prospected for the copper, but found none. By spring their provisions had run out and they started down the river again, prospecting as they went. They found indications of gold near the mouth of Stewart River, but could take no advantage of this till they had obtained provisions. They had to make their way nearly 2,000 miles to St. Michael, near the mouth of the Yukon, and on their way back met McQuestin and Mayo, who had meanwhile gone into the service of the Alaska Commercial Company.

When about 400 miles up the river and near the mouth of the Koyukuk they encountered an Indian having some gold which he said had come from the mountains in that vicinity. So they spent two years prospecting in that region, but with no results. Meantime, McQuestin and Mayo had gone up the Yukon and established Fort Reliance, six and a half miles from the stream which is now known as the Klondike. Harper and his companion joined them a little later and formed a trading partnership. The region near this stream was known only as a fishing and hunting ground, and no one thought of prospecting there then, for the beds were formed of uninviting dirt and nothing but surface prospecting was done. Harper had written concerning the traces of gold to some of his old comrades in British Columbia, where he had mined for years, and some of them made their way to the new diggings. Early in the eighties gold was found in the Stewart River, and it was about this time that rich quartz fields were discovered in the vicinity of Juneau, on the coast, and the attention of the outside world was mainly directed towards them. In 1886 Harper erected a trading post at the mouth of the Stewart for the benefit of the thirty or more miners who had been induced to go into these regions, but in the same year coarse gold was found on Forty Mile Creek. Coarse gold is the miner's delight, and as soon as the discovery became known, the Stewart River diggings, the product of which in 1885 and 1886 was estimated at $300,000, were deserted for

Forty Mile Creek, and Harper moved his trading post to that point; this was the beginning of the settlement of that name. The same year the Klondike stream, which then appeared on the maps as Deer River, was prospected for several miles, but no gold was found. On the other hand, gold was found nearly the whole length of Forty Mile River and in all its gulches. The news of this discovery was brought out by Tom Williams, who died at Dyea from the effects of cold and exhaustion endured in crossing the Chilkoot pass. His information caused several hundred men to go to Forty Mile from the Pacific Coast.

The only mining done on the Stewart was on the bars of the river. The bench and bank bars were all timbered and frozen so that to work them it was thought would entail a resort to hydraulic mining, for which there was no machinery in the country. During the fall of 1886 three or four miners combined and got the owners of one of the little river steamboats to allow the use of her engines to work pumps for sluicing with. The boat was hauled up on the bar, her engines detached from the wheels and made to drive pumps manufactured on the ground, thus supplying water for a set of sluice boxes. With this crude machinery the miners cleared $1,000 in less than a month, and paid an equal sum to the owners of the boat as their share.

But scarcely anything was heard of these discoveries by the outside world, though the Canadian agent reported them to his government. Few miners were there, the season for work was short, and the little gold which came down attracted no attention, while many rich mines were being discovered in Colorado and California.

Not long after the discovery of gold in Forty Mile Creek a few miners crossed the narrow divide which sep-

arates the headwaters of Forty Mile from those of Sixty
Mile and discovered gold on Miller and Glacier creeks.
The former had already been prospected three different
times and given up as worthless, but it turned out to be the
richest creek in the region and enjoyed that reputation for
years. In 1891 gold was found on the headwaters of Birch
Creek, which flows into the Yukon about forty miles below
Fort Yukon. According to the story which came down
the coast, this discovery was due to Archdeacon Macdonald,
a Canadian missionary on the Peel River, who in connection
with his missionary labors traveled over much of the
country. In coming from the Tanana River he picked up
a nugget in one of the gulches of Birch Creek. He told
some of the miners and a party made a search. While they
failed to find the place answering the missionary's description they found gold. This was the beginning of Circle
City, on the banks of the Yukon, about 200 miles below
Forty Mile and only a few miles by portage from Birch
Creek. During 1893 the Klondike stream was again prospected, but nothing was found. But Circle City attracted
to it many of the old miners who had had poor success on
other creeks and most of the newcomers. These, however,
were very few until 1894.

My partner had learned the story of some of these discoveries while at Juneau and during his unsuccessful venture inland. He returned to California in the hopes of
providing a good outfit, but was obliged to prospect and
work in the mines, trusting to luck to raise the necessary
money. Attracted by the stories which came down, several
hardy miners from California went up to the Yukon regions
in 1894, but Joe remained behind and worked hard to secure the means which he had learned by observation and

experience were required to prospect in such a wild country. Late in the summer of 1895, a lot of gold came down to San Francisco from the mouth of the Yukon, and for the first time Alaska began to attract a lively attention in the mining camps of the Rocky Mountains and along the Pacific Coast. Joe was greatly excited but knew it was too late that year to venture safely into the new El Dorado. When we became fast friends he saw the advantages of forming a partnership with me in the enterprise.

It was then November, and we wished to be ready to start by the first of March. He said it would be no use for us to try to start earlier, for owing to the difficulties of travel before the Yukon broke up no time would be gained, while a good deal of needless hardship would be incurred. It was fortunate for me that I had a companion who knew something of the route and what to expect. It would have been just like me to start in with little thought of provisions and with an inadequate outfit of clothing and supplies. We worked along till the end of the year making our plans, and early in January we bade good-bye to Colorado and started for San Francisco to secure our outfit and passage.

I have seen many statements of the outfit a man needs in going into the Alaska mining regions, but I have never seen one that enumerated all the things which a man wants after he is there. It must be borne in mind that he is going to a place which is practically cut off from the outside world for the greater part of the year and which is very little better, as far as supplies are concerned, at any time. All this may be remedied some time, but I was going in before the attention of the commercial world had been greatly attracted to the region. While one with money enough in his pocket can travel all over the United States and want for nothing, when he crosses the mountain passes or goes up the Yukon to the interior of Alaska he needs to have with him all that he is likely to want for a year. He may want it very badly and in vain, and still have any amount of gold in his pockets.

We secured a cheap boarding place near the wharves in San Francisco and soon set to work to collect such articles as Joe's experience and the best information we could obtain from every possible source convinced us would be necessary. After taking out of our capital what was needed for passage, living expenses till March, and quite a sum for expenses on the way, we concluded we might with the remainder purchase enough clothing and provisions for a year, or more, besides the necessary hardware.

I have a list of some of the things we purchased and others I have supplied from memory. The following is about what we took in the way of provisions:

Flour,	800 lbs.	Bacon,	300 lbs.
Corn Meal,	50 "	Dried Beef,	60 "
Rolled Oats,	80 "	Dry Salt Pork,	50 "
Pilot Bread,	50 "	Roast Coffee,	50 "
Baking Powder,	20 "	Tea,	25 "
Yeast Cakes,	6 "	Condensed Milk,	50 "
Baking Soda,	6 "	Butter, hermetically sealed,	40 "
Rice,	100 "	Salt,	40 "
Beans,	200 "	Ground Pepper,	3 "
Split Peas,	50 "	Ground Mustard,	2 "
Evaporated Potatoes,	50 "	Ginger,	2 "
Evaporated Onions,	20 "	Jamaica Ginger,	3 "
Beef Extract,	3 "	Evaporated Vinegar,	12 "
Evaporated Apples,	50 "	Matches,	25 "
Evaporated Peaches,	50 "	Candles, 2 boxes containing	
Evaporated Apricots,	50 "	240 candles,	80 "

Dried Raisins,	.	.	20 lbs.	Laundry Soap,	.	.	15 lbs.
Dried Figs,	.	.	20 "	Tar Soap,	.	.	5 "
Granulated Sugar,	.	.	150 "	Tobacco,	.	.	30 "

In the hardware line our outfit was of a more miscellaneous character and as complete as we knew how to make it, and everything came in handy. We purchased as follows:

1 Hand Saw.
2 Shovels.
30 pounds of Nails (assorted sizes).
½ dozen assorted Files.
2 Handled Axes.
2 Draw Knives.
1 Jack Plane.
1 Brace and 4 Bits.
3 Chisels, assorted.
2 Butcher Knives.
2 Hunting Knives.
2 Pocket Knives.
2 Compasses.
1 Set Awls and Tools.
150 feet of ⅜-inch Rope.
1 Medicine Case.
15 pounds of Pitch.
20 pounds of Oakum.
Pack Straps.
2 Gold Pans.
4 Galvanized Pails.
1 Whetstone.
2 Picks and Handles.
2 Prospector's Picks.
2 Grub Bags.

2 Hatchets.
1 Whip Saw.
2 Scissors.
Fish Lines and Hooks.
1 Gold Scale.
1 Chalk Line.
1 Measuring Tape.
2 Money Belts.
2 Cartridge Belts.
2 Gold Dust Bags (buckskin).
2 Pairs Snow Glasses.
6 Towels.
1 Caulking Iron.
Knives and Forks.
Table and Teaspoons.
2 Large Spoons.
2 Bread Pans.
Granite Cups.
Granite Plates.
2 Coffee Pots.
2 Frying Pans.
1 Stove (Yukon).
4 Granite Buckets.
1 Camp Kettle.

I have no exact record of the wearing apparel that formed an important part of our outfit, but it was ample. There is nothing in the following list which will not come in very handy if a man intends to move around in the rain storms of summer and in the frigid weather of an Alaskan winter:

3 Suits Underwear, extra heavy.	2 Pairs Leopard Seal Waterproof
2 Extra heavy double-breasted Flannel Overshirts.	1 Pair Hip Boots. [Mittens.
	2 Pairs Rubber Shoes.
1 Extra heavy Mackinaw Over-shirt.	2 Pairs Overalls.
	1 Waterproof, Blanket-Lined Coat.
1 Extra heavy all-wool double Sweater.	2 Pairs Blankets.
	1 Fur Cap.
6 Pairs long German knit Socks.	1 Wool Scarf.
2 Pairs German knit and shrunk Stockings, leather heels.	1 Pair Leather Suspenders.
	1 Extra Heavy Packing Bag.
1 Mackinaw Coat, extra heavy.	1 Suit Oil Clothing and Hat.
1 Pair Mackinaw Pants.	1 Doz. Bandana Handkerchiefs.
4 Pairs All-Wool Mittens.	1 Canvas Sleeping Bag.

Any woman who thinks of going to Alaska can read this list intended for a man and govern the selection of her garments accordingly.

Our outfit, which altogether we estimated would weigh about 3,200 pounds, embraced other little odds and ends, personal effects, and so on. We each had a rifle, and we also provided ourselves with revolvers. We haunted grocery stores and clothing houses for over a week, and as our purchases were delivered I began to get a dim realization of what Joe was preparing for. Still I was often surprised at the wholesale manner in which he bought. One day he bought a medicine chest, which looked like a miniature drug store. It had been recommended to him by a physician. It took up a lot of room and it was about the only thing that we did not use in our subsequent wanderings. The trouble was that we did not know how to use it. Some of the remedies might have been for blisters or cramps or any other human ailment so far as we knew. We managed

to sort out a few remedies with which we had some famil-
iarity. We found that a few stock remedies, such as most
persons are accustomed to use, are about all that it is worth
while to carry over the mountain trails and long voyages
by water. In winter a hot drink of tea did us more good
than anything else, and in summer a few quinine pills were
taken as bon-bons.

"Over a ton and a half," I said when the collection was
completed.

"You will think it weighs five times that before you get
it on the Yukon," remarked Joe. "But it's a mighty good
outfit, and I hope we shall get it there all right."

Joe was sometimes vague as to the details of some of the
difficulties for which he was so carefully providing; and
though a faint suspicion would now and then arise in my
mind when he confined himself to general statements in
answer to some of my questions, I quieted my misgivings.
I think even he had no clear conception of the magnitude of
some of the dangers and hardships we were destined to encounter. "It'll be the roughest roughing it you ever saw,"
he would say. "But you've got grit, and that's more than
half."

CHAPTER III

A T the time we started for Alaska there were but two
general routes from the Pacific Coast of the United
States to the gold regions of the Yukon. The first
was by the way of the Yukon River, and that means a journey of about four thousand five hundred miles, all by water,
at such times as the sand bars do not obstruct navigation.
This voyage can only be made between the middle of June
and the first of September, and it usually requires forty
days to reach Circle City. The other way, which is shorter
and quicker, if conditions are favorable, can be undertaken
much earlier in the year, and is by the way of Juneau, Dyea,
and the mountain passes to the lakes and upper waters of the

(58)

ALONG THE DYEA TRAIL

A lone gold-seeker crossing the Dyea River on his way to the Gold Fields.

In Camp on the Dyea River After a Day's March

Yukon. The fare from San Francisco by way of the Yukon is about three hundred dollars, and a charge of ten cents a pound for freight over the amount allowed for personal baggage. From San Francisco to Juneau the fare is fifty dollars, and the freight charges amount to but little. After reaching Dyea the charges for packing and ferrying are extravagant. One can spend as much as he likes. There is no limit to what the Chilkoots will try to make out of a person disposed to give.

We were too impatient to get into the country to wait for the water route, and I should have dreaded its monotony. I looked forward to the overland route with pleasure, especially that part of it supposed to impose the obstacles at which Joe had so vaguely hinted.

We sailed out of San Francisco harbor on March 15th. We were not the only gold-seekers aboard. Still, we were not crowded, and our quarters were comfortable. Port Townsend, the " Key City of the Sound," is the port of entry for the Puget Sound customs district, and point of departure of the mails for Alaska. Here we transferred to the Alaska steamer which came from Tacoma and Seattle, and fell in with a few more Alaskan adventurers.

The voyage from Port Townsend, which we left on the 20th, to Juneau, is one of the most varied and delightful that any coast line affords. I do not believe there is another journey on the face of the earth, the first half of which is so enjoyable and the second half so dismal, as the journey from Port Townsend to the Yukon *via* Juneau and the passes. For two thousand miles the vessel steams through land-locked channels, straits, and passages. The landscape is wonderfully beautiful all the way, and the traveler never ceases to wonder at its variety.

All the upper end of the Puget Sound is dominated by Mt. Baker, an extinct volcano over ten thousand feet high. We crossed the Strait of Juan de Fuca, close-walled on the southern side by the Olympic range, and touched at Victoria on the southern point of Vancouver Island. We then skirted the shores of San Juan Island through Active Pass, and entered the Gulf of Georgia, which is a great inland sea with the snow-capped mountains of Vancouver Island continuously on one side, and the Cascade Peaks on the other. Rounding Cape Mudge, we entered Discovery Passage, which is, at points, less than half a mile wide. At Queen Charlotte Sound there is a forty-mile gap in the island belt, and the swell of the outer ocean is felt. Those subject to *mal de mer* disappear for a time, but that is the only place in this salt water voyage of two thousand miles where any discomfort need be expected. We soon entered the narrow way again, steaming through Lama Passage, which is beautifully wooded, revealing here and there glimpses of the aborigines and their totem poles. Having crossed Millbank Sound we entered the great scenic regions of the trip. The shores, which are seldom more than two miles apart, rise abruptly for over a thousand feet, rugged promontories underneath whose shadows limpid mirrors lie; while above them rise the snowy ridges, glistening with glaciers and cascades.

After passing Fort Simpson we entered Alaskan waters. The coasts continued mountainous and the scenery became more grand. A little above Fort Wrangel we reached the region of tide-water glaciers, whose bergs sparkling along the sound, and on every foot of the shore on both sides, is a suggestion of the wonders of this mighty land of the north. Mountains rear their snow-capped summits far into the sky,

and, peering through the clefts once riven by some great
shock of nature, we see other ranges, over-topping ranges,
frowning darkly or standing with a ghost-like whiteness;
and, nearer, the mighty glaciers glow in all their varied
tints. We passed inlets, where

> . . . "the channel's waters spreading
> Turn toward the land, and find it
> So entrancing in its fairness,
> So stupendous in its grandeur !
> Find its ice-bound coast so willing
> To receive their bright advances,
> That they lie in sheets of silver
> At the foot of lofty ice-peaks."

On the fourth day out from Port Townsend we steamed
into Gastineau Channel, and soon arrived at Juneau, the
metropolis of Alaska. We had feasted on the delights of
the voyage, and the disagreeable portion was to come.
Nature has a way of evening things up, and though sometimes the process is so long that we do not realize it, her rigid
law of compensation is always in force.

We disembarked at Juneau with our precious supplies.
It is a queer metropolis, lying at the base of precipitous
mountains about three thousand feet high, and the flat plain
between the shore and the base of the mountain seems very
narrow. It is now well built up with houses, though it contained at that time only about two thousand people. Its
streets are narrow, crooked, and muddy, and here and there
the tree-stumps remain unpleasantly in the way. It has a
court house, several hotels and lodging houses, theaters,
churches, schools, newspapers, a hospital, a fire brigade, and
a brass band, but more saloons and dance-houses than all the
other institutions put together. Among its more modern
improvements are water-works and electric light plants.

Adjoining on the east below the wharf is a village of Taku Indians, and on the flats at the mouth of Gold Creek is a village of Auk Indians, back of which we get a glimpse of totem poles over the graves of the dead, and hung with offerings to the departed spirits. As we pass along through Third and Stewart streets, in the heart of the city, we find the Indians squatting about their wares, fish, vegetables, berries, and curios, and in the larger stores are fine displays of furs. One can get about everything he needs here, and a good deal more, especially in the lines of gambling, drinking, and dance halls. Such, in brief, is the metropolis of a country larger than Germany and Austria-Hungary together.

Juneau is essentially a mining town, owing its supremacy to the adjacent quartz mines which have much more than paid the cost of Alaska, to say nothing of its seals and valuable fisheries. Until recently the territory's reputation as a gold country has been due to these mines. It was about twenty years ago that a party of Indians brought a bit of gold quartz to Sitka, where a merchant grub-staked Joseph Juneau and Richard Harris, and sent them in search of the ore. Although this was the beginning of Juneau, it was three years later before the place took its name. The settlement was first named Harrisburg, but the mining company which had named the district the Harris Mining District gave the name of Juneau to the town. Miners flocked to the new camp, but many came too late to find claims there, and crossed over to what is now known as Douglass Island, then an untouched wilderness. After they had staked out claims they sold for something less than five hundred dollars, and a corporation, mostly of California men, finally secured it. It is now the site of the famous Treadwell gold mills, the largest plant of the kind in the world. About a million of dollars has been spent on the plant, at which six hundred tons of ore are milled daily at a cost of about one dollar and twenty-five cents a ton. The ore varies in value from three dollars to seven dollars a ton. The supply seems inexhaustible. The company is capitalized at five million dollars, and has paid nearly four million dollars in dividends. Joseph Juneau died a poor man.

Being the center of such an industry, and also the chief rendezvous of the miners going over the passes into the interior, Juneau City will doubtless maintain its supremacy as Alaska's metropolis. The news of the Yukon discoveries has wrought a great change in the place since we went in, and promises to work greater. Joe was perfectly at home in this region, where he had worked during his former sojourn in Alaska. I played the part of the tourist, he of guide. While waiting at Juneau we purchased a couple of sleds well adapted to Alaskan uses, and with these our outfit seemed complete.

From Juneau to Dyea is one hundred and eighteen miles up Lynn Canal and the Chilkoot and Taiya (Dyea) Inlets. The route by Dyea and the Chilkoot Pass was the old reliable one, having been used by the Indians for years, and the one which most of the gold-seekers we had encountered were taking. There are two others, the Skagway over the White Pass and the Dalton trail from the Chilkat Inlet. The first was thought by some to be the easier route, and was the one generally chosen by those who were experimenting with horses in this rough country. It is about seventeen miles from tide water to the summit of the White Pass, and about four miles of this is through a flat timbered valley. The summit is about two thousand six hundred feet above tide water, and the remainder of the route until it joins the Chilkoot trail is over marshes and an undulating rocky surface exceedingly difficult for pack animals, and with very little soil. In 1896 this trail attracted little attention. Its prominence was to come the following year.

If the Alaskan traveler is to experiment with horses, and the temptation is certainly great in view of the unreliability of the Indians, he had best try the Dalton trail, which takes its name from Jack Dalton, who went to Juneau many years ago, as one story goes, because he was accused of stealing horses. He was innocent of the charge, but he took vengeance on the man who had accused him. His trail affords a tolerably good road for two hundred miles from tide water. The first forty miles from Chilkat Inlet is on a river flat with an easy grade, thence to the divide, which is three thousand feet above the sea level. Another divide is crossed twenty miles further on the watershed of the Alsek and Chilkat rivers. The rest of the trail to the Five Finger Rapids is a succession of valleys with hardly perceptible divides. It is said that in summer a man with a saddle horse and pack animal can make thirty miles a day on this trail. Dalton is one of the most expert of Alaskan trailers.

But it is the Dyea route which concerns us, and thus far it has remained the most practicable one. We left Juneau for Dyea on March 25th, on a fair-sized steamer, but quickly encountered different conditions from those which had previously afforded us so much pleasure. We should have reached Dyea in twelve hours, but there seemed to be a hurricane trying to get out of the canal, which some have called the grandest fiord on the coast. There are a few indentations on the coasts, which are made up of abrupt palisades varied with glaciers and forests. The water is very deep in the channel, and a strong cold wind sucked down between the cliffs of either side, and tossed us about in the most boisterous fashion. Drifting icebergs from the Eagle, Auk, and Davidson glaciers added to the confusion. After pitching about helplessly for some time, we put up in a little bay, and lay over there one day. Meanwhile most of the wind seemed to have worked itself out of the channel. Thus we did not arrive at Dyea till the 27th, and after picking up on the way a party which had been wrecked on a small sailboat and had lost most of their provisions.

Dyea is an Indian word meaning " pack " or " load." Certainly you would have thought it a very appropriate one if you had seen the gold-seekers and their belongings dumped on the beach, almost every man and woman with provisions for a year or more, while some of the dirtiest-looking Indians on the face of the earth hovered around like evil spirits. There was a small improvised wharf, which was of no use, as there was too little water in the channel to permit the steamer to come up, and her cargo was discharged by scows and small boats.

The beach was flat and covered with small rocks which the people there, who make their living by unloading cargoes and packing over the trail, leave just where Nature dropped them. It might hurt their business to remove such obstructions to convenience and safety. The steamer anchored about two miles from the village, it being low tide. Boats were lowered and the unloading commenced, the contents being dumped on the rocks, anywhere to get rid of them, and there was considerable confusion.

After our goods were deposited and had been sorted out, the next thing was to get them up above the reach of the tide. We worked like beavers, and so did the others. With a little high-priced help from the Indians, we managed to carry everything back about a mile from the beach, where we found a place to camp. There we set up our tent, and made preparations for the season of roughing it before us. About ten inches of snow covered the ground, and it was quite soft in places. While we who had been used to a miner's life did not mind it much, there was a noticeable change in the faces of those who were less inured to hardships. It is not pleasant to leave the steamer and to begin living in a tent pitched in nearly a foot of snow.

When we had settled ourselves as comfortably as we could, and had taken the opportunity to observe our surroundings, we were struck with the transformation which some of the women had undergone. Generally speaking, their dresses had disappeared, and they came forth in bloomers, and many of them in the regulation trousers of the other sex. It does not do to be " squeamish" in Alaska. There are obstacles enough to travel, without the incumbrance of skirts. The women were of all ages under fifty, and, as we gradually learned, the majority of them were unmarried, at least had no husbands with them, and their destination was the dance halls of Circle City and Forty Mile. They were not as a rule an attractive lot for fastidious people to encounter socially, but out of about thirty women, four or five were wives traveling with their husbands, or daughters with their fathers, and were very respectable and well-appearing people, with marks of refinement which their life in mining camps had not obliterated.

But there is little time to observe human nature. There are over three thousand two hundred pounds to get over the trail somehow. On our two sleds we could draw a

fair load over good roads, but the advisability of securing
Indian packers for the bulk of the provisions was naturally
suggested. A few of the gold pilgrims started at once to
pack their goods further up the trail before camping. A
feverish haste will always be noticed among such pilgrims,
though it helps but little in the end.

In a short time a dirty one-eyed Indian came towards
us, and in English which just escaped being unintelligible
asked if we had packing to do. He knew well enough we
had.

" How much you give to summit? " he asked.

According to the ethics of the trail the price for packing should not be bid up. If one party put up the price in
order to secure quick service, every other Indian on the trail
would know it in an inconceivably short space of time, and
all would throw down their packs at once, contracts or no
contracts. They would refuse to carry for less than the
man in a hurry was willing to pay. One man who had
plenty of money, it was said, bid up the price, and as a result
received a very cold ducking in the creek. So we offered
the Indian the prevailing price, which was seventeen cents
a pound, and he promised to be on hand with twenty-five
Indians early the next morning.

" You may see that heathen in the morning, and you
may not," remarked Joe, as the Indian slowly loafed away
towards the little village of about three hundred Chilkoots.

We cut some hemlock brush and laid it on the snow in
the tent, put our blankets on it, and filling our pipes sat
down near the opening of the tent, Joe on a box of soap, I
on some evaporated apricots.

" Do you see that notch up yonder? " said Joe, blowing
a cloud of smoke from his mouth. I saw it, though it was

hardly distinguishable in the whiteness of the towering mountains.

"Well, this truck of ourn' has got to go up through there."

I never slept better in my life than I did on those hemlock boughs laid over snow. We were up bright and early to be ready for the Indians. There were no signs of them. We finished our breakfast, and packed the sleds which we intended to draw ourselves. Then we took down our tent, but no Indians came. I grew impatient, but Joe seemed not at all surprised. After a time he went down to the Indian village, but came back alone, saying the Indians were not all up. As they showed no indications of taking off their clothes when they retired for the night, I concluded that getting up could not be a long process. But it was over an hour before an Indian appeared, and then there were less than a dozen.

"Where are the others?" I asked sternly of the one-eyed Chilkoot.

"They come bimeby," he remarked indifferently.

The wretched-looking Siwashes poked around among the packs, hefted them critically, then jabbered away among themselves, and finally informed us that they objected to some of the articles unless an extra price was paid. The very Indians we had engaged were dickering with other parties in the same way. I tried threatening one of them, but it had no more effect than if he had been an iceberg. Joe laughed at me, while the Indians stood about chattering in a language that is perfectly inexpressible in any phonetic signs we have. No one would ever take it for speech but for the slight motions of their lips, and the convulsions in the throat. "A confusion of gutturals with a plentitude of saliva — a moist language with a gurgle that approaches a gargle," is the best description of it I have ever heard.

None of the Indians seemed to be in the least hurry to start; indeed, they did not appear to care whether they started or not. Once in a while the one-eyed fellow would come and demand more on some flimsy pretext or other. Finally my patience gave out completely. I told Joe that I would rather pack our stores over a dozen Chilkoot passes than fool with heathen like these. So, after losing considerable time, we concluded to do our own packing, and I think some of those fellows went away actually relieved. They are too lazy to regard the loss of work as anything but a blessing. So far as I observed them, they had one virtue, and that was a remarkable regard for other people's property. They will not steal, but their word is absolutely worthless. They have no conception of the obligations of a contract. After demanding exorbitant pay, and being promised it, they will delay starting to suit their own feelings, and will throw down their packs at the slightest provocation. They will even trudge along with them for a long distance, and then, after demanding extra pay, will drop their burdens and return with no pay for what they have done. No one can afford to engage them for any but short distances, for the point is soon reached when they have eaten up all they started with.

These people may be interesting to ethnologists, and they may seem promising material for devout missionaries, but for the man who is in a hurry to get to the gold regions of Alaska they are more often a hindrance than a help. Where one cannot depend on horses or dogs, he will save his temper by depending on himself. He will also save a lot of money and a large percentage of his provisions.

CHAPTER IV

LIFE ON THE TRAIL — STRANGE SIGHTS AND SCENES —
STORM BOUND IN SHEEP CAMP — A WOMAN'S AD-
VENTURES AND EXPERIENCES.

Along the Famous Dyea Trail — Walking Twenty Miles and Making
Four — Snow, Boulders, and Glaciers —Exhibitions of Grit — Tent-
ing in the Snow — A Democratic Crowd — The Yukon Stove —
The So-called Gridiron — Beans and Bacon — "It will be New On
the Yukon" — Asleep on a Bed of Boughs — What a Trail Consists
of — A Crack Two Miles Long — Pleasant Camp — Sheep Camp
and the Faint-Hearted — A Discouraged Man and a Resolute
Woman — Going Over Anyhow — Not All so Brave — Having a
Good Cry — My Theory as to the Fortitude of Some Women —
Throwing off the Fetters of Civilization — Two Weeks of Storm —
Monotony and Silence — An Active Glacier Entertains Us — Nature's
Untamed Moods — Sunshine at Last — Now for The Chilkoot!

THE beginning of the trail over Chilkoot Pass does
not give any indications of the difficulties a little
further on, especially under favorable conditions
in the latter part of March. The streams are still frozen,
except in open places, and the trail along their banks is covered with snow, which in most places has become solidly
packed. In the early winter the snow is apt to be soft and
deep, while in the summer the trails are soft and slippery,
and streams with treacherous bottoms must be forded.
The water is considerably colder at all times than any manufactured ice water, and the current is swift and strong,

being abundantly fed by the melting glaciers and rains that never end till one has forgotten when they began.

"Does it always rain here?" I once heard a traveler ask of an Indian.

"Snows sometime," replied the native, in the most matter-of-fact manner. Before we got through the pass we found that it could do both at the same time without showing any signs of exhaustion.

Joe superintended all the preparations. We increased the loads on our sleds to 400 pounds each, and found that we could pull them very comfortably for the first five miles, the river being frozen and the track hardened by those who had gone ahead. At the end of five miles the way became more difficult, and, coming to a spot well timbered and watered, where several others had camped, we unloaded, cached our goods, and returned to camp for another load. We saw that we could not make the four trips necessary to bring up all our goods without working half the night, and we were tired enough to stop when we returned from the third load, but concluded to keep on.

The Dyea Valley is an old river bed full of huge boulders, which make a summer trip over the trail exceedingly difficult. Even in winter they are serious obstacles, as there are places in the river which do not freeze, and unless the snow is deep the sledding is very rough on the banks. On either side, high up on the mountains, the tops of which were hidden in the clouds most of the time, were small glaciers cutting down through the scraggy growth of spruce and hemlock. Back and forth through this desolate valley we tramped, continually meeting others engaged in the same work.

There is no time to stop to cultivate acquaintances.

Occasionally we came up just in time to help a man right his overturned sled, or to extricate a woman who had stepped into a treacherous drift or fallen into a little crevice. Here and there along the way tents were passed, as well as caches of provisions, which were left unguarded without incurring serious risk. But in Alaska all provisions must be cached to be out of reach of the dogs. They are the only thieves.

Many strange sights are witnessed even in these days, when the gold fields at Forty-Mile and Birch Creek are attracting fortune-seekers. We met a young woman who was going in with her husband, slowly working her way toward the pass. She was trudging along with packs of over forty pounds on her back, and her face bore the marks of refinement. The grit and nerve displayed on every side were marvelous. Some men preferred to make short marches and piled on their backs sixty or seventy-five pounds, keeping up a brisk gait for a mile or so, then striking camp, and in the same way bringing up the remainder of their outfits. That is the hardest way and nothing is gained.

It was very late before we arrived with our last load and had our tent again set up in the snow. Those who have not tried it can hardly imagine what it is to tramp twenty-five miles, half the way pulling four hundred pounds, in an intermittent snow storm, over a road which, while smooth for Alaska, would be deemed almost impassable in New England.

Yet there was a novelty in the experience which was exhilarating, so that it did not fatigue us as much as it might otherwise have done. Having put up our tent and cut a few scraggy hemlocks, we trimmed off the tops for a bed and used the stumps for a fire, not so easily started with green wood in a snow storm. It was a very democratic gathering. There were no formalities, no hint of conventionalities of any kind. The picturesque element was not lacking, and the ludicrous side of life was ever present. Looking a few feet up the hillside through the flying snow I caught a glimpse of a woman who, attired in her husband's trousers, was turning flapjacks on a " Yukon stove," utterly unconscious of the ridiculous appearance she presented. The " Yukon stove," by the way, is a small sheet iron box with an oven at the back and a telescope pipe. Novices sometimes have to study a moment to decide which is the oven and which is the fire-box. This simple arrangement is set on a " gridiron," that is, three poles about eight feet long, so that when the snow melts underneath, the poles continue to form a support for it. Necessity is nowhere a more fruitful mother of invention than in Alaska.

Joe and I confined ourselves to beans and bacon, a staple dish in these regions; indeed, an odor of beans and bacon predominates in nearly all the camps along the trail. We lighted our pipes and sat close to the little stove to dry our clothing. Mingled with the sighing of the wind and the soft beating of the snow on the tent, came the shrill voice of one of the dance-house girls singing a hackneyed air.

" It will be new on the Yukon," observed Joe, as he threw himself full length on the bed of boughs, and he was asleep before I had time to follow. I went out and carefully brushed the snow off the roof of the tent before retiring, for I had learned the importance of such a measure in roughing it in an even milder climate. If the interior of the tent is heated, the snow falling on the outside will, of course, become damp, and, later, when the fire has gone down or out, and the interior has become cold, the damp snow will freeze so hard that it is almost impossible to take down the tent. Many found this out to their sorrow when the next day they started to move ahead. The storm had been a cold one, and it was hours before they could pack their tents, and then they were weighted with ice and extremely difficult to handle. People can cause themselves a world of trouble in Alaska by neglecting a few details.

We were four days in moving our stores to Sheep Camp, which is about seven miles further on. For the first two miles we could haul about three hundred pounds, but through the cañon it was only by the greatest exertion that we could pull one hundred and fifty. The trail was much better from Pleasant Camp, on the other side of the cañon, to Sheep Camp, but it was up-hill all the way. It snowed continuously, sometimes gently, and occasionally furiously.

A trail in Alaska should not be confused with the ordinary highway of settled states. When a trail is spoken of as existing between two points in Alaska it has no further meaning than that a man, and possibly a beast of burden, may travel that way over the natural surface of the ground. There is a very strong improbability concerning the beast, unless it be a dog. The path may consist of nothing more than a marked or blazed way through an otherwise impenetrable wilderness, and unless it is used more or less continuously the traces are apt to disappear in one of Alaska's seasons. No eager prospector stops to make it any easier for someone else. A man carrying his food, his cooking utensils, and working tools on his back, has no time nor disposition to cut down trees. When he comes to an unfrozen stream he wades it, or if a tree has fallen across it, so much

A Supper of Beans and Coffee

A party of gold-seekers eating their supper at the entrance to Miles Cañon.

the better. The Chilkoot trail possesses the advantage of having been used by miners since 1880, but it was laid out by Indians, who are too lazy to improve it; and, besides, they make a living because it is almost impossible for pack animals to go over it. The opening of Alaska may put an end to all this, so far as the Dyea trail is concerned.

Dyea Cañon is a crevice in the mountains about two miles long and fifty feet wide, with a raging river at the bottom. The topography abruptly changes. Great boulders are piled in confused heaps, and the snow-laden stumps of trees and upturned roots stick out in fantastic shapes. We kept to the ice when we could, but frequently took to steeper and rougher paths. For a short distance the grade is about eighteen degrees, until an elevation of five hundred feet is reached, and then the trail descends slightly to Pleasant Camp, which is not far from the mouth of the cañon. It is a spot which is anything but " pleasant," according to the significance of that term in civilized regions. It is applied here because a few trees have had the good fortune to get a living there, and they afford a kind of shelter and a convenient place for a camp.

The trail from Pleasant Camp to Sheep Camp was fairly good, at an average elevation of five hundred feet, and with but few sharp pitches. The camp itself is in a valley or cañon about half a mile wide, with very high, steep, and rocky mountains on either side. The white summit of the Chilkoot towers three thousand feet above, but we caught only glimpses of it in the fickle storm. No timber grows above us. It is a frowning picture and it tells on faint hearts. As we slowly dragged our loads, we met more than one man who had turned back, not caring to brave the pass for all the gold that might be on the other side. Alaska is no place for a man who, becoming discouraged at the first serious obstacle that presents itself, leaves a camp where he sees women keeping up hearts as strong as iron, and turns his back.

Sheep Camp is a favorable place to discover the difference in men and to see what some women are made of. We came across one man completely disheartened and limp, right at the foot of that great climb of three thousand five hundred feet, pleading piteously with his wife to turn back, while she, not half his size, but with wonderful nerve, bustled about their snowy camp in the bitter cold, constantly wearing a smile and cheering up her forlorn mate in every possible way. How will she get him over the summit? I thought. But she did. She just told him that she was going over anyhow, and that if he wanted to go back he could. She had a woman's shrewdness. She knew that, much as he feared to go ahead with her, he would not dare to go back without her.

Shortly after pitching our tent at Sheep Camp I looked out and saw a slim woman swinging an axe at a small hemlock. Her tent was near by and she seemed to be alone. With a spirit of gallantry, which, I am glad to say, is never altogether lost in mining life, I walked over and offered my assistance. She wanted the tree for a fire, and I soon had it in front of her tent ready for a blaze. She had been making trips to the summit of the pass all day, carrying packs of twenty-five pounds, and was then preparing the camp for her husband, who had gone to the summit with the last load. Her clothes were wet through; she was lame and tired, but she laughed good-naturedly as she told me some of her experiences on the awful trail, how she had slipped off a log and fallen into the river and an Indian had pulled her out by the collar of the thick coat she wore.

But it must not be thought that all women along the trail were as brave as this. There were exceptions. I saw one sitting down and having a good cry, crying for home and other women to talk to, perhaps, for carpets, and baker's bread, and the gossip of the city, and the comforts of civilized life. Her husband, who was pretty blue himself, was trying to comfort her. I noticed that she still clung to her petticoats. One could not fail to notice many instances, however, in which the women seemed to show a fortitude superior to the men. It was a revelation, almost a mystery. But after a while I began to account for it as the natural result of an escape from the multitude of social customs and restraints which in civilized society hedge about a woman's life. Hardened miners enter on the Alaskan trail as a sort of grim business, something a little worse than they have been accustomed to, and yet much the same. The stimulus received from the novelty of the situation is much less than in the case of a woman, especially one who has not been used to roughing it. She steps out of her dress into trousers in a region where nobody cares. Her nature suddenly becomes aware of a freedom which is in a way exhilarating. She has, as it were, thrown off the fetters which civilized society imposes, and while retaining her womanliness she becomes something more than a mere woman. Her sensitive nature is charmed with the new conditions, and her husband, who has had the advantage of no such metamorphosis, sits down, tired and disheartened by the obstacles in his path, and marvels at his wife as she drags her heavy rubber boots through the snow and climbs with a light heart the precipices of mighty mountains.

The weather was fairly good while we were bringing our stores up to Sheep Camp, but as soon as we had them settled there and were ready to begin on the summit it became ferociously cold. The mercury fell to eighteen degrees below zero, the snow flew at intervals, and at times the wind would swoop down through the valley like an avalanche, rolling from the great peaks above us. On one side of the valley is a large glacier. We could stand at the entrance of our tent, looking across the cañon, and see it very plainly, about two miles away. A wall of ice eighty or ninety feet high marked its lower end, and occasionally a great piece of ice would break off and come rolling down into the valley. The earth would tremble and the roar of the mighty crash was like a peal of distant thunder through the mountain gorges. Twice while I was watching I saw great pieces of ice many times larger than the great skyscraping buildings of Chicago break away and come tumbling into the cañon below.

The scenery was sublime, but the weather continued abominable and we were detained at this camp for two weeks. Few thought of venturing over the summit under such conditions. The wind must be still and the sky clear. Once, when the prospects seemed brighter, we strapped on our packs and started out, but soon it began to storm again. We met a party of Indians and prospectors who had started earlier and had cached some of their goods at a point well up on the trail and were going back to wait again. They warned us that it was dangerous to attempt an ascent, but as we had light packs and the wind was blowing in our direction we decided to push ahead. The trail grew worse, the wind increased and sifted the snow across the track so that we could not fail to recognize the serious dangers of a misstep. And so we followed the others back to camp.

It was a very dreary camp during those two weeks. There was no laughter there. The everlasting hills and the apparently everlasting storm hung over the little valley like a harsh penalty. Difficult as it is to follow the trails, there is nothing so hard as to keep still in these regions, especially when the mercury is far below zero. We got along very comfortably, however, as our tent was a good one and we had plenty of blankets. There were about a hundred others in the camp, but they kept closely to their tents most of the time. Indeed, when the wind went down the stillness over that little clump of white habitations among the stunted trees was almost appalling. No hum of industry or sound of sociability disturbed the silence. Cut off from the world, a man feels himself dwindling into a mere atom amid these silent, everlasting hills. He feels almost like speaking in whispers when, suddenly, on the oppressive stillness there breaks a sharp report like a clap of thunder, and it goes on roaring, and dies away grumbling and murmuring amid the mountains. Then all is still again. A glacier has moved. Here is where Nature is working. She is young yet, the hills have not been ground down. But in her youthful, untamed moods she is terrible.

The anomaly presented by the region forced itself more clearly upon us when we considered that we were practically in the same latitude as St. Petersburg, where the brilliant court of a great empire is held. We were still eight hundred miles south of the Arctic Circle. We were hardly five hundred feet above the sea level, but in an inhospitable region, where heroic courage and endurance are requisites; a wilderness with the snow and ice around and above us.

At last the clouds passed away, and the sun shone out for a time with dazzling brightness. The white peaks above us fairly glowed. The little camp was alive.

CHAPTER V

THE DREADED CHILKOOT PASS — HOW WE CROSSED IT
— SLIDING DOWN THE MOUNTAINS AT LIGHTNING
SPEED — "THERE COMES A WOMAN."

A Steep Trail — Climbing the Mountain Forty Times — Some of the
Difficulties — Missteps that are Dangerous — Straight up over
Seven Hundred Feet — An Obscure Summit — Facilitating the Re-
turn — Trousers Fortified with a Canvas Patch — A Slide in the
Trench — Tobogganing Outdone — A Collision — Out of Sight in
the Deep Snow — "There Comes a Woman" — Down Like a Flash
— Runaway Sleds — An Alaskan Sunburn — Snow-blindness — A
Painful Experience — On the Summit at Last — A Grand Spectacle
— Turning Sleds Loose down the Mountain — Bounding over
Crater Lake — Lake Lindeman — Observing the Timber — The Ir-
responsible Indian — Signaling by Burning Trees — Ice-sledding
across Lindeman — Lake Bennett — Flapjacks and Congratulations.

FROM Sheep Camp to the summit of Chilkoot Pass is
about four miles, and we determined to carry all
our things up on our backs. The trail was so steep
most of the way that it would have been impossible to haul
more than a hundred pounds on a sled, and added to this
would be the weight of the sled. The latter part of the
way is altogether too perpendicular for comfortable sledding. It is a steady ascent from the camp to the " Scales,"
which is a flat place at the foot of " the last climb." The
grade from the camp to Stone House, so called because
nature seems to have arranged the rocks with more sym-
metry than usual, and that is saying very little, is from

(85)

twelve to eighteen degrees; from there to the " Scales " it is about twenty-five degrees, and from that place to the summit about thirty degrees, though the last ascent is nearer thirty-five. The ascent is one thousand nine hundred and fifty feet in the first three miles, and one thousand two hundred and fifty in the next mile.

This does not look great on paper, and it is not; for mountain climbers are every day ascending steeps as great and twice as high. But they are not compelled to take along all they are to have to eat, to wear, and to use for a year or more. Therein lies one of the main difficulties in proceeding to the interior of Alaska. If one could depend upon warehouses within easy reach, could buy what he wanted as he journeyed from place to place, traveling in Alaska would have a few pleasures in it. At least it would not be difficult.

Joe and I were compelled to make forty trips over these steep places to get our outfit to the summit, and climbing a mountain forty times with a heavy pack on the back is different from climbing it once almost empty-handed and for fun. Many took all their goods to the Stone House at first, and then by another stage carried them to the " Scales "; then by another to the summit. We adopted different tactics. Having strapped our packs on, we continued to the foot of the last ascent, and there if the weather was bad we would leave them, otherwise we continued on to the summit. As the wind was blowing most of the time, this resulted in our having most of our outfit at the foot of the final ascent before we had many opportunities to view the summit, or any at all to indulge in a view from it.

The trail up to the " Scales " looks smooth when the snow lies deep over it, but it is, nevertheless, difficult, and by a single misstep the traveler may find himself buried to the armpits. Underneath are great masses of rocks, and part of the way fallen trees, but the timber belt ends completely at Stone House. One of the difficulties in the ascent lay in successfully passing those who were descending for another load, for the way is exceedingly narrow, and one must not step out of the trail except with the greatest caution. Occasionally a man would find himself at the bottom of a crevice forty feet or so below the trail, and he could make his way back only with the greatest difficulty.

The last climb of nearly seven hundred feet up a mountain peak that seemed to rise almost straight before us was the hardest of all. The trail winds in zigzag fashion in and around the boulders and over the glacial streaks, but at this time it was covered with snow, in some places fifty feet deep. In the steeper places steps were cut in the ice and snow, and in taking a pack up one was compelled to lean forward and use his hands on the icy steps. Occasionally a tired man would make a misstep, or his foothold caved off, and down the precipice he rolled, landing in the soft snow, from which he had to extricate himself and again attempt the tiresome climb. Its was drudgery in its simplest and purest form. One hundred pounds was the most that either of us could take, and then it required an hour to cover that seven hundred feet to the summit, which we generally found covered with a blinding snow storm or bathed in an ice-fog.

Fortunately, in returning we could make up for lost time. So steep and so treacherous was the trail, and so many were working up it, that the descent by the steps for another load was as trying work as the ascent. The grim mother of invention again came to the rescue. Nearly everybody fortified the seat of his trousers by sewing on a piece of canvas, and as there was a short cut back to the bottom of the trail, straight and smooth but too steep to climb, it was brought into use for the purposes of returning, a trench being formed thereby.   One would sit down in this trench at the top, and just hold his breath till he struck the bottom.   He need not hold it long.   It took less time to slide down than it takes to tell of it.   Once started there was no opportunity to stop, and no time to consider such a question. I remember that at the first trial I picked myself out of the snow and thought I would give up that sport.   It seemed a little too much like riding an avalanche bareback.   I was so much larger and heavier than the rest that gravity gave me a greater speed.   In places the ditch was as much as four feet deep, but in other places it was shallow, and there was danger of jumping the track.   Once I ran into a little man and was thrown completely out of the groove.   Down the mountain side I plowed, plunging entirely out of sight in the soft snow at the bottom.   I picked myself out and was not in the least hurt.   The little man righted himself somehow, and came down the groove in good order.   After awhile the experience began to have the flavor of true sport, and the more we tried it the better we liked it.

The women were a little timid at first, but they looked as if they would like to try it.   " I'll try it if you will," they kept saying to one another.   Standing at the bottom and seeing men come down the seven-hundred-foot groove, it looked easy, but when standing at the summit and looking down was something appalling.   Finally, as we were about to start up with a pack, some one shouted, " There comes a woman."

We could see her fidgeting a little at the top; then she wrapped her coat about her, dropped into the trench, and down she came like a flash. She picked herself up out of the snow rosy and smiling. Then this method of descent became general. They seemed to enjoy it as much as the men, but most of those whom I saw going down were of the dance-hall variety. It appeared to be a little too much for the staider matrons, even in men's clothes.

Occasionally, on our way back to Sheep Camp for a load we also saved a little time by securing a ride on some one's sled. There was one hill, quite steep and over a mile long. By having one man to guide the sled, and another to run a stout stick down through the center for a brake, a small load of men could slide to the bottom in a very short time, and generally without mishap. An experienced man will guide these sleds with a pole about six feet long very cleverly, but the inexperienced sometimes make bad work. There were runaway sleds about every day, and generally some one was hurt. But in such places nothing is serious, so long as a man escapes with his life.

It is, however, in the milder winter months only that the difficult ascent can be varied with such amusements as these. After the snow has melted the trail becomes one of confused boulders, roaring streams, and creviced glaciers. To be sure, we suffered from the cold, and sometimes severely, but, on the whole, going over the summit is much pleasanter at this season than in the rains of the summer months, when the trails quickly become muddy and the streams must be forded.

On my trip over I suffered from sunburn more than anything else. It may sound strange to speak of sunburn when clambering over snow many feet deep, but when in Alaska the sun begins to shine, it is with a blazing fierceness. My epidermis was well hardened before I started for

Alaska, but some of the time, while working over the pass, my face became so swollen that I could hardly see out of my eyes. It was exceedingly painful, and often kept me awake nights when I was very tired. When the wind blew and the snow flew, my face would smart as if burned by steam. Many of us learned to blacken our faces with burnt cork or charcoal, and this served not simply to protect the skin somewhat, but to protect the eyes. We were gruesome objects with our black faces and goggles. Snow-blindness was another serious danger. Snow glasses are an absolute necessity in Alaska, and especially when going over the snowy passes in the full blaze of the sun; and one must be very careful about taking them off. Occasionally, when several of us would be trudging up the steep path together a cry would be heard. Some one had suddenly become snow blind, and had to be led back to camp. Such unfortunates would suffer intense pain, and would not regain their sight for three or four days.

But at last we have reached the summit of that snow-wrapped peak towards which we have been making our way for twenty-three days. Fifteen miles in twenty-three days! After such a journey there should be something besides the mere consolation of having at last conquered the obstacles in the path. There is. It is a great temptation not to throw off the snow-glasses, as we stand on that dazzling summit. The clouds have been blown away for a time. The whole scene lies under the fierce sunlight of an Alaskan April day.

And what a picture! It seems not of this world; it is so strange, so unique. Almost at our feet is the little armlet of the Pacific which we left nearly a month ago, and beyond that and this side of the great Pacific a hun-

dred miles away, stretch the snow peaks and their shining
glaciers.

> "Silence reigns! the awful stillness
> Like a phantom presence lingers
> All unseen, but felt so plainly
> That it seems to touch the senses.
>
> .   .   .   .   .
>
> "Far away the mountain ranges
> Pile in wild unclassed confusion,
> Ragged peaks, extinct volcanoes,
> Rounded knolls and wave-like hillocks
> Clustering near or stretching outward
> Far beyond our wondering vision:
> Snow-clad all, or maybe shining
> Underneath an icy garment.
> Glacier, cliff, and mountain shoulder
> Leaning close against the other,
> By the ice-keen chisels blended,
> Until ice and stone are welded
> In a firm eternal union.
>
> "Crash and boom! the silence wakens
> With a shock, whose mighty roaring
> Rends the clouds with thunderous pealing!
> Sends its varying detonations
> Rolling o'er the bay's clear surface!
> Bounding forth o'er mountain summits
> Where their echoes catch its thunders
> And repeat them loudly, wildly,
> As if Nature's fierce artillery
> Joined its mightiest cannonading
> In one grand, triumphant salvo!
> In a thousand-voiced announcement
> Of an iceberg's bold departure
> On its evanescent journey."

Turning in the other direction we behold the hills melting away into the great watershed of the mighty Yukon,
which runs its winding course to the Bering Sea three thousand miles.   At our feet lies the first of the frozen lakes; a

body of water lying in an old crater and now covered with ice and snow. This is the next stage of our journey, and the old adage that it is easier to fall than to climb was illustrated in Chilkoot style. The descent to the lake, which is five hundred feet, is smooth and straight, and the Indians, who were packing for parties on the trail, securely tied their packs to sleds, mounted them as a clown would mount a circus donkey, and off they went. The sleds shot down the decline with terrific speed and bounded off on to the frozen lake, sometimes going eight hundred yards before stopping. But for the snow they would have gone much further. Sometimes a sled would swerve a little or strike a slight obstacle and the Indians would fly off into the air and roll like bundles to the lake. A perpendicular bank about six feet high stretches around the lake, and this the sleds would clear with a long leap to the ice below, and he was a good Indian who stuck.

As the sleds seemed to go equally well without Indians as with, we concluded to let ours go alone. They behaved nicely, and clambering down the decline after them we drew them on across the lake, where they were unloaded, and we then pulled them bck for another load and a slide. At the end of the lake we cached our provisions and pushed on with our tent and a few articles to Lake Lindeman. The trail at this season is not difficult, as trails go in Alaska. The lakes were frozen and the only impediment on them was the snow, which in places was soft and wet. The lengthening days were beginning to have their effect on the lower lands. Crater Lake is not more than a mile in diameter, and the outlet is over a lava bed of rough boulders. Long Lake lies a little lower, and is studded with glaciers. The traveling becomes tedious, difficult, and slow, and the greatest care must be used in places, the dangers of which may be hidden by the weakening snow. After passing Deep Lake, we follow a dim trail, almost indiscernible at times, and then, from the top of a rough little hill, Lake Lindeman lies below.

It is said to be less than ten miles from the summit to Lindeman. It seems twice that distance, but we managed to bring up our entire outfit in four trips, and were the best part of three days in doing it. In the summer we were told the natives maintained what were called ferries on this chain of little lakes, but the charges were enormous and many preferred to keep to the trails, trying though they were.

From the Stone House to the vicinity of Lindeman not enough wood can be found to start a fire. At first we came to little clumps of short, scrubby pines or spruce, scarcely three feet high and twisted into all sorts of fantastic shapes by the winter gales, but around Lindeman could be found a few fair-sized trees, though few were over thirty feet high. They are mainly confined to varieties of spruce, yellow cedar, hemlock, and balsam fir, but spruce everywhere predominates, and its lumber resembles that of southern or pitch pine. The hemlock is less plentiful. White spruce is the staple timber, and though in some places near running streams it attains the height of from fifty to one hundred feet, it is most commonly found below forty, and averaging about fifteen inches at the butt. It is a fairly clear white wood, straight grained, and easily worked, light, and yet very tough. It endures the weather well, and a log house built of it is good for over twenty years. It abounds in a light and delicate looking gum, and those addicted to the chewing-gum habit can always be sure of a supply.

Good timber, however, was not plentiful at Lindeman, even at this time. Much of it had been burnt off. In the summer, we are told, when the Indians are resting on their journeys and are pestered by insects, they set fire to the leaves and twigs about them and then sit in the dense smoke which keeps a few of the mosquitoes at a distance. After his rest the native goes forward without extinguishing his fire, and as the vegetation is rank and inflammable in the long summer days, the fire quickly spreads to the trees and to the forests. The Indian also has a way of signaling by burning trees. When in a locality where he expects to find his friends or family, he sets fire to a tall spruce, and then calmly sits down and watches the horizon for an answering column of smoke. The wind will fan these flames into a fierce forest fire in a short time, and the Indians are too utterly indifferent to think of putting them out.

Some gold pilgrims, worn out by the arduous tramp over the pass, pitched their camps at Lake Lindeman to await the breaking up of the ice, meanwhile entering upon the construction of a boat which they fondly hoped would diminish the tediousness of the further trip. But the ice was in such excellent condition here and the timber so poor that we decided to push on.

Lake Lindeman is a narrow piece of water six miles long, hemmed in with ragged hills. It is close to the boundary line between the territory of the United States and that of Queen Victoria. On the cone of an immense boulder on the left, as we looked down the frozen lake, fluttered the Stars and Stripes, and from another staff close by waved the ensign of Great Britain. Both had been tattered in the gales from the great regions of the North.

A stiff breeze was blowing in our direction as we started

A Tired and Disgusted Party of Gold-Seekers

Looking for hotel accommodations on the Dyea Trail. The signs "Hotel," "Lodgings," "Meals," and so forth indicate that these accommodations are to be found only in the snow-covered tent.

from the head of the lake. The snow was not deep except in spots; so, rigging up sails on our sleds, we fastened them together, and away we sped with a load of one thousand two hundred pounds. This was sport. Taking a position on the back of the sleds we used two long poles as a rudder, though it was a severe task on the arms. Occasionally we would run into a drift of snow and the speed would slacken, or we might stop altogether while the wind tore over our sails in a threatening manner. Then we would jump out, pull them beyond the drift, jump on, and resume our steering. In this way we made the length of the lake in forty minutes. Others adopted the same tactics, and the scene of these ice sleds sailing over the lake, which seemed like a great cañon, was indeed picturesque, and very much pleasanter than the raft trips made later in the season, when the wind is likely to " kick up " a lively sea and drench the poor gold-seeker and his goods. He has usually by this time become so hardened and so accustomed to the ways of the country, that he does not mind such a little matter as a wet skin, and a camp in the snow or on the spongy lowlands.

The portage from Lake Lindeman to Lake Bennett is along a rocky canal which plunges into a cañon filled with boulders. The stream cut through a wall of granite and basaltic formation for three-quarters of a mile, and has a fall of forty feet. The latter part of the portage is over a sandy ridge, away from the stream and much better traveling.

Here many of the gold-seekers decided to camp and build their boats, but as the weather was fair and the traveling on the ice easy, we concluded to push to the other end of the lake, or further, before going into camp. Lake Bennett, so named by Schwatka after James Gordon Bennett, is thirty-four miles long, and from one to two miles in width.

About fourteen miles down, the southwest arm of the lake joins it, and from its hills fierce winds usually blow. Thus the trip over the lake is much more comfortable on the ice than on the water. We made the first trip in one day. The wind favored us, and we exchanged services with a man who was endeavoring to take in some horses, which helped us very materially. On the second trip, however, when compelled to depend on ourselves, we had head winds, and we were three days in making the single trip. It was hard work at that.

At Caribou Crossing, which separates Lake Bennett from Tagish Lake, we learned that there was some open water beyond. The crossing is a neck of sluggish river, and is so named because the caribou use it in their migrations south in the spring and north in the fall. The ice and snow were growing very soft under the sun of the lengthening days, though the air from the peaks continued cold. We determined to halt a Tagish Lake and build the craft upon which were to depend to take us down the upper waters of the Yukon.

"I guess the worst is over for a time," said Joe that evening, as we sat by the little box of a stove devouring flap-jacks as fast as they could be cooked. We both were hungry and kept well ahead of the stove.

"Our health has been good, anyhow," I remarked; "but I don't believe there is any worse traveling this side of the moon. And there is one consolation, I'm thinking, Joe, whatever society we have will at least be made up of persons of grit. Anybody who gets over here has got to be made of stout stuff, even though it is put together wrong. If you had just sat down in 'Frisco and told me in detail what this tramp would be, I think I should have looked on it as a rather long and at times agreeable method of premeditated suicide."

"Well, it may amount to that yet," said Joe, as he turned over another flapjack, eagerly waiting for it to brown. I had finished mine, and was patiently waiting for my turn to brown another.

CHAPTER VI

CAMP LIFE IN ALASKA—WE BUILD A BOAT TO CONTINUE OUR JOURNEY—ADVENTURES WITH BEARS.

Our Camp at Lake Tagish—Building a Boat—The Saw Pit—Preparing the Trees—Whip-sawing—Its Effect on Character—An Accident—Almost a Quarrel—A Case in Which Angels Would Lose their Amiability—Spoiling the First Log—"Work it Somehow"—The Dish-Rag and the Dog—A Bargain—Adventure of a New Yorker with a Bear and Three Cubs--An Excited Man—He Empties His Gun and Nearly Kills His Dog—I Lend Him My Rifle—The Bear Finally Gives It Up—Catching the Cubs—Tough Hams—Our Triumphant Return—An Old Timer's Bear Story—Face to Face with a Wounded Bear—Playing Possum—Just in Time—A Narrow Escape—"Don't Go Off Half-Cocked."

IT was the first of May when we went into camp near Tagish Lake, which is usually reckoned as about sixty miles from Dyea. Although we had made much better time after crossing the Chilkoot, we had averaged less than two miles a day on the whole tramp, and now we were destined to lie in camp for an indefinite time while building our boat and waiting for the river to be safely free of ice. But this, bear in mind, was before anything was known of the Klondike. While some were hurrying along as fast as they could, and faster than was safe, the majority were taking time, and really enjoying their rough fare in camp after the ordeals of the pass. The location was very good for camping purposes and as four of five other parties were there building their boats we did not lack for company. We were also afforded a little opportunity to study the methods of boat-building in these primitive regions. I knew nothing at all about the construction of boats and Joe's experience had been small. Very soon I came to the conclusion that all the knowledge about boats there was in the whole camp would not have taken a man far out to sea. But Joe pretended that he knew all about it, and I had the greatest confidence in his judgment, mainly because he had been over the route before.

The first essential in building boats *a la* Yukon is to know what constitutes suitable trees, and the next is to find them. Two logs would be sufficient, if they would cut nine-inch boards, but the great majority of the trees will not allow it. After roaming about for some time Joe found three which he thought would do, and these we cut down and dragged to a place near the lake.

The next essential is a " saw-pit." As little boat-building had been done at this lake we could not avail ourselves of what someone else had left, but had to construct a pit of our own. We hunted about for four trees near the beach, standing as nearly as possible in the same relation to each other as the corners of a rectangular parallelogram. These, when found, we cut off about six feet from the ground, thus constituting the four legs or support of the platform. The tops of these stumps were then hollowed out so that logs could be laid across each pair, that is the narrow sides of the parallelogram. We fastened these cross-pieces, after a fashion, with spikes, and the saw-pit was complete. The only difficulty about this part of the process is that it is hard work, and takes time, and generally has to be done either while it rains or while it snows. The man who travels in

Alaska only when the weather is good will make about a mile a month, on an average. And it is a country of magnificent distances.

The pit being ready, we squared off the butt ends of the logs and spotted them, that is, cut them the right length, and straightened them as well as we could with an axe. Skids were then placed against the pit and a log was rolled up to the platform ready to be sawed; also two others to serve as a sort of foot-rest for the victim destined to stand above. We then peeled off the bark and sap-wood, and with a chalk-line marked off two slabs.

"You see," said Joe, "that will give you a good place on which to stand and see the chalk-marks when we come to saw off the boards."

It looked very reasonable, like very many other theories which can be found without taking the trouble and risk of going to Alaska. We put a wedge under the logs so as to prevent them from rolling while sawing off the slabs, and then the sawing began; also the trouble.

A whip-saw is a long, coarse-toothed saw, tapering to one end and with handles fixed to each end at right angles. It is an invention of the tempter. It ought to be suppressed. No character is strong enough to withstand it. Two angels could not saw their first log with one of these things without getting into a fight.

I learned this gradually, however. I had allowed Joe to boss all proceedings, and when he said that I might stand on top while sawing off the slabs, I thought, perhaps, that out of the goodness of his heart he was granting me a considerable privilege, for the man on top has only to pull up the saw while the one below pulls it down and does the cutting. So up I climbed, and, taking my end of the saw with a light heart, we worked away at the butt end of a log for a while, and finally got the saw started on the chalk line. As a matter of fact, we both were green at this business. Pretty soon I was startled at hearing Joe swear. This was unusual. He was a man who swore only on great occasions.

"What's the matter?" I asked, looking down, and seeing Joe's face distorted and his eyes blinking.

"You mind your own end of it," he answered back, rather spitefully.

I kept on pulling up the saw with a feeling that I was doing my duty, when Joe shouted savagely:

"Say, don't you know a chalk-line when you see it?"

"I'm not doing the sawing," I replied, "you pull the saw down, and if you don't keep on your mark I can't keep on mine."

"Well, you just keep her running on your line and I'll look out for the under one," he retorted. I have not quoted him exactly. There are certain figures of speech used by men of strong natures, when angry, that look somewhat harsh in print. I tried to pull the saw towards the mark, and did so, but soon it got to running the other side; then I steered it back, and so it went, wobbling around the line, till Joe, firing another chain-shot of forceful expressions, gave the saw a spiteful pull. The wedges slipped from under the slippery log I was standing on and it shot off the pit, saw and all, with a suddenness which would have turned a firecracker green with envy. I came down on my back on one of the little stumps under the pit. Joe stood watching me for a moment as I sat there rubbing several of my shorter ribs.

"You're a dandy," he said, as he walked over and extricated the saw.

I felt that he was to blame for giving the saw such a spiteful pull, and my first impulse was to get up and have it out with him. We had been good friends for a long time. We were " pardners " in all that that word signifies in a mining camp. We had shared all the hardships of the tramp, and I would have risked my life any day to save his, and I knew he would have done the same for me. We had braved the Chilkoot together and the severities of camp life in the snow, and here we were at odds over sawing a log; at odds before we had sawed five feet for the first slab. And we were to saw enough boards to build a boat.

" See here, Joe," I said at last. " If I am to kill anyone over this business I'd rather it wouldn't be you. Suppose I swap off with someone in one of the other parties, and then you or I can have it out with some other fellow."

But we finally made up, rolled the log up to the pit again and resumed. We managed to keep quiet for a long time under the greatest temptations. No two green men can follow a chalk line on their first log. One will be on one side of it on top and of course the saw will run on the other side on the bottom. The first log is nearly always spoiled and boards three-quarter-inch on one edge and one and a quarter on the other will be the result. Such boards will not do for water-tight joints. We spoiled our first log and had several wordy tussles, and lost four or five days, and, I am afraid, came near losing our immortal souls. But finally we got down to work and towards the end sawed out as nice lumber as could be had at a sawmill. I found that the man on the under side had the worst of it, after all, for in pulling the saw down the saw dust spurts into his eyes, and the chalk-line is a more troublesome thing to contend with than when on top. It was more trying than the Chilkoot Pass. Others had similar experiences, and some of the boats turned out in that camp were fearful and wonderful to behold. Some of them looked like coffins; but we discovered afterwards, when we came to some of the rapids, that looks did not count.

After one of the days of hard work, the one in which we had at last completed the sawing of the logs, and while I was washing the supper dishes in the lake through a hole in the ice, I began to reflect. The experience of whip-sawing had developed elements of danger which I had not suspected in the beginning, and I was now in the dark as to what new surprise might be lurking in the building of the boat, now that the lumber was ready. Joe was sitting in front of the tent, enjoying a smoke and the scenery.

"Do you know how to put this lumber together?" I asked.

Joe twisted one leg over the other with the air of a man who knew exactly what was to be done, and was just self-sacrificing enough to impart a little of his knowledge to the ignorant.

"It's easy enough," he said. "You see, in the first place, we must make the frame of her. We'll take some small poles and set them about two feet apart. The bottom piece must be 'half-scarfed,' or 'half-checked'; that is, cut through at each end half way, at an angle at which the upright pieces are to stand. Midships the ribs will be nearly straight up and down, while at the bow they will be much more inclined. The bottom and sides of the ribs must be nailed firmly together, and then the boat is ready to be built. A platform of saw-horses and two planks must be made, and over these the ribs will be laid, bottom up. for that is the way she will be built."

"I hope that's not the way she'll sail," I said.

"The center plank, or keel piece," continued Joe, without noticing such a trivial interruption, "must be nailed down to the ribs first, and each rib then put in its proper place from stem to stern. Each bottom-piece must be nailed on in turn and brought up close. By the way, Bill, did you bring a boat-clamp?"

"Not that I know of."

"I knew we'd forget something we would need, but we can work it somehow."

I suggested no objections, having by this time learned that about the only way to do things in Alaska was " to work it somehow."

"When it comes to putting on the side planks," continued Joe, "the ribs will have to be shaped a little, so as to bring the planks up close to them, so as not to have them rest on sharp edges, for, you see, I am going to give her a pointed nose and a square stern."

"That seems reasonable and commendable," I said, as I threw the dish-rag at a dog that was sticking his nose into one of the kettles, and which thereupon picked up the rag, ran off a little distance, and began to eat it up. I was beginning to learn something of the ways of the country.

"A stem-piece must be firmly attached to the keel-piece," continued Joe, "and over this, to protect the bow of the boat, must be fastened a strip of tough wood, about three inches thick by four wide. Then comes the caulking. Anybody can do that."

We had cut our lumber twenty-six feet long and eight inches wide. I suggested to Joe that the lumber did not seem to me long enough for a boat to take us and all our provisions.

But Joe had been down the river before, and he quietly "allowed" that he knew what sort of a boat was needed. In fact, I think he rather resented my criticisms, for he made the proposition that he should build the boat himself, and that I should look after the camp, do the cooking, and so forth. I agreed to the bargain readily, for I knew that these duties would give me much spare time, and my hunting instincts had been aroused by an occasional glimpse of game in the woods. So Joe kept at work on the boat, and nearly every day I shouldered my rifle and disappeared in the woods. Grouse and rabbit were plenty about this place, and I brought in a great many, so we would have lived quite like epicures had I made fewer disastrous experiments in cooking. One day I ran across two mountain sheep, and I saw a good many moose and bear tracks, but they were difficult to trace, for the snow was nearly off the ground by this time and everything was beginning to look green.

One day I started out with two other boys in the camp, one a fellow by the name of Cook, from New York. We were simply after any game we could find. Coming to a small hill in the timber, we separated, I to go one side, Cook the other, and the third fellow was to go to the top. I had gone on slowly for perhaps half a mile when I heard Cook's dog barking, and then Cook began shouting for us with all the strength of his lungs. I started on a brisk run, imagining that he must have come across a dragon by the way he was shouting. The other fellow came tearing down the hill, too, and when I reached them they both were looking up a tall spruce and the dog was dancing about in a perfect frenzy.

Hanging to the limbs near the top of the tree were four

bears, an old one and three cubs. Cook had never seen a bear before outside of a menagerie, and his excitement was such that he could hardly tell one end of the gun from the other. But according to the ethics of the woods they were his bears. His dog had treed them, and it was his privilege to do the shooting. His desire was to kill the mother and catch the cubs alive. He walked off a few steps and aimed, but I could see the muzzle of his gun wobbling like a weather-vane. He had a good, clear chance, but he did not hit her, nor anything else. But the next time he fired he crippled her, and down she came with a tremendous thump at the foot of the tree, where she picked herself up and faced the dog, which, more brave than discreet, pitched into her. She gave him a savage little cuff, which sent him rolling through the underbrush, and Cook, who was scarcely thirty feet off, fired again and missed her. The dog began to dance around her again, and at Cook's next shot the dog ran away with a yelp. The bullet had grazed his neck.

Cook was getting more excited than ever. He emptied his gun, and though the poor bear was too crippled to keep her feet she was still lively. I was longing for one shot at her, but I gave my gun to Cook, and after he had nearly emptied that the bear gave up the ghost.

" Cook," said I, " if it takes two guns for one bear, what would you do with two bears and one gun ? "

" They die hard, don't they ? "

" Unless you hit 'em."

Then we turned our attention to the cubs. The other fellow volunteered to go up the tree, and when he had climbed as far as it would hold him, he cut off the top, and down the cubs came, one of them getting his back broke. We rushed in to catch the others, and they scratched and bit like demons. The one I had caught hold of was particularly ferocious, and I carry on one hand a scar which he gave me. Cook had a tussle with his, but he was better at catching them alive than shooting them, and, after skinning the old bear and appropriating the hams, we started for camp, leading the two cubs, while the dog urged them on from behind.

On the way, Cook slipped in crossing a ravine, dropped his cord, and in a twinkling his cub was up a tree. We had to cut off the top of that one also before we had him again. We found the hams too tough to eat. That night one of the cubs broke his chain somehow and got away, so Cook had only one cub and a bear skin to show for all his shooting.

Our exploit aroused considerable interest in the little camp that night, but Cook didn't enjoy it, as much sport was made of his marksmanship. These brown bears will sometimes fight very fiercely, and a man needs to keep a cool head and to be a good shot.

" It would 'a been all day with you," said one of the old-timers who was coming in with us, " if you had shot like that when meeting the brown bear I once did. I was down at Cook's Inlet, washing gold from the beach sand, last year, and, a cold snap coming on, we were obliged to close work. I had two Indians with me, and as they were anxious to make a trip up the bay for some traps, and possibly to get some bear meat, they asked me for my Winchester rifle in exchange for a large single-shot. I complied, like a fool, and one day when I had got back to the cabin from prospecting, and it was too early to turn in, I went out and sat down not far from the beach to see if there were signs of the Indians returning. Suddenly I was thrown into a flutter by seeing two big brown bears walking leisurely along in my direction, not two hundred yards away. I crawled along in the grass to the cabin, and got the Indian's rifle, putting some extra cartridges in my pocket. I now wished for my six-shooter. I crept down towards the bank, and, sitting down in a cutting, tried to keep myself cool. Presently the nose of one of them came into view, a short distance from where I sat, and he saw me, and gave a deep angry growl. I had a good shot at his head, and he fell in his tracks. Then I started down the beach for the other. The report had alarmed him, and he was scampering away. I dropped on one knee, took a slow aim, and fired. He wavered a bit; evidently, the ball had struck home, but he turned in around the bank before I could get a second shot. I tried to track him, but couldn't, and I concluded he had some hidden shelter. I finally turned towards the cabin, and put the hammer of the gun down. I had hardly gone fifty yards, however, when, rounding the edge of some scrub bushes, I came right on the wounded bear, lying in the grass. He jumped to his haunches, his mouth streaked with foam, his eyes glaring defiance, and his whole air was so ferocious, and I had been taken so by surprise, that I have to confess I turned and ran. The bear gave instant chase. When I had gone some distance I tripped and fell, and, looking back, expecting to see the bear close by, I saw that I had gained on him. I recovered my courage, and thought that if I fired and missed I would still have time to run on. But I waited too long. When he came within a few feet he raised himself on his haunches, and I pulled the trigger, but, to my horror, it failed to act. I had, in my excitement, forgotten that I had put down the hammer. Before I had time to recover myself he hit me a terrible

blow on my left side. Instinctively I turned my face downward and played 'possum. He came up, sniffed about me,
clawed me once or twice, and walked off a little ways. My
gun had been thrown off somewhere in the grass and was
out of reach. I lay there for a minute, and finally the bear
came back and clawed me some more. I was beginning to
think he was going to turn me over, when I heard a shot,
and the big bear dropped beside me. The Indians had
come in just in time. When I got up I found that the blow
of the bear had torn clear through my clothing and made
an ugly wound in my side, which was bleeding freely. If
I hadn't played 'possum I should have been a dead man."

Every one appreciated the moral of this tale. When
you are gunning for bear in Alaska, or anywhere else, do not
go off "half-cocked." There was very little game of this
sort about here, nor, indeed, is there much anywhere near
the gold regions. The forest fires started by the Indians
drive away the good game, and the pest of the mosquitoes
in the summer is trying to the bears. In some parts of
Alaska there is a variety of bear called "silver-tip," which
is very ferocious, and does not wait to be attacked, but
attacks on sight. The miners, unless traveling in groups
and well armed, give it a wide berth. Though I saw many
moose tracks while I was on my excursions, I never came
across one. It usually requires a three or four days' hunt
to come up with them. There are two species of caribou in
the country; one, the ordinary kind, much resembling the
reindeer, and the other called a wood caribou, which is a
much larger and more beautiful animal. The ordinary
caribou runs in herds and is easily approached, and, when
fired at, jumps around and is as likely to run towards one
as from him. At last, when several have been killed, the

rest will start on a continuous run, and may not stop for twenty miles. The Indians kill them in large numbers sometimes, even when they have meat enough. They are rarely found, I was told, in two successive seasons in the same place.

The mountain sheep which I found around here were pure white in color, but otherwise they resemble very much the gray ones found in the lower latitudes. But they have finer horns, more handsomely curved.

CHAPTER VII

A DANGEROUS VOYAGE—OVERTURNING OF OUR BOAT—
LOSS OF AN $800 OUTFIT—WE ESCAPE WITH OUR
LIVES—HUNTING FOR A CAMP THIEF.

We Name Our Boat the *Tar Stater*—More Handsome than Adequate
— Drifting amid Scenes of Wild Grandeur—Magical Vegetation—
Fifty Mile River—At the Mouth of the Cañon—We Conclude to
Pack Around—Several Boats Go Through—The Trail—An Offer
to Take the *Tar Stater* Through for $5—I Am Invited to Ride,
and Accept—A Quick Repentance—Discarding Gum Boots—A
Serious Catastrophe—At the Mercy of the Current—Clinging to
an Overturned Boat—Over Again—Saved—A Four-Minute Ex-
perience —The Milk is Spilled—Loss of an $800 Outfit—Recovering
Our Boat—Towards White Horse Rapids—Disappearance of the
Sugar Saved from the Wreck—I Am Mad—Strapping on My
Gun—Looking for a Camp Thief—Sympathy for Us—A Phase
of Yukon Life.

WHILE I was acting as chief cook and wood-cutter,
and was making excursions for game in the
country, Joe kept himself busy with the boat,
and I helped only when it was ready for the caulking. It
was finished in about ten days, and was a very good specimen, considering the tools we had to work with. I thought
it looked small for the purpose of carrying our large outfit
through very rough water, but Joe insisted that it was large
enough, in spite of the warnings of one of the old-timers.
But Joe had been over the river as well as the old-timer,
and he was satisfied. I was a fair swimmer, and I knew

that I could get out of any place that he could, so I kept still. We named her the *Tar Stater*, in honor of Joe's native State. Every boat on the lake had a name, and one could see all sorts of clumsy-looking boxes carrying the names of all the States in the Union and of prominent men from George Washington to Grover Cleveland.

The ice continued to block the lake, being five or six feet deep in places, but the weather suddenly growing warmer, it broke and it seemed safe for us to embark. As we piled in our effects I saw that the boat was going to be pretty full, but Joe persisted that he knew what we wanted, and so off we started, working our way through the cakes of ice, and finding no very open water till we reached the lower end of the lake, which is about twenty miles long. Running out from it are long arms, the most prominent of which are Windy Arm and Taku Arm, reaching far up between the terraced and evergreen hills. The group lies in a depression between the coast range and the main range of the Rockies, and altogether it is a very picturesque region, abounding in striking promontories with a continuous fringe of wooded landscape along the banks, and back of them the impressive mountains seamed with little glaciers — gleaming like silver ribbons — while, breaking out here and there, little rivulets leaped down precipitous heights and sometimes rose to the dignity of torrents. Mile after mile of wildest grandeur glides by like a continuous panorama.

At the mouth of Windy Lake are three small islands, and beyond them tower mountains of limestone and marble, and the beach abounds in marble of various colors. When we come to a little clear water we find it so transparent that we can peer to the bottom of the lake and see the fragments of marble scattered about. From the junction of Taku

Arm, of which little appears to be known, to the north end of the lake, the distance is about six miles, and the width for the greater part of the way is over two miles. It is a fine piece of water, but apparently very shallow.

At the lower end the river issues from it and flows six miles to Marsh Lake. It is not more than 150 yards wide, and some of the way not more than six feet deep. On its bank, about one and a half miles from the lake, the Canadian police and customs officers are stationed. On the other side are the Tagish houses, or council houses of the little band of Stick Indians which wander about the lake country, and which, until recently, were not allowed by the Tlingit tribes to come down to the coast to trade. The buildings, though the only ones in the interior of Alaska with any pretensions to skill in architecture, are little more than rough enclosures, and the natives are exceedingly poor specimens of humanity. They have a simple way of disposing of their dead, and one of their burying-places can be seen from the river. The departed one is laid on a pile of dried logs which have been smeared with grease. A fire is then started, but the remains are seldom thoroughly burned, only charred, and over this they hold their funeral services, which are too complex for the civilized mind. It is their delight to go to a funeral, and when they are employed in packing for the miners or upper Yukon travelers they will, on hearing of a death, at once drop their packs and not return till the funeral is over.

A little distance below the Tagish houses is the entrance to Lake Marsh, so named by Schwatka after Prof. O. C. Marsh of Yale, but most of the miners call it Mud Lake, though there is no good reason for such a name, and it is possible that it was originally given to the lower part of Tagish Lake, which is shallow and in places somewhat muddy. Lake Marsh is about twenty miles long and two miles wide. Its shores are low, flat, and stony, and the waters are shallow. The boat must be kept to the left bank. When we went through, it was still full of ice, though it was rapidly disappearing under the sun, which was now approaching its long summer course. Along the shores the vegetation was springing up as if by magic under its continuous warmth, while the rivulets formed by the melting snow and glaciers tumbled over the rocks of the hillsides, falling in glittering cascades. The surrounding region appears low to us after what we have passed through, but it is picturesque in any season, the great terraces rising to high ranges on either side and not more than ten miles away. Prominent on the east stands Michie Mountain, five thousand five hundred and forty feet in height (so named from Professor Michie of West Point), and on the west Mounts Lorne and Lansdowne, six thousand four hundred, and six thousand one hundred and forty feet high, respectively. Wild fowl are plentiful along the flats, but nothing alive abounds like the mosquitoes, which begin to come up in swarms from the swamps.

The traveler finds the names of all the prominent features of the landscape of recent origin. Nothing more clearly indicates the newness of the country. Of course the natives have long had their names for the prominent objects, but they are seldom adopted by explorers. It is easier to go over the Chilkoot than to pronounce them as they pronounce them, for there is nothing in the English language sounding like their clicking syllables.

Near the foot of Marsh Lake a stream called McClintock River enters, and its valley is but yet little known, though it

RAFTING DOWN THE YUKON

The mining outfit of these two Klondikers, consisting of provisions, arms, camp equipage, dogs, and so forth, is piled on to their rude raft.

seems to be large, and it evidently pours in a quantity of the dirt that forms the shallows of the lake.   The outlet of the lake is called Fifty Mile River, and it is here that the descent of the Yukon may be said to commence, though it is many miles further before the great water course really begins. Here the water flows northwesterly through the great valley with a current of three miles an hour.   From here on we had open water, and it was a welcome relief after working our way through so many obstacles.   But in the springtime the banks of the river are constantly caving in and dumping trees into the stream, which is shallow in many places. Often we had to poke the nose of the *Tar Stater* out of the mud, for in many places the current seemed to run directly over these bars.   The salmon struggle up to this point, and some of the largest are found here in season, but they never have the strength to get back, and in the summer large numbers of the dead and dying are found here.

After a rapid run down this stream, which twists and turns like a huge serpent in distress, the current becoming swifter and swifter, we came out into a wide sweep of the river where the water is still and gives little evidence, except a dull roar, of the dangers ahead, till the two frowning walls of the cañon appear.   The river above the cañon looks about five hundred feet wide, and it is eight or ten feet deep.   All this has to pour between two bluffs only about seventy-five feet apart, and rising in perpendicular grandeur for a hundred feet on either side.   We found many boats along the west bank, and so we landed to take a look at what was before us.

Climbing to the top of the bluff, we gazed down upon the mighty current rushing in a perfect mass of milk-white foam with a roar intensified by the high walls of rock.   The

water was boiling through it at such terrific speed that it
ridged up in the center, while along the perpendicular banks
it whirled in huge eddies which had a very threatening look.
The clouds of spray gave the water level a snowy appearance.   The cañon is about a mile long, and while we stood
there we saw several boats go through at the speed of a race-
horse.   But though they bobbed about like chips, they were
generally managed cleverly, and ran through safely.   By
hard work they were kept in the middle of the channel, but
occasionally one would get to one side, and be caught in the
eddies, and whirled around past all control.   It was then a
matter of luck if they went through without a mishap, for
there was the greatest danger of their being dashed against
the steep basaltic sides and smashed.   But while we looked
all passed safely through, though we could see that some
shipped considerable water in the big waves.

"Pretty stiff gallop through there, ain't it?" remarked
Joe as we turned to go down the bluff.

"I don't know what you think," said I, "but I know too
little about managing a boat to run her safely through there.
Besides, Joe, the *Tar Stater* is too heavily loaded to meet
those waves gracefully."

So we finally agreed to pack our goods around.   The
portage path is over the east bluff, is about a mile long, and
the trail is comparatively good.   This does not mean that it
is easy.   It leads over a high ridge just the length of the
cañon, and then descends abruptly with a dizzy incline into
a valley, then, after continuing for some distance along the
cascades, it ascends a sandy hill.   It is very difficult, for
many trees had fallen across it so that it resembled crossing
a lot of hurdles.   It leads much of the way through brush
and wooded patches, where the mosquitoes filled the air and

made life miserable. One knows how to fight a big enemy, but a myriad of persistent little ones completely unnerve a man. On the first trip I took my clothing, bedding, and gun, and Joe took a one-hundred-pound sack of sugar and part of a sack of beans. This promised to be a slow process, and on our way back, as we saw another boat go through safely with a whole outfit in less time than it took us to fix a single pack on our backs, Joe began to get braver.

"I know the *Tar Stater* will ride as well as that coffin did," said he.

Our boat was certainly handsomer than many that went through without mishap, but I still clung to the idea that it would not be well to try her till she had been lightened considerably. When we reached the bank again, we were approached by two men who were making it a business to take boats through at five dollars each. They wanted to take ours. I asked if she ought not to be lightened more, but after looking at her critically they said she was all right, indeed, was a pretty trim-looking craft. They had taken seven through safely that day, and seemed so confident of their ability that we made the bargain with them, and, as we must give them the same, loaded or empty, we foolishly decided to let them take her as she was. It would take two days to pack our things around the cañon, and as several of our camp friends had gone through we wished to keep pace with them. One of the men asked me if I would like to ride through, and I told them I would not mind if I should not be in the way.

"Jump in," they said, while Joe strolled up to the bluff to watch us.

We pushed off, and in two minutes my heart failed me, and I would have given all the gold I ever expected to get in

these regions had I staid out.   Return was impossible.   As
we rounded the corner, and looked down through the cañon,
I made up my mind that some fine work would be done if the
Tar Stater went through those waves all right.   I quickly
pulled off my gum boots, thinking that if I should need to
swim I would get along better without those, and then into
the yawning chasm we shot, drawn by a force nothing could
resist.

There is a popular summer amusement called " Shooting
the Chutes," very exciting and very exhilarating, I am told.
A boat-load slides down an incline, and splashes into the
water.   But just imagine a boat hurled along on a ridge of
water running a mile in three minutes, and twenty times as
long as your amusing chutes.

The two men started in to manage the boat cleverly
enough.   Not far from the entrance the boat seemed to
take a fall of several feet, while all the waters in creation
seemed to have fallen into a space seventy-five feet wide.
The moment we struck the first high wave we shipped some
water, at the second we shipped more, at the third it poured
in around the whole outfit, and at the next we were full, and
over we went into the ice-cold water with the worst part of
the cañon before us.   The boat turned toward the side I
was occupying, and I sprang out so as to avoid being covered
up.   The moment I struck the water all fear was gone.   It
was easy swimming, for the current took one along whether
he would or not.

When the boat came up she was about ten feet from me,
and it was not easy to reach her, for struggling against the
current was another matter.   Finally I caught hold of the
stern and climbed up.   As I was swept by one of the other
fellows, I got hold of him and pulled him in so that he could

climb up, and a little afterwards the other man was able to reach us.   There the three of us were riding on the bottom of the boat, which was whirling about in the wildest manner. As straight as a crow flies runs the cañon for an eighth of a mile.   The roar was like a cannonade.   On the top of the bluffs which fled by us grew dense forests of spruce which shut out the sun, and a weird darkness pervaded the deep and angry channel.   The boat shot forward with lightning speed, leaping like a racer or bucking like a mustang, now buried out of sight in the foam, and now plunged beneath a terrific wave.   We clung desperately to the bottom as helpless as flies.

A moment later we came to the worst place in the current, where there are three heavy swells, and where those who are steering boats through incline a little to the left to avoid the roughest part.   But the current was steering us, and into the swells we dived.   The waters swept us from the slippery keel as if we had been so many leaves.   Again we struggled in the current, and again we caught on to the whirling boat, for after the swells the water became smoother, and in a twinkling we shot out of the cañon like a rocket, amid the reefs of boulders and bars thickly studded with drifts of timber.   Two men were waiting at the foot of the bluffs in a boat, and when they saw us come out they rowed after us and took us in.   Thus we left the *Tar Stater*.

I had looked at my watch, which fortunately I carried in a rubber sack in my pocket, when I got into the boat at the upper end, and I looked again as we climbed into the boat which had come to our rescue, and saw that we had had a little over four minutes of experience.   Some of the boats go through in three minutes.

Wet and shivering, I sat down on a rock on the bank and felt very blue. Ten minutes before we had boasted the best outfit that any two men we had seen were bringing in; everything we would need for the next eighteen months. It was worth over $800, according to the way things sold in Alaska, and we had lost very many things which could not be bought on the Yukon. All we had left was the sack of sugar and a few beans; nothing to cook them in. We had no tent to sleep in, and we were two hundred and fifty miles from Juneau and five hundred miles from the nearest trading post down the river.

As I sat there Joe came down with a grim expression on his face. He had stood on the bluff and had seen us go under. He knew now that we had been too heavily loaded.

" The *Tar Stater* is down yonder somewhere," I said, with a despondent gesture towards the rushing river. I thought I would not be rough on the poor fellow.

" Well, the milk is spilled," he said, giving the forlorn bag of beans a kick.

" And this region doesn't flow with milk and honey," I added.

We walked along down the river, and about a mile and a half below we found the *Tar Stater*, bottom up, and her nose tucked into a crack in the rocks by the bank in such a manner as to be held fast. She was somewhat strained, and needed recaulking. We dragged her up to the rocks, and Joe looked at her mournfully. I could not withstand the temptation.

" The *Tar Stater* is a dandy in rough water," I said, and I could see that Joe was badly hurt. Then I was sorry, and tried to make amends by saying that she would have gone through with flying colors had we only taken the precaution to carry part of the load around the cañon. " She is too trim for heavy work," I added.

On the next day a boat was overturned in running through, and two men were drowned. It was a sad ending to the hard voyage of two gold-seekers, but all along the river are the little marks which tell of similar cases. There were several parties camped at the lower end of the cañon, including some of the friends we had made at Lake Tagish. They were very kind to us, so that we managed very comfortably while we were getting our boat ready. This did not take much time, and, having secured a set of oars, we loaded in all that remained of our costly outfit and proceeded down the river.

Below the cañon there is a stretch of somewhat milder rapids, or cascades, for nearly three miles, and then after a little smooth water we arrived at the White Horse Rapids, which are justly considered more dangerous than the cañon, but it is less on account of the swift current than of the formation of the passage, it being full of sunken rocks. It is, on the whole, the worst piece of water on the Yukon, and no one should ever attempt to take their outfit through. Of course, we were no longer hampered in this way.

In coming up to these rapids one must land on the west bank, which is formed of steep rocks, and the place is very difficult either for managing a boat, or for getting a burden up to the portage. Many drag their boats over the trail, but it is difficult work and requires several men to pull a loaded boat around in a day. To get the boats up over the rocks the miners had constructed a crude windlass. But most of those on the way with us determined to carry their goods around, and then shoot the rapids in empty boats.

We lined the *Tar Stater* down the side, and then went

up to watch proceedings and to help one of the other boys down with his boat. We were gone some little time, and when we returned to our boat the sack of sugar was missing. I was mad. Some villain had stolen the most valuable part of the provisions we had saved from the wreck; that was about all we had left of that eight-hundred-dollar outfit. I strapped on my six-shooter and went hunting for that sugar with a vengeance. Theft is one of the worst crimes a man can commit in this country, and it is not common. Only tenderfeet who have not outgrown the privileges of life in civilized regions will dare commit it. Generally, anything can be left with perfect safety on the trails, providing it is out of the reach of dogs. There are no storehouses, and traveling necessitates leaving articles of value all along the route. Traveling would be impossible but for a rigid regard for other people's property. It is the unwritten law of the land, and it comes as naturally to the Indians as to any one. Morose, superstitious, utterly ungrateful, and never to be believed, these Indians rarely touch a thing that belongs to any one else. They will leave their own belongings all along the trail, and they will be often passed, but no one thinks of touching them. They know they will be there when they return.

I knew it was some white man who had taken the sugar, and I went through the boats with fire in my eye. It would have been easy to find it had it been there, but it was not. On the other hand, everybody was in perfect sympathy with my attempt to find the thief, and if he had been found they would have given him, then and there, what, in the parlance of the Yukon, is called a " jig-in-air " at the end of a rope. It was lucky, perhaps, that I did not find him, for I was in a dangerous mood. I could have shot him dead and no one

would have said a word against it.   I should have been criti-
cised if I had failed to.

Two or three boats had gone on through the rapids, and
the thief had evidently taken the sack just as he was putting
off, in the expectation of escaping safely.   It would not
have been so serious had he taken something from a party
that was well-stocked with provisions, but taking it from
us who had lost nearly everything but that, was sufficient
to raise the indignation of the whole camp to the boiling
point.   The fellows offered us all we wanted.   We suffered for nothing.   We could make ourselves at home in
any tent there.

There are some rare qualities in the rough breasts of the
pilgrims of the Yukon, a consideration for the condition of
others which is not always found in a softer climate and in
an easier life.

CHAPTER VIII

SOME THRILLING EXPERIENCES — DISCOVERY OF THE
THIEF — HIS SUMMARY PUNISHMENT — PICTURES BY
THE WAY.

Through the White Horse Rapids in an Empty Boat — Close Shave for
the *Tar Stater* — Rough to Experience but Interesting to Watch —
Overtaking Three Boats — I find the Sack of Sugar and the Thief
— Swift Preparations for a Lynching Bee — "Say the Word and Up
He Goes" — I Refuse — "Nothing Less Than Fifty Lashes, Then" —
I Administer Them on the Thief's Bare Back — The Victim Becomes
a Good Citizen — Lake Lebarge and Tagish Indians — Eggs for a
Change — In the Twilight of the Midnight — Nature in Her Great
Work — Cutting Down Hills and Valleys — Where Eagles Nest —
Twisting and Turning — Five Fingers — Rink Rapids — Arrival at
Fort Selkirk — A Touch of Civilization — The Route Marked with
Graves of the Fallen — Reflections on the Journey.

THERE were, as I remember, six boats with ours at
the entrance of White Horse Rapids, and we all
went through in safety, but it was a thrilling experience. We were swept along over the raging torrent,
which here and there throws white spray into the air, a
fact from which the rapids take their name. The foaming
waves seem to come from every direction. Ragged rocks
hang over the passage, the current sucking in under them,
and at times we could have reached up and touched the
rocks with our hands had we cared to. We had too much
to do for amusement of that kind. The rapids extend
straight away for nearly a quarter of a mile, and then take

an abrupt turn to the right. It is after passing the turn that the most dangerous part is encountered.

With a stream that is two hundred yards wide, full of ugly boulders, coupled with a fall of two hundred feet in five-eighths of a mile, it is no wonder that this stretch of river has become the terror of Alaskan gold-hunters. If the current in the cañon appeared to speed along with the swiftness of an arrow, that in the rapids seemed to equal the flight of a swift bird. The last hundred yards of the journey was particularly dangerous. At the spot called the "White Horse" the waters tumbled and tossed in most fantastic fashion, piling up the spray in long white columns ten or twelve feet high. There is a sheer fall of nine feet at that point.

"Joe, we're goners sure," I shouted, holding on in terror. But the *Tar Stater* took the plunge in a way that gladdened our hearts. True, it seemed that we would never come up; and, when we did, it looked as though we would never come down. Into the air the bow went, and when the boat again struck the water flew over us in a torrent. We thought that the next moment would see the *Tar Stater* sink, but she did not. I think it was the swiftness of the current that kept her afloat. At any rate, we reached shore safely, but wet through to the skin. If anybody imagines that shooting the White Horse Rapids is easy or pleasant he is very much mistaken.

There may be some pleasure in boasting of having shot these fearful waters, but it is the height of folly to run the risk. Many go through safely in empty boats, but they are at the mercy of as angry a bit of water as there is in Alaska, and there are a great many such places. The summer before we went through, it was said that thirteen persons lost their

lives there, and all because they preferred to take the risk
than to drag the boat around.   It requires but a minute or
so to shoot through, but days to get an outfit around.

Terrible as is the experience, there are few places more
sublime to the view.   Standing on the bank in safety, the
eye is charmed by the waters that leap and foam around
the highly-colored rocks.   You may watch it for hours
and turn away with regret, and if the eye wanders off it
rests on the somber stretches of trees, in their varying colors,
the luxuriant grass, and the tundra, while standing like
ghostly sentinels over all are the snowy peaks in the distance.   Everything is on a grand scale, and one acquires a
faint realization of what this planet must have been in those
untrimmed, uncut, glacial times when the earth was dotted
with raging waters like these, and mammoths stalked or
crawled about the gloomy hillsides.

Below the rapids the river flows swiftly on for several
miles, much of the time between gravel banks, but the
water is smooth, the banks one hundred and fifty yards
apart, and no obstacles except bars appear; so we made good
progress.   The current becomes less and less as the river
turns northward through the same wide valley.   The bluffs
along the bank are of white silt, which gives a cloudy yellow
tint to the waters.   About thirteen miles down we come to
the mouth of the Tahkheena River, a muddy stream about
seventy-five yards wide, flowing in from the west.   Its
sources are near the Chilkat Pass, and its waters flow through
a large body of water named Arkell Lake, not far from the
Dalton trail.   It is said to have been formerly used by the
Chilkat Indians in reaching the interior, but now it is
seldom used, though its waters are said to be navigable from
the head of the lake down.

Our little party of six or seven boats kept close together as we drifted down the rapid stream, and, towards evening, as we were looking along the banks for a good place to camp, we came upon three boats and a little camp back from the bank. I had not forgotten the sugar; neither had the others. We disembarked with assumed indifference, but I immediately raised some consternation by going through the boats. In one of them I found a sack of sugar.

In less that a minute that boat and the man claiming it were covered with a dozen guns, but I was somewhat surprised to see my friends put a rope around his neck and lead him struggling towards a tree. The day before, when I was boiling with rage, I might not have said a word. I knew how heinous the crime of theft was considered in Alaska. But now I was somewhat taken aback by the swiftness with which my friends proposed to mete out justice. The man could say nothing. He was badly frightened, and those who had been with him on the bank made no protest; and, if they had, we were too many for them.

The rope was thrown over the limb of a neighboring tree, and a half a dozen men caught hold of it ready to pull.

"Hold on a minute, boys," I said. "It strikes me it's pretty tough to hang a man for stealing a sack of sugar."

"Hang the man who steals anything!" said one of the old timers.

"But I don't want to be too cruel on the fellow," I replied. "He may know better next time."

The poor fellow was trembling like a leaf. His face was ghastly pale, and he looked at me with beseeching eyes.

"Wal, it's your sugar," said one of the men, "and all you've got to do is to say the word and up he goes."

"I won't do it," said I. "Settle it some other way."

"He's got to be punished somehow," said the old-timer, in a determined tone, "and, if you don't want to have him pulled up, you'll have to give him the lash. We sometimes does that."

"All right," I said, knowing that some form of punishment would certainly have to be administered.

So they made him take off his clothes down to his bare back, tied his hands together, and swung him up so that his toes barely touched the ground.

"Nothin' less than fifty lashes," said the old-timer, handing me a piece of rope. So I began to lay it on, and the more I did so, the more I began to think he deserved it. He stood it remarkably well, but finally began to cry with pain, and I stopped.

"Nothin' less than fifty," shouted the old-timer.

So I kept on till the number was reached. It was a pretty tough-looking back he had when I finished, and he drew his shirt on with the greatest care.

I came to know that man very well later on. Strange as it may appear, we grew to be friends, and he made a good citizen of Alaska. I never knew of his again taking a thing belonging to another. These primitive methods of punishment are quite effectual, after all. There would be fewer burglars and sneak thieves in the States if the lash were used publicly, instead of the so-called enlightened method of retiring them to a rather agreeable life in a prison, to which they take their own evil natures, and where they exchange lessons in criminality with their prison associates.

Proceeding a few miles further, we arrived at Lake Lebarge, which lies nearly north and south, surrounded by mountains, those on the southeast presenting very abrupt and castellated forms, with summits of white limestone. It is thirty-one miles long with an average breadth of nearly five miles. Its southern half is somewhat wider, but then it narrows down to about two miles for a distance of about seven miles, and at the north end expands to about four miles again. The western shore is indented with shallow little bays. Just before reaching the place where it narrows there is a large island, the southern end flat, with gravel banks, and the other end rocky. The rocks are a bright red, and makes a very pretty picture against the other colors along the shore.

The lake is about two thousand feet above the sea-level, and we found it rough sailing most of the time, though the wind held in our direction. Its rough water is usually dreaded by miners, who sometimes are forced to camp on its banks for several days, till the wind goes down. The whole valley seems to be a great trough, sucking inland the southerly winds, which are apt to prevail in the summer months.

It is a favorite spot for the Tagish Indians, exceedingly filthy and degraded creatures, who will bargain almost anything they have for a little whisky, for which they have acquired a taste through the expanding trade of our Christianized countries. The missionaries came at the same time, but their efforts have little effect on them. To them, the greatest importation of civilization is " fire-water."

We made good progress on Lake Lebarge, in spite of its roughness. Other names have been given this body of water, and the Indians have one of their own. Its common name is derived from one Mike Lebarge, who not many years ago was engaged by the Western Union Telegraph Company, exploring the river and adjacent country for the purpose of connecting Europe and America by a telegraph line overland, except for the short distance at Bering Strait.

The days had become so long by this time that we could travel nearly all the time, stopping only now and then for a square meal.   It will be difficult for anyone who has not been in the Arctic regions to form a good idea of the picturesque features of a sail along one of these lakes at this time of year.   The shore of the large lake is fringed with a line of trees, which stretch back over the low hills, but over the tops of these trees towers the white line of mountains miles away.   And above these mountains is the canopy of heaven. Around this circles the blazing sun, hour after hour.   One does not realize what a relief the darkness is till he comes to a region like this, at a time when there is no darkness.

On we drifted, over the ruffled waters, taking a cold lunch when hungry, but without any adequate realization of the time of day, unless we looked at our watches.   Finally the sun set, and Venus was the only star which became dimly visible in the twilight of midnight.

About half way down the lake is a large bare rock, where flocks of gulls make their home.   Eggs are a great luxury in Alaska, and we laid in as good a supply as we could and feasted on them for several days.   One can scarcely appreciate the amount of pleasure there is in instituting a little variety in Alaskan diet, for the appetite knows no bounds, and the staple food is extremely limited in variety.   Besides, since the loss of our outfit we had been obliged to use our money to buy what stores the others could spare, though they were very kind, and would have given us food at any time had we asked it.   I kept my eyes on the shore most of the time, in the hopes of seeing game, and although I found enough to provide us with many good meals, I could not fail to notice that it was becoming more and more scarce.

The Lewis river, as it flows out of the lake, is about two hundred yards wide, and for about five miles preserves this width, and a swift current of from four to six miles an hour. It then makes a sharp turn about a low gravel point, and flows for a mile in a direction opposite to its general course, when again it sharply resumes its way northward.   Twenty-seven miles down we come to a great tributary from the southeast, the Teslin River, as it is now called, as it drains the great Teslin Lake; but the miners call it by its Indian name, the Hootalinkwa.   Schwatka called it the Newberry, and Dr. Dawson had given it the name of Teslintoo; from which it appears that names in Alaska are sometimes uncertain, and time alone will tell which name will prevail.   We were told by the Indians that gold could be found on this stream, but few explorations of it appeared to have been made.

The water of the Teslin is of dark brown color.   Indeed, one cannot fail to notice, at least in the spring of the year, the amount of dirt these streams are carrying down. It is another feature of a fact that strikes a traveler at every point, the immense amount of work that Nature is doing in these regions.   The country in the section we have recently passed is extremely mountainous, with torrents plunging down through the rough valleys from the eternal snows. The water in the lakes appears to be remarkably clear, but as soon as we touch any of the connecting streams we notice that they are so full of sediment that one cannot see an inch below the surface.

If a basinful is taken out and allowed to stand until it clears, a thick deposit of mud is found at the bottom.   The current boils and flows very rapidly, and as the boat glided along a sound was heard almost like that of frying fat.   It was only the constant friction on the boat of the immense amount of large particles of earth which the water was carrying in suspension. This is noticeable all along the river, and is an indication of the wearing-down process that is constantly going on in this great country. It furnishes the reason for the shifting bars which exist on the lower Yukon, and for the difficulties that prevail at its mouth. When time has done its work, the shores of Alaska, about the mouth of its great river, will be pushed out much further into the Pacific.

As we proceeded down the river we easily saw whence comes all this material. Along the silt and sand bluffs, loose material is constantly falling into the stream. These little landslides, occurring all the time, except in the months when everything is frozen, result in an immense amount of dirt being dumped into the river. We should be surprised if it were measured. I had read how Nature worked through countless ages, but I never realized the extent, the capability of the mighty forces, till I took that first trip down the upper Yukon region. But while we see Nature working in an earlier process than that to which we are accustomed, one is appalled to think how long she has been working even here. For all those mighty cañons which we have seen, and through some of which we have barely escaped with our lives, have been worn out by the torrents. These great rocks and boulders, which fill the stream and around which the swift current plays, have been rolled down from the mountains by the receding glaciers.

We found these huge boulders a great obstacle all the way down this part of the river. Sometimes it was all we both could do to handle the boat. The current would carry us against them before we could stop it, but we managed

much better than some of our friends with loaded boats.
Many of them bumped into the rocks, and one man lost
nearly half his outfit.

About thirty-three miles below the mouth of the Teslin
River the Big Salmon pours into the Lewis. Thirty-four
miles more and we come to the Little Salmon, which is sixty
yards wide at its mouth, and is shallow. Here the valley
becomes so broad that no mountains are in sight, only low
hills, at a distance from the bank. The Lewis makes a
turn to the southwest, and after running six miles it turns
again to the northwest; then, at the end of seven miles, to
the southwest again, around a low, sandy point. Thus we
proceeded for twenty miles or more, without gaining more
than five in our northern course. The first turn is around
Eagle's Nest Rock, which stands up on the slope of the
eastern bank, and in it is a huge cavern, where it is said gray
eagles rear their young. It is composed of light gray stone
and rises fully five hundred feet above the river.

About thirty miles further on, another river, the Nor-
denskiold, draining a chain of lakes far to the westward,
empties into the Lewis, which continues its course with a
width of from two hundred to three hundred yards, occasionally expanding as it flows around little islands. Its
course is very crooked, and near the mouth of the Nordens-
kiold it winds under a hill, and away from it several times,
once for a distance of eight miles, and after making all
these turns it has gained but a mile. From this the river
flows on in a straight course to the Five Finger Rapids.

We did not stop to look at this place, but ran right in,
and soon were bobbing about like a chip on the whirling
current. It is a cataract of ferocious mien, but not at all
dangerous, as a boat can be easily kept away from the haz-

ardous points.   As in the Grand cañon, the water rolls away from the sides and is ridged in the center.   Just before entering the rapids there is a whirlpool, which is studiously avoided, though it is not dangerous.   If a boat gets caught in it she is liable to be whirled about in it for some time before being released.

The current continues very rapid for six miles below Five Fingers, so-named because of the five large rocks standing in mid-channel, and then we began to hear the roar of the Rink Rapids.   They make a great deal of noise, but are not dangerous, as the only obstruction is on the west side, where the water pours over the rocks.   On the east side the current is smooth and the water deep, and a boat can run through without the slightest difficulty.

For fifty-eight miles, the distance between the Five-Finger Rapids and the place where the Pelly River unites with the Lewis and forms the great Yukon, no streams of any importance appear.   The river continues through a pleasant landscape for the whole distance without the slightest indication of civilization.   About a mile below the rapids the stream spreads out, and many little islands appear.   We passed in and out among these islands for about three miles, when the river contracted to its usual width, but islands and bars were common all the way, and the current is about five miles an hour.

After passing a long bank called Hoochecoo Bluff, the river again spreads out into a very archipelago.   For three or four miles it is nearly a mile from bank to bank, but so close and numerous are the little islands that it is often difficult to tell where the shores of the river are.

At the confluence of the Pelly and the Lewis the country is low, with extensive terraced flats, running back to rounded hills and ridges.   The Pelly is about two hundred yards wide at its mouth, and from here these great waters flow swiftly on in an uninterrupted course one thousand six hundred and fifty miles to the Bering Sea.

The Yukon, below the junction, averages about a quarter of a mile wide, with a current which carries everything swiftly along. It is dotted by many little islands, and we quickly came to the ruins of old Fort Selkirk, a trading post which was established by the Hudson Bay Company in 1848. Indians pillaged and set fire to it in 1853, leaving nothing but the remains of two chimneys, which are still standing. The place has been put to some later uses, however, an English church mission and an Indian village being established there, and for some time Arthur Harper, whom we have already mentioned as a pioneer in these regions, maintained a trading post there.

Here we were enabled to use some of the money we had brought along in case of emergency, and which we had saved by packing our goods, in the purchase of new supplies, but it did not enable us to put in all we could wish, for goods are high after they have been brought up the long Yukon. But we were glad to have a tent again, and some articles which are a prime necessity in such a country. We felt as if we had again come in touch with civilization.

We had made good time from the lakes and were in good health, but it had been a long, hard voyage, and it always will be, in any time of the year, till modern methods of communication have overcome some of the terrible obstacles. All along the route we had noted the graves of those who have been lost in previous years on this route. Both Indians and white men have fallen in the struggle to press into the great valley of the Yukon by the Dyea trail. And we heard of others, besides the two drowned in the cañon, who lost their lives that same spring in which we came in. One man was killed in the Five Finger rapids, but Joe and I were safe at last on the waters of the mighty river, and he who will never stop to think of an overruling Providence in the feverish rush of life in the busy centers of the United States, must in these immense regions, where he feels so small, where he finds so little to measure himself by, feel a sense of gratitude filling his whole being as he stands strong and unhurt at the end of such a voyage.

CHAPTER IX

LIFE ON A YUKON POST—OUR FIRST GLIMPSE OF THE
KLONDIKE—HOW MINERS ADMINISTER JUSTICE IN
ALASKA—THE PLAGUE OF MOSQUITOES.

The Latest News — The Swift Yukon and Its Branches — The Upper
Ramparts — White River and Its Probable Sources — Stewart River
and the Tales of Indians — Reports of Prospectors — Sixty Mile
Creek — Passing the Mouth of the Troan-Dik or Klondike — Its
Various Names and How They Were Obtained — A Peep at the
Moose Pasture — Moose Skin Mountain — Old Fort Reliance — Forty
Mile and Its Institutions — Justice as Administered at Miners'
Meetings — A Little German's Trouble — French Joe's Experience
— A Tailor and His Bill — The Canadian Police — A Plague of
Mosquitoes — How They Operate and How Their Bites Work —
Old Pharaoh's Troubles Not a Circumstance — What Miners Suffer
— No Preventive Sufficient — Tough Miners Sit and Cry — More
Indian Tales — Bears and Dogs in a Frenzy — Frost Comes as a
Blessing.

THERE were many inquiries at the trading post as to
the news of the day. Not having been burdened
with a heavy outfit after leaving the cañon, we
were among the first to put in an appearance at the post that
spring. In the winter months the posts along the Yukon
are practically cut off from civilization, and they can only
imagine what is happening as the world moves rapidly on.
No hermit is so secluded. But naturally we had little of
recent date to tell. Nearly three months had elapsed since
we had set out from San Francisco. Joe, who took more interest in political affairs than I did, in reply to many ques-

(141)

tions narrated to eager listeners events on the Pacific coast which had then receded into the forgotten past. An old newspaper which we had brought in, wrapped about some of my clothing, was read with all the eagerness with which a starving man would eat. This serves to show how remote Alaska is from the world most of the year.

We were still about three hundred and eighty miles from Circle City, to which we were destined, and which was then the center of the mining interest in this great territory. So with our new supplies and a few tools needed by the prospector, we resumed our way. Below the fort and for a distance of ninety-six miles to the mouth of the White River, the Yukon maintains its width of from four to six hundred yards, and its course is a little north of west. The current continues swift, over four miles an hour on the surface, and so numerous are the little islands that there is no part of the river where one or more cannot be seen. Gravel bars abound, but cause no trouble. It is a broad, majestic, hurrying river, displaying some of the grandest views eyes ever beheld.

We drifted on with but few stops, and those were brief. It made no difference whether it was night or day — it was nearly all daylight then. The circling sun would dip behind the hills or the bluffs along the river for a little while, and a sort of twilight would fall on the majestic scene, the heat would suddenly disappear, and for a couple of hours the frost in the ground would fill the air with a cold moisture. Then the sun would come up again, and for twenty hours pour its blazing heat on the broad valley. Under its influence the grass rises to phenomenal height, and so bright a green is seldom seen. All day long, and night, too, birds with unfamiliar voices were singing about us, seeming to

A Long and Hard Journey Over the Skagway Trail
Entrance to the cañon. Two Klondikers with heavy packs making
their way on foot through the deep snow.

mock the trials of mankind and their greedy rush for gold, and occasionally we caught sight of a bit of game — a moose too far away for us to reach, or a duck, too hard a shot for me with a rifle. Had we possessed the proper weapon we could have feasted on ducks and geese. They are very plentiful, and every Yukon man should have a shotgun. We stopped upon the banks but little, never except for a substantial meal, for the mosquitoes make camp life an excruciating experience. Joe slept while I managed the boat; and then he took his turn at the oar, and I would catch a nap.

Upper Ramparts is one of the most picturesque places in Alaska. Steep basaltic bluffs tower like monster cathedrals along the banks. The lights and shadows work unique effects among their rocks, standing out like minarets from the walls.

About thirty miles below the fort a little stream called Selwyn River enters the Yukon from the south. Good timber abounds in its valley, and we saw men getting out the logs ready to float down the river to places where they are needed for houses. White River comes in from the west about seventy miles further on, and after the Yukon has resumed its northerly course. It is a powerful river, about two hundred yards wide at its mouth, and it plunges down loaded with silt over ever-shifting bars, the main channel being not more than a hundred yards in width. The current is not less than ten miles an hour, and its name is derived from the milky appearance of its waters. With numerous other creeks so much easier to ascend, this river has been neglected by prospectors, and its source is somewhat problematical, though the Indians say that it rises far inland near an active volcano. For aught that may be known, the richest gold fields in the world may lie near the sources of this great watercourse so turbid and rapid at its mouth.

Between White and Stewart rivers, ten miles, the Yukon spreads out to a mile in width, and is a maze of islands and bars between wonderful banks.

The Stewart River enters from the east through the middle of a wide valley; the current is slow and the water dark colored. While camping here for a brief space we encountered a small party of miners who had been prospecting on the river above. They had found considerable gold on the bars, and were returning for provisions, but they told us that it would depend upon how other points on the river turned out whether they returned to the Stewart. They had done most of their digging in the bars along the river, and had not explored the creeks running into it.

The current above, they told us, is swift, and it is necessary to pole boats up the stream. The banks for some distance from the mouth are steep and uninviting. Further up they found bars and the river bottom covered with grass. They had been compelled to go into camp about forty miles up, because of high water, and, while there, had found plenty of game, including moose and bear. The fish were also good. They said that on some of the upper bars they had found gold which yielded over twenty dollars per day, but they found the digging was irregular because of the high water at times. From what information they had acquired from the Indians, who declined to ascend the river, there exists a very savage tribe of Indians, holding the country around its sources. They are at war with the other Indians lower down, occupying a stronghold in a mountainous wilderness, and they will not permit any white man or other Indian to enter their territory. They make their

living by hunting, occasionally bringing their furs down to
the trading points, getting guns and such cther things as
they desire in return. These Indians, it is said, are met
about two hundred miles up the river. But there are few
things more unreliable than Indian stories. White prospectors have not met these Indians in their explorations.
At some time they may have existed there, thus giving
ground for the tradition. The prospectors had no information which could tempt us to turn aside, and we concluded
to waste no time on the river.

About twenty-three miles below the Stewart a small
stream enters from the west, called Sixty-Mile Creek. We
are now in the region of the miners. This stream has been
prospected all the way to its sources, and gold had been
found nearly everywhere, but not in rich quantities except
on two creeks. A few miners were working there. For
some time after the discovery of Miller and Glacier creeks
the diggings there were considered the richest in the region,
but the more recent discoveries on Birch Creek had drawn
the miners in that direction, and the year before a rich spot
called Mosquito Creek, an appropriate name for any creek
in the river, had been discovered running into Forty Mile
River. At the time we came into the regions this creek
was making the sensation.

So we pushed on, passing Indian River, a stream
destined to gain great notoriety, but then considered of no
particular account. A little further on we passed another
stream about forty yards wide at its mouth, which emptied
into the Yukon from the east. The Indians called it Troan-
Dik, or Thron-Diuck. As to how the Indian appellation of
this stream should be spelled, and what it means, there is
considerable uncertainty, which, however, is not strange

considering the difficulty of putting into English characters anything which an Indian pronounces, and the further difficulty of securing from an Indian of these parts an intelligible idea of what he means by anything he says in his own language.   According to some, the name of this river means " water full of fish."   According to others, it takes its name from the fact that, the stream being swift, the Indians have to set their salmon traps or nets by driving in stakes with a hammer, and so they gave it the name Troan-Dik or Hammer Creek.   The sure thing about it is that it seems to have something to do with fish.   The miners, probably in an effort to cast into phonetic English the Indian pronunciation, had in 1896 fallen in the habit of calling it Clunedyke. It should be remembered that when one of the natives of this region pronounces one of his words he does it as if he were doing his best to strangle himself with it, and the effect is as if he just barely escaped doing it.

In 1883, when Schwatka rafted down the Yukon, he camped at the mouth of this stream, and according to his reports he found that the traders called it Deer Creek " from the large number of caribou or woodland reindeer seen in its valley at certain times of their migrations."   The valley looked as though it might abound in moose and caribou, and for years it had been a favorite fishing ground for the Indians who were waiting for the salmon to run up.

We floated by in blissful ignorance of what lay under the tundra of its creeks, and no one would have suspected that in a few weeks there would be a lively city on the swamp near its mouth, and that a pushing civilization would have transformed the Indian's Troan-Dik and the miner's Clunedyke into Klondike, a word which philologically means absolutely nothing except that your practical civilization does about as it pleases in naming things, and that when it does it that ends the matter.

The Indian name for one of the landmarks near the mouth of the stream is, when translated to the best of human ability, Moose-Skin Mountain, a name that is likely to adhere to it, unless at some time some one finds something there except the mountain, and practical civilization takes liberties with the native appellation.

I could not fail to notice as we floated past this region, the river being quite narrow here, its inviting aspect for hunters and fishermen, and but for the fact that we were now anxious to arrive at the center of the gold diggings we might have stopped a day to see what we could bag in this moose pasture.

Proceeding on, we passed old Fort Reliance, an old private trading post of no great present importance, the stream flowing in from the east called by Schwatka the Chandindu, and a little over thirty miles further we come to Forty Mile, which for years had been considered one of the richest sections in the territory, and had been one of the chief attractions to those who had braved the difficult trails from the coast.

Joe and I landed here, and for the first time entered into the vortex of white civilization on the Yukon. Forty Mile contained nearly a hundred log buildings, and such are the most palatial residences in Alaska. Some of them had cost over ten thousand dollars, for even logs are dear here, though they are so abundant. The town is situated on the south side of Forty Mile River at its junction with the Yukon, and the Alaska Commercial Company has a station here which was located by McQuesten shortly after gold had been found on the creeks above. It is in the British

Territory, and a few of the mounted police were at hand, but the diggings are mostly located across the border line, which crosses the stream about twelve miles from its mouth. The best mines are sixty miles up stream, but Forty Mile is the headquarters.   At this time it was the second place in size on the river, contained a sawmill, several blacksmith shops, restaurants, billiard halls, saloons and dance halls, of course, and a few bakeries.   It also contained an opera house, and here, a little later, we found some of the women who had come over the pass with us singing the same old songs we had heard at San Francisco, and had heard once in awhile during the journey.   They had had a hard time of it, but they received "big money" for the display of their talents.   It is one of the peculiarities of mining regions that much of the gold goes to those who do not dig it.

At the time we were at Forty Mile, miners' meetings as a means of settling disputes were being brought into disrepute.   For a long time they had answered very well, as the miners in the district were few and acquainted with each other.   But as the influx of all elements began with the reports of discoveries on Forty Mile River, and saloons increased in number, disputes became more frequent, and miners' meetings became a mere burlesque.   We heard of several cases which had been thus tried.   In one instance, a poor little German was passing quietly along the street one day, and a big ruffian, who rather prided himself on his capabilities as a bully, drew out and struck the little man a blow that paralyzed him.   He was powerless to help himself; he could not match his strength against that of his assailant; and so he consulted a German friend of his as to what he should do in the matter.   The friend suggested a miners' meeting, which was called at once. Now what do you think the miners' meeting did. They fined the plaintiff twenty dollars for calling the meeting, and the fine was expended for drinks on the spot, the meeting being held in the saloon, and the chairman being the proprietor of the place.

Another instance reported was that of four miners who were partners in four claims. These did not return more than expenses, and they decided to sell. One of the partners was going to Forty Mile for something or other, and the others instructed him, if he could, to sell out for the whole lot. He asked them what was the lowest they would be willing to take for their interests, so that he might have something to go on. After consultation they decided that five hundred dollars was the least they would be willing to take, but at the same time instructed him to get all that he could. At Forty Mile he sold the four claims for two thousand eight hundred dollars — seven hundred dollars apiece. He handed the three partners five hundred dollars each, and put the one thousand three hundred in his own pocket. Soon after they discovered this fact, and called a miners' meeting to make him divide even. The meeting by resolutions decided that:

" As long as they got their five hundred dollars apiece, it was none of their business what he got."

Again, a miner, commonly known as French Joe, a French Canadian, was going down " the creek," as it is termed, to Forty Mile. While passing the cabin of a certain miner he was asked where he was going.

" To Forty Mile," he said.

" Well, you're going by Dick Robinson's; will you take down these two ounces and give it to him? "

" Oui—certainment, M'sr."

The two ounces were weighed out and handed over to Joe, who carried them down and faithfully presented them to Robinson as directed, with the explanation that they had been received from the miner.

"But," said Robinson, "he owes me three ounces."

Joe was pained and surprised and a little indignant at his reception.

"I don't know for dat.   He gif me two hounce—der she was.   Dat's all I know for."

"But he owes me three," said the persistent Robinson.

"Vell, dat may be.   She maybe he owe you tousan'. He giv me two hounce — dere she is.   You got two hounce?"

"Yes; there's two ounces here."

"Vell, dat's all he gif me."

"But I want my other ounce."

"Vell, sacr-r-r-e " — the Frenchman was becoming warm — " perhaps next time you see him you ask him about her.   I give you two hounce — dat's all I got."

Robinson called a miners' meeting to decide whether or not Joe should pay him the extra ounce.   Eighty-two miners attended, and after much discussion, in which Robinson admitted having received the two ounces from Joe, six voted that the Frenchman should pay the extra ounce and five that he should not.   The rest, as Joe explained, " didn't giv dam no how — one vay or de other."

So the Frenchman was compelled to pay the extra ounce, with the costs of the meeting added, amounting to nearly one hundred and fifty dollars.   Joe remarked afterward, in telling the tale of his misfortune:

"By Gar, dat satisfy me with miners' meeting.   I don't vant any more dem things."

What first brought the miners' meetings into disrepute was the result of one held at Forty Mile in June, 1896, or shortly before our arrival. A tailor there had demanded payment of a bill of four dollars and fifty cents from a barber. The barber put in a counter bill which fully paid the tailor's bill. The tailor called a meeting to decide between them.

The meeting gave the tailor one dollar and fifty cents, and one of its members then gravely proposed that he be fined twenty dollars for calling the meeting. This was just about to pass unanimously, as things sometimes do at miners' meetings, it being sufficient only to have a mover and a seconder, when another member stood up and protested against this action, urging that if they fined a man for calling a meeting the poor man would have no way at all to get justice. They had awarded the man one dollar and fifty cents, and the imposition of a fine would be manifestly unfair. The meeting saw the force of this and let him go.

The barber then rose, and slowly, deliberately, and with a picturesque profusion of profanity and an eloquence of metaphor that did credit to his originality, requested all present to go — not to any more frigid clime. He would go down the river on the underside of a log, he observed, if the worst came to the worst — but as for that dollar and a half, they could—! !

A committee was forthwith appointed to try and collect the amount adjudged due. They could, however, find no one who owed the barber anything, or, if he did, was willing to pay it over to them. It was well known that if they tried to enforce payment from the barber he would apply to the mounted police for protection, and of course their action in so doing would be punishable. The absurdity of the

situation dawned on the parties to the affair, and miners'
meetings fell below par.

This and similar cases brought the miners' meetings
into such contempt that all in the country were quite ready
to join in their obsequies when the Canadian police instituted a different condition of things. All seem to be
heartily glad that they had been abolished. They
seem to be particularly pleased with the fact that a man's
just rights do not depend upon his personal popularity, that
his title to his claim is not based on the number of times he
treats when near the saloon, nor yet upon the quantity of
whisky he drinks, or any kindred merit, but simply and
purely on his just and legal rights, whether or not all in the
country are his friends or all his enemies. In the first stages
of settlement, however, these miners' meetings and the laws
they made answered the purpose better than anything else
could. There is a sense of justice among the miners which
is not always found in society, and it would not become per-
verted except for the introduction of elements depending
less on their hands and muscles than on their wits.

The general course of Forty Mile River as far as the
boundary line, a distance of twenty-three miles, is southwest, but after this it runs nearly south. The miners work
their way up in small boats. It is about one hundred and
twenty-five yards wide at its mouth, and all the way the
current is strong with many rapids. Eight miles from its
mouth is a placed called the Cañon, though it is simply a
crooked contraction of the river with high and steep banks
for a distance of about a mile. At the north side there is
plenty of room for a trail along the beach.

The rumors of the rich finds at Mosquito Creek had
been one of the incentives in our coming to Alaska. Joe,

who had followed reports closely, had never ceased to urge upon me the possibilities of this creek whenever I had shown an inclination to turn aside and travel into regions unknown. Here was where he expected to make his fortune, but when we had worked our way to the object of all our exertions we found that gold was being washed out plentifully, but the creek was completely occupied, and, of course, we had no money to go into a speculative business. The law allows a claim of one thousand three hundred and twenty feet measured in the general direction of the stream, and the few who had been in the country at the time of the strike had taken all the claims, although the rule up to that time had been claims of five hundred feet only. Such was the condition of things at Mosquito Creek.

But we found mosquitoes. They are no more abundant there than anywhere else, so far as I have seen in Alaska in the summer months, but they had a better chance to prey upon us. We had had our trials with this pest on our voyage down ever since the ice had melted, but it was not till we were camped around the headwaters of Forty Mile River that we began to realize their capabilities as thorns in the flesh and destroyers of the soul. For he is a pretty good missionary in Alaska who will not swear once in a while in the mosquito season.

These insects, which are apparently no larger than the ordinary mosquito of lower latitudes, are several times as venomous. They begin operations about the first of June, and close them about the first of September, and during that brief season they make up for any lost time that the latitude imposes. They seem to thrive on any ordinary smoke. They revel in fire unless it consumes a whole forest. One may hurl a blanket through a cloud of them, but ranks are closed up and the cloud is again intact before the blanket has hit the ground. All day long, and of course in July that means for about twenty-four hours, they are on the alert, always after anything that has blood in its veins. Any one who reads the Bible in this region in the summer must wonder at the weak nature of Pharaoh. There surely never could be a plague like this.

They rise in vast clouds from the peculiar moss along the banks and creeks, and their rapaciousness knows no limits. They have been known to drive men to suicide, and the sting of a few dozen will make a man miserable for days. I have seen tough miners sit and cry, and it is a common sight to see them so worn out and nervous that they can not sleep even after they are protected from them. My wrists have sometimes been so bitten that for days they were too lame for me to work to any advantage.

It is absolutely essential to wear cheese cloth or mosquito netting of some kind for a protection, but in the summer time, when there is scarcely a breath stirring, this of itself becomes almost unbearable. They pile themselves upon any netting worn over the face so thickly that it is difficult to breathe, and they will make so much noise that it is sometimes difficult to converse unless one almost shouts in his neighbor's ear.

The tent door must be covered with netting, there must be netting over the bed, netting must be worn while at work, gloves must be worn on the hands, everything must be done to prevent these insects from devouring the body and wearing out the nerves. Like everything else in Alaska, the mosquitoes are on a large scale. I do not wish to make it out any worse than it is, for the reality is bad enough. Any one who goes to Alaska will at times be impressed with the paucity of the English language as a medium of expression. I wish those scientists who write so learnedly upon the benefit of the mosquito as an antidote for malaria would take a trip to the Yukon regions in summer. They have something to learn.

The Indians say — and it is more readily believed than most Indian stories — that they have known bears and dogs to rush madly off cliffs when frenzied with a swarm of mosquitoes, and that native horses will break harness and run madly away, and that dead bears have been found in the woods swollen by the bites of these insects. But one thing is certain, the miners in their work along the creek suffer agonies from them, no matter how well protected. A strong wind is always welcome, and a frost seems like the soft, comforting touch of Nature, although it may be the forerunner of a long winter and a season of deprivation.

CHAPTER X

ARRIVAL AT CIRCLE CITY — DANCE HALLS AND OTHER
PLACES OF AMUSEMENT — THE YUKON SLED —
ALASKAN DOGS AND THEIR PECULIARITIES.

Pushing on to Circle City — Some of the Yukon Creeks — Old Man
Rock and Old Woman Rock — A Flight of Native Fancy — The
Poor Man and His Scolding Wife — His Last Resort and its
Petrifying Results — Prospecting American Creek — Our Lumber
Venture — A Thunder Storm and a Wreck — Escaping on the
Tar Stater — Arriving at Circle City — Our Reception — Some of
the City's Institutions — Convenience of the Saloons — No money
but Gold Dust — How Purchases Are Made — The Dance Halls —
The Relaxation of Faro — Dogs Invade Our Boat — Their Thieving
Propensities — Faithful Workers — Their Enormous and Indiscrim-
inating Appetite — Eating Their Harness — An Arctic Turnout —
The Dog Whip and Its Uses — The Yukon Sled — " Ouk," "Arrah,"
and " Holt."

INDING no promising opportunity for suddenly becoming rich on the creeks of Forty Mile, as all the
best locations appeared to be occupied, we concluded
to return to the town and to push on towards Circle City,
which was reported to be flourishing in the most magical
manner, and where wages were high, whether the mines
proved profitable or not. We each located a claim, however, on one of the Forty Mile creeks least prospected.
There could be no doubt that there was gold enough in
that section, if the mines could be properly worked. One
man we saw had cleaned up $50,000 as a result of three

(158)

months' work on his claim, but much dead work was necessary and heavy expenses were to come out of this.

Circle City is about two hundred and twenty miles further down the Yukon, which continues in its same general character much of the way. A large number of streams flow into it, all called creeks, although they are of considerable size. Small steamers could make their way up them but for the bars at points.

Where the river cuts the boundary line it flows between two large rocks, one called Old Man Rock, on the west side, and the other, Old Woman Rock, on the east. These respectful appellations are the translations from Indian names, which, as we afterwards learned, are derived from a legend, indicating that even in the dull intellect of the natives there are occasional flights of the imagination, such as among other more promising aborigines have been woven into graceful song and stirring epics. This legend, as it has been culled from natives by traders who are not experts in legendary lore, and which therefore may be somewhat misty in spots, runs something like this:

In remote ages there lived here a powerful tshauman, which is the equivalent in the speech of these interior Indians to the word " shaman," — medicine man — used by the tribes of the south coast. These medicine men are the magi, or wise men, of the Alaskans, and by their absurd manœuvers exercise a wonderful influence over the superstitious natives. In this powerful tshauman's locality there lived a poor man who, like Socrates, had an inveterate scold for a wife. He bore his troubles for a long time without murmuring, in the hopes that she would relent, but time only served to increase the infliction. At length, his patience weakening under the unceasing torment, he com-

plained to the tshauman, who, of course, went through some
of the motions common to all powerful wise men in his
position, and then sent the poor man home, telling him that
in a short time all would be well.

Soon after this the poor man went out to hunt, and
remained away for many days, endeavoring to secure some
provisions for home use, but without avail. He returned,
weary and hungry, only to be met by his wife with a more
than usually violent outburst of scolding. This so pro-
voked him that he gathered all his strength for one grand
effort, and gave her a kick that sent her clear across the
river, which is here about half a mile wide. On landing,
she was converted into a mass of stone, which remains to
this day as a monument to her viciousness, and a warning
to all female scolds. Of course, it was the tshauman who
effected the metamorphosis, and there is some doubt as to
whether it was he or the enraged husband who did the kicking, but it makes little difference, as the husband could
not have done it had not the tshauman rendered some mirac-
ulous assistance.

Like a great many other ancient legends, important
features are left unexplained, as, for instance, how it was
that the husband, after kicking his spouse across the river,
was himself turned into a mass of rock. The Indian intellect, having gone thus far in its flight of poetic fancy, doubtless become quite exhausted, and was unable to proceed.
Perhaps the old man was petrified with astonishment at the
remarkable effect of his kick. From an artistic standpoint,
it will be seen that it lacks some of those rare qualities of
those northern legends which the genius of Wagner has set
to soul-stirring strains. But it is a remarkably sublime
fancy for a Yukon Indian.

Going on a few miles, we came to American Creek, and Joe's disposition to prospect got the best of him for a while. It looked promising, so we entered and spent a few days there. We found gold, but none of our diggings averaged more than five dollars a day, and it would be better to work for wages, which were reported to be at least ten dollars a day at Circle City, than to bother with dirt of that kind.

Having learned that good logs were in great demand at Circle City for building purposes, we stopped on our way down the river at a place where the timber was particularly good, and constructed a raft of fine spruce timber. But we had proceeded but a little way with this down the swift current when we were caught in a thunder storm, which came up suddenly, and, like everything else in this great country, operated on a large scale. In these silent solitudes a clap of thunder caroms through the hills in mighty reverberations, and the claps follow on each other's heels so rapidly, and their reverberations become so confused, that they seem to be tearing each other and the hills into fragments.

The roar was deafening, the rain was blinding, the wind was like the blast from a mighty air pump, driving the murky waters of the river into a frenzy. The *Tar Stater*, which was tied by her nose to the raft, danced about, while the water swept over the raft, nearly taking us from our feet. Desperately we poled along, trying to keep in the stream, but, in spite of all efforts, the raft ran with fearful force on a bar, and instantly began to break to pieces. We had barely time to jump into the boat and cut the rope before being thrown into the river. With great difficulty we worked toward a partly sheltered bank, and there awaited the passing of the furious storm. That ended our lumber venture, and towards evening we continued our way down in the boat.

After rowing about one hundred and sixty miles from the boundary line, we drifted into the Yukon flats and the center of a great mining district, that of Birch Creek and the upper Tanana. Circle City, the metropolis of this great region, and then claimed to be the largest log city in the world, makes a brave front on its bluff, overlooking the river. At the time we reached it it was the booming town of Alaska, and had nearly a thousand inhabitants. It had more during the winter, but at this season many of the miners had gone over to the creek, which is reached by a six-mile portage, to work their claims.

It was early in July when we arrived in sight of this place, and during the twilight hour, that brief space of time during the summer months when the sun dips below the horizon, spreading the whole sky above with a wondrous mellow light. We anchored our boat out from the shore in a sort of slough, and went up to see the city.

The places of business face the river, and were going at full blast. There was a theater, four large warehouses, three stores, and three blacksmith shops. We counted twenty-eight saloons and eight dance halls. Back of these were log houses, interspersed with tents, laid out in fair order, and altogether presenting a very comfortable appearance for these regions. Our approach had been noted from the shore, and there was a general gathering to welcome us, for the appearance of a boat on the river, no matter how small, is an event in this far-away center of civilization. It was a cosmopolitan crowd of men and women from everywhere in North America, a sprinkling of dirty Indians, and a crowd of howling dogs.

The stores and saloons are the only places to go to. If seeking information, it is found there. If looking for a friend or acquaintance, the chances are that he will not be at his cabin, but in the saloons or one of the stores. Nearly all the men congregate in the saloons, tell yarns, play cards, and occasionally drink too much, though a man without gold dust is not in danger of it, for prices are high. The tenderfoot will doubtless expect to see men going about with a gun and knives stuck in their belts, but, rough as humanity is here, it generally has an orderly appearance.

There is no specie except such as newcomers manage to bring in over the passes or up the river. Everything is transacted in gold dust. Every man and woman carries a buckskin sack, and when they enter a store to make purchases they throw out their sack of dust, and the amount of the purchase is weighed out in front of the purchaser. The seller never cheats himself, but makes sufficient allowance for poor dust. For instance, a man who puts twenty dollars' worth of dust in his sack, and goes from place to place making purchases, will find that he gets but about eighteen dollars' worth of goods for his twenty dollars. Sometimes in the stores the dust on five hundred dollars' worth of sales will weigh up to five hundred and twenty-five dollars, but, of course, it works both ways in the long run. It seems to be more the custom of the place than a trick of dishonesty. But the dust and the scales are always in evidence, even if it is nothing but a spool of thread that is desired. Go into a saloon and buy a cigar, and fifty cents worth of your dust is weighed out; if a man drinks, fifty cents' worth of dust goes out of his sack for one of the worst mixtures that ever was labeled whisky.

A dance hall at Circle City at this time was not such a

den of wickedness as is generally supposed by those who read
newspaper accounts of life in these far-off mining camps. In
1896 the Alaska places had not become sufficiently attractive to draw thither in large numbers the professional rough
element.   It is rather one of the institutions of society as
it must exist here, among hard-working miners, like the
blacksmith shop, or the schoolhouse which sets back among
the cabins.   It is a community of men, rough in aspect,
but not wholly vicious.   After long seasons of hard work
in the mines up the creek, or after tiresome journeys over
steep and dangerous trails, in the solitudes of the great forests, or among the mountains, even the rasping music of a
dance hall sounds sweet.   The rough miner delights in a
bit of a square dance, or the enlivenment of a reel, or, possibly, if his early education has not been neglected, of a
waltz or polka.   He knows that he is in a society which
cares nothing about the cut of his clothes, and is not critical
about the grace of his step.   A touch of feminine life, even
if not all that the fastidious or the strictly moral might
desire, comes like a warm breath from the southern latitude over the frozen hills, a reminder of the city life in
the States.

Of course, the miners have to pay well for it, as for
everything else.   Before he leads " one of the charming
young ladies " into a set on the floor he must dig a dollar's
worth of dust out of his sack.   The young lady gets a quarter of it, and the house, which takes the rest, furnishes the
pair a drink if they call for it.   The miner need not pull off
his big boots and put on pumps, or even take his hat off,
and he can swing his partner with all the gusto of which
he is capable.   Every set he dances in costs him a dollar,
and a round dance the same.   The man who plays the violin

on the roughly-improvised platform receives anywhere from twenty-five dollars to forty dollars a night. He does not need to suffer the hardships of working a claim, but the chances are that he has one, and that someone is working it for him.

If the miner does not take to dancing he can seek relaxation at the faro table. If he loses, as he probably does, there is more dust in the hole on his claim up the creek; if he wins, so much the better. Under such conditions, and leading a life which for many days in the year is full of hardships, he seeks amusement when the chance offers, and is satisfied that he is getting his money's worth, no matter what it costs. Every one is on a perfect equality. The college man, if he happens to be here, is no better than anyone else; a man with thousands of gold dust tied up in his belt exhibits no haughtiness; indeed, in the busy season, he may not be able to buy a lodging, and may pay for the privilege of sleeping on the dance-house floor " after the ball is over." Here the socialist might see the realization of some of his dreams of equality, but there are precious few, I imagine, who would have the fortitude to brave the dangers of a miner's life under the midnight sun, to enjoy the realization of the dream.

After observing something of the town, and making some arrangements for a temporary abode, Joe and I went back to our boat, where we learned other facts concerning the ways and possibilities of the country. While we were away the dogs had swam out to our boat, chewed off the rope by which it was held, and dragged it ashore. There they tore open every sack of provisions we had, and, when we approached, were having a regular feast. They had even chewed up some of the flour sacks and the dishrag, the flavor of which was undoubtedly agreeable to them. Everything in the boat was wet, and the damage we figured up to amount to forty dollars. Everyone who gets along well in Alaska must have a proper understanding of dogs, and a few facts concerning them may be established at this point, though the pioneer may not acquire a complete knowledge of them until he has been some time in the country.

Dogs are fed here but once a day, unless they find an opportunity to feed themselves, and they rarely let an available opportunity slip, even if they have to bite through a tin can or climb a pole. They are fed dried fish, whenever it can be obtained; if unobtainable, bacon and flour. All provisions must be set up on a cache, and that should be as high as possible, or they will climb up to it when there is no one at hand to disturb them. They will lie down innocently enough near a tent, watching and waiting for hours for the owner to leave and give them a chance to ransack it. I have known them to come into my tent, go up to a boiling pot of beans on the stove, push off the cover, take out the piece of bacon, and walk off with their tails curled up over their backs in the most nonchalant manner.

But they are too precious to shoot. They are a prime necessity in Alaska, and are sometimes worth almost their weight in gold. They do nearly all the packing in the summer, and they will carry from forty to fifty pounds, keeping up with a man. In the winter they do all the freighting, haul all the wood, and carry the mails. Harnessed tandem to sleds — and I have seen twenty in a single string — they will go anywhere, ninety miles from Circle City to the mines, or a thousand to Juneau, and if a man wishes to take out for a drive one of the few young ladies of the city who conforms to his ideas of respectability, and whose acquaintance is, therefore, of considerable value, he rigs up a couple of dog teams, for Yukon sleds hold but one, and off they go. But there is very little driving for pleasure over the Arctic snows, though the experience is not without its delights, so unique are all the conditions.

I met one young lady who had become enthusiastic over dog-sled rides for pleasure. Her father owned a fine team of native dogs and she had a good Yukon sled. The winter before, when the weather was clear, and often when the thermometer was hovering far below zero, she used to bundle up in her fur parka and moccasins, slip the dogs into their harness, and streak off across the frozen flats, going many miles before she returned. Squeezed down into the little box of a sled, wrapped in furs so that she could hardly move, and so that little but her eyes could be seen, she flew along after the scampering dogs, up and down, over the deep snow.

"Tip over? Oh, yes, many times," she said, laughingly, "but that's a part of the fun. And sometimes I would have to get out and run along with the dogs. Those rides did me more good than any sleighride I ever had over your smooth, monotonous roads after a big horse. These dog turnouts are positively delightful."

Two good dogs will haul from five to six hundred pounds on a good trail, and run twenty-five miles in six hours, and they will haul a man from forty to fifty miles a day and show little sign of weariness. A native Yukon dog is much more valuable than any importation because they endure the climate so much better. The natives are of all colors, and most of them have very long hair, as fine as wool. They look like wolves, but they rarely bite or bark at persons. They simply howl. They are faithful to the last degree

in their work, and have that single failing — they are born
thieves.

Buckskin moccasins are provided by many owners to
keep the feet of the faithful little animals from becoming
raw and sore on the ice and snow.   They are made like a
child's stocking, about nine inches long.   Sometimes pack-
saddles are used, whereby a dog can carry from ten to
twenty pounds, besides drawing a sled.   A dog harness
commonly weighs a little over two pounds.   The collar,
which is usually made of leather, faced with sheepskin, and
stuffed with deer hair, slips over the dog's head — fumbling
with buckles would be severe on the fingers in Arctic
weather — and on each collar are rings, to which the traces
are attached.   These traces are usually made of heavy web
material, otherwise the dogs would eat them up.   They
have an insatiable appetite for leather, and will devour their
collars if they are allowed a chance.   They have to be kept
separate when harnessed, or they will eat each other's collars, and when the web traces become oily they will eat
them.   They are so adroit that, sooner or later, even with
the most careful master, they will devour their trappings.
An Arctic appetite is something enormous in a man, but it
is completely distanced by that of a dog.

An old prospector in Alaska told me that once when he
was driving a pair of native dogs one of them slipped his
collar while he was camping for the night near Fort Yukon,
and ate up a pair of large gauntlet gloves, all the leather off
a snow-shoe, a whip, and a part of the handle, a long leather
strap on a gun case, and the leather binding on the canvas
case, and badly chewed a part of the harness.   When the
man got up in the morning the dog was asleep, and never
showed any signs of the night's dissipation.   But these dogs
will do a good day's work on four pounds of dried fish.

A Hard Place on the Trail

Packers transporting the goods and outfits of gold-seekers over the Skagway Trail.

They do not drive themselves. A good leader is generally placed ahead, but dogs will often lie down in the trail unless kept going. They are driven with a dogwhip, a device which is a miracle in the hands of an expert, but a dangerous thing in the hands of a novice. It has a handle about nine inches long, and a lash about thirty feet long, and weighs four pounds. The lash is made of folded and plaited seal-hide, and for five feet from the handle averages about one and a half inches in diameter; then, for fourteen feet, it gradually tapers off, ending in a single thong half an inch thick and eleven feet long. When traveling the lash drags along at full length behind, and, when the driver wishes to make use of it, he gives a skillful jerk and twist of the wrist which cause the lash to fly forward, the thick part first, the tapering end continuing the motion till it snaps at full length ahead. Sometimes it is merely snapped over the heads of the dogs as a reminder or warning, but a skillful driver can pick out any dog in a team and touch almost any spot on a dog's back, and, if hit just right, the fur will fly. But till the driver is used to the management of this weapon, he is liable to receive most of the injury himself, for when awkwardly thrown the lash may wind about him like a snake and inflict painful injuries on his own face.

The standard sled for an Arctic traveler consists of a narrow box four feet long, the front half being covered or boxed in, mounted on a board eight feet long, resting on runners. In this box the passenger sits, wrapped in skins so that he can hardly move, with only his head and shoulders projecting. In front and behind and on top of the box is placed all the luggage, covered with canvas, and securely lashed, to withstand all the jolting and possible upsets, and the snow-shoes are kept within easy reach.

The dogs are harnessed to the front of the sled, sometimes each by a separate trace. The nearest dog is about fifteen feet from the sled and the leader, with bells on his neck, as far off as the number of dogs in the team. They are guided by the voice, using husky Esquimaux words, " owk " — go to the right; " arrah " — to the left; and " holt " — straight on. If the driver runs ahead on snowshoes, as is frequently required, the dogs will follow him.

CHAPTER XI

GUARDING AGAINST EVIL-DOERS — LIFE IN A GOLD-SEEK-
ER'S CABIN — HOW IT IS BUILT AND FURNISHED.

W E found society at Circle City not at all bad for a
mining town. Being on the American side, no
authority existed there except miners' law, but
under that one must walk straight as far as honesty goes.
With all the idleness, drinking, and gambling, there was
less crime there than would be found in most cities of its
size in the United States. Cabin doors were nearly always
left unlocked, and in them bags of gold and other valuables
were left when the owners were away. The Miners' Association was more feared by evil-doers than any courts or
police would have been. To be sent down the river in a
small boat was to delinquents a worse punishment than im-

(173)

prisonment, and it might happen that no boats were available and the evil-doer would depart on a log. Depart he must. To be turned out to shift for one's self in Alaska is no laughing matter.

In minor cases simply involving disputes over money or claims, the miners' meetings appeared to afford satisfactory justice, and they had not become liable to some of the abuses noted elsewhere. When such a meeting is called all the miners at hand assemble, a chairman and secretary are appointed, and the plaintiff is called upon to state his case. Then the defendant is heard, and any other testimony introduced. The assembled miners act as the judge and jury together, can ask all the questions they desire, and make any motion they please. Any motion that is carried for the disposal of the case settles it, and a committee is appointed to see that the judgment is carried out. So long as the majority of the miners are actuated by a sense of seeing fair play for every man, no court could be more efficient or just. The element of danger comes when a little frontier politics works its way into the system and justice is defeated by some man of influence, who more than likely may be a saloon-keeper. But so far as I witnessed the operation of justice in Circle City at this time, it was adequate and fair. There being no police force at hand, as over the Canadian border, and the authority of the United States being too far off to be effective, the miners fully realized the importance of not abusing their own authority, and of being fair and just to all concerned. The judgments rendered would sometimes appear curious to an outsider, but when all the conditions of life in these regions were taken into account, their rationality would become apparent.

It was a miners' law that no pistol should be carried in

the city, and it was obeyed. A spirit of good feeling and good comradeship prevailed. There was a sort of feeling that the dangers of existence here were too many and too real to have them aggravated by any unnecessary outbreaks of the evil side of human nature. Questionable as some of the characters were in this booming town, there were many respectable families there, the education of the children was provided for, a good hospital was among the institutions, and it was as complete a town as one could expect on the Yukon, founded as it was but two years before, and rising so suddenly to importance in 1896.

Joe, with the restlessness of an old prospector, was inclined to make for the mines at once, but as wages were averaging about twelve dollars a day in the city, and as our supply of money had run low because of our misfortunes on the trip, I was disposed to work awhile in the city, and acquire some shelter and provisions for the winter. So we concluded to separate for a time. I was handy with carpenters' tools, and with the axe, and quickly secured a job putting up log cabins, for which there was a great demand at this time. One could fairly see the city spread out and grow. Lots in good locations were selling for five thousand dollars and over.

Log houses may be made pretentious or otherwise, depending upon the uses to which they are to be put. An ordinary dwelling for the accommodation of two or three people need not be large — fourteen feet by sixteen feet in the clear, that is to say, built of sixteen feet and eighteen feet logs. To a lumberman or carpenter the building of such a cabin is an easy matter, and a green hand who is handy can learn very quickly how to put it up. There are two things to remember. The cabin must be built to keep

the cold out in the winter, and to keep the mosquitoes out
in the summer.   For this the cabin must be equally tight,
for wherever a draft can get in a mosquito will find its way,
too.

No foundations are needed.   The only preparation is
leveling off the frozen ice and " muck," as it is called.   The
logs must either be cut and floated down the river, or can be
bought as they lie in the water ready cut in proper lengths.
The average size of these logs is seven inches in diameter,
and the length varies considerably.   The cabin should be
seven feet high to the roof line, and so will require at least
forty-eight logs — that is twelve a side for the walls.
Smaller logs are used for the gable ends and the roof, and
some pieces of cut lumber will be needed for the tables,
stools, and bunks.   It costs not less than five hundred dollars to build a log cabin complete, as prices run on the
Yukon.

The first thing to do is to " spot " the logs.   By this a
lumberman means to strip off the unevenness and skin them
on the top and bottom sides about three inches wide, so as to
insure their lying close together when placed one upon the
other.   All the logs must then be " notched " at the end,
half-way through, beginning five inches from the end.
Each notch will have to be about seven inches wide and cut
half-way through the log, so that when a similar notch is
cut in another log the two can be fitted together and be level
top and bottom.

Several sacks of moss must be gathered in readiness, and
then the miner is in shape to commence building his home.
The two side beams are laid in place and the two end beams
are put across, the notches of the side beams fitting into
those of the end beams so that a solid rectangular frame is

formed.   Moss must now be spread all along the top of this
frame of logs.   It should be laid evenly, about three inches
thick, and in such manner that when the next frame of logs
is in place the joints of the notches will be held about half
an inch apart.   The reason for this is that, as the log house
is built up higher and higher, the weight of the upper logs
will gradually squeeze down the lower ones until the notches
are a close fit, and in so doing must squeeze the moss between
the logs, making it airtight and mosquito-proof.   This looks
like a very trifling matter, but it is one of those little things
upon which the comfort of the whole cabin will depend.
There are many little matters like this which are of the
greatest importance to him who winters on the Yukon.

The walls are built up solid like a box to the proper
height, and the windows and doors are put in afterwards.
When the proper height for the window is reached, vertical
saw-cuts should be made in the log the width apart of the
window-pane.   These cuts are merely a convenience, so
that when the cabin is finished it will be an easy matter to
insert the saw and cut down through the logs on each side
the square spaces into which the window and door are to fit.
The same saw-cuts must be made at the height of the top
of the door for the same reason.

The logs are laid up by means of skids and block and
tackle.   When the walls have been raised to the height of
six feet, the roof logs are laid, those at the ends being
shortened to correspond with the pitch desired to be given
to the gable.   This is a part of the work which needs a
fairly good craftsman.   To the top of the roof, that is to the
ridge-pole, the cabin is usually eleven feet high — in other
words, the gable or slant of the roof is four feet high, measured perpendicularly.   The logs for these gable-ends must

be cut in the proper lengths.   The first one will be about twelve feet and the top only a few inches long; the others between will be graded in size.   In order to hold these logs in place one over the other, wooden pegs or dowels must be made and driven in tight.   The dowels in each lower log should fit snugly into the upper ones, and be made long enough to allow for the moss between the logs, and to let the upper logs press the lower ones together.   When the logs are all in place for the gable ends, they must be " sniped " off; that is to say, all the ends of these logs must be cut off on the proper slant.

When the roof logs have been laid and a ridge pole is in place, a rough roof of split poles is laid, the poles extending from the ridge to one or two feet over the side walls, forming eaves.   The poles are secured in place by logs laid across them transversely, through which pegs may be driven into the poles of the roof and logs of the superstructure. When this has been done, the poles are covered with earth and moss to the depth of a foot or more, thus forming a substantial, tight roof that excludes both wet and cold.   In making the roof care is taken to leave a vent at the top in addition to the hole for a stove-pipe.

A cabin built in this fashion, whether at the claim in the mines, or in the city, usually serves only as a temporary shelter, and when circumstances warrant it a more imposing and permanent structure may be built.   Should the claim prove profitable, such a cabin will serve later on as a storehouse, or should a better abiding place be desired in the town, it may serve as an ell to the larger building.

Rude bunks are made in such a cabin, and a door made of whip-sawed lumber is fitted to the opening.   A fire is built in the center to warm the interior, smoke making its escape through the central vent in the roof. The stove is commonly used in camp huts for cooking only, and is not sufficient for warmth in severe winter weather. Such a cabin, while not inviting, is not an unhealthful shelter. Having been built of green logs, its walls will be ice-coated throughout the winter whenever the fire is out, as the moisture is drawn from them when the fire is burning.

The interior of the cabins is pretty much the same everywhere. The beds or bunks are always opposite the door, across the far end of the cabin, the table is always under the window, and the stove on the far side from the window. Three or four-legged stools and a few boxes complete the furnishing. All the furniture is to be made by the miner, and having built his cabin this cabinet work will not be difficult. For the table, two horizontal props driven into the side of the cabin and supported by slanting struts are all that will be necessary. On the horizontal props the table-top of planks must be nailed. The tables are usually large enough for four people, one at each end and two at the free side.

The bed is a shelf across the back end of the cabin, is usually divided in the center, and so wide that two men can sleep on each side of the partition. It is made in the simplest way by placing a pole horizontally across the end of the cabin, say four feet from the back wall, and joining the ends between the chinks of the logs in the side walls. The partition in the center can be made to afford additional support. Some people put the slats for the bed across — that is to say, width-wise — but there is more spring, more ease and comfort if they are placed lengthwise. The mattress is nothing but moss and straw well bedded down.

In building a new, substantial, and better arranged log

house, the first business is to carefully select the logs. Drift logs are preferable, being dried and seasoned. In the absence of such the bark is peeled from green logs, and they are cut to the desired length and hewn square with adze and broad axe. When the foot logs have been laid — preferably the largest and soundest obtainable — joists fashioned from whip-sawed lumber are laid in mortises made in the foot logs, and secured thereto with wooden pegs driven through holes which have been bored therein. At the corners the logs are mortised so that their round or square sides fit closely upon one another. But when laid up a coating of moss or mud is used to fill up all the interstices. Openings are left in the sides and ends for such doors and windows as may be desired. When the side walls have reached a height of six or eight feet in the clear above the floor joists, a second series of joists for a ceiling and the floor of an attic may be laid if desired.

Having raised the walls to the required height the roof construction is begun. Two forms are in use in such buildings — one of the kind already described in the temporary cabin, the other built of whip-sawed timbers covered with split shakes laid like shingles. In this form of construction the gabled ends of the building are built either of squared logs laid one upon the other and pegged together, and with ends sawed at an angle corresponding to the angle of the roof, or are built of a frame work of whip-sawed lumber, and the space between the joists and siding stuffed with moss.

When duly enclosed the spaces between the joists are filled with earth and moss, and the floors laid. The roof is fitted with a galvanized chimney, and when the ceiling has been finished the house is ready for habitation. In such a house access to the garret is had either by a ladder nailed against the wall, or a narrow stairway, according to the fancy of the builder. Glazed sashes are fitted to the windows so as to make them double, and battened doors are hung with strap hinges. Most of the Yukon houses are but one story in height, but some are two. In nearly all the roof projects from three to five feet over the front entrance, and a storm shed is erected by standing poles upright from the ground to the roof as close together as possible. By having the opening into this storm shed at one side, the entrance to the dwelling is protected from the wind and drifting snow. Such a dwelling as this is a palace on the Yukon.

The poor resident in town or the new prospector at the mines is fortunate to have a tent over his head. While lumber is plenty, cabins are expensive when labor is twelve dollars a day and over, and when logs sometimes have to be hauled some distance by dogs. One must have begun to take out gold dust in good paying quantities before affording the luxury of a good log dwelling.

At the time we reached Circle City the demand for capable workmen for building purposes was altogether out of proportion to the supply. The trading companies had large buildings contemplated, and any one who could swing an axe handily was a skilled workman and commanded large pay. The very lowest that was paid was ten dollars a day, and few could be had to work at that figure. To those who were skillful in fitting windows, doors, shelves, and the like, as high as an ounce a day was paid — seventeen dollars being the recognized value of an ounce of gold on the Yukon.

It was indeed a bustling scene which Circle City presented in the early summer days of 1896. The banks of the river and the streets of the town were covered with logs. Chips were scattered everywhere, and the sound of the axe and the saw mingled with that of the squeak of the violins in the dance halls and the howl of the dogs. The Birch Creek mines were rich and gold dust was plenty. There was no such thing as an idle man if he had any disposition to work. People talked glibly of the coming metropolis of the Yukon. No one could have imagined a livelier place of its size. Neither could any one in the busy place anticipate that within a year it would be as dead as a door post—almost a silent city.

CHAPTER XII

WORK AND WAGES IN ALASKA—AGRICULTURAL POSSI-
BILITIES IN THE ICY NORTH — COST OF LIVING.

Misleading Rate of Wages — Cost of Bringing Provisions to the Yukon
Valley —A Sample Price-List at a Circle City Store —Value of Fresh
Meat — A Roast of Beef — A Woman Who Baked Bread at a Dollar
a Loaf — Fourteen Loaves a Day on a Yukon Stove — Monotony of
Diet — Ordinary Laws of Agriculture Upside Down — Difficulties
of Raising Garden Stuff — Plenty of Berries in the Summer — A
Dream of Agricultural Possibilities — Deceptive Flatlands — Nig-
gerheads and How They Grow — Grass That Makes Poor Fodder —
A Question of Transportation — Has Not Been Regarded as a Poor
Man's Country — Competition in the Stores — Jack McQuesten —
A Great Night at Circle City — Order of Yukon Pioneers — An
Indication of the Hardships of Alaskan Life.

IT may seem to many hard-worked individuals earning
no more than two dollars a day in the thriving cities of
the United States that the mining centers of Alaska
must afford a man a fine opportunity, when labor is so scarce
that it commands from ten dollars a day upwards. But
scarcity does not figure in this amount hardly as much as
the cost of living. Circle City was more or less regularly
reached by the Yukon steamers from St. Michael, and the
trading companies have stores there, and, moreover, in the
summer of 1896 there had been no great rush for the gold
fields and the town was not faced by any prospects of
scarcity of provisions. There was every promise of abundant stores at Circle City then. But to appreciate the high

(183)

cost of provisions, even when they are plenty, it must be remembered that almost everything, except gold, must come from the Pacific ports of the United States by the way of St. Michael or Juneau, and that the freight charge on the river route is about one hundred and twenty-five dollars per ton, while no one could bring over the pass more than the main things he needed, and sometimes, as in our case, failed to do that.

While I was at Circle City, in July of 1896, the following prices were prevailing:

Flour, $8 per hundred weight.
Bacon, 40 cents per pound.
Ham, 40 cents per pound.
Beans, 15 cents per pound.
Oatmeal, 15 cents per pound.
Rice, 15 cents per pound.
Sugar, 25 cents per pound.
Crackers, 25 cents per pound.
Butter, $1 per pound.
Soda, $1 per pound.
Coffee, $1 per pound.
Tea, $1.50 per pound.
Condensed Milk, 50 cents per can.
Vinegar, $2 per gallon.
Corned beef, 50 cents per can.
Baking powder, $1 per pound.

Dried fruit, 30 to 50 cents per pound.
Potatoes, 25 cents per pound.
Condensed potatoes, 30 cents per pound.
Eggs, $2.50 per dozen.
Lemons, $3 per dozen.
Sulphur, saltpeter, alum, $1 per ounce.
Cathartic pills, $2.00 per box.
Overalls, $2.50 per pair.
Hat, $5 and up to $15.
Shoes, $6 to $10.
Cheese Cloth, 25 cents per yard.
Common white cotton cloth, 25 cents per yard.

No cloth could be obtained for less than twenty-five cents per yard. The price of better qualities ranged accordingly. Anything like a comfortable outfit for the winter cost at least five hundred dollars at these prices, and it must not be supposed that work was possible every working day in the year. The expenses of living while working must, of course, take away much of the extra money earned, though one confine himself to the simple necessities of life in such a climate.

One must kill or buy of the Indians all the fresh meat he enjoys. The awakening from a dream of a juicy beefsteak is very painful. The only fresh beef that I ever heard of in Circle City was brought over the summit and killed at Forty Mile, and a piece weighing ten and a half pounds was brought down and raffled off for the benefit of the Circle City Hospital. In this way the piece sold at the rate of nineteen dollars and twenty-seven cents per pound.

Moose, bear, caribou, and mountain sheep furnish the only fresh meat to be obtained, and as a rule they must be hunted. Everyone was too busy for sport then, so at times such meat was very scarce. It readily brought twenty-five cents per pound by the quarter, and sometimes the price was much higher. Up near the mines, if one were a good shot, he could secure a good supply of game and caribou meat. As I am fond of hunting and claim to be handy with a rifle, I went in search of game quite often between working hours when I was at Circle City. It was daylight all the time. I had very good luck in running on to bears, but as their hide is of no value except when they first come out of their holes, and as they are generally pretty lean, and always tough, they are hardly worth the powder and ball. One day when I was out hunting for caribou I came across a black bear and shot him, but he was useless.

As an indication of the cost of living at Circle City, at this time, I may cite the enterprise of a woman with whom I became acquainted, and who was one of the pioneer female gold-hunters in this section. Mrs. Wills had lived in all portions of the West, from New Mexico to Washington, and had followed various occupations. But the collapse of one of her enterprises in Tacoma had necessitated a new move, and she fixed her eyes on Alaska.

She went first to St. Michael, and obtained employment as a cook. She earned good wages, and, being an excellent cook, soon became a favorite. Hearing so many stories of life on the Yukon, she soon concluded that the Simon-pure pioneer life of Alaska was to be found only upon that river. Much to the regret of the boarders, Mrs. Wills resigned her position as head of the culinary department in the boarding-house at St. Michael, and took passage on the river boat to Circle City. She took with her the regulation camp outfit, and soon pitched her tent at Circle City. What to do was the next question. After a few days of investigation she concluded that she would set up in business for herself. The very next morning the Circle City bakery took rank among the flourishing institutions of what was then the chief city of the land of the midnight sun.

In her camp outfit she had a sheet-iron camp stove and two baking pans. The two pans were all that the oven would hold, and for that reason her " bakings " were limited to two loaves at a " batch." But a ready market was found for her bread at fifty cents a loaf. The miners soon learned that Mrs. Wills could " double discount " them when it came to a matter of baking bread, and before the week was over the demand for Wills's loaves was such that the price went up to seventy-five cents, and a few days later to one dollar, and there it remained for the season.

By working fourteen hours a day she could turn out twenty-four loaves, and in the meantime, while the oven was doing its share of the work, Mrs. Wills filled in the time washing, ironing, and mending. Buttons were sewed on at two bits a button, and double that price was charged for patches. The day's baking was always sold out a day or two in advance, and customers had to wait their turn. On more

ON THE MOVE

A long pack train of heavily loaded horses *en route* to the Gold Fields.

than one occasion men fought for the right to the next loaf,
and, to obviate further difficulties, Mrs. Wills each afternoon sold twenty-four slips of paper, numbered from one
to twenty-four. The first slip sold was No. 1, and so
on in rotation, until the last fellow had to take No. 24.
Each slip was redeemable next day in bread, and No. 1
called for the first loaf out of the oven, and so on down the
line to the end; and when No. 24 was out the bakery closed
for the night.

When side issues, such as washing and mending, did not
encroach too much on spare time, Mrs. Wills would bake a
pan of biscuits and a batch or two of cake. The biscuits
went lively, and the cake sold at one dollar and fifty cents
a pound. Six mince pies, made of moose meat, sold at
Christmas time for five dollars each. But Mrs. Wills was
too busy with plain baking to give much attention to the
fancy end of the art. Her laundry business was less flourishing, for the requirements of the miners in this direction
are not large. Starched shirts were almost as scarce as palm
trees.

The monotony of the ordinary Alaskan diet is something
which requires a strong stomach and the patience of Job. I
did not appreciate this till afterwards, when wintering in
the Klondike, for a tenderfoot will gaze in wonder at the way
vegetation grows here in summer, and he is apt to be deceived by visions of fresh vegetables of marvelous size and
delicious flavor. But all the ordinary laws of agriculture
are turned upside down. With the sun shining throughout
the twenty-four hours, the plants, never resting at night,
hurry on with a feverish haste to maturity, but few have
time to ripen. The summer lasts no more than eighty days,
on an average, and though measured in sunlight, it is equal

to one hundred and twenty days of the growing capabilities
of the Middle States, the rapid growth of plants gives them
such a weak vitality that the first breath of frost lays them
low; and a frost may occur at any time during the summer.
A snow storm in August is not unusual.

I have seen lettuce raised in excellent condition along
the Yukon, but as the seeds will not ripen and few importa-
tions are made, such a luxury is scarce.   Cabbages will
thrive mightily, producing enormous leaves, but, alas, they
never form heads.   Russian turnips, however, seem to be
just suited to the short and vigorous summer season.   They
will grow to average five pounds in weight.   Radishes will
flourish to a certain degree, but potatoes are about as un-
suited to the soil and climate as Florida oranges are to
the Northern States.   The tubers attain such small size
that it takes many to make a meal, and even then much
work must be expended in protecting the vines from the
early frosts.

Evenings when the sky was clear and frost was threatened, I have seen those who were trying to raise a " little
garden stuff " go out and carefully suspend blankets or
heavy ticking over the vines and plants.   It would protect
them somewhat, but would never save them entirely.   Even
success to this degree is possible only along the river bottoms; nothing can be done back in the hills, where the industrious miners must spend their time.   And when a
woman can get a dollar a loaf for her bread, and a miner
can get ten dollars or more a day in the hills, there will be
little fooling away of the summer season in nursing garden
stuff.

But Alaska has some products of her own which may
vary the epicure's diet in the summer.   Every third bush

is a berry bush, which produces white and purple flowers, and then berries, of the richest hues. The berries ripen in two months after the first leaves appear. Cranberries from Alaska have been considered desirable delicacies in the San Francisco markets for many years; they are brought down by the steamers in crates and boxes at a season of the year when cranberries are not in market on the Pacific Coast. They are small, wild berries, not much larger than peas; but they are deliciously flavored and highly prized in their native country. The Indians and new settlers eat them freely in summer, and make jellies and preserves for winter use. Blackberries and huckleberries are as abundant in a large part of the country as on Long Island or the mountains of Georgia and Carolina. Nearly all of our common berries are found in parts of Alaska — red and black currants, wild strawberries, raspberries, gooseberries, and dewberries, and many others that are indigenous only to Alaska, such as the roseberries, mossberries, bearberries, and salmonberries. All of these are eaten fresh by the natives, and preserved by crushing and drying them. On the coast of the mainland and on the islands the inevitable oil of Arctic regions is utilized even in preparing the berries for eating. It is not uncommon to find the natives greedily eating a dish of crushed strawberries or blueberries, mixed with sugar and seal-oil — a combination that is sufficient to nauseate most Americans.

The agricultural possibilities of this region of long winters and short summers have recently been painted in hues which my observation there inclines me to think are much too rosy. The Secretary of Agriculture has made a prediction that before many years Alaska's grain and food products will more than equal in value all the gold which is now supposed to be hidden beneath the surface. He says:

"The soil of Southern Alaska, along the coast, is rich and best suited for barley and oats. Fish will be an important feature of the Alaskan's diet, and thus the race will become a seafaring one, well suited for the United States navy. If we send to the people now living there commissioners who can teach them in a practical manner how to raise these and other foods profitably, I believe the country will develop rapidly. Grass is abundant, and can be easily cultivated further, and by a special process we can teach the Alaskans how to make hay even in the worst kind of Alaskan climate, where it rains a little every day. We would introduce whatever vegetables could be successfully cultivated, and make the best of the soil, now so rich already.

"The winters need not be especially hard, for food will be abundant in the summer, and can be easily stored away for winter consumption. In barley alone a tremendous traffic could be built. More than enough barley to feed a greater population than is probable in a number of years to come can be successfully raised, and that is grain for which there is a constant market. I repeat, Alaska's agricultural possibilities will yield her more money than will ever be taken out of her gold mines."

The realization of a dream like this would be a great thing for Alaska, but it is largely a region of icy mountains. Comparatively speaking, the flats near the rivers are of exceedingly limited area, and many of these are less attractive than they look. There are great stretches of tundra covered with clumps of grass which have sprung up sometimes on fields of solid ice. White people here call these grassy inventions of human torture "niggerheads," but the term is weak. It is not half bad enough. Call them the vilest thing you can think of. Why is it necessary for Madam Nature to utilize every wretched spot of the earth's surface? Here, for instance, was once a pond of water, and that became frozen; then a root of some kind crawled from the margin out on to the ice, and the wind carried dust from the hills and bits of decaying moss from the trees, and small leaves to this venturesome root. The little rootlet thrives under this covering, and soon a little mound is begun, and some seeds are blown along, and lodge in this little mound, and they sprout and grow a little the first year; the dead shoots catch more decayed or decaying stuff, and the mound grows higher and more seeds are lodged upon it, and more grass grows, and perhaps a weed, and thus each year adds to the height of the mound. And it widens only so far. When it has attained about a foot of breadth the heat of the sun can no longer penetrate to the center of the mound and it ceases its lateral growth, but grows higher, and the grass grows stronger because the sun's heat can warm all sides of the cylindrical mound.

From all along the margin these mounds have started and grown, and from these other mounds have started and grown, but the ice foundation is always there, and in time the pond is covered with these mounds a foot or less in diameter and usually more than a foot in height, and the long grass stands up in summer, looking like a meadow. It has a distinctly agricultural look from a distance. One might think that a thousand cattle could be fattened on this level meadow in a summer.

In winter this grass falls and tangles one's feet, and when you want to walk through one of these flats you must step over these mounds and place your foot between them, and you sink in the ooze that has collected there, until your foot touches the ice, and if you have far to go you become very tired, and if a foot slips or you stagger from any cause, down you go. Sometimes you think you can walk on the tops of these mounds, but you cannot. They sway under you and down you go on your knees in the mud between them. In time you quit trying to do so, and stick to the trail, if there be one, no matter how deep the water and ooze may be.

The result is that the miners and other residents of that country keep as far away from a niggerhead swamp as they conveniently can, avoiding it as they would the plague.

For the rest of the country, the surface is covered by from one foot to two of moss, and, underneath, the everlasting frost. On this a scrubby growth of trees is found, extending up the mountain side to an altitude of from one thousand to one thousand five hundred feet above the river. It is this which appears to those passing down the river in boats to be a continuation of the good timber seen along the banks. Timber that is fit for anything is scarce.

Some of the islands of the Yukon have a very rich soil, but they are locked in ice usually from October to June, and, owing to the swiftness of the current, Yukon ice is not apt to make good skating. I once heard a woman describe it as an ice house blown up by dynamite. There may be throughout all Alaska room for a thousand farms, but the Indians would be altogether too lazy to work them — they would die first — and a white man who would begin farming there when gold could be shaken out of the sand-bars all along the river would be set down as a man of unsound mind.

The Alaska Commercial Company has had a couple of acres in a favorable spot near Forty Mile in cultivation for

several years. The have sown oats, but they say they have
never ripened. They made fair fodder. Good fodder for
cattle could be had in this way by importing barley and oats,
but the seed would have to be brought in every season, as
there is no kernel in the pod or shell. Those contemplating
taking horses or cattle into the country for other purposes
than slaughter should go in a couple of years in advance, get
a favorable piece of land, clear it, and prepare for the cultivation of such fodder as this. Otherwise, they will have
to import all their fodder.

Horses have been in use at Forty Mile for several years,
but the owners depend largely on the trading companies
for the food for their subsistence. Mr. Harper has had
a few horses at Selkirk for several years, the fodder for
which he cuts from ponds in the vicinity. On this they pull
through the winter, but they are not in a condition to do
any work.

Throughout the Yukon valley, wherever the soil is rich
and fertile, a great variety of grasses grow, and cover the
land with heavy mattings of vegetation. They constitute
the coarse varieties, but many of the finest grazing grasses
are seen, such as the blue joint, which reaches a height of
four or five feet, and the blue grasses. One would think
that no better forage for cattle could be desired than what
is furnished by these grasses in the Yukon Valley and
along the coast, and that, so far as food is concerned, pigs,
cattle, sheep, and goats could live and grow fat in the
valleys.

But grasses of such rank growth do not seem to afford
the proper nourishment for our domestic animals, even if
secured in good condition, and that is difficult, in view of
the frequent rains. Of course, for the greater part of the

year these fields are buried under tons of frozen snow, and
the animals must be housed.   To care for them is not easy
or inexpensive in such a climate.

Much more can be done for the opening up of Alaska
by improving the means of transportation so that the regions
of the Yukon may be accessible, instead of inaccessible, for a
greater part of the year.   With the Yukon open only long
enough to enable a steamer to make two round trips from
its mouth to the upper trading posts, and with the old Indian
trails, fit only for Indians and dogs, and with a population
which must import the greater part of what it consumes,
the problem resolves itself to the simple proposition of transportation.   Alaska cannot be successfully developed so long
as tough moose hams will fetch forty dollars apiece in the
winter.

While, therefore, the high rate of wages prevailing at
Circle City might make Alaska seem to those who have
never been in it like a great country for a poor man, it had
always been a poor country up to the summer of 1896.
There were plenty of old miners about there who had been
on the Yukon for years and had barely made more than
their " grub."   When one is making money rapidly the
temptation always is to spend it with a lavish hand.   But
even if one lives economically, he needs to strike a rich vein
of gold in order to acquire wealth.   I could see that if Joe
and I were so fortunate as to get together two thousand
dollars by working at high wages during the short summer,
it would be scarcely enough to pay for taking a winter's
outfit to the mines and putting up a poor shelter there, for
provisions become several times more valuable by the time
they are hauled over the rough trails to the mines.

The list of prices already quoted in this chapter were

reasonable enough for Circle City at that time, and their apparently high cost was not due to scarcity, but to the value of articles after they have been carried over four thousand miles, a third of the way against a swift river current. There was a fair competition among the stores, and at the head of one of them was Jack McQuesten, an old pioneer in the country. He has been in Alaska for over a quarter of a century, and was really " the father of the country." He had come in contact with nearly all the men who had risked their lives in the search for gold in its frozen soil, and had ever been their friend. It has been said that he has out-fitted, supported, and grub-staked more men, and kept them through the long winters when they were down on their luck, than any other person on the Yukon. Hundreds of men now on the river owe all the success they have to his help, and they know it and appreciate it.

It was a great night at Circle City when he was pre-sented with a gold watch and chain, bearing the insignia of the Order of Yukon Pioneers. It was said that the watch cost five hundred dollars, but McQuesten's bill for enter-tainment was probably much more than that, for there was no half-way business about his generosity, and the boys needed no gold dust when they stepped up to the bar.

The Order of Yukon Pioneers was started in 1890, and was composed only of the men who had been in the country since 1887. It had a very limited membership, therefore, till the rules were changed so as to make men eligible who had been in the country before 1893. They have a lodge at Circle City and hold meetings every Tuesday night. It levies on its members for the care of the sick, for the relief of widows, and the sending out of the country of those who had been broken down by hard work and privations. It is an influence for good, and is also an indication of what sort of a life these pioneers were compelled to lead in a country which is supposed to be lined with gold.

CHAPTER XIII

WE REACH THE GOLD DIGGINGS — LOCATING A CLAIM — HOW GOLD IS MINED — THE MINER'S PAN, ROCKER, AND SLUICE BOXES.

The Trail up Birch Creek — Some of the Gulches — Great Cost of Wood — The Process of Placer Mining — How the Prospector Works — Testing the Dirt — The Miner's Pan — The Trick of Shaking Out Gold — All the Fascination of Gambling — Nature Holds the Cards — Placer Mining Conditioned by the Climate — The Old Process of Sun-Thawing — Soil That Resists Picks, Dynamite, and Hydraulics — Where Fire Burning is Necessary — Burning at Night — A Long Process — Sinking through the Muck — Rockers — Sluices and How They are Constructed — Nature Caught in the Act — Claims Regulated by the Miners Themselves — The Birch Creek Yield of Gold.

GOLD-seekers were continually going back and forth from Circle City to the diggings on the upper waters of Birch Creek, and in this way I occasionally heard from my partner, who was working most of the time on other claims for wages, for the season was not propitious for prospecting. This is easier done after the freezing weather comes on. As I had managed to locate a very good cabin in town for our needs while there, and had earned a fair sum during the early part of the building rush, I determined to carry over a light store of provisions to Joe, as he wished to remain on the creek during the winter and prospect as opportunities offered.

Birch Creek empties into the Yukon more than a hundred miles below Circle City, but in its tortuous course its upper waters flow but six miles from the town, though the headwaters are back in the mountains from sixty to one hundred miles away. The short portage across the neck of land to the creek is not difficult, though low and wet in places in the summer, and a hotbed of mosquitoes. They were almost unendurable unless a wind was blowing. I have seen strong men on the trail through these swamps driven to the verge of hysterics by the swarming pests. The trail up the creek leads through a wild country, and by the time a winter's supplies have been dragged over it to the camps they are worth something. If taken in a boat they must be pulled against a swift current and sometimes up rapids. By carrying only a pack I made fair time over the rough trail.

In an earlier chapter I have alluded to the discovery of gold in this region, an Episcopal missionary having picked up a nugget in returning from the Tanana River district. This was in 1891. By 1894 the district had been pretty thoroughly explored and had yielded large results. The gold consisted of coarse flakes and nuggets; forty dollars a day was made by some men, and all did well. The drift is not as deep here as in some other streams, and water can be applied to greater advantage. I found Joe on one of the farthest of the most remote creeks, nearly a hundred miles from Circle City. On some of the nearer creeks I passed they were taking out gold in good quantities, particularly at Deadwood Gulch, a little stream ten miles long. Mastodon is a rich tributary, but the very rich claims are rare. It was asserted on one claim there that they had taken out gold enough to clear one thousand dollars a day for seven weeks. On Miller Creek there were claims to be had where a man could easily pan out from six dollars to ten dollars a day, but they were not worth owning in such a region, for more can be made in wages on the richer claims.

The district was in its most flourishing condition in the summer of 1896. Most of the gulches were then running, miners were working on double shifts, night and day, which at this season in this latitude are very much alike, and large profits were reported. On Mastodon Creek, which seemed to be the best producer and which was thoroughly staked, over three hundred miners were at work. There was every evidence that the creeks would continue to pay well for five years, and after that were the untold possibilities of hydraulic mining, which might without difficulty except that of expense be introduced by tapping some of the creeks near their head.

If some of these claims which are discarded as practically worthless could be set down in a place nearer transportation facilities, and in a kinder climate, so that they could be worked continuously, they would yield fortunes. Joe had proceeded to a creek where the ground was undoubtedly rich, but it was an expensive job to work it. By the time wood had been cut by men receiving twelve dollars a day, and hauled a distance of six or seven miles by dogs, it was worth about sixty-five dollars a cord. It is clear, therefore, that a claim must be very rich in order to pay the large expenses of working it. If a miner is paying the expense of having his provisions brought out from Circle City, it costs sixty cents a pound in summer and fifteen cents in winter, the trail being so much easier in the latter season.

In order to well understand the recent progress of mining in Alaska, a few facts as to placer mining in general,

and as to the processes in the frozen north in particular, is
necessary. The process in Alaska is peculiar, and the
novice should give it some study before he starts in to make
his fortune. It is the desire of the expert prospector to
locate over river gravel, and he has a theory that the short
side of the bends in the river will prove the richest. Free
or native gold, such as is found in placer mines, is supposed
to be brought down in the course of ages from a " mother
lode " by the action of running water or glaciers. The
sands and rocks of river beds, dry creeks, and gulches, therefore, are the places which secure the attention of the experienced prospector. He observes the characteristics of
the loose rocks in ravines and gulches, or in any place where
matter is left after freshets have subsided. The natural
presumption is that, if the bed of a river flowing through an
open country yields fine gold dust, larger grains will be
found in the nearby hills and mountains from which it
flowed. The heavier particles are, of course, looked for near
the probable source. Sometimes gold is in dust too fine to be
readily distinguished by the naked eye, or the dirt is so
combined with it as to make it deceptive, and the prospector
must proceed with the greatest care and skill.

Having secured a place which may give the desired
promising indications, because of surface conditions, which
are apt to be deceptive in Alaska, the next thing is to begin
sinking a shaft to get down to bed-rock * so that the value of
the diggings may be determined. In a climate where the
temperature runs down to sixty degrees or more below zero
in a winter lasting for nine months of the year, water in
large quantities is scarce except in the short summer. Snow

* Bed-rock. Solid rock lying under loose detrital masses, such as sand
and gravel. Detrital matter consists of particles broken or worn away from
the land, and carried along by the streams to be deposited elsewhere.

may be melted for testing, and there have been instances in very rich claims in Alaska mines where a miner could wash out in his cabin enough to pay his help for taking out the frozen dirt.

Both in prospecting and in sinking his shaft the miner makes frequent use of his pan, which is broad and shallow and an inseparable companion. After clearing off the coarse gravel and stone from a patch of ground, he secures a little of the finer gravel or sand in his pan, fills it with water and gives it a few rapid whirls and shakes, which brings the gold to the bottom of the pan on account of its greater specific gravity. Many miners prefer to sink the pan of dirt under water and shake it there, in such a dexterous manner as gradually to throw the lighter dirt off into the stream, but this cannot be practiced to a great extent in Alaska unless a large tub of water is used in the cabin. Many old miners believe that under-water panning is so much better that they use such tubs in winter. An old and skilled miner will sometimes shake out more gold in a day than a beginner can in a week from the same quantity of dirt. There is a trick about it that comes only by experience, and out of the same gravel a greenhorn may not get fifty cents' worth of gold where an experienced man would get a dollar. A good man can pan a ton of gravel a day, but it is hard, back-breaking work. There is the fascination, however, of ever watching the yellow color as the dirt washes away, and it will keep a man at work till he finds himself exhausted. It is the same fascination that is felt by the confirmed gambler, for every pan of dirt is a gamble. Dame Nature is dealing the cards. Will the player make a big stake, or will he lose ? Having won it from Nature by hard work, he will very likely lose some of his winnings in an ordinary gambling game.   He lives in an atmosphere of chance.   What comes easy, goes easy.

After the pan is shaken and held in such a way as to gradually wash out the sand and gravel, care being taken near the end of the process to avoid letting out the finer and heavier particles which have settled to the bottom, all that will be left in the pan is whatever gold there may have been in the dirt, mixed with black sand, which is nothing but pulverized magnetic iron ore.   Should the gold thus found be fine, the contents may be thrown into a tub of water containing a pound or so of mercury.   The gold coming in contact with this forms an amalgam.   When enough of this has been formed it may be fired or roasted.   First it is squeezed through a buckskin bag to work out all the mercury possible, and what comes out is put back in the tub, while the contents of the bag is put in a retort, or, what is more probable in a mining camp, is put on a shovel and heated till the mercury has evaporated.   The gold will remain in a lump, though with more or less mercury combined with it.   This washing process must be continued after the layer of best paying dirt is reached, for in no other way can the pay-streak be followed.

While this is a process characteristic of all placer mining in Alaska, it is conditioned, like everything else, by the climate and the soil.   When gold was first discovered in the Yukon valley the great drawback in successfully operating the rich placer mines was found to exist in the auriferous gravel being frozen into a solid, compact, adamantine mass, which the rays of the summer's sun could never melt, and with which the methods usually employed in washing out gold were totally ineffective.   There seemed to be no end of the depth to which the frost penetrated the earth's surface, as the deepest shaft or prospect hole has yet to reach unfrozen gravel except in certain localities, and in such places no one has been able to account for the strange phenomenon. Various ways were tried by the miners of ten years ago to expedite the slow work of the sun in thawing out the congealed mass. Picks were found to be of no avail, as the heaviest blows would produce but little more impression than it would have done on a solid block of granite. Dynamite was experimented with, but a heavy shot resulted in blowing out only a " pot hole," and had no effect whatever in loosening the surrounding gravel. Hydraulics were proven equally futile, the stream from the giants serving only to bore a hole in the bank against which it was directed. In fact, the only manner by which the shallow or summer diggings could be worked at all was to strip or burn off the heavy coating of moss covering the earth, thus allowing the sun to reach the gravel beneath. This in a day would thaw to a depth of three or four inches, and after the frozen muck under the moss had been thawed out and thrown aside, the sun could then work on the gravel. As fast as it thawed it could be shoveled into the sluices, and another like amount would be workable the day following. But it was an unusual summer season that would permit of more than ninety days' work at the sluices, and claims that would not pay an ounce to the shovel were abandoned.

Then came the discovery of the Birch Creek mines, and the problem of profitably operating the mines in the winter time solved itself as a simple matter of necessity. With the pay-streak located from fifteen to twenty-five feet beneath the surface, it would have been impracticable and almost impossible to remove the barren earth lying above it. Prospecting had to be done by burning holes in the gravel.

A huge pile of logs would be fired on the spot where it was proposed to sink and allowed to burn over night. In the morning a foot in depth, possibly, would be found to have been thawed out, and this was shoveled aside and a fresh fire kindled. By continuing this operation a number of days, the shaft would finally reach the pay-streak, and then it became a comparatively easy matter to ascertain the probable worth of the claim. If the gravel panned an ounce or two a day, more fires were built at the bottom of the shaft, and " drifting " was begun with the pay-streak, the latter being followed the same as in a quartz lode. The night is the time employed to " burn," the fires being heaped up with logs just before the day's work is finished. These last all night, and by morning, if the amount of fuel has been properly gauged, nothing remains but the dying embers and hot ashes; the smoke and gases have all escaped, and the work of shoveling the loosened gravel begins without delay. As the shaft sinks a windlass is erected over the opening, and as fast as the bucket is filled the contents are hauled to the surface and dumped in a convenient place for washing the following season.

When the drift has reached a short distance underground the bitterly cold weather of the winter has no terrors for the placer miner, and he prosecutes his work in comparative ease and comfort. As distance from the shaft is gained, a wooden track is laid on the floor of the tunnel, and a car pushed by hand is employed to convey the gold-bearing gravel from the ever-receding breast of the drift to the primitive hoisting works.

Who it was who first conceived the idea of drifting under the muck banks and thawing the frozen gravel by means of log fires would be difficult to determine, but who-

TESTING A STREAM FOR GOLD

A gold-seeker panning for gold in a small creek in the Klondike Gold Regions.

ever he may be, he deserves a monument as a perpetuation of his memory. The ability to mine in the winter has lengthened the mining season from three to eight or nine months. As soon in the fall as it becomes cold enough to freeze the water and prevent the shaft from filling up, then the winter miner begins his labors only to cease in the spring when the water begins running again. During the cold weather he has hoisted the muck to the surface, and there lies on his dump many tons of gravel wherein may be a small-sized fortune as a compensation for his work of the winter. Exposed to the sun, the gravel quickly thaws, for it has frozen again after being cast upon the dump, and then it is shoveled into the sluices, and the glittering yellow grains of gold are caught by the riffles, finally finding a resting-place in the buckskin sack of him who has toiled so unremittingly to wrest them from their gravelly bed. Placer mining in such a country, therefore, is a long process, involving much hard work under very uncomfortable conditions, and a great consumption of fire wood, which in most places is very expensive. This was particularly the case on Birch Creek.

Six, eight, ten and twelve feet of the surface is decayed vegetable matter and alluvial deposit of sand in the clay. termed by the miners " muck." As soon as gravel is struck, prospecting is commenced; that is, a pan or two of the dirt is washed to determine whether it is worth " keeping " or not, as the refuse is thrown on one side of the hole and the pay-dirt on the other. Near to and on bed-rock the " pay " is found, which is generally not more than two or three feet thick.

All the way through the so-called muck which lies on the surface are found trees lying in every direction, and they appear to be similar to those growing on the hills to-day, but these logs and roots have evidently been deposited there a long time. While bones of animals now common in Alaska are found in it, there have been found at the same depth bones of other animals belonging to much lower latitudes to-day. Well preserved horns of buffaloes have been found. Occasionally, in a part of frozen pay-streak nearly twenty feet under the surface, bits of bones will be found with parts of the flesh still clinging, but they quickly crumble when exposed to the air.

It must not be thought, however, that the difficulties of the Alaskan gold-seeker are all overcome by simply sinking a hole through several feet of frozen earth by the process above indicated. The time it takes to sink a hole is measured by its depth, as fires thaw on an average about a foot a day. But should a hole be sunk in a claim without finding a good pay-streak, the process must be repeated in another locality. One claim-holder may locate at the very first hole, while another, on perhaps as good a claim, may have to sink a dozen or more, bearing in mind that his living expenses are all this time enormous, and, if he is hiring men at twelve dollars or more a day, his profits are by no means measured by the amount of gold he takes out in a season.

After the pay-streak, which is seldom more than three feet in thickness, is struck, the fire must be continued on the side of the shaft showing the best indications. This is also a slow process, only a few inches being thawed out in a day. This process is continued in the direction of the best pay, a distance which is governed by the thickness of the crust on top. If this is twenty feet, you may drift thirty feet with safety, when a new hole or shaft has to be sunk and the drifting continued. In this way the pay-streak is taken from underneath the surface in the winter until the water begins running in the spring, finds its way into the shafts, and hinders operations to such an extent that they are closed. Preparations for the erection of dams are then made and sluice boxes procured.

The washing process was in full operation at the Birch Creek mines in the early summer of 1896, when I made my trip through them, and the miners were hoarding their dust in anticipation of having a good time at Circle City in the winter. So in the case I have mentioned, where gold was taken out at the rate of one thousand dollars a day for seven weeks, it must be remembered that these miners had done a great deal of hard work before they had taken out any. They were simply cleaning up the dirt they had so laboriously and expensively accumulated. After taking out their heavy expenses and what they squandered at the saloons and gaming tables of Circle City, it will not appear strange that many old miners had been operating in this region for several years, when gold was everywhere, and still remained comparatively poor men.

In placer diggings where sluicing may not be possible, what are called " rockers " are used for cleaning up. A rocker is simply a box about three feet long and two feet wide, the interior fitted with a sheet-iron division punched full of quarter-inch holes, so placed as to make the first division very shallow. The lower part is fitted with an inclined shelf about eight inches lower at one end than at the other. Over this is laid a heavy woolen blanket. The whole is placed on two rockers much resembling the rockers on an old-fashioned cradle. This arrangement is set up on two lengths of wood convenient to the water supply. Having put some pay-dirt in, with one hand the miner rocks the cradle, and with the other he pours in water. The finer

matter with gold falls through to the blanket, which holds
the fine particles of gold, while the coarser particles of dirt
are washed on and out of the box, which usually has some
mercury on the thin slats over which the refuse runs to
catch any gold that may have escaped the blanket. Of
course, any large nuggets will be held on the iron division.
At intervals the blanket is taken out and washed in a barrel
of water containing mercury.

Sluicing is always employed wherever possible, as it is
much more rapid, and, when well arranged, more
economical. It requires a good supply of water, which can
usually be obtained on most of the Yukon creeks during
the summer season from the little rivulets running from
the melting snows and ice above. But the construction of
sluices is generally an expensive operation, as if mill-sawed
lumber is used it must be brought from a great distance, and
if whip-sawed lumber, it requires much labor. In either
case the cost is considerable.

A sluice box is about ten inches in width and twelve
feet in length, the boxes so made that they fit into each other
like the joints of a telescope. In these are placed what are
called riffle bars, which are strips of wood about one inch
square and eight or ten feet long, nailed together at their
ends so as to be parallel with each other, and about one-half
to three-quarters of an inch apart. These are placed longi-
tudinally in the sluice boxes, which are set up so as to have
an incline of two or three inches fall per foot of their length.
A common method of arrangement is to place the slats cross-
wise at suitable intervals, or to bore shallow holes in such
order as to catch heavy particles. Into this system of boxes
a stream of water is directed, which must be of sufficient
volume to carry with it the gravel and dirt that are in the
dump.

As soon as the sun has attained sufficient force to thaw out the surface of the dump, it is shoveled into these sluice boxes. The water carries down with it to the tailings, as it is termed, the refuse — that is, the gravel, sand, and other matter which is not wanted. The gold and the black sand, or pulverized magnetic ore, owing to their much greater weight, fall between the riffle bars and are held there.

As soon as the riffle bars are filled, so that there is danger of the gold passing over and downward to the tailings, the flow of water is stopped, and what is called the clean-up is made; that is, the riffle bars are lifted out and the contents of the sluice boxes gathered and the black sand and other refuse separated.

To one who has made a study of the gold leads of the mountains of the Pacific coast, the conditions of the placers of Alaska make an interesting study. Gold leads have been associated with glacial action, and in Alaska the frozen placers are in close proximity to the active glaciers grinding down the quartz-ribbed mountains and depositing the heavier substances in the furrows carved out at their feet. No matter how ancient, therefore, the gold deposits in Alaska, they are recent as compared with those which till lately attracted the attention of the world. The frost has not had time to leave the ground yet. The glaciers are still at work. The Yukon miners have, as it were, caught Nature in the act.

Little or no attention had been paid to the rocks about Birch Creek, all the work being devoted to the gravel washed down from the sides of the gulches. Miners' laws governed the district. In each gulch prospectors were at liberty to stake out claims not already taken, the size of the claims being decided by a vote of the miners in each gulch

according to the richness of the gravel.   When a prospector
had staked out his claim, it was recorded by one of the
miners elected by those at that gulch, and that was sufficient to secure him a title.   Securing a claim was much
the easiest part of it, for the district is a large one, and
traces of gold could be found almost anywhere, but the difficulty was to secure one that would pay for working when
owners on the rich claims already worked to some extent
were offering twelve dollars a day for laborers and furnishing the timber.

These Birch Creek mines are on American territory, and
only need economical working to make them as profitable as
any mines in Uncle Sam's domains.   Cheaper and better
transportation facilities are required, so that the cost of provisions and of fuel shall be much less, and so that wages may
come down.   As it was, in the summer in which I spent a
short time there, the yield was put down as five hundred
thousand dollars, which was large considering the number
of claims that were really worked and the number of men
employed.   Most of this sum came from a half dozen mines.
Many, under the existing conditions, could not be thoroughly worked, and many more, of course, will not pay
when the cost of everything is so high.   But in two years
these mines had built up Circle City into a lively town, the
second place in population in the whole territory of Alaska.

CHAPTER XIV

MY VOYAGE DOWN THE MIGHTY YUKON — INCIDENTS
AND EXPERIENCES DURING THE TRIP — IN THE
SHADOW OF THE ARCTIC CIRCLE.

Down the Yukon River — Yukon Steamers — Flat-Bottoms and Stern-
Wheels — Carrying Machine Shops Along — A Perfect Labyrinth of
Water — Going Wherever Its Varying Moods Take It — Barren Islands
— Fort Yukon — Lazy and Filthy Natives — Trading for Curios with
Yukon Indians — Birch and Beaver Creeks — A Sudden Change —
Out of the Flatlands into the Ramparts — Some Good-Looking
Creeks — The Munook — The Great Tanana River — Wooding Up
— Indian Settlements — The Women and Children — Dogs Galore
— The Inevitable Cache — Nowikakat — Short Cut Portages to the
Coast — Thrilling Journey of a Party of Miners — Almost Ex-
hausted and Starved — Perils of Traveling in Alaska.

A S little could be done to advantage in mining till winter set in, and as, when I had returned to Circle
City, a favorable opportunity was offered me to go
down the river on one of the returning steamers, I rented
my cabin, for which there was demand enough, and set out,
pleased with the chance thus afforded of studying the
mighty stream and the possibilities of its tributaries. Such
steamers as plied on the river previous to the summer of
1897 looked fairly well from a distance; the greater the
distance the better they looked. They were of the stern-
wheel, flat-bottom variety, and but for a somewhat pretentious smoke-stack would have looked like small barns
built on scows. The rush of people as a result of the gold

discoveries on Birch Creek had brought two larger and somewhat improved vessels up the river, but they were still of the stern-wheel variety, and indeed nothing else seems to suit the conditions. The old steamers on which the pioneers had to depend were usually without staterooms, except for the use of the officers and employes, and temporary quarters were fitted up on accompanying barges when there was a rush of travel. At such times apartments were partitioned off with canvas on the barges and fitted up with rude bunks, supplied with bedding by the passenger himself. These scows were sometimes harnessed and trussed to the front of the steamer and pushed ahead in a clumsy fashion. Two years ago half a dozen dirty little " wheelbarrows " plied up and down the murky stream, making semi-occasional trips to Circle City, sometimes apparently attempting to go overland in the effort to shorten the journey. They were good boats, as boats were known to Yukoners, and the pioneers of that country were thankful when the Circle City excitement induced the building of one or two additional steamers of increased power and capacity.

The machine-shop is a necessity to every Yukon River steamer, for there are no repair shops along the stream, nor at either end. If a rudder post is bent or a shaft broken, the repairs must be made on board the vessel, and such repairs are made in surprisingly short time. The passenger soon learns that there is no use in being in a hurry.

It was on such craft as these that the Yukon pioneer was compelled to travel up and down the river, but he was duly thankful for the opportunity, without reference to the possibility of going in comfort. Inured to the hardship of travel on foot over ice and snow, any means of locomotion other than his own legs was a welcome relief, and he could wrap his blankets about him and lie down on the floor, on the table, anywhere, and really enjoy life.

Below Circle City the river spreads out into what are known as the Yukon flats, and it has the appearance of flowing all over the country. When once well into this maze of narrow channels and bars, one has little idea of what part of the river he is in or where the banks are. There is nothing permanent about the banks. A new channel is liable to eat its way almost anywhere, and the current is quite as fickle, though it rushes along everywhere between the flat islands, which stretch as far as the eye can see in any direction. One has a feeling that he must be nearing the mouth of the Yukon. It is a perfect labyrinth of water. Some say the river here is ten miles wide, and others say fifty, and others guess anywhere between those figures. No one seems to know, and it would be difficult to imagine any one making the effort to find out. There is a suspicion that the river has no defined main banks, but just goes wherever its varying moods take it. It has all the appearance of having given up trying to be a river at all.

Many of these islands are merely wide stretches of sand and gravel, some of them covered with desolate-looking ridges of drift-wood. On others tall grass flourishes, but they are nothing but swampy lands. At high water the little steamers could pick their way through these channels with no difficulty with an Indian pilot at the wheel, but in low water the task is much more difficult, and one of the amusements of a trip is an occasional struggle of the little boat to pull her nose out of sand and try again, only to ground it somewhere else.

But the current nowhere abates its swiftness, and it is less than a day's ride to Fort Yukon, which lies just above

the Arctic Circle.   It is a curious geographical fact that the
river here, after having pursued a steady course towards the
northwest for some seven hundred miles, turns abruptly
to the southwest, just as if it had suddenly changed its mind,
a thing that it seems quite capable of doing at any point
along the flats for three hundred miles.   It is here that it is
joined by the Porcupine, which comes in from the northeast, and the new turn the river takes is evidently a joint arrangement of the two currents, the Porcupine having the
best of it.

There is a class of Indians about Fort Yukon trading in
curios and the like, and its individuals will do almost anything but work.   While I stopped there, one of the trading
companies was endeavoring to put up some log warehouses.
It was a convenient place for wintering provisions, for often,
late in the season, as was afterwards more fully developed,
the steamers find it impossible to cross the bars above the
fort, and are compelled to leave their cargo in log caches
here.   The overseer of the company which was putting up
these buildings had orders to hire all the Indians needed for
help, but he could not induce them to work, though he
offered them five dollars a day.   All they had to eat was
fish, but they subsisted on this and took it easy.   They take
no thought for the morrow.   One white man, his wife, and
two children, were the only white people there at that time.
It is the most forlorn of places, close on to the Arctic Circle,
and on the bank of a river which, spotted with dreary
islands, stretches away as far as the eye can see in nearly
every direction.

For something over a hundred miles after joined by the
Porcupine, the Yukon flows a little south to westward, maintaining its character for uncertainty.   The boats keep to the

channel along the south bank, but where the north main
bank is keeping itself is purely problematical. Channels
separate and appear to start off like other rivers bound for a
sea in some other parts of the world, while others are coming in at various places. The islands gradually become
larger and make a somewhat better appearance.

Birch Creek, the upper waters of which flow within a
short distance of Circle City, empties into the Yukon about
forty miles below the fort, and, according to the maps, the
Tadrandike empties on the opposite bank from the flat lands
of the north, but one would have to go out of the river's
course to find the mouth of this stream. About sixty miles
further on Beaver Creek flows in from the south. A little
time before this had been the scene of a great stampede of
miners from the upper Yukon. Gold had been picked up
there and many flocked in, but the excitement had proved
to be without cause, and the disappointed gold-seekers
gradually scattered back to the old diggings.

Soon after Fort Hamlin is passed, the maze of islands is
left behind. The mighty river " gets itself together "
again; the banks become higher and the mountains begin to
appear. It is a great relief after steaming for nearly four
hundred miles through a bewildering maze of water and flat
islands. The change is so great as to almost impress
one with awe. These miles of dreary flat lands are suddenly succeeded by what are called the Lower Ramparts,
and the Yukon Rapids sweep between bluffs and hills, which
rise about fifteen hundred feet. The river is not more than
half a mile wide, and seems almost as much underground
as one of the upper cañons. The bed is of granite, and the
current has worn it away on both sides so that there are two
good channels.

Some promising looking streams enter the river along this stretch of mountainous banks, but they are so common as to attract little attention from those on the river boats. One of them, however, was soon to spring into importance, for at this very time an Indian half breed named Munook was stumbling on his way to a rich discovery on one of its upper tributaries, and in another year, on one of the high and more beautiful spots on the south bank of the river, was to spring up a lively mining town called Rampart City.

The Tanana River, which flows in from the picturesque country to the south, is the largest tributary of the Yukon, and at its mouth seems the larger river. But it is from this point over one thousand three hundred miles to the headwaters of the mighty Yukon, and in its course it has flowed clear around the Tanana, which heads up directly to the territory of the gold diggings of Forty Mile and of Circle City. The Tanana brings down a vast flood of water from the mountainous regions of the interior, and yet it is only recently that a white man dipped his paddles in it. The late explorations have shown that it is a river of remarkable power and possibly of unnumbered treasures. It is navigable for steamers for nearly two hundred miles, for which distance the current is quite slack. Then it becomes swift — swifter than that of the Yukon, it is said. All the way on the left hand are rugged mountains and the most sublime scenery, while on the right hand, or to the south, the mountains stand at a distance. Colors of gold have been found in all of the many creeks which empty from glacial sources into the river, but no one has yet sunk a hole to bedrock. Nearly all of the prospecting that has been done has been by those who have crossed over the mountains from Forty Mile or Circle City.

In 1896 the junction of the Yukon and Tanana showed signs of becoming the important trading point it now is. There has long been a trading station there of the Alaska Commercial Company, and now the settlement of Weare holds an important point at the very junction.   Geographically, this is about the center of the great territory, though it is over eight hundred miles in a straight line from the old capital of Sitka.   A short distance below, St. James Mission, attached to the Episcopal Church, has for some years been successfully maintained, and the changes which have been wrought upon some of the native children are certainly noticeable.   As a general thing the Indians which are encountered along the Yukon River are no improvement over those farther up.   Though they are classed under different tribes they appear quite similar until we reach the point where the true Eskimo makes his appearance.   They have some good qualities and are exceedingly useful in the trade of the lower Yukon.

Along the banks of the various places are wooding stations, where the Indians cut up timber for firewood for the steamers, which, however, are compelled to stop much more frequently in facing the swift current up than on the downward passage.   The appearance of a Yukon steamer is a great event at these remote settlements, and the whole population within reach of the sound of the whistle flock down to the banks.   If wood is needed, a line of Indians, carrying the sticks in the primitive way, file over the gangplank and scamper out again, and for such services they are paid fair wages, but their disposition is to trade.   They take various articles, and many prefer to take it out in something to drink.   One thing they never take is soap, and yet that is what they most appear to need,

These settlements are for the most part all alike. They are thickest about places where the companies keep their stores, and these become the trading centers. The natives live in huts and tents, and there is the inevitable crowd of dogs, which, upon the advent of a steamer, line the bank and howl. It is the most dismal din imaginable. Along the banks also will be seen in season big salmon hanging from long poles drying in the sun. The children are not quite as thick as the dogs (nothing is in Alaska, except the mosquitoes), but they toddle about in their dirty garments as if life were something of a delight. The women come down the bank carrying queer baskets of trinkets, mostly of their handiwork, which gives evidence of an enormous amount of patience and skill in the use of crude materials — baskets of unique shape woven very fine from some of the long grass of the valley, and dyed in the most striking colors, moccasins of rare quality, and so on.

Wherever there are settlements, and where there are none, for that matter, the cache appears. These curious log boxes on stilts are sprinkled all over Alaska, for dogs are everywhere and the cache is an absolute necessity. They must be made to hold whatever is fit to eat, and a good deal that is unfit, for the dog will eat both. The cache is the lock and key of Alaska. And the only thief is this little animal, which will in harness haul his master for miles over the Arctic country, and then go to sleep in a snow bank.

One of the important stations which we come to in passing down this part of the river is Nowikakat, about seventy miles below the mouth of the Tanana. It is situated on the north bank and upon a fine bay, which is connected by a narrow entrance with the Yukon. In passing it is easy to judge of the nature of the soil from the crumbling banks. Layers of sand show the deposits of annual inundations.   In many places where the bank has been undermined these layers may be counted by the hundred, and all the way great masses of dirt from the banks are hurried off by the swift current to the sea.

When the river has flowed on in its westward course to within about eighty miles of the sea, it takes another sudden turn and proceeds southward, for two hundred miles, parallel with the coast.   This turn is made where the Koyukuk enters from the north, and, as above at the junction of the Porcupine, the river dodges off in another direction like one billiard ball hit by another.   The Koyukuk has been well explored, but not very thoroughly prospected. Gold has been found in large quantities on it, and as much as a hundred dollars a day has been made on some of its bars by the use of a rocker.   But little or nothing has been done on its important creeks, though the presence of coarse gold in the bars would imply unusual richness somewhere further up.   The river at its mouth is shallow, and for some distance up has many of the characteristics of the Yukon and Tanana.   About a hundred miles from the mouth the mountains begin to hem in the banks, but it can be navigated for nearly five hundred miles.   This accessibility should make it attractive to prospectors, for the headwaters lie in the same belt of mountains that hold the gold-bearing creeks of the upper Yukon.   The worst thing against it is that so much of it lies above the Arctic circle.

The Yukon, after its union with the Koyukuk, flows with a still swifter current along stretches of uninviting country, among marshy islands and sloughs, and at one place is only about fifty miles from the sea.   Two trails or portages from the river to St. Michael or Unalaklik have been in use for some time by the Indians and missionaries, but either is a hard road to travel, especially in the summer, and dangerous after the winter sets in. Winter, however, is the time when it becomes useful as a short cut from the interior after the river has frozen at its mouth. A party of miners once tried to reach St. Michael over this route and had an exceedingly hazardous trip. It teaches the lesson that traveling in Alaska is perilous unless amply provided for. They had only a few blankets and barely enough provisions for the trip. They walked over the frozen sloughs with the ice cracking under them at every step. Sometimes they had to lie flat on their stomachs and creep along, pushing their blankets ahead of them, in order to keep the ice from giving way under their weight. They knew that if any one went through that would be the end of him. There would be no possibility of getting him out. One of them gave out the first day, and they divided his load among the others and helped him along as best they could.

The first night they slept in an abandoned Eskimo winter house that was full of mice and vermin. That is, they stayed in it, but slept little, because the moment they dropped off the mice began nibbling at their noses and running down their necks. The next night they stayed in one of the inhabited Eskimo houses, and it was a million times worse than the other. There were seventeen of them crowded with ten Eskimos into an underground hut, without a breath of fresh air, and with all the bad smells imaginable reeking off the filthy Indians. They gagged and stifled and suffocated all night long, and the next night they took to the open. It was storming, and bitter, bitter cold. Five of them had only four blankets between them, and they were so near freezing that they were afraid to sleep. They stumbled and crept along, uncertain whether or not they were even going in the right direction. On the second day after the first night they slept out another man broke down. He was a man of fine courage, but so utterly spent and ill that they could scarcely get him along. He would stumble and fall in his tracks, and before they could reach him he would be asleep from exhaustion. Much of the time that day they had to carry him in their arms. Nearly all day there was an awful storm of howling wind and snow and rain, and all were wet to the skin. But they kept right on as rapidly as they could make their way across the tundra, and when night came crawled into the shelter of a lake bank and made a fire. They had run out of provisions and had left only a flapjack and a sliver of bacon for each. They put the sickest man into the middle of the group and all huddled around him, trying to keep him warm through the night.

It was a sorry-looking crowd that left that camp the next morning. They knew not where they were, or if they were going in the right direction, or how soon they might have to lie down and die of exhaustion and starvation. But they drew up their belts, set their teeth, took the sick man on their shoulders, and started on. The weather was not quite so cold as it had been. It was warm enough to rain, and the water was just pouring out of the sky. At last they reached the top of the first hill and saw St. Michael below them. They were six days traveling that one hundred and ten miles.

The portage from Nulato leads to Unalaklik and is the least difficulty, but neither of these trails offers any advantages except as a short cut to the base of supplies. At this

point the river flows within about fifty miles from the sea
and not much further than that from St. Michael, but it is
about six hundred miles to that port by way of the river.

Alaska is a difficult country to get into, and equally difficult to get out of. The erratic Yukon has all the appear-
ances of having met the latter difficulty. During its long
course it runs towards every point in the compass, and in
some places seems to be running in all directions at once.

CHAPTER XV

STILL JOURNEYING ALONG THE DREARY RIVER — SIGHTS
AND SCENES ON THE WAY — HABITS AND PECULIAR-
ITIES OF THE INDIANS.

Holy Cross Mission — Soap at Last Has Legal-Tender Value — Some
Domestic Scenes — Close Race with the Climate — The Sisters of
St. Anne — Mass in a Log Church — The Untutored Innuits —
Their Unpleasant Environment — Queer Heirlooms — Geese and
Ducks Find a Favorable Abode — The Trip to the Coast — St.
Michael — Why Ocean Steamers have to Anchor a Mile and a Half
Out — Alaska Commercial Company — Fort Get-There — A Lone
Government Official — The Question of Transferring Cargoes —
Characteristics of the Natives — Watching a Chance to Reach the
Yukon's Mouth — Difficulties of Getting in with a Load — Breast-
ing the Swift Current — A Hard Nut to Crack — Returning up
the River.

A S we proceeded down the river towards Anvik, the
high ground ceased to come down to the water's
edge, and the flat lands began to reappear, though
the horizon is met by low hills some distance away. At
some points rise lofty clay cliffs, made up of various colors.
Spruce and fir trees, poplars and willows, are sprinkled
along, but they do not extend back far into the country,
which rapidly becomes more and more marshy and dreary.
While stopping at Anvik, our attention was divided between the strange old trading station, with its storehouses
on stilts, and the ancient Russian mission, with its silver
candelabra, luminous wall paintings, and sacred relics.

Much more progress seems to have been made with the natives at the Holy Cross Mission, a short distance further down, though I think they must be a better class naturally. Here a cake of soap seems to have considerable legal-tender value, and some of the children are attractively clad in the garments of civilization, and wear clean faces, as well as the inevitable Innuit smile. The buildings of the Holy Cross Mission are well constructed, and include a church, two schools — one for boys, another for girls; a convent, and the necessary outbuildings for a well-ordered farm. Large cultivated fields adjoin the establishment, and in them vegetables of prodigious size are grown, as well as strawberries. But it is a close race with the climate. Upon the hillsides, in well-kept terraces, the more delicate plants are grown, and in the dooryard sweet mignonette, phlox, pansies, violets, nasturtiums, marguerites, dahlias, and other homelike flowers flourish in the summer months, nurtured by the slender hands and tender solicitude of the Sisters of St. Anne. These heroic women have immured themselves in this inhospitable region, and have undertaken to subdue nature and nature's children by gentle persistency, and their efforts are telling in the manifold results to be observed about them.

But being unfitted for Innuit life by these civilizing influences, the wonder is what is to become of them and their acquirements in such a country.

The school has its press, and has issued several volumes in the native tongue.

There is the great log barn, with its well-filled hay-loft, and even a cow; the haystack outside, and various other evidences of rural domesticity and comfort. There are the wofully homely but peachy-cheeked native girls, neatly clad in their uniform ginghams, with a delicious French accent in their very precise English, the source of which becomes apparent in conversation with these sisters of St. Anne. And all these wonders compensate the traveler for the delay of several hours usually made there for the purpose of obtaining wood, cleaning boilers, and giving the passengers a pleasant diversion. It has grown to be the custom of the mission to hold special services whenever a vessel is in port, and the chorus of fresh young Indian voices in the mass rings from the organ loft in the church of logs with much impressiveness, set in these unique surroundings in a desolate country.

These Innuit people are a queer lot, the untutored housed in their squatty mounds of earth, the entrances to which are holes under ground, and subsisting on mixtures the flavor of which nearly kills a white man. They are, however, as a whole, much superior to the Indians of the interior, being a trifle less lazy. They are used by the companies to man their steamers, but if one can shirk work he will. They seem to look on the industry of the white man as a great exhibition of foolishness. They live in a country which in summer is a great flat swale full of bog holes, slimy and decaying peat, innumerable sloughs, shallow and stagnant, and from which swarms of mosquitoes rise to fairly destroy any animal life. The insects come out of their watery pupæ with the earliest growth of spring vegetation, early in May, and remain in clouds till destroyed by the frosts of September. The natives seldom go into the woods at this summer season, and their dogs, though protected by their long hair, sometimes die from bites about their eyes and paws. Close-haired beasts, like horses and cattle, could not live a month, unless protected by man.

In the winter and early spring fierce gales of wind at zero temperature sweep over these flats of Alaska in constant succession, and, although it is in this season that land travel is easiest, it is full of dangers to any but the natives, who are muffled in their skin parkas. Their undergarments consist mostly of a skin shirt, which is handed down from one generation to another, but it is difficult for an inexperienced white man to tell whether the odor of one of these garments belongs to the present owner or to one of his more or less remote ancestors.

The bluffs which here and there come down to the river are desolate enough, with their barren slopes, but they give the only indication that the country is not all under water. The channel zigzags from side to side in a way common to such swift bodies of water, which are constantly washing out and building up bars and islets, and sweeping down in its resistless flood an immense aggregate of soil and timber. The banks, where they rise above this surging current, which runs at an average of eight miles an hour, are continually caving down, and so sudden and precipitate are these landslides sometimes that any craft in their way is liable to be destroyed.

When the Yukon has in its tortuous career again turned towards the coast, it manages somehow in the course of over one hundred miles to empty itself. It makes a very bad job of it. It breaks up into a labyrinth of blind, misleading channels, slough and swamps, which extend over an immense territory with a most mournful and distressing prospect. The country itself is scarcely above the level of the tides, and is covered with a monotonous cloak of scrubby willows and rank sedges. It is in summer water, water — here, there, and everywhere, — a vast inland sea, filled with thousands and thousands of swale islets scarcely peeping above the surface.

Myriads of geese, ducks, and wading water fowl resort to this desolation, where in the countless pools and the thick covers of tall grass and sedge they are provided with food and protection from their enemies. With good luck and a good pilot, the steamer finally works its way out by the northern channel, and reaches the sea at Kutlik, which is a meagre settlement where the steamers take on drift wood. The rest of the trip is along the coast. A voyage in one of these small, flat-bottom boats of the Yukon, is a good deal like knocking about the Atlantic on a plank, unless the weather is very favorable. In this region it has few such agreeable moods.

A cursory glance at St. Michael harbor tells why the question of getting supplies up the Yukon is a serious one to overcome, even were the other conditions partially favorable. The harbor is but little more than a crescent on the shores of Norton Sound. It is neither deep nor well-protected. The port itself is on an island, about five by eighteen miles, shaped something like an ink spot, and separated from the mainland by a narrow slough. The hills of the mainland are some four or five miles back from the shore to the south. At the other points tundra is broken only by rolling hills, which are hardly more than large mounds.

Ocean steamers have to make a wide detour away from the mouth of the Yukon on account of the dirt it has been pouring into the sea, and St. Michael is the only place where they can get within a hundred miles of it, but steamers drawing over twenty feet anchor about a mile and a half, even, from St. Michael, and none of the vessels lie in nearer than half a mile from the Alaska Commercial Company's wharf. The port is a clustering village of some thirty or more small houses. and is nearly wholly given over to the interests of the Alaska Commerical Company. Scattered huts and Eskimo dwellings make up the rest of its entirety. Half a mile further on is now Fort Get-There, headquarters for the North American Transportation and Trading Company. The island is undoubtedly of volcanic origin, it being nothing more than volcanic rock and tundra, entirely treeless, and, even at this season, dreary-looking. The tundra is nothing but the moss and peat covering rock. Soil there is none. The tundra may vary up to two feet in depth, but below this it is frozen solid at all times of the year. Imagine agriculture where the plow would turn up ice and frozen moss at from eight inches down beneath the surface. In spite of this the grass is almost knee-deep, and bright-colored wild flowers are luxurious in their growth and profusion. Innumerable small ponds break the surface, filled with water which seeps through the moss, and which is neither palatable nor good. It appears to be impregnated with alkali. All the water used by the Commercial Company's post is brought from the mainland by boat. That at Fort Get-There is said to be filtered from the ponds.

The first settlement here was made by the Russians in 1836. At the time of the purchase of Alaska this fort and post were a part of the transfer, about one hundred thousand dollars being paid for the buildings and fortifications. The United States must have let their interest go by default, as now all that is left is a small blockhouse and half a dozen small cannon, and even these are a part and parcel of the Commercial Company's post. Our lone government official, deputy collector of customs, has his office in a dwelling rented from the Alaska Commercial Company.

St. Michael is eighty miles, at least, north of the pass by which the steamers enter the river, and the river proper is over a hundred miles further on, as we have seen, the extent of its delta being second to none in the world. After an ocean steamship reaches St. Michael the question of getting its cargo ashore and up the river commences in real earnest. Everything has to be lightered from the boat to the warehouses, which, with the present improved facilities, is tedious and exasperating. A small launch and two scows have constituted the outfit. Lighterage is also subject to the conditions of the weather, for the wind frequently blows here at a terrific rate. When the river steamers are in they take in cargo alongside the ship, which greatly expedites matters. Having been loaded, the river steamer must watch its chance to cross Norton Sound to the Aphoon Mouth, and thence over a hundred miles to the main river. This must all be done between June 15th and October 1st. Sometimes the river starts freezing by the middle of September, and St. Michael's Bay has never been opened before June 18th. The sound freezes over early in winter, and seldom is opened before June 20th. One of the inhabitants very tersely puts the situation thus:

" For nine months it means from thirty to sixty degrees below, and everything frozen over. For two months it's mosquitoes, and for the other one month, it depends on the weather whether it is fog or sunshine." In spite of this, the people here do not seem to be particularly discontented. For ages the natives have lived in these ice-bound regions of the north, and have met and overcome the most inhospitable conditions that could confront human beings. Physically. they are good specimens of manhood. Mentally they are far superior to most savage tribes. In their domestic pursuits they are skilled to a degree that challenges admiration. They are inventive, and out of the slender resources of their native land they have gathered much that would be accounted wealth if the arts of civilization had not intruded. They have learned to tan the hides of the seal and walrus into leather that is waterproof and resists wear like iron. With it they construct their kyaks and canoes and their summer dwellings. Out of the walrus tusks they fashion implements of the chase, and ornament them with faithful likenesses of the animals, birds, and fish with which they are familiar. Ivory-carving is an art with them. The women sew, and make the fur garments, and boots and shoes that are worn by all. They are a merry race, giving themselves up to pleasure completely when the season for labor has passed. Honest and truthful to a degree, they are trustful of the stranger, and hospitable, too, though to the newcomer their hospitality is sometimes oppressive.

The journey from St. Michael to the mouths of the Yukon, and thence up its swift current, pushing a barge, is a much longer and more serious task. We were fortunate in connections, and the little stern-wheeler and barge were soon loaded, ready to make the spurt across the sound. The weather was caught in a favorable mood, and we were quickly in the safer waters, where narrow banks like dikes rise out of the sea and extend oceanward for miles, inclosing the channel.

These narrow strips of land resemble great wharves or breakwaters when seen from the ocean side. The practical navigator anchors his craft in the lee of these banks to wait

CROSSING THE SKAGWAY RIVER

The bridge consists of the trunk of a single tree over which two gold-seekers are making their way. This is only one of many similar places along the trail.

a favoring tide, and when it rises pushes his vessel forward with all possible speed to cross the shallows at the entrance, nor stops until the first station of the journey up the river is reached at Kutlik.

Only at high tide, or when the river is very high, is it safe to push loaded boats over these bars, for once caught on them it may be a matter of weeks before the boat can be got off and the journey resumed. There is more or less of this all the way up the river. As one traveler expressed it, " it is touch and go, or touch and not go," much of the way. There can be no time-table.

The river proper is not generally entered until the second day out from St. Michael. During all this time the steamer has been winding in and out, seeming never to directly approach the range of distant hills that marks the beginning of the mainland, yet ever coming nearer through the sinuous channel. Suddenly the steamer emerges from the narrow and shallow way into a broad, swift-moving current confined between something like banks, and pointing a long, straight, dreary course toward the mountains. The pulse of the engines quicken, there is a straining of timbers, and with quick leaps forward the steamer breasts the mighty current, and backward from her bow the white foam curls as she rushes onward.

But it is up-hill work. Occasionally the strong machinery, which takes up most of the room in the boat, will break down, and the machine shop, which has to be a feature of Yukon craft, is kept busy. Or perhaps the wood gives out before a station is reached, and the crew, and, possibly, the passengers, are brought into service to cut a fresh supply from the banks. As the little steamer puffs along the incidents observed in coming down the river are re-

peated.   The natives throng to the landings, and when vil-
lages are passed, the Indians and dogs line the banks, in
picturesque confusion.   There is a sort of delight in riding
swiftly down the current while these scenes are passing in
panorama, but in struggling up, day after day, the monotony is tedious, though everyone tries to make the best of it.

There can be no question that the river route to the gold
regions of the upper Yukon, with all its drawbacks, and the
length of time it consumes, is the least dangerous, the easiest
and the most agreeable.   It must in the future be made to
play a great part in the development of Alaska, and yet,
for commercial purposes, it is a hard nut to crack.   It is a
strange river in a strange country.

If Alaska still belonged to Russia, and development had
to come from Kamschatka and Siberia, its position would
be right enough, but it is wrong end to for the United States.
Access to it involves the crossing of two turbulent seas, the
North Pacific and Bering Sea, three thousand miles to a far
northern point, then in a horseshoe route up and south
again, over a rapid current and shallow and shifting bed
that at the best has but little more than four months per
year of ticklish navigation.

Even with improved facilities it must always be expensive business to carry freight so long a distance.   All efforts
to improve the channel must be wasted, because of the swift
nature of the river, which is continually pouring down silt
and constructing its own shallow channels.   In some places
the navigable way is here to-day and gone somewhere else
to-morrow.   It is almost impossible to mark a channel at the
mouth, for the movement of the ice in Bering Sea is continually changing the depths at this point, so that what
might be the channel one season would not be the next.

From this cause, and high winds making it too rough for river steamers to cross the intervening eighty miles from St. Michael to the mouth, there is much delay here, and it would be impossible to fix regular dates of sailing. To deepen one of the channels sufficiently to allow ocean vessels to enter the mouth of the river would be very expensive, and even when done could hardly be expected, under the conditions, to be permanent.

In spite of all the difficulties, the transportation companies have struggled nobly to provide for the necessities of the increasing population at the mines, and it remains the only way by which provisions can be carried in in large quantities. To the people there these little river steamers mean life, if winter is to be spent in the interior, and unless winters are spent in the interior there can be no development of the mines. It is then that the digging must be done.

Meeting with generally favorable conditions on our way up the river, we arrived at Circle City in good time. Joe was down from the mines for another load of supplies, and he informed me that so far as he had worked the ground where our claims were the prospects were good, and he proposed to stock up with provisions and continue the work through the winter. It seemed best for me to continue on the steamer up to Forty Mile and seek to make some arrangements, if possible, for the working of our claims there before returning to Circle City for the winter. So up the river I went, little dreaming of the events which had thrown the miners of the upper Yukon into a fever of excitement.

CHAPTER XVI

ARRIVAL AT FORTY MILE — WONDERFUL STORIES OF
NEW DIGGINGS — HO ! FOR THE KLONDIKE ! — MAD
RUSH OF EXCITED GOLD-SEEKERS.

Something Has Happened — Forty Mile Almost Deserted — A Genuine
Stampede — The Discovery on the Thron-diuck or Klondike —
Henderson's Find on Gold Bottom — He Returns for Provisions —
Meeting Cormack's Fishing Party — He Tells of His Discovery —
Cormack Concludes to Find Gold Bottom — Over the Trail — Re-
turns to His Fishing Camp — Prospects a Little on His Way —
Stumbles on a Good Pan on Bonanza Creek — Claims for Himself,
Tagish Charlie, and Tagish Jim — Siwash George's Reputation for
Truth and Veracity — Where Did He Get the Gold ? — Tremendous
Excitement — Forty Mile Deserted — Old Miners Lack Faith —
Skim Diggings — Highly-Colored Tales — I Conclude to Go and
See for Myself — Poling Up Stream — Returning Prospectors Shoot
By Us — "It's a Big Thing, Boys" — Never Mind the Blisters —
Tired and Footsore — A Lively Camp — Trying to Sleep — Ten
Dollars to the Pan.

WHEN we reached Forty Mile it was at once apparent that something had happened to that lively
little settlement with which we had become acquainted a few weeks before on our swift trip down the
river. A great change had come over it, and we were not
long in discovering the reason. The greater part of the
place had vanished, moved bag and baggage to the " Thron-
diuck," the moose valley forty miles above. It was here
that we heard the story of the " Klondike " discovery.

There is some dissimilarity in the accounts of how the

discovery was made, but the most reliable seems to show that the credit for it in the first instance should be given to three men, Robert Henderson, a Canadian, a native of Prince Edward Island, Frank Swanson, a Norwegian, and another man named Munson, who, in July, 1896, were prospecting on Indian Creek, which, as will be observed by the map, empties into the Yukon some twenty-five miles above the Klondike.

They proceeded up the creek without finding sufficient to satisfy them until they reached Dominion Creek, and after prospecting there they crossed over the divide and found Gold Bottom, where they got good prospects and went to work. Gold Bottom is a little creek whose headwaters are very close to Dominion Creek. It flows northward, emptying into another creek, which, in turn, empties into the Klondike about twelve miles from its mouth. It is said that the attention of these prospectors was first directed to Gold Bottom by the stories told by Indian fishermen. But these stories had often been told, and little confidence was placed in the acuteness of the Indians of this region in noticing traces of the yellow metal.

The prospectors kept at work for some days with results that seemed promising, but, provisions running short, Henderson retraced his steps to the mouth of Indian Creek, leaving the other two at work. From the mouth of Indian Creek he went up to Sixty Mile, but failing to obtain a supply there he had to make for Forty Mile. On the way down he passed an old mining comrade named George W. Cormack, a native of California, who had associated with him two Indians, Tagish Jim and Tagish Charlie, natives of the upper waters of the Yukon. Cormack was what is known as a " squaw man," having, like many other pioneers in the

country, married an Indian woman, and thus having become more closely associated with the "Stick" Indian ways.
He was commonly called "Siwash George." With his Indian associates he had been fishing near the mouth of the
Klondike for some days, but without much success, as the
salmon did not run up well in the summer of 1896. He
had heard stories of the Indians as to traces of gold on the
creeks emptying into the Klondike, but like most of the old-
timers had paid little attention to them, and in his Indian
life had looked upon the salmon season as a time when the
energies must be expended in laying up a store of fish for the
winter.

The scene as Henderson came drifting down the rapid-
flowing Yukon towards the little camp near the mouth of
the Klondike, where Cormack and his associates were conducting their unsuccessful fishing operations, may be easily
imagined. Here with majestic swiftness the great river rolls
between its steep banks, on which plants and flowers flourish
in the colors and exuberance characteristic of a Yukon
summer. To the voyager it was a weird, picturesque scene,
as the sun cast a flood of light on the sweeping river and the
steep mountains, fringed with green and tipped with streaks
of white, and fell brightly on the camp of Cormack, his Indians, and his dogs. An opportunity for a brief companion-
ship in these solitudes is seldom missed, and Henderson
steered to the camp, where items of news were exchanged.

It is one of the articles of the miner's code that he shall
proclaim all discoveries made by him as soon as possible,
and Henderson, who had already dropped the word to a few
at Sixty Mile, to which place he had first gone for provisions, but without success, at once advised Cormack of the
discovery on Gold Bottom, and advised him to try there.

Making inquiries of the local Indians as to the situation of Gold Bottom, Cormack learned the route to it, and, along with the two Indians mentioned, started, climbing over the ridge which divides the valley of the Yukon from the valley of the creek now called Bonanza, down into that creek and up it to the rich stream now known as Eldorado. It was a rough, agonizing journey, but Cormack and his Indians were hardened to such conditions. They went up it about three miles and then followed the ridge dividing its waters from those of Bonanza until they struck the watershed between Indian Creek and Klondike, along which they traveled until they reached the head of the creek that they assumed to be the Gold Bottom. They went down, found Swanson and Munson at work, but Cormack was not satisfied with the prospects there. They were fair, but not sufficient to justify the conclusion that placers of exceeding richness lay in streaks under the frozen soil. Often had prospectors been tempted into these hills only to work their way out in disgust to seek provisions. Cormack determined to return to his fishing, prospecting the creek from its head downwards, as it lay in the direction of his camp.

He found nothing of note until he came down about midway, where from a little nook in a bend of the creek he panned out a good prospect. This encouraged him to try again. He did so, and in a few moments panned out twelve dollars and seventy-five cents, which he put in an old cartridge shell and corked with a piece of stick. This was on August 10, 1896. The next day he staked discovery claim and No. 1 below for himself, No. 2 for Tagish Charlie, and No. 1 above for Tagish Jim. He then made his way down the creek as fast as possible and went down the river for a supply of provisions.

On the way he met several miners and informed them of his discovery. At first they would not believe him, as his reputation for truth was not above par. These miners said they could not tell when he was telling the truth, if he ever was. Yet there was no question about the man having the twelve dollars and seventy-five cents in gold. The only question, then, was, Where did he get it? He had not been up the Sixty Mile, nor yet the Forty Mile, and he must have got it somewhere near where he was engaged in fishing, and that was right at the mouth of the Klondike. There must be gold there somewhere.

Then followed the excitement. It takes very little to start a stampede of miners. Boatload after boatload of men went up from Forty Mile. They went up any how and any way, starting at all times of the day and night. Men who had been drunk for weeks and weeks, in fact, were tumbled into the boats and taken up without any knowledge that they were travelers. One man, it was related, was so drunk that he did not realize that he had left Forty Mile until he was more than two-thirds of the way to the Klondike. Yet this same man is settled on one of the best of claims.

In less than three days every boat had gone from Fort Cudahy and the town of Forty Mile, and only enough people were left to watch the business houses and the police barracks, while a few who could not obtain boats were acting in the most distracted manner. No one knew anything about the richness of the new discoveries; they only knew that a man had been there and had come away with a few gold nuggets.

I knew enough of miners' stampedes not to be greatly interested in the new development at Forty Mile. I was aware that there had been at that place a lot of miners who had been having poor luck, and leading a very unsatisfactory existence. They were the bluest of the blue, for they had been tramping over the rough trails in the country back from the Yukon in the hopes of making a strike, had failed, and were, as the winter season approached, completely disgusted with the country. Those who had been working for wages in some of the paying mines were better off, but the moment the Klondike news came they threw up their jobs, and some owners of the mines on Forty Mile either stopped work or sold out their claims, and departed with the rest. A large number of them rushed off without provisions or the means to obtain them.

Very soon some of these came down the river, having located claims, and then it was learned that there was really something on the Klondike worth traveling after. " It's a big thing," they said. " Everybody is finding big pans." They were speaking comparatively, for none of the really big finds had been made as yet. The surface pans were large as compared with those that the miners had been accustomed to in the region. It was easy enough to find gold, but the thing was to find it fast enough to pay. A " grubstake " strike, by which one might succeed in obtaining a winter's outfit, was something. All the returned miners could say was that the surface was good, and " if it went down it would be the biggest thing on earth." There was a belief among those remaining at Forty Mile that they were only what are called " skim diggings." This impression was intensified by a few old miners who had come back either in disgust or highly skeptical. They said the valley was too wide, that the willows did not lean the right way, and that the waters did not taste right. It was simply another crazy stampede. Some of them did not even wait to stake out a claim, while others staked them and sold them for what they could get, thinking themselves in luck to do that. The creek had been staked principally by " chee-chacoes," as the Indians call them, or tenderfeet. So little faith was shown at Forty Mile that some of the claim-holders could not obtain " grub " at the stores in exchange for their prospects.

But more and more highly colored tales began to come down, though no one, so far as we could hear, had reached bed-rock as yet, and I determined that I would put out and see for myself. I knew it would be an impossibility for one man to work a boat up the rapid Yukon, so I picked out a helper, with whom I was well acquainted, from among the feverish throng that were waiting for a chance to go up. We threw a tent, a stove, and a month's provisions into a boat, and started off, but before we had got far we overtook two men who insisted that their happiness in this world, and, perhaps, in the next, depended upon our taking them along with us. They would pull the boat, do anything, if we would only let them come in. So we did.

Working up stream with a loaded boat is a laborious undertaking. The current is too swift to permit of rowing or paddling except for occasional short stretches, and so we had to pole most of the way, and when that failed we had to tow or " trick " the boat along. These two men would grasp the tow line and pull with all their strength, for they were anxious to make the best time possible, but neither of them were experts in handling a boat in the peculiar methods required on the Yukon. My brief summer's experience, however, had been of value to me, and we worked along in fair order, but most of the time in a drizzling rain.

It was very dismal. We camped wherever the lengthening nights overtook us, and generally on a gravelly bank, for the heavy moss on the top of the banks overlooking the river is full of water. We ate hurriedly, slept little, and hour after hour dragged the tow line over rough places on the shore, the boat all the time pulling a dead weight against us.

Long before we reached the Klondike many boats passed us loaded with men who had been to the new diggings and were returning for provisions. They shot by us gaily in a five-mile current in strange contrast to the men on the tow line, who, with blistered feet, were slipping and sprawling along the rocks on the bank.

" Hurry up, boys. It's a great thing! " they shouted as they shot past, as if we could hurry any faster against that current.

" Five dollars to the pan, boys," shouted another, " but take it easy, for there's lots of good claims there," and we pulled away on the tow line harder than ever.

" Hello, Bill, is that you? " came a voice from another boat later on, and I recognized a man with whom I had become acquainted on the trip in, and who had stopped at Forty Mile. " It looks good," he shouted. " Yes, I've staked. Will sell for one hundred dollars, for there are more claims there. Take some grub over the mountains and look around a little. I'll be back shortly."

I made up my mind that it was no wild goose chase. I could take that man's word, for he was an old miner, and not easily deceived. " It must be a big thing," I said to my companions, and they pulled and poled with renewed energy. How exasperating a five-mile current can be when it is against one, and there is gold at the other end! Never mind the blisters on the feet and the sore hands!

Never mind stopping to eat! We munched crackers and kept on pulling and poling.

On the third evening we reached the little native village at the mouth of the Klondike. When Joe and I had gone past there in the early summer there had been but two white men in the village. Now they were camped all about the banks. We were too tired and footsore to attempt to go over the mountains that night, so we put up the tent and dragged our boat up on the beach. Some of the men who were camped there had been over the trail, and had come down for more provisions which they had left in caches, or in the native huts, while some were bound down the river to Forty Mile, like those we had passed on the way. Others had just arrived and, like ourselves, were waiting to go over the trail. We had a bite, a little hot coffee, and then a pipe, then sat and listened to the stories of those who had been in. These stories, however, did not agree. Some said they were not coming back, that the Klondike couldn't " hold a candle " to Forty Mile Creek, others spoke of big strikes, but we were shown little gold. They had just staked out their claims and were going back for supplies.

All night the boats kept arriving and pulling up on the gravelly beach. They came from Sixty Mile, Stewart River — from everywhere in this part of the Yukon valley, and when we wondered how they came to hear of it we found that they had been sent for by their friends on the stream. The natives had been used as messengers.

Then we were startled by a wild whoop like a Comanche yell from the brow of the first rise of the mountain over which the trail comes from Bonanza. Then came a volley of yells, and a stranger would have thought that a whole band of savages were pouring down the hill after us. We looked up through the bushes to see the rocks tumbling and rolling down with them. The yells increased; and rocks and men came down faster and faster till they reached the bottom a few yards away. Of course we knew what was up. They had just come in from the creek. We were up and shouting, too.

"How is it?" everybody asked as the men came nearer.

"Ten dollars to the pan, right in the bank of the creek on No. 11."

"Above or below?"

"Oh, below, of course. Nobody has done any panning above."

It is, of course, understood that when a discovery is made on a creek that claim is called "Discovery Claim," the next above is called "No. 1, above," the next one down stream "No. 1, below," and so on as far as claims are made either up or down.

The little camp of scattered tents was at once alive with eager men. The returning miners were seized and buttonholed, to use a polite expression which is sometimes out of place in Alaska for want of buttons. More wood was thrown on the fire, the coffee-pot was put where it would boil quickly, and the frying pan was soon doing its duty, while the visitors squatted around and were pumped for information.

We were told that three men on Bonanza Creek worked out seventy-five dollars in four hours, and that a twelve-dollar nugget had been found. Nothing had yet been done except to pan, though two men with two lengths of sluice boxes had taken out four thousand dollars. The gold is coarse. That was enough to set the miners wild.

It was evident, from the ferocity with which the men

attacked the solid food, and poured down the boiling-hot black coffee, that the trip to the creek was not exactly a picnic, though they say it is " fair." We knew enough to know that in Alaska that word applies to any place where a man can go without breaking his neck.

In a little while I saw a few men slipping away from the small crowd clustered about the fire, and in a few minutes the sound of stones and rocks rolling down the mountain side was heard again. But there were no yells. No one was returning. Here and there a man had slipped away and strapped on his pack, and was climbing upward, clinging to the small bushes, working slowly, but going on persistently. They could not wait a moment after hearing the stories of those wonderful pans.

I knew we were too tired and footsore to attempt to make the climb till morning. If we had attempted it we should probably have had to stop somewhere on the mountains without water. Still, we regretted that we could not push on. My companions showed no signs of being sleepy, although I knew they needed rest like myself. Finally we got into the tent, rolled ourselves in our blankets, and tried to sleep, but every once in a while another boat would scrape on the gravelly beach, and more men would come up and cook a meal, or hurriedly shoulder their packs and scramble on up the steep trail.

While I lay there, almost ready to drop off and forget about the wonderful pans, I heard a noise in the tent. Some one was moving about. But I recognized the sound. I have already related a few facts concerning the Alaskan dog, and there is no mistaking that peculiar, gentle sound of a pan being licked by a " huskie." I picked up a hatchet and threw it at the dark object, but it did not hit him.

Nothing but a rifle ball would hit one of these dogs.   The hatchet made a big hole in the tent, but time was too precious to waste in sewing it up.

Finally, I fell asleep, only to be awakened by more boats grinding on the gravel, more Comanche yells, more men clambering up the mountain, more stones rolling down to the beach.

CHAPTER XVII

MY FIRST TRAMP IN THE KLONDIKE GOLD FIELDS —
WHAT A PLACE FOR GOLD! — A PEEP INTO THE
SLUICE BOXES — I STAKE A CLAIM.

Preparations for a Start — Over the Mountain into the Swamps — A
Hard Tramp — Cranberries to Quench Thirst — A Mysterious Pup
— The Klondike Valley from the Summit — Glimpse of the Arctic
Rockies — "All the Goold in the Worruld" — An Old Story —
Hurrying On — On Bonanza Creek at Last — Calculating the Dis-
tance — Blowing a Little — Looking for Henry Ward Beecher — A
Disgusted Irishman — Too Tired to Keep On — A Look at the
Gravelly Bar — I form a Poor Opinion — Ready to Change My
Mind — Too Tired to Care — Forgetting One's Name — Chilled
Through — Nuggets Fished Out with a Shovel — Washing Out
the Gold — Objects of Suspicion — Pushing on for a Claim — Indi-
cations Do Not Count — I Stake My Claim — Starting Back in the
Rain — Over the Trail Again — Our Turn to Yell.

B Y the time daylight had found its way into the valley
our breakfast was disposed of, and the dishes set
away out of the reach of the dogs. We cached
most of our provisions, and fixed in small packs what we
deemed necessary for the next few days. Then we set out
over the trail, taking our turn at tearing up the little bushes,
and making the stones rattle down the mountain side. I
had become accustomed to climbs of this character during
the summer, and, difficult as it was, I could by this time regard it as quite the usual thing. My companions also had
good muscles and lungs, and made no complaint. Besides,

there were those stories about those wonderful pans of gold, and there was no time to lose — at least, that was the way we all felt about it.

After going half a mile or so the trail became less precipitous, and undulated through a patch of wind-swept spruce and cottonwood. The ground was covered with moss of that large variety which lies all over the Yukon valley and hills, while everywhere were clumps of cranberry bushes, the berries being just in their prime. Huckleberry bushes also abounded. In a little while we came to a swamp with a wealth of hummocks. The water in the trail was over ankle-deep, but there was no use trying to walk outside of it, so we splashed along, and soon came to comparatively dry ground again. Some of my companions grew very thirsty and looked about for water, but none was to be seen. That in the swamp was not fit to drink. On we went, picking a few cranberries by the way to relieve thirst, and causing the grouse to flutter from among the bushes, for berry time is their feasting season.

We met a returning party, and were told that we should find a spring just before we reached the summit, but we forgot our thirst a moment while they told more tales of the great strikes of gold on the creek. We pushed on, finding no spring; others came down the trail, and some overtook us. We saw a down-trail man take an up-trail man to one side and evidently whisper some advice. Once I heard the word " pup " mentioned. In Yukon parlance that means " gulch." Every creek has its pups, and if any of them become of considerable importance they may have pups also. The natural conclusion was that some of the prospectors had struck it rich on one of the pups of the Bonanza. Of course, I was then in utter ignorance of the nature and locality of that particular pup.   The world was to learn about it later on.

We finally reached the longed-for spring, and indulged in a little rest, for we greatly needed it.   People never know what work is till they have followed an Indian trail in Alaska for half a day.   As we hurried on again to the summit we encountered returning men about every half mile, and they told of rich prospects being found in different places along the creek.   Some of them thought they existed only in spots and on the rim-rock,* others were sure the creek was good from source to mouth.   Now and then one assured us that it was all a fraud, and that the men who claimed to have got big pans never got them.   These pessimistic prospectors always looked weary and fagged out, and I knew they had had no breakfast, and perhaps had no supper the night before, and probably did not sleep much.   In the first place, doubtless, they had met poor luck in panning the surface dirt, and, being without provisions, they had naturally taken a very gloomy view of the whole subject.

On the summit we dropped down exhausted and took another rest.   As we toiled upward the trees had become fewer, more scrubby and wind-swept, and at the top they permitted a view of what lay about us.   The Klondike Valley made a beautiful picture in the foreground.   We looked up the valley and could see the windings of the silvery thread of water for fifty miles, and where it came out of a gateway in the mountains fully one thousand feet in depth, with the two sides so exactly alike and so evenly inclined that one could hardly help believing this to be an engineering feat of the Titans.   Beyond this, and one

---

* Rim-rock.   The edges of the channels worn away in the rocks by streams of former ages.   Within these channels the auriferous detritus was accumulated.

hundred miles on either side of the round-topped mountains which form the foothills of the Rockies now, but did
not once, as they are evidently a more recent formation and
upheaval, lay the Rockies, peaked and pinnacled and jagged
beyond description.   Every ravine visible could be traced
by its string-like glacier, and as you followed one upward
with your eye you could see the side ravines coming in like
branches of a tree.   In some cases these branches are sufficiently numerous to give the appearance of an outline
drawing in chalk of a leafless tree.

I suppose if one should live constantly where such views
were ever before his eyes, they would become commonplace
enough.   When at home in Vermont I used to hear of
people who seemed to be overcome by the majesty of the
White Mountains, and who, sitting on a rock on Mt. Washington, would break out with one of David's majestic psalms.
What would they do in the Arctic Rockies ?   They are
wonderful, when one stops to look and to think, but these
men who were passing up and down over the trail seldom
did such a thing as that.   Big pans of gold !   That is the
vision before them, and one who lies tired, bruised, and
footsore at the summit, looking off on the wonderful scene,
cannot help but wish that the Creator had put all the gold
away down deep in the bowels of the earth, where man would
never have known of it.   Doubtless it was a foolish thought,
for that yellow metal will work wonders on the mind which
may be unaffected by a view of these snowy billows of the
Arctic Rockies.   The Indians have been going over such
trails all their days, and yet they are the dullest, dirtiest,
most unemotional creatures under the sun.

But we must move on !   Never mind the mountains !
It was to seek the golden creek and its pups that we were

climbing over these rocks, and we forced our tired muscles into action and again struck into the trail.

After winding along on the summit for about a mile, we began the descent, which is gradual for a half mile and then becomes steep, then steeper, and, further on, most steep. Again we were clinging to the bushes and rattling down the rocks. As we descended the rain began to fall — one of those Alaskan drizzles, in which water takes the place of the atmosphere. Nature does nothing by halves here. The trail became very wet, soft and slippery, and we slid and rolled along till someone declared that he must rest. All were willing, and we crawled under the limbs of the largest spruce we could find and tried to keep out of the range of the drops from its branches.

Presently we heard someone struggling up the trail. Soon a rough and jovial fellow of Hibernian mould came into view.

" Are ye there, b'yes, and have ye ary a match ? "
We had.

" And which way might ye's be goin' ? " he asked, as he drew at a pipe of over-moist tobacco.

We pointed down the mountain.

"To Bonanza, is it? Begorry, ye'r right. I'm after thinking all the goold in the worruld is down there, but it's a domned rough counthry."

Oh, yes; he had a claim, but he had not worked it. He took one as near to the discovery as he could, set up his stakes, and ran for provisions, like most of the others. He had no idea what there was in the dirt he had staked off, and he would not have for weeks, even if he worked, but — " all the gold in the world was there." I had heard of such places before. He told us to hurry, as there were many ahead of us, and then he puffed along up the trial, and we straightened up and slid and tumbled along down. It did not matter if the rocks were a little hard and sharp when a slip was made and one of us came down with undue haste. We were going to a place where there was all the gold in the the world. An old story.

Finally we reached the bottom, our necks still unbroken. We were not at Bonanza yet. It was only one of her pups which crossed the trail, something as yet of no consequence. We brewed a little tea and ate some bread, that is, we called it bread. "Anything goes," as the gold hunters say, in Alaska.

Soon we pushed on towards the creek, the trail being ankle-deep, and more, with slush and mud. It was one of those tundra bottoms, which at a distance have such a fine agricultural aspect, a tract of "niggerheads," and to walk across such a place is one of the most fatiguing exercises a man can take. Finally, after a mile or so of it, we arrived at Bonanza Creek. It looked very little like a gold-bearing stream. A little washed gravel could be seen, but few glimpses of quartz were to be had, and there was nothing at all that an old miner would call an indication. It was no wonder that prospectors had waded and tumbled over these places and left them in disgust to the Indian hunters and fishermen. We said to ourselves that if anyone had got ten dollars to the pan out of this stuff, there ought to be a million tons of gold within twenty miles of such a place.

We got out of the trail — if there was one — and had to wade the creek and walk the banks; then wade again, and so on very slowly, watching the location notices. At last we found one, No. 64, which told us the distance to Discovery Claim, for ten and a half claims make a mile.

That means about six miles, on paper, but several times that on foot.

We plodded on, climbed over rocks, slid down rocks, tumbled up against rocks, and met two men.

"How far is it staked?" I asked, in a weary and disgusted way.

"Why, my number is 45; several men ahead of you; just stop at Discovery and look in the sluice box; two Siwashes packing dirt in buckets; George shoveling tailings."

George Cormack, as I have said, was the discoverer of gold on Bonanza Creek. We thought we would stop and look in the boxes, if we ever got there.

The men passed on, and we toiled ahead over a long tundra bottom. A man ought to find "all the gold in the world" to compensate him for such a tramp. The mountain trail was a positive delight to this.

"Say, let's blow a little," exclaimed one of our company.

Certainly I was willing to "blow" a whole lot — indefinitely.

A venerable Irishman, apparently a tenderfoot, came plodding along, falling over hummocks and sinking knee-deep in the mud beneath the weight of a heavy pack. Altogether he presented a most discouraged and disconsolate appearance.

"'Av ye's seen onything of thot man Beecher?" he asked, as he came up.

"What Beecher?"

"Hinry Wa-r-r-d Beecher."

"No. What do you want of him?"

"I'd loike to shpake wid 'im wan minnit. They do be tellin' me he wunst said there was no hell," and he dropped his heavy pack and wiped the dripping perspiration from his flushed face.

" Is it gold ye's do be afther here ? " he then asked.

" Yes," I replied, with as little enthusiasm as possible.

" All the saints help ye! " and he shouldered his pack again with a sigh and groan.

The last number noticed was somewhere in the twenties; two miles and more from George's. One of the men said he could go no further that night. I looked at him and thought so too. He insisted that we should go on and leave him, but right down in my heart I felt like doing nothing of the kind. I was tired enough myself. He looked thoroughly exhausted, and I doubted if he would have had the strength to make a fire if we left him. It was almost dark.

I could have crawled under a rock, under anything, and gone to sleep at once, but his condition required a warm fire and a hot drink. So we got wood, not particularly dry, made a roaring fire on a sandy spot, and brewed a pot of tea. Then we shoved our feet to the fire and meditated.

I thought after a while that I was rested a little, but when I tried to get up I could hardly stand. I wanted to take a look at a gravelly bar a few yards away before it became too dark, so I hobbled down to it, and found nothing but comminuted micaceous schist, with some glassy quartz, such as is always associated with these stratified schists in sheets and intervening layers. The mica was muscovite, and I thought the whole arrangement must belong to the Silurian age; that is, I thought so when I was too tired to think clearly about anything. I might change my mind when I could see the rocks adjoining these schists. But it was a matter of indifference to me whether I changed my

mind or not. If I did, all I felt like asking was that I could
do it lying down. I began to believe that I wouldn't stand
up for anything — not even for my native land. What a
place for gold !

When I started out, I regretted that Joe was not with
me to share in the fortunes of the great strike, but it would
have taken many days to reach him and to return. Besides,
I knew that as soon as these stories reached Circle City there
would be another rush. My best lay was to push in and get
a claim, and let Joe keep on working his. But now I was
glad Joe was on Birch Creek. Any one who had seen the
diggings on Forty Mile, and on the tributaries of Birch
Creek, would think all these fellows running up this Klondike waste had been driven out of their wits by the mosquitoes. I could dig a hole two feet deep in this stuff with
my hands, and the quicksand would run right in and fill it
up. Who would think that such loose stuff was full of
gold? I thought to myself that I would not wash a pan of
it if the owner would give it to me; but I was ignorant as to
who the owner was, and too tired to care. I hobbled back
to the fire and thought some more. We were all thinking
or trying not to think. No one said a word.

I spoke to one of them twice before he answered. He
remarked that he guessed he had forgotten his own name. I
was not surprised. He was too tired to remember such a
trifle. One by one they rolled themselves up to sleep
almost anywhere. I looked around for a soft spot, threw
my blankets down, and myself upon them. As I dozed off
the words of the Irishman we had met on the mountain,
" All the goold in the worruld is there," ran through my
brain and gradually faded into indistinctness as sleep overcame me.

We awoke just as the daylight was beginning to work its way into the valley, and found that we were chilled through. A white frost spread over everything, but after a cup of hot tea and a little bread we felt better. Sleep had done us some good and we moved on up the trail, making very good speed—as speed goes on an Alaskan trail. About a mile from George's we met more men, and one of them pointed to a spot where he had washed a dollar from a pan of the loose stuff he called gravel. It did not appear to have a washed pebble in it. But they had washed it out, and, like so many others, were rushing back after provisions.

At last we reached Discovery claim, where George was at work. We took a look in the sluice boxes, and there was certainly plenty of gold there. Some one asked him why he was shoveling the tailings up on to the hillside, and he replied that there was five dollars to the pan where the tailings dropped, the tailings, be it understood, being the refuse dirt falling at the end of the sluice. He put his hand in one of his pockets and drew out three nuggets worth about twenty-five dollars.

" Fished 'em out of the bottom of the creek with a shovel," he said.

" Jimminy-crickets," observed one of my companions. I thought so, too.

" Well, I'll be hanged," said another newcomer. He looked like a fit subject for the operation. Still, we all did, for that matter. After one has traveled a little in the moose tracks of such a region as this, he cannot step out into a civilized community in the same clothes without being an object of suspicion.

We picked up our blankets and what little we had left

to eat, for we had shared with those who passed us on the
trail, with hardly enough to keep them alive, a good deal of
what we started with.   They were in a hurry and had already staked out their claims.   We walked back a ways to
cache the remnant, far enough, one would suppose, to be
out of the reach of the dogs at Discovery claim, but if we
had stopped to think, we were aware that the dogs would get
at it, no matter how far we went, unless it was put up high
enough.   Still one always has a natural disposition to avoid
building a cache right over a dog's nose.   This done, we
started on and found it very much easier without our packs.
The creek bottom gradually became wider and the hills on
either side lower, and it was plainly to be seen that the
greater part of the rush into the region had been along
there.   It was fair to presume, therefore, that the best pay-
dirt would be found there, but I thought to myself that
there is no telling in such a field as this.   Indications do
not indicate, in the Klondike.   The only thing to do is to
stake anywhere.

After a while we met more men, who said that the creek
was at least staked up above 60.   One man informed us
that he obtained twenty-five cents to the pan on 60.   The
trail wound along over acres of tundra flats, and I thought
what a fine moose pasture it was, and expected to see a
moose, but they had evidently been frightened away by all
these people rushing in here and digging in the dirt.   There
were plenty of moose tracks.

As we passed along I noticed a pup which seemed to
have a more inviting look for a gold-seeker.   It certainly
appeared more like a gold stream, but, of course, like all the
rest at first, we rushed with the herd.   Before we got to the
fork we met more men and learned that it was staked up

into the seventies. The trail did not reach above the forks. Even the moose had deemed it wise to go somewhere else.

At last we came to the end of the claims and added ours, blazing trees, and putting up our notices. Then we rested a little, and looked around. We had no pans, and, in fact, did not think of washing out any gold. It was all a chance. Gold might be there and it might not. It certainly looked little like it. Then we started back and reached our caches at dusk in a rainstorm, built a fire, cooked what we thought would appease our appetites, rigged up a blanket tent, and went to sleep. We had seen the place where there is " all the goold in the worruld."

We felt much better — tolerably well in the morning. We were all foot-sore, but a little breakfast — all that we had left — with some strong coffee, straightened us up, and we were ready for the weary tramp back to the river over the trail. As we traveled along we met plenty of gold-seekers, all of whom asked about the same questions.

" Oh, yes," we told them, " it is a big thing."

We had no gold to show, but we told them about the five-dollar tailings, and the nuggets fished out with a shovel. We noticed a few men on their claims, but they were cutting logs for houses and were not prospecting. Some were working along with big packs, having been over before, and were now getting provisions in for the winter.

Back we climbed over the summit, and I stopped to look again at the picture. The sun was shining, the day was quite warm, and the ground was dryer than when we went over. We could lie on the ground, pick berries, and eat our fill. When at last we arrived in sight of the camp on the river near the Indian village, we, in our turn, yelled like Comanches and jumped and tumbled down the hills with the rattling rocks.   There was an ever-accumulating crowd there, and we were quizzed and " pumped."   We told what we knew, which, after all, was very little, and, as when we went over, we noticed that here and there a man slipped away, and soon we heard them toiling up the bluff and the rocks came rolling back down to the bottom.   We slept soundly that night, and I would not have had energy enough to throw a hatchet at a dog if one had tried to eat up the tent.

CHAPTER XVIII

THE DISCOVERY OF ELDORADO — THE FOUNDING OF
DAWSON — CONFUSION AND QUEER COMPLICA-
TIONS OVER CLAIMS — "THREE INCH WHITE."

W E took life as easy as circumstances allowed for
the next two or three days; indeed, we made
ourselves think we were actually deriving some
pleasure out of it, for, while an ever-increasing number of
feverish men were landing on the gravel beach and hurrying on to the new region, and an ever-increasing number
were returning over the mountain trail, we were in the delightful position of having staked our claims and of having about a month's provisions at the foot of the trail. We
could feed the newcomers with interesting stories of what
we had seen, and hear the latest news from those who were

coming out.   We ate as much as we thought we could afford to, and nursed our feet a little.   The tow on the river and the tramp on the trail had been a severe ordeal for them. As the time was fast approaching when the Yukon would freeze over, and running ice had already increased the difficulties of navigation, many participating in the rush determined to wait for the ice so they could sled their provisions up the creek.   In fact, quite a village of tents was springing up not far from the mouth of the Klondike.

But dragging loads over the rough ice of these rapid streams is, on the whole, not much of an improvement upon packing over a mountain and swamp trail, so at the end of four days we strapped on packs three times as heavy as those we had first carried, and started out.   It makes a great difference in carrying a pack on a trail whether a person is in a hurry or not.   Having our claim, we could afford to proceed leisurely and rest when we felt like it, without being harrassed by the feeling that we might be too late.   We even stopped occasionally to break up a rock to see what it was made of, and I admired the scenery to my heart's content.   We chatted with those whom we met, and still made about as good headway as when we first went over, and we camped at the same places.

Once, while we were resting, a party of Indians carrying heavy packs overtook us.   Following them came the owner, looking very weary under an extremely light burden.   He said he had hired the Indians to pack his supplies over; " and," he added, " I got it done cheap, too."

" How much a pound? " I inquired.

" I don't know."

" Then how do you know it's cheap? "

" Oh, any packing is cheap over a trail like this."

When we approached the creek again we learned that big strikes had been made on the " pup " that had looked so promising to me on our previous trip, and that I had been tempted to ascend and test. It seems that a party which had rushed in when the news of the Bonanza was noised around had worked up the creek till their provisions had run out. They were about to turn back and go to the nearest trading post for provisions, when they met and joined another party having more provisions than they needed. While they were cooking their supper near the mouth of the pup, one of them suggested that they walk up the bed about a mile and wash a pan of the gravel. They did so, and were amazed when one of the pans yielded over six dollars. They at once staked out claims, and, returning, told others. This had been the significance of the whispered communications we had noticed between the parties we encountered on the trail when we first came over.

We resolved to go up the creek and see for ourselves. So, in the morning we pushed on and camped at its mouth. It had been named Whipple Creek, after the discoverer, and no longer bore the obscure name of " pup." I ascended it, and found some men washing out gold where the discovery was made, and I washed out a pan myself. It contained about a dollar. The others seemed to get about the same. Going on up the creek, I found it staked for much more than half its length, and I concluded that I would rather hold the claim I had than exchange for one here. Bonanza and this new creek were in the same district, and no one was entitled to stake more than one claim in a district. Not long afterward, parties buying some claims on the new creek named Eldorado.

The next day we heard of another rush for creeks in another section. We joined in this, too, and tramped up the Bonanza to the forks and thence over the mountain to Gold Bottom, where the earlier discoveries of Henderson were made, and thence down to Hunker Creek, to which the new rush was directed. Hunker empties into the Klondike about twelve miles from its mouth. By the time we reached there the creeks were well staked, and so we went over to the Indian River district and prospected along there for a day or two without remarkable results. The snow began to fly, and we finally made our way back to the Yukon to await developments. During this tramp we met the same obstacles and had similar experiences to those recounted in the previous chapter.

In the meantime we found that a new metropolis had sprung up on a low stretch of ground on the banks of the Yukon, just below the mouth of the Klondike. A clever man could see that this flat was about the only place available for a city in that rugged region, and there was a clever man there who saw it. In fact, the honors of the discovery of gold in this district must be divided between Joseph Ladue, who had fitted out Henderson, of whom we have spoken, and Cormack, to whom Henderson told of his findings on Gold Bottom Creek. At the very time Cormack was washing his first pans of gold in Bonanza Creek, Ladue, who had not yet heard of Cormack's find, was coming down the Yukon to locate a town site at the mouth of the Klondike. He had heard from Henderson.

Joseph Ladue is, as his name shows, of French extraction, and was born in Plattsburg, N. Y., about forty-four years ago. His grandfather was a French Huguenot, who, driven from home in the early persecution of his church, settled with many others of that sterling faith in Canada. He removed across the line into the United States and located at Schuyler Falls, about ten miles southeast of Plattsburg, where Joseph Ladue was born. His mother died when he was seven years old, and his father, a stone-mason, married the second time. Young Joseph Ladue was strong and active for his years, and a neighboring family, the head of which was James H. Lobdell, took a liking to the lad, who had found some things not altogether to his liking at home, and who was ready, at the age of nine years, to accept the adoption of his neighbor. Joseph was therefore brought up under the influence of Mr. Lobdell and his wife — good, old-fashioned Methodists — who sent the young man to school and gave him work on their farm until he grew to an age when he was ready to look out for himself. Upon the death of his father in Iowa, in 1874, Joseph decided to go West and look after the small estate of his parent.

The affairs of his father's estate having been administered, and his attention being at the time attracted to new discoveries in the Rockies, he started for the Black Hills with a fixed purpose of becoming a miner of gold. He arrived at Deadwood in 1876 with about one hundred dollars in his pocket, full of grit, industry, honesty, and determination. The town was enjoying a boom, and the young man at once started in for himself by securing little jobs as a contractor for moving houses and doing other public work. Meanwhile he was constantly on the watch for better employment, his ambition being to secure a place in a quartz-mine. The only place he could find came in about a month in the shape of a job as engineer in the mine at four dollars per day. The young man had never run a steam-engine, and was utterly unfamiliar with mechanics, but his natural aptitude stood him in good stead, and he accepted the place and for eighteen months held it successfully.

In 1878 he was advanced to the position of foreman or superintendent of the "night shift" of miners in the famous Hidden Treasure mine, which was a most profitable producer of gold. His pay was now five dollars per day, and he spent all his leisure time in studying the secrets of gold-mining. Mr. Ladue so thoroughly familiarized himself with gold-mining that he was fully competent for almost any task that might be offered him, and he was soon offered, and accepted, the place of superintendent of a sixty-stamp gold-mill at the wages of ten dollars per day. After a year in this employment he decided to strike out to make a fortune, and for some years followed the adventurous life of a prospector in Arizona and New Mexico. He there found several promising prospects, and for one of these, in New Mexico, which subsequently failed to meet his expectations, he, unfortunately for himself, refused an offer of twenty-five thousand dollars.

After two years of this hard, but practical, experience, he decided to strike for the newly-discovered mining country in the British Northwest Territory adjoining Alaska. He made the long and tedious journey to Juneau, and was one of the first prospectors in that new country. He then passed over into the interior, and it is a significant fact that he was hunting for gold as early as 1882 within six miles of the present rich mines of the Klondike. If he found little gold then, he acquired a great faith in the richness of the country and in its future. He did not fully explore the valley of the Klondike, because it was his belief as an experienced miner that it was not of the right sort.

When Schwatka made his famous voyage on a raft down

the Yukon in 1883, he ran across Ladue at Charley's Village. With a partner he was prospecting the streams in that vicinity, which is about fifty miles above where Circle City was founded later. Ladue was familiarly known among the Indians as " Joe," and he was in great favor among them.

For fourteen years, with a determination that never faltered, and a confidence in his ultimate success that was never diminished, Ladue lived in the dreary wilds of the Northwest. Up to five or six years ago his headquarters were at old Fort Reliance. Every year he added to his capital by prospecting and trading, until at last a business opening presented itself in the purchase of a profitable sawmill at Fort Ogilvie, forty-five miles up the Yukon from Fort Reliance.

Here the enterprising young man remained for five years, earning money and carefully saving it, but his faith in the golden resources of Alaska never abated. He met a young Nova Scotian prospector named Robert Henderson, in 1893. Henderson was about the same age as Ladue, and in the solitary wilderness of the frozen North they established a warm and lasting friendship. For three years the thrifty Ladue furnished the necessary implements, tools, and provisions of a prospector to Henderson — " grub-staked " him, in the mining vernacular. Indications of gold were found in many places, but nothing of great value until one day Henderson came into Ladue's sawmill camp radiant with smiles and carrying a small bottle. He held it up to Ladue, filled with bits of yellow metal. It was the gold he had panned out of Gold Bottom Creek, one of the tributaries of the Klondike. This was on the twenty-fourth day of August, 1896. On his way to Ladue, Henderson had told

Cormack, as already related, and Cormack, on the twenty-sixth, as the story goes, made his strike on Bonanza Creek.

Ladue, who knew only of Henderson's find, saw that his time had come. His keen eye for business was wide open now. He did not rush into the gold-diggings, for he foresaw the enormous value of the town site at the place where he knew that a prosperous city must be located. He sent Henderson with four horses and four men back across the country eighty miles, to the new gold-fields. He himself took a raft loaded with lumber and went down the Yukon by the quickest route, landing August 28th, and located the town site of Dawson City, on the only site in that rugged country that had been left open for it. He built a store and hastened to Fort Cudahy, forty-five miles distant, to make the official entry in the British Land Office. Having secured this great prize, he looked over the gold country and carefully selected and quickly purchased some of the richest claims that could be found. He built a sawmill, which was soon running day and night, and earning a little fortune every twenty-four hours, in a region where the timber limit extended fifteen miles.

Thus was Dawson started. When the gold strikes were made, in the latter part of August, there were not half a dozen white people in the Klondike Valley. In a month there were a thousand. The lumber mill did a big business, and Ladue made thousands of dollars by selling cheap pine lumber to the miners at one hundred and forty dollars the thousand feet. The increasing cold made no difference to the crazy miners at Dawson City and in the cabins along Eldorado and Bonanza Creeks. By October about six hundred claims had been staked out up and down both sides of the creeks. The Canadian mining laws made five

AN EXCITING TIME

Arrival of the first Yukon steamer at Dawson.

hundred feet along the creek or river bank a single claim, and one man was allowed to locate but one claim in each district.

Putting up a cabin in Dawson was expensive business. Logs, which in that region means poles from four to six inches in diameter, sold generally from four dollars to eight dollars apiece. A man really needed almost as much money as he would to put up a brownstone residence in New York in order to secure a building which would have any of the comforts of a home. The timber had to be hauled about twenty miles, and the so-called hotels, which were soon open, were little more than moderate-sized log houses, admitting of a few box-stalls. People who arrived late had at once to set about finding a way to protect themselves from the winter blasts.

What a hustling there was for lumber to build shanties and cabins ! It was growing colder every day, and many men paid over two hundred dollars the one thousand feet for lumber. Laborers that got a few dollars a day in August now were snapped up at fifteen and eighteen dollars a day. The native Indians sold fur garments for one hundred and fifty dollars each, or for some gewgaws that were more precious there than diamonds are here. Lots were soon selling in Dawson from two hundred and fifty dollars up to ten thousand dollars. The Alaska Commercial Company and the North American Transportation and Trading Company quickly prepared to concentrate their forces and supplies there. Moose meat was sixty cents a pound, and all canned goods seventy-five cents per can. The companies adopted a cash system, and carried as large a stock as could be brought up. The government consisted of a gold commissioner and the chief of the mounted police. New enterprises sprang up every day, and, of course, the saloon predominated.

Naturally, in such a rush of business and fever of speculation, there existed much confusion. Men who had been in a chronic state of drunkenness for weeks had been pitched into boats as ballast and taken up to stake themselves a claim, and claims were staked by men for their friends who were not in the country at the time. All this gave rise to much confliction and confusion, there being no one to take charge of matters. The land agent not being able to go up and attend to the thing, and the Canadian surveyor not knowing what to do, the miners held a meeting and appointed one of themselves to measure off and stake the claims, and record the owners' names, for which he got a fee of two dollars, it being, of course, understood that each claimholder would have to record his claim with the Dominion agent, and pay his fee of fifteen dollars.

Just how it happened no one seems to know, but it was said that the men who were selected to measure the claims, somehow slid in a forty, instead of a fifty, foot rope, thus making the claims considerably short. Others have an idea, which is not entirely without reason, that when the claims were first staked off, the excited miners, being anxious to secure all the room possible, would, in their measurements, which were sometimes made at night, stretch the line a little. The one taking the next claim would begin where his predecessor left off, and stretch his line more or less, according to his sense of morality.

However it happened there was considerable uncertainty, and the miners finally petitioned the Dominion land surveyor to come up to Bonanza Creek at once and settle the complications that were arising. One of the late arrivals was an Irishman, who, when he found he could not secure a claim, went up and down the creek, trying to bully the owners into selling, boasting that he had a " pull " at Ottawa and threatening to have the claims cut down from five hundred to two hundred and fifty feet. He came along one day and offered to wager two thousand dollars that within a year they would be reduced to two hundred and fifty feet. One of the men to whom he had made this offer went to the Dominion surveyor and asked about it.

" Do you gamble ? " asked the surveyor.

" A little," was the reply.

Then the surveyor told him that he was never surer of two thousand dollars than he would have been if he had taken that bet.

This ran to such an extent that the surveyor put up notices to the effect that the length of the claims was regulated by act of the Parliament of Canada, and that no change could be made except by that Parliament, and telling the miners to take no notice of the threats that had been made.

A fellow known as Jim White located a fraction between Nos. 36 and 37, thinking that by getting in between he could force the owners to come to his terms, forgetting that the law of this country does not allow any man to take more than he has a right to. For three or four days this state of things kept the men in an uproar. The surveyor was making his survey, and getting towards Nos. 36 and 37; when he approached them he delayed operations and went up to No. 36, finding there would be no fraction, or, at least, an insignificant one of inches.

He worked along slowly, and in the meantime the owner of No. 36 became very uneasy, and White also. The officer set in a stake down in the hollow until he saw how much of a fraction there was. It was only a few inches. He was purposely very deliberate with this portion of the work, and the man who was with him seemed to have quite a difficulty in fixing the stake. Then the officer went down, with the remark that he would do that himself. He had made it a rule never to tell anyone whether there was a fraction until it was marked on the post.

While he was standing by the post Jim White came up to him. He had a long way to go down the creek, he said — and he did not want to wait any longer than was necessary.

"Well," said the surveyor, "I can't tell you just yet exactly how much of a fraction it will be — but something about three inches."

This is why Jim came to be known as "Three Inch White."

He resurveyed the whole group of claims, and the result was a lot of fractional claims, which were open to entry. This occurred at about the time some of the later arrivals of the early winter were looking for places, and they grabbed these fractional claims on the rich creeks as fast as they were declared open. These fractions varied all the way from three inches to forty feet, and were valued accordingly. Of course, no one could work the narrower ones, but they were desirable property to the adjacent owners, who either bought them outright or formed a partnership with their owners. In one case it was reported that a fractional claim of five inches sold for five hundred dollars, after the richness of the adjacent claim had been determined.

In locating a claim on Canadian creeks, a man is supposed to measure five hundred feet the way the valley lies,

and then run across from base to base of the foot-hills, or
from rim-rock to rim-rock. It must be marked by four
legal posts at the corners. Posts must be at least four inches
square. One post must be marked "initial post," and on
that post a written notice must be placed, stating number,
length, and general direction of claim, the date of notice,
and name of locator. All placer claims must be recorded
in the mining recorder's office of the mining division in
which such claims are situated within three days after location thereof, if within ten miles of the mining recorder's
office; but one additional day is allowed for each additional ten miles. The recorder must be furnished with
the following particulars in writing: Name of claim,
name of locator, number of free miner's certificate, locality of claim, length in feet, period for which record is
required, date of location. Placer claims may be recorded for one or more years on payment of fees — two
dollars and fifty cents for each year. After the miner
has located and recorded his claim, he, or some one on his
behalf, must work it continuously during working hours;
and, if unworked on working days for a period of seventy-
two hours, except during sickness or for some other reasonable cause, the claim will be considered abandoned and forfeited. Leave of absence for one year may, however, be obtained by any free miner, upon his proving to the gold commissioner an expenditure equal to one thousand dollars in
cash, labor, or machinery on a claim, without any return of
gold or other minerals in reasonable quantities.

CHAPTER XIX

RICHNESS OF THE KLONDIKE GOLD FIELDS—THE GREAT
WINTER EXODUS FROM CIRCLE CITY—FIRST RE-
SULTS FROM TESTING PANS—MINERS WILD WITH
EXCITEMENT.

Realization of the Richness of the Klondike Claims—Why old Miners
were Skeptical—How Tenderfeet Suddenly Became Rich—Selling
Claims at Low Figures—Cutting Logs to Get Provisions—El-
dorado All Staked—Great Stroke for Some Men—Circle City
Skeptical—The First Big Pans—Excitement at Circle City—A
Mad Stampede—Scarcity of Dogs—Dogs at $2.50 Per Pound—
Some Big Strikes—Grumbling Canadians—Bed-Rock on El-
dorado—Lippy's Bargain—Nothing Like It in the History of the
World—Pans of Dirt Worth Five Hundred Dollars—The Miners
Simply Staggered—Mrs. Berry Picks up $50 in Nuggets While
Calling Her Husband to Supper—Scarcity of Labor—Hunting up
Claims—Gold Everywhere—Opening Up New Territory.

I
T was many weeks before anyone had a proper realization of the richness of the newly-discovered placers,
and for a long time all the excitement was confined to
Bonanza Creek and its tributary, Eldorado. Those who
staked claims were, of course, met with the same conditions
imposed upon all placer mining in Alaska. There were
several feet of frozen muck and gravel to be worked out
of the way by the slow process of burning before anyone
could say what lay at bed-rock, and many old miners who
had been over the ground laughed at the idea of rich placers
in such a locality, and did not even take the trouble to join

in the rush, while others who did looked about in a knowing way and departed without staking any claims.

Stampedes had occurred so often, and had so generally
proved unprofitable, that the old miners had become weary
of them. They had, in their more tenderfooted days,
rushed from Forty Mile to Sixty Mile, to Beaver Creek, to
Birch Creek, and a lot of other creeks, in which the Yukon
Valley abounds. The fact was that there was some gold
almost everywhere, and when anyone stumbled on a spot
containing a particularly rich deposit near the surface, there
was the natural temptation to believe that the whole creek
was made up of such material. The miners had become
so tired of this unsettled state of things, the fatiguing journeys, and loss of time, that they were disposed to regard with
discredit any reports of rich finds, and when they heard
that " Siwash George " had struck gold on the " Thron-
diuck," it was enough to make the soberest of them laugh.
Even had Cormack's reputation for truth and veracity been
first-class they would have doubted the value of his discoveries on the creeks of a river which they had so often
prospected without success. They just lay back and
allowed the tenderfeet to rush in and stake to their heart's
content up and down this moose pasture, and that is the
reason why so many old miners were " left," and why so
many new-comers suddenly became rich.

But there were, as I have said, a great many miners
about Forty Mile and adjacent diggings who had been working in poor luck and were sick and discouraged of the whole
country. These constituted the greater part of those who
first rushed into the Klondike. It was to them a last chance,
merely, and a mighty poor-looking one at that. They had
nothing better to do, and so rushed in.

Yet the way they sold their claims in the first weeks succeeding the stampede is evidence of their lack of faith in them. They had no money, or very little. Two-thirds of all the claims could have been bought in September by those who would have provided " grub " for the claimants for the winter. As some of the poorer ones were unable to raise on their claims sufficient provisions to enable them to go to work, they sold out cheap to anyone who came along with a little dust. Claims which were afterwards worth thousands could have been picked up by the dozen in September and October for a hundred or two dollars. Many were sold, and old miners who had clambered over the trail and staked considered themselves exceedingly fortunate in receiving that small amount, and congratulated themselves that by their rush they had at least made enough to provide themselves with a small supply of winter provisions. They knew that to hold their claims, build a cabin, and convey their tools and supplies over the rough trails to the new creeks would cost them several hundred dollars, and that the claims must yield something over ten dollars a day to pay at all for working them. They had not a particle of belief that the creeks would yield such a return. They looked with pitying eyes on the tenderfeet who were greedily acquiring claims in the new district, and were confident that in the course of the winter they would discover the difficulties of working placers in Alaska, and in the spring would somehow work their way out into other districts with no money and little to eat, sadder and wiser men.

Only a few men remained on the creek after staking. Most of them came back to Dawson, where affairs were already becoming lively, and either sold out or went to work for what they could get. Even the discoverer, Siwash

George, had been compelled to cut logs for the new mill before he could get a few pounds of provisions to enable him to begin work on his claim. The fishing having totally failed him, he got together as many provisions as he could, and in the first part of September, with his wife, his Indian brother-in-law, and another Indian, he set out for his diggings. He was short of appliances, and managed to put together only three lengths of sluice-boxes, a very defective apparatus, to wash what gravel he could before the ground froze up completely. The gravel itself he had to carry in a box on his back for a hundred feet. Notwithstanding all this, it was soon reported that he had washed out one thousand four hundred dollars by the first of October, and it was known that he had as yet come nowhere near bed-rock.

Up to this time the rush had not been so great as to take up all the available claims on the creek, but the news was reaching both down and up the river, and boat loads of men continued to arrive. Once landed they made a bee-line over the mountain. One of the greatest rushes was soon after I returned from the creek, and soon after the discovery of Eldorado. The little steamer Ellis landed with about one hundred and fifty excited men, who poured over the trail. Eldorado was staked in a jiffy, and many of these turned out to be the lucky ones. They set about making preparations for the winter, such as building cabins and getting ready to sink holes on their claims. The pans averaged about three dollars, with prospect of improvement.

What a stroke this was for some of the men may be seen from a single instance. One of the men on the boat had come from a little village in Cayuga County, New York. He was a cash boy in a Buffalo dry goods house ten years ago, and went West as a tramp, riding on freight cars. He learned something about mining in the gold district of California, and more in a spirit of recklessness and adventure than anything else, he joined the Yukon mining rush in 1894. He had a terrible experience with cold and hunger for two years, and suffered more in that time than many men do in a lifetime of hardships. He was too poor to go back to the United States, and so he stayed on the Yukon. He tried gold mining in fifty different spots, and lived on half raw salmon for days at a time. He said he was about to commit suicide in September, when he realized that another long and dreadful winter was beginning. A friend told him to go up to Klondike and make one more trial anyhow, for there were rumors at Fort Yukon, where he was at the time, that the diggings were good on the Klondike. He sold his rifle for passage on the last boat on the river before navigation closed. In two weeks he had made his claim to five hundred feet along Bonanza Creek and was working in the cold and ice to get out the golden nuggets. When, the following spring, he went back to the United States, he had with him about thirty-five thousand dollars, and he had worked but thirty feet of his claim.

Although news of the finding of gold on the Klondike and of the rush there had made its way down to Circle City, it at first created little attention. A few miners who were in straits came up on the boat, but the majority remained, and Circle City began the winter as lively a town as ever. On November 23d a man by the name of Rhodes, located at No. 21, above the Discovery, on Bonanza, obtained as high as sixty-five dollars and thirty cents to the pan. This was the first large pan of any importance, and Dawson was thrown into a blaze of excitement. The news spread up and down the river like wild-fire, and more men hastened in. Some of the old miners who had gone away without staking began to come back. In a little time the news reached Circle City, but nobody would believe it. Yet this claim on Bonanza was the one which really proved the value of the district. The owner was in the habit of cleaning up a few tubfuls of dirt every night in his cabin and getting enough to pay his workmen at the rate of one dollar and fifty cents an hour. In that way he discovered the richness of the dirt. Melting water enough to pan out gold under cover was a slow process, but he found that the soil paid him to do it. Others began to adopt similar methods.

Claim No. 5, Eldorado, next produced a pan of fifty-seven dollars. This was succeeded by one of upward of eighty dollars. Then came one of one hundred and twelve dollars. Soon after, claim No. 16 showed up a pan of two hundred and twelve dollars, and this it was that caused the intense excitement in that country. The news went down to Circle City early in December, and it at once emptied itself and came up to Dawson. The scenes of the Forty Mile rush were repeated. The miners came up any way they could, at all hours of the day and night, with provisions and empty-handed.

It was a great day in Circle City, so they said, when the news of the Klondike richness came with such force and authenticity that even the skeptical old miners began to believe it and quietly made their plans to go up the river. It was carried down by J. M. Wilson, of the Alaska Commercial Company, and Thomas O'Brian, a trader, and they also had with them some of the Klondike gold. When it was seen that a few were starting, of course, nothing more was needed. It at once grew into a stampede. The price of dogs jumped almost out of sight. In a few days they were so valuable that they began to be sold by the pound, first at one dollar and fifty cents a pound, and then as high as two dollars and fifty cents. One man told me that he saw one dog sold for twenty ounces of gold dust, and, as in trade an ounce is worth seventeen dollars, the dog sold for three hundred and forty dollars. The purchaser was determined to go, and he had the money. He was bound to have dogs no matter what they cost. It was a melancholy time for the Circle City saloon-keepers, who saw the signs of prosperity vanish, but many of them joined in the rush for the new diggings. It was a melancholy time, also, for those who had failed to go up when the river was open, and now had not the means to buy the fancy-priced dogs, for they were too wise to think of setting out without at least four months' provisions, and it required dogs to drag that quantity over the rough ice of the Yukon in the face of the biting blasts of the dead of winter. Yet it was the greatest exodus that was ever known on the Yukon. As many as four hundred men and women worked their way up, and none of them lost their lives, though several had their faces and toes frozen.

Dawson fairly leaped into importance. By the time the Circle City contingent arrived greater discoveries had been made, and the value of the diggings surpassed all the dreams of the most sanguine. But locations on the Bonanza and Eldorado had been staked weeks before. A good many Canadians and others who, at Circle City, had out-Americaned the natural, native-born Americans in their protestations and professions of Americanism, came up to Dawson, which is in Canadian territory, in this rush with certain expectations in realizing something in the new finds by reason of their nationality, and made loud professions of loyalty, cursed their luck, and declared it strange indeed that a Canadian or a Briton could not get a foot of ground in his own country.

In December bed-rock was reached on No. 14, Eldorado, and dirt of surpassing richness was found. Other holes began to go down in a hurry — that is, as fast as the slow process of burning them out would admit. Pans were taken out occasionally and tested, reaching from five to a hundred dollars, and yet the workers could scarcely believe it. They had an idea that they must have struck an unusually fine piece of dirt. In a hole eighteen feet deep, on Eldorado Creek, two men struck a pay-streak that went five dollars to the pan on the average of the testing they gave it, and, without knowing it, they went on shoveling out into the dump dirt which was rich in gold.

Many of those going in early, of course, had endeavored to secure claims on Bonanza, but they could not be had, so they rushed up the Eldorado. When Professor Lippy, one of the fortunate ones, arrived there, this creek was staked up to No. 36, and he took that. But a man who had staked No. 16 wished to go further up the stream, and they exchanged. When Lippy first struck the rich pay-dirt on his claim, the man he had traded with was " joshed " by the boys without mercy. He looked rather sober, but he, too, could laugh after all, for his claim turned out to be very valuable.

It was difficult for anyone to realize the richness of the dirt, and even late in the winter claims were sold for a price ridiculously low, considering what was in them. The miners were continually expecting to meet a limit to the richness. Finally, pans as rich as five hundred were discovered, and nuggets containing gold worth as high as two hundred and thirty-five dollars were brought to light. Claims jumped up enormously in price, but still many sold out for a small fraction of the value of dirt that lay in the frozen dumps which they had so laboriously dug out of the earth. Nothing in the history of the world had ever been found to equal, or, in fact, to anywhere near approach the yields taken from pans gathered indiscriminately. In an early day in California the best claims ever discovered had run but thirty-five to forty cents a pan, and these were considered marvels of richness. Alder Gulch, in Montana, had been thought for years to have contained the richest gravel ever dumped into a sluice-box, but even that was insignificant when compared with not only one but many of the claims on these two tributaries of the Klondike, which was worked in a haphazard fashion.

But what was thought to be a profitable season in those days could scarcely equal a few days' work in the new Eldorado. Think of a pay-streak nine feet thick, one hundred and fifty feet wide, and five hundred feet long, every pan of which, so far as could be ascertained by sinking prospect holes to bed-rock in various parts of the claim, would contain over one dollar in gold, some of them as high as two hundred and fifty dollars. Nor was this the exception, but the rule. On one of the Bonanza claims a doubting Thomas was asked to go down the shaft, pick a pan of dirt at random, and then test it himself. He did so, and with a pan and small prospector's pick he dug out a piece of gravel on the very upper edge of the pay-streak, then another small amount a foot lower down, then more was taken still lower down from the opposite wall of the shaft, and so on until the pan was filled by the time bed-rock was reached. Ascending to the surface, ice was melted until sufficient water was secured to wash the gravel, and with his own hands the contents were panned out. The task was of but few moments' duration, and his doubts were entirely removed, as at the bottom of the pan was found enough gold to more than cover a ten cent piece, and it weighed two dollars and twenty-seven cents.

When it is remembered that dirt that averages ten cents to the pan is considered very rich, what must it be when it runs four and five dollars to the pan? On No. 6, Eldorado, all the men that could be had were given employment during the winter at one dollar and twenty-five cents an hour, and some fifteen or twenty prospect holes were sunk to bed-rock, and the pay-streak located for a width of one hundred and fifty feet, and averaging three feet in thickness the full length of the claim. Pay-dirt was encountered immediately under the muck, which in that locality is about nine feet thick, running from eight to twenty-five cents to the pan, but the pay-streak was not considered to have been struck until seventy-five cent dirt was reached. Pans taken from the bed-rock on this claim simply staggered the miners, as they not unfrequently ran as high as one hundred and fifty and two hundred dollars.

The owner of this claim, Clarence Berry, worked his claim more extensively than most proprietors, and his expenses ran as high as one hundred and fifty dollars a day. He settled with his employes every evening after working hours, using only a pan and some water secured by melting ice to wash out the amount necessary to pay his labor. One evening when Mrs. Berry came down from the cabin to call her husband to supper, while waiting for him to come up the shaft, she picked up over fifty dollars in coarse gold and nuggets that were lying loose in the gravel just as it came from bed-rock, not five minutes' time being occupied in doing it.

The effect of such results as this in the camps along the creeks was to make it practically impossible for an owner of a claim to secure men to help in working them. Some old miners would not work for any price. Sometimes it was possible to rope in a newcomer and get him to work for a few days for fifteen dollars, and a few old miners worked on shares for a time and made good money, but they soon dropped this to hunt up claims of their own. It is impossible to work these Yukon placers successfully without help.

The result was, that while many of the claim-owners were lying idle waiting for someone to work their ground, the men who were competent to do it, because they understood the process and had the necessary provisions, were prospecting among the creeks to see what they could find. In the end, perhaps, nothing was lost by it, for it served to open up a much larger district than anyone had supposed possible, and other creeks came forward to share the honors with Bonanza and Eldorado.

CHAPTER XX

WINTER IN THE KLONDIKE — CAMP LIFE AND WORK — A MINER'S DOMESTIC DUTIES — CHRISTMAS IN A GOLD-SEEKER'S CAMP.

THERE is but one thing more dreary than camp life and work in the gold-bearing placers of the regions of the Arctic, and that is camp life and work in the same regions when the placers bear no gold. There is less difference than one might suppose. It is undoubtedly a great relief to feel all the time that, as a result of hard drudgery, rich dirt is being heaped up, and that in the spring, after the long winter night is over, shining gold dust and nuggets will buy some consolation in a milder region where life is worth living. If there were no use for gold except to spend it in Alaska, none of it would be dug there. It is a splendid country to leave whether one has gold dust or not.

When the middle of October came we were nearly cut off from the rest of the world. Of course we heard from Circle City and Forty Mile occasionally, through those who came into the Klondike during the winter. Immediately after the discovery and my short stay at the mouth of the creek, I had taken an opportunity to send word to Joe, advising him to come up, as I thought the prospects looked promising, and meanwhile I set to work to construct a place in which we could make life endurable for the winter on my claim. It was nothing more than a hut backed up into a crevice in the side hill, but I had neither the time nor the means to put together anything more substantial. By a liberal use of moss, which is the cheapest article in Alaskan regions, I flattered myself that I was at least providing for myself a warm place, even though the logs were green and the ground of the cabin frozen.

As the nights lengthened, loneliness settled down like a pall over the desolate gulch. The snow fell nearly every day, mantling the great frowning hills. It was a scene of solitude, and a time of deep silence broken only by the wailing of the wind through the little spruce trees scattered about on the hillsides. Miners, muffled up in their thick winter clothing, passed up and down, and I had some neighbors on the creek, but there was little time for sociability. Nearly every one was busy working to bed-rock, setting their cabins to rights, or getting their provisions up. When the few rich strikes had been made, all who could redoubled their efforts at their own shafts. When digging for gold with a feverish rush and attending to household duties besides, there is little time for sociability, and we were too busy

READY FOR WINTER

A wayside cabin on the Skagway Trail, made of whip-sawed boards. The chinks between the logs are filled with mud and moss.

to think of the outside world. It would have done us little good if we had, for there were no mails that we knew of. According to the established regulations, mails were supposed to be brought in from Juneau every six weeks, but time-tables are of no value in these regions any more than they are for the Yukon boats. No one wrote letters, and there was hardly a bit of reading matter in the whole camp except the labels on some of the boxes in which provisions came. If one wishes to realize how interesting they can be, let him camp in a gulch somewhere in latitude sixty-four, North America. A trademark on a pick handle becomes fairly eloquent in that solitude. Two fellows named Dick Butler and Charley Myers had been prospecting in the country for some time, and a friend of theirs in Seattle one day had the forethought to wrap up a few newspapers and send them in by one of the slow mails. These boys had about the only library in the diggings in those old Seattle papers, and the miners congregated from all the creeks and read them, advertisements and all. One day when a crowd was in the cabin Butler said:

" Boys, I don't mind your reading the papers, but I think you ought to remember the fellow who sent them to me. I'm going to put up a little contribution box," and he left a bottle near the papers. They did not forget it, and dropped in their nuggets. When in the spring the bottle was sent to the Seattle friend it contained nearly four hundred dollars' worth of the shining nuggets.

After Joe arrived with a part of the Circle City contingent, life became a trifle pleasanter for me, for it was easier getting along and we could talk, though he was naturally uncommunicative. But when men who never had more than a few hundred dollars all their lives are faced with the prospect of making a few hundred every day, they are too restless to converse, or to think of letters or reading matter. Gold, gold was the one topic of interest in that gulch. There were fires to build from the pitch pine, and then when the ground had been thawed and loosened, the alluvial was dug out and put in piles, either in a warm cabin or left out to freeze. Then the fires would be started again, and more digging would follow. Then on alternate days ice was melted, and the water used for panning the gold. Sometimes a half ton of gravel would be worked over in a day by those anxious to get out the rich metal. It grew dark at two o'clock in the afternoon, and lamps and candles were lighted. Then there was water to be made by melting ice and snow for washing and drinking purposes, besides a round of domestic duties in our cabins.

It was hard work day after day. We never knew when Sunday came, and there were constant disputes as to the day of the month. We had no time for games or for melancholy, for we were all so weary from hard work when night came that sleep at once overcame us. In December and January there was scarcely any light, and very little work was done. Some miners built their cabins over their claims, and by building a hot fire in the cabin kept the ground more or less thawed all the time. They would go down through the floors of their habitations to dig gold from the ground some fifteen feet or more below. How tired every one got of canned food and salt meats! Many a time that winter I would often have gladly given one hundred dollars in nuggets for a slice of beefsteak. It did seem at times as if all the riches we were taking out were not to be compared with even the lowliest home in civilization.

Domestic duties were by no means light for two hungry

men during that dark winter, when the thermometer registered far below zero, hour after hour, and day after day. It was easy enough to make beds in Alaskan diggings—your sleeping bag can be chucked anywhere except out doors — but making a fire or making bread is a different matter.   Some of the most trivial precautions are neglected at one's peril.   In their eager pursuit of the golden dirt, too many of the tenderfeet that winter neglected to perform those little duties which were necessary for comfort, and which unperformed might lead them to within an inch of losing their lives.   Every day, as regularly as it came around, I shaved splinters from the wood that we had cut, to be dried on the Yukon stove for starting the fires the next day.   Without these dried splinters it was next to impossible to start a fire when everything was covered with snow.

It was a question whether the gold dust or some of the bread made in that camp had the greater specific gravity. It is fortunate that in such a climate the digestive organs are equal to almost anything.   They will seize with avidity the coarsest and hardest material, and clamor for more. There is no possibility of getting the appetite into a less active state, so that food will stay by a little longer.   It is like a roaring lion seeking what it may devour.   A winter in the Arctics, devoted to digging dirt out of a frozen hole, is the only complete dyspepsia cure I ever saw.   It will either kill or cure; indeed, it can do both.

I became quite an expert in making bread, which in Alaska always means baking-powder bread or biscuit. Some miners brought in a little yeast and tried to raise bread in that way, but it was soon discarded for baking-powder.   My method was simple.   I would take a quart of flour, throw in a couple of tablespoonfuls of baking-powder and about a half a teaspoonful of salt, and mix till quite stiff with water, which had to be previously obtained by melting snow or a fragment of a glacier.   Then I would grease the tin with the best grease that was obtainable, and which usually was very poor; but little things like that are not worth a passing thought in an Alaskan camp.   Having a red-hot fire in the little Yukon stove, I would push the tin into the oven, and in half an hour take out a loaf of bread which, in the ravenous condition of our appetites, would make our eyes water.   The only difficulty was that a loaf would disappear at every meal, so that as long as our supply of flour continued abundant I was compelled to bake two or three times a day.

At evening, and that meant whenever we decided to quit work, for it was night nearly all the time, I would often make a few biscuit, though sometimes we were so tired that we would eat something cold and immediately go to sleep. My biscuit were concocted by nearly the same formula as my bread.   Having put a quart of flour, two tablespoonfuls of baking-powder, and a half teaspoonful of salt together, I would mix it while dry with lard, if I had any, but more commonly with bacon fat.   This I stirred in with water, and rolled out the stiff dough on the smooth side of a slab.   The rolling pin I had manufactured from a section of a spruce pole.   Then I would cut the dough into circles with the top of a baking-powder tin, and bake about fifteen minutes.

But while we could eat enough of these to make a meal in any ordinary climate, they were used only to piece out, as it were.   They had to be accompanied with some such staple article of diet as flapjacks, or bacon, and beans or oat meal.

No game came within sight during that long winter, and we were too busy to look for it till our provisions began to run out and it was difficult to obtain any more.

The prices we had to pay for some of the mere necessaries of life would drive the ordinary housewife into nervous prostration. I have spoken of my biscuits and bread as a great success, and so they were for the country, but they were always hampered by the quality of the flour. For this stale commodity we paid sixty dollars for a hundred-pound sack. Codfish cost us forty dollars per hundred pounds, pork sixty cents a pound, bacon eighty cents. Sugar was sold only in twenty-five-pound lots for eighteen dollars. There were a few potatoes to be had for sixty-five dollars a hundred pounds, and we had very few of them. Dried fruits ranged from seventy cents to a dollar a pound. Now, when you consider that a man could barely keep his appetite easy on four pounds of provisions a day, you will appreciate the fact that high living is not always indicated by the size of the bill.

Of this monotonous diet of stale and canned stuff two men disposed to be economical would require about five dollars' worth a day to be even tolerably comfortable. Think what a variety of dainties in the way of food they could revel in " back in the States." The miners of the Yukon, by the way, always refer to the United States as " back in the States"; and that word " back " is significant. It indicates the feeling which is unconsciously uppermost in the hearts of the majority, the purpose to get " back." They are only waiting for the gold, and the old fellows who have been in these regions so long have stayed because they failed to find enough gold to make them a comfortable fortune over and above what it cost them to winter. And a good many have stayed because they could not find gold enough to enable them to get out.

The prices which provisions commanded were far from being the only expense. Common flannel shirts were eagerly bought at sixteen dollars each, while rubber boots, that are absolutely necessary for placer mining, sold for forty dollars a pair. Moreover, it required something like thirty cords of wood for each man to work his claim during the season, and, if this were not cut from the claims by the men themselves, it had to be hauled from Dawson. On many claims the wood was exceedingly scarce; in fact, on most of them there was none at all.

Slabs from the Dawson City sawmill were used for fires in most of the mines, and immense numbers were bought at fifty cents each, while sawdust brought twenty-five cents a sack. All buying was done with gold. We became as used to handling gold dust at Klondike before the winter was over as a miller does to handling meal.

Occasionally, when the weather made working in the mines uncomfortable or impossible, we would get completely worn out with the tediousness of life and tramp down to Dawson to see what was going on and to get a bit of recreation — anything to break the monotony. With little to carry, and thoroughly prepared for the weather, we could work our way along comfortably, observing what others were doing farther down on the creek, and then pursue our way down the frozen river. One of these trips we took about Christmas time, but no one would have known it at Dawson, which was then a city of a few log cabins and a host of tents. Hundreds of people were too busy keeping themselves warm to celebrate, but a good many miners were down, and there were many who were staying there working in the sawmill, or clerking in the stores, or in the various saloons and restaurants and dance halls. These institutions were active, but no more so than at any time. When the old miners came to town they celebrated anyhow, irrespective of the day of the month or of the week.

Still, Christmas was not entirely forgotten in this region, and there is a feature of the life on the Yukon which should be mentioned. It is all the more noteworthy because it is so rare. The little mission stations along the Yukon make slow headway among the natives, but they still afford a flickering gleam of a higher religious enlightenment. I heard of a Christmas celebration down the river which afforded a glimpse of the life of those who face the severe climate for something besides gold. The story was told by the wife of a man connected with the post in that locality.

The first Christmas she spent in the Yukon district had been two years before, when, with her husband, she lived in a log house at Fort Cudahy, about fifty miles below the mouth of the Klondike. There was but one other white woman there, but it was a comfortable little community, and the gold fever had not become epidemic. Two of her husband's bachelor friends were invited to spend Christmas Day, and she made extensive preparations for a feast that would be a real Christmas treat. Turkey? They do not wander around the Klondike waiting to be shot for Christmas tables. Mince pie and plum pudding? Not on the Yukon. The dinner consisted of a huge haunch of roasted bear meat cut from the carcass of an animal that had been killed hundreds of miles away, and they were glad enough to get even such meat. Bear meat is very much like roast pork, and, if tender, is quite a dainty dish when properly prepared.   They sat and talked all day with the wood blocks heaped up on the blazing hearth, and the rough log walls of the house reflecting cheerfully the light from the flames that danced and sparkled around the chimney corner. Outside it was a very cold, cold world.   Christmas weather in the Klondike is not comfortable.   The wind howled around the log house and the snow fell, steadily accumulating until it made a thick white covering that effectually kept any drafts from finding their way in.   The thermometer outside registered fifty degrees below zero.   But inside they were as cosy and warm as any eastern home heated by modern appliances could be, and in their quiet way, though many thousand miles from what they really called home, they enjoyed themselves and were happy.   The men were certainly grateful for some homelike fireside to gather around on that Christmas day in the Yukon.

Her Christmas day of the winter when we were there was different from the previous one, and approached somewhat nearer to the ideal Christmas of the East.   They actually got up a party at the post, and had a Christmas tree, and games, and a real old-fashioned time, indicating that the Klondike region had advanced some in civilization.   It all came about through the efforts of the Rev. James Naylor, an Episcopal minister who had buried himself in the Klondike, and had devoted his life to work among the Indians and half-breeds there.   He had gathered at the post a numerous contingent of little half-breed children, who had been Christianized and partly civilized and made permanent attaches of the station.

Having taught them the meaning of Christmas, Mr. Naylor decided to show them that it was a time to be joyful by giving a party in which Santa Claus was to make his initial bow to a mixed audience of whites and half-breeds, and go through his customary performance of distributing toys and other gifts.   The weather was all that Santa Claus could have desired.

But where could they get toys in that region, where every one was only too thankful to procure sufficient to eat and wood enough to cook it when procured?   It happened in a strange way, but it is perhaps not so strange when one observes how many seemingly useless things gold-seekers bring into this country.   One man with a trading instinct had come into the Klondike region late in the fall, and had stuffed into his pack several toys and other nicknacks where he ought to have put food.   But it came out all right. Every white mother in the country around was willing to pay its weight in gold for any pitiful looking toy that bore the trademark of a city store.   The man sold his toys and candy at his own prices, and was not such a freak after all. In this way Santa Claus was enabled to keep his contract with the little folks in the Klondike that year.

When the day came and the people around drove over to the mission where the party was to be given, the thermometer was at its Klondike lowest, and frost-bites threatened any nose that showed itself beyond the fur.   Teams consisting of half a dozen dogs were rigged up, and women and children enveloped in furs to their eyebrows climbed in, and off they went over the hills and the frozen river with the dogs trotting along at their best pace to the door where Mr. Naylor awaited them.   Inside all was merriment and laughter.   The members of the little half-breed colony, about a score of children, were in such a state of gleeful expectation that they were ready to stand on their heads at the slightest provocation, and they did this at every fresh arrival.   They were all gotten up in their Sunday best, but some of the white children who had come in had to waddle about in their fur boots.

Nothing like that Christmas tree was ever seen in the Klondike before. There were real dolls gaily attired, and with real eyes and noses instead of the featureless baseball heads with which the Klondike children had been forced to satisfy themselves. There were horses and wagons, dancing figures, and tiny drums, and other contrivances which bring joy to the juvenile heart, no matter in what latitude it beats. The toys were packed in bags made from mosquito netting, which was the only material available. Then Santa Claus came down and distributed them. How the little eyes of the half-breeds stuck out! They thought he was the genuine article. He was gotten up for Yukon weather in a great furry " parka," with the hood turned up around his face. In lieu of a genuine white beard he had powdered his own beard with flour, and no one of the children knew who he was, so effectually was he disguised. He distributed the toys to the great delight of the little half-breeds, who, after a time, could scarcely express their feelings, even by standing on their heads.

After that they went in for a series of old-fashioned games, of which blind-man's-buff proved the favorite. The mission house was built of rough untrimmed logs, like all the best houses, but some attempt had been made to decorate the interior, and with light and warmth and the merriment of happy children, it needed no very great stretch of the imagination to forget the white and frozen earth outside, and fancy ourselves at home again. The party broke up about midnight — the first genuine Christmas party, so far as I have heard, in the country of the Klondike.

CHAPTER XXI

ALASKAN WEATHER — ON THE VERGE OF STARVATION—
HOW WE PULLED THROUGH — DANGERS OF WINTER
TRAVELING — PAINFUL EXPERIENCES.

The Paradox of Alaskan Weather — A Difference in Humidity —
Miners' Thermometers — Time to Take Care of One's self — Seventy-
two Degrees below Zero — Sunset and Sunrise — Dangers on the
Trail — We Discard the Hut and Take to the Tent — Building
Fires in the Morning — Hearing One's Breath Strike the Air — An
Involuntary Bath — Painful Experiences — Eyelids Freeze To-
gether — Protection against the Bitter Cold — The Parka and Its
Uses — An Alaskan Opera Cloak — As a Frost Protector — Care of the
Feet — Snow Shoes — Shortage in the Food Supply — How it Seems
to be without Salt — Sold for Its Weight in Gold — The Pulling-
Through Process — Northern Lights as a Compensation for a Win-
ter in Alaska — Their Brilliancy.

THE weather in the Alaskan latitudes is, like many
other features of the country, not readily appreciated and understood by those who have never been
there, but have simply read about it. I have suffered more
from the cold in Colorado than I have in the Klondike; and
more from the heat on the Yukon than I have in Colorado.
In Alaska in the winter of 1896 snow did not thaw a particle,
except a little while during four mild days in February,
from the time in November when everything froze up till
the middle of April. Most of the time during what we
call the winter months the mercury was far below zero, and
the lowest that I saw recorded was seventy-two degrees.

In a general way, this paradox of the weather may be explained as simply a difference in humidity.   In Arizona, for example, the hot weather is dry, and the cold weather is apt to be damp.   In Alaska the hot weather is damp, and the cold weather dry.   When the thermometer registered eighty-five degrees one summer day on the Yukon, the air was filled with a hot moisture; not a breath was stirring, and the sun shone on with no interruption from clouds for twenty-two hours.   A person could hardly breathe, and I saw men quit work who would not think of doing so were the mercury thirty degrees below zero.   The cold weather of the Klondike does not seem cold in a still day, and yet there are many days when a man can step out of his cabin and freeze his nose before he can count sixty.   One who takes thoroughly good care of himself need not suffer seriously from the cold in Alaska.   Otherwise, he is sure to suffer.   Indeed, he may freeze to death by overlooking a few essentials.

There were not half a dozen regular thermometers in the camp that winter, but the specific degree of coldness did not worry the old miners, unless their mercury bottles froze up.   Then they knew it was time to take care of themselves.   These mercury bottles are the miners' thermometers.   They have need of quicksilver in separating their fine gold, and so they always have it at hand.   They take a little bottle of it with them when they are traveling, and when the mercury freezes they generally, unless in a great hurry, or in a tight place with no provisions, go into camp and wait for the weather to moderate, for it indicates a temperature of at least forty degrees below zero.

The winter of 1896-97 was said by the old-timers to have been a remarkably mild one.   It was true that it began so, and the average temperature did not fall permanently below zero till in November. But it made up for this delay in March. The coldest day, according to my observations, was on the 15th, when the mercury stood seventy-two degrees below at eight o'clock in the morning. From the 4th of March till the 23d it was never above fifty degrees below. It was quite cold some days in January and there were many days below fifty degrees.

It may be imagined that weather of this character is not exactly propitious for gold mining, and very little was done. Of course, the man down in the hole could stand it very well, shoveling up the embers of a night's burning, but the man at a windlass at the top was in a less agreeable position. But he was, on the whole, much better off than the man in the shaft, who, when work was over, frequently came up hot and perspiring, and the cruel blasts chilled him through in an instant.

In the Klondike region in midwinter the sun rises from 9:30 to 10 A. M., and sets from 2 to 3 P. M., the total length of daylight being about four hours, but the sun never rises but a few degrees above the horizon, and many are the days when it is wholly obscured. The wind blows almost constantly, and while the snow seldom falls more than three feet on the level, it is always present from early October to April. When the reader couples a condition like this with the fact that day after day mercury will remain frozen if left outdoors, he may begin to imagine the desolation of a life amid the lonely gulches of the north, far from all that civilized people are used to.

The changes of temperature from winter to summer are rapid, owing to the great increase in the length of the days. By May the sun is rising at about 3 A. M., and setting about

9 P. M., and by June it is rising at 1:30 in the morning and setting about 10:30 P. M. Either in summer or winter the resident of the Yukon must be prepared for the greatest changes. When the sun shines the atmosphere is remarkably clear, the scenic effects are magnificent, all nature seems to be in holiday attire. But the scene may change very quickly; the sky becomes overcast, the winds increase in force, rain begins to fall, the evergreens sigh ominously, and utter desolation and loneliness prevail. These treacherous conditions will lure many a brave fellow to death upon the lonely trails. The soft autumnal languor of that lonely land may change within an hour to the darkness of the swirling storm. When Nature thus changes her smiling mood for the tempest's frown, the mountain trail becomes charged with terrible dangers.

In the winter this danger is increased. A storm may break from the clouds, and for many long hours the frigid blasts, filled with swirling snow which cuts like a knife, will overwhelm the brave traveler unless he is prepared. The native Indians will stick a couple of poles in the snow and hang their blankets up against the wind, and let the snow drift over them. Usually they will come out all right, but they are accustomed to the climate and its hardships, and no newcomer should be caught in such a predicament. It means death nine times out of ten.

Joe and I managed to endure the winter very comfortably, though we quickly discarded as a habitation the little hut I had constructed out of green logs. We set up the tent in front to live in and used the hut as a sort of store room for tools and the like. It was too small for comfort, and the air became too intolerable for two persons in the long nights when vents had to be closed to keep out the cold. We moved the stove into the tent and enjoyed life much better. Little by little the snow banked around it and over it, so that after a time it was quite warm, though, of course, much cold air came in at the entrance, no matter how well closed. After the fire went out at night it cooled off very quickly, and it was as cold as out of doors, but the tent kept off the wind. One could hardly get under blankets enough to keep warm, but with a pair of blankets and a good robe I was more comfortable than those who were using sleeping bags. During the summer when I went down the Yukon, I traded with some Indians and secured several fine lynx skins. I had them made into a robe at Dawson, and the whole thing cost me about seventy-five dollars. It was eight feet long and seven feet wide, and lined with a heavy woolen blanket. Before I had lived through half that winter I had made up my mind that I would rather throw away my gold mine than that robe. It was worth more than twenty blankets for comfort, and some of the miners in the camp offered me twice what I paid for it.

But in spite of all the precautions we took, and the care we exercised in small details, we could not fail to suffer some. It was rather cold getting up and building a fire when the thermometer was fifty degrees or more below zero. It was all the more trying because I had slept as warm as toast in the robe. Mornings when it was so very cold, and no wind was stirring, it was as still as death, and I could actually *hear* my breath strike the air. There was a sort of a crackle when the warm breath met the cold atmosphere, and it was at first painful to draw such cold air into the lungs. But, strange to say, I was never troubled with a cough, and never felt the slightest touch of a cold until late in the season, after the ice had begun to break up. One day, when coming up to camp from Dawson, I slipped and fell in the river, and neglected to change my clothes. I worked several hours after reaching camp, and, after drying a little before the fire, rolled up in my blanket and went to bed. Instead of killing me, it only gave me a slight cold for a week.

I had a much more painful experience in January, when I started out from Dawson to pull a sled load of provisions up to the camp. When I had gone a few miles I became so cold that I could not pull the sled. It was too far to go on, so I left the sled there and walked back to Dawson. In that way I could keep tolerably warm, for one can keep warm if he moves fast enough, but if he stands still he will freeze. My eyelids kept freezing together, but I had to be very careful about pulling off my gloves to thaw them apart. I did it as quickly as I could, but several times my hands nearly froze before I could get them back into the big mittens. When I reached Dawson City the thermometers registered fifty-eight degrees below.

One need not fear these uncomfortable experiences if he be properly dressed and prepared for them. A common winter dress of the mines is a garment that the native Alaskans sell. It is a blouse of heavy skins, with trousers of seal. These are fastened close about the body, which is enveloped in two or more suits of heavy underclothing. For footwear, low boots of tough walrus hide or rubber boots are worn. Mittens and hoods of bear or dog skin are essential.

But the great institution in Alaska, so far as wearing apparel is concerned, is the " parka." Whenever the coat of arms of the territory come to be designed, there are four objects which should be worked in somehow; these are a cache, a dog, a mosquito, and a parka. If that is not enough the artist might put a glacier in the background. The parka is of Indian origin. No matter what part of the great territory the Indians come from, or to what tribe they belong, they wear this garment. It is made like a big shirt, coming down to the knees, and with no opening front or back. It is just slipped on over the head, and attached to it is a hood, trimmed around the face with fur. The Indian parkas are usually made entirely of fur, the fur being inside, and the sleeves, especially of the parkas of the lower Yukon Indians, are made so large that if they wish to pull their arms inside they can do so with no trouble. They can snuggle down in these garments until completely out of sight.

The Yukon miner and trader has adapted the Indian style to his own uses, and the usual parka is made of blue denim or overall cloth, with a bit of fur around the opening of the hood. When the temperature is fifty or sixty degrees below zero, however, the all-fur parkas are better and are common. These garments are useful not only to keep out the cold, but to keep the frost off. For when one goes out in severe weather the breath congeals in a white mantle all over the parka. Going indoors, it of course thaws, and if one stays long he throws it off. Going out again, it freezes stiff. But it keeps the clothing underneath in good condition. It is a sort of " opera cloak." If one leaves his tent to go down into the city of an evening, he slips on his parka. If working, the under coat may be dispensed with; not so the parka. As a frost protector it is as valuable then as it is when going to the theater or the other places of amusement.

In severe weather — that is, when the mercury is frozen — the hands, face, and feet must be watched closely.

Otherwise they will have a tendency to freeze before you
are aware that they are cold. I used to wear a heavy pair of
woolen stockings which came up to my knees, over them a
pair of fur socks, and then moccasins. One will make a
track in the snow as big as that of an elephant, but none too
big to enable one to get along comfortably. Indeed, snowshoes are generally needed, for the snow never packs solid
except in the trail, and a person will drop clear to the bottom
of almost the deepest snows if he steps out of the road,
unless he has on snowshoes.

There was some difference of opinion in the camp as to
the advisability of wearing whiskers during an Arctic winter, and there certainly are two sides to the question. Shav-
ing oneself is not an easy process when living in a tent, and
when the air is apt to be chilled by the blasts which find
their way in. Moreover, whiskers are of some protection
to the face and throat when facing such blasts outside.
But, on the other hand, this very protection becomes a
nuisance of the most exasperating character. I have
spoken of the way in which the frost congeals upon the
clothing. But that is not a circumstance to the freaks it
will play with a heavy beard. It will settle in and through
it till it becomes a solid mass of ice, and cannot be thrown off
like a parka when entering a warm room. The only thing
to do is to sit over the fire and let the glacier on your chin
melt. In view of this inconvenience, the majority of
miners keep their whiskers trimmed very short in winter,
and allow them to grow in the summer as a protection
against mosquitoes. Then they are a real blessing, and
many times a man will wish himself as hairy as a baboon.

Towards the end of winter the food supply in camp and
at Dawson ran very low, — a common spring complaint

A Rest After a Day's March

A party of gold-seekers just after pitching their tent on the Skagway Trail.

in the upper Yukon region. Although the trading companies had concentrated what supplies they could at Dawson, the discovery of gold had taken place so late in the summer, and had been followed so quickly by ice, that by March there was much difficulty in getting anything. A few supplies were brought up from Circle City, and a little flour was dragged up from Forty Mile. It was also possible to buy a little caribou or bear meat occasionally, but by the time the snow began to melt there was practically nothing in the camp but beans, and fully two hundred men lived on these for several weeks. We nearly starved, or, at least, we thought we did. It would not have been much of a job to get together a million of dollars' worth of gold dust along the creek, but such a thing as a good square meal was not to be had. It is fully as unpleasant to be without salt as it is without flour, yet salt was so scarce that it could be obtained only in the most insignificant quantities and at the most exorbitant price. It was actually worth its weight in gold to some of the miners. A party on the creek ran completely out of this article, though they had a fair amount of other provisions. They said they really felt as if they should die did they not obtain salt somehow.

Near them was another party having salt, but they refused to part with any of it. It was insisted that it ought to be shared, and that the party having it must sell at a fair price. It was ascertained that the party owning the salt had very little gold dust, and those without salt had an abundance. So it was finally arranged that the owners of the salt should part with a portion of it, and that it should be weighed against the precious dust. Thus was salt actually sold for its weight in gold.

When matters reached this pass the provisions became

to a certain extent common property. No one was allowed to starve so long as anything was left in the camp. Meanwhile the cold remained intense, and our appetites knew no bounds. But we never quite reached the starving point. That has always been the way on the Yukon. Every year the people there come near to starvation, but they pull through somehow. This "pulling through" process cannot be appreciated by simply reading about it. It must be experienced.

There is one spectacle which compensates one for these long, cold winter twilights and contingent hardships; one thing which is worth the spending of a winter in the Klondike, or any part of northern Alaska, the nearer the Arctic Circle the better. It is not the gold. The more I reflect on this life and the hereafter, the more I am in doubt as to whether the gold in the frozen placers of Alaska is in itself worth going after. But the aurora of Alaska is worth seeing, even if you have to live on short rations of bacon and beans for three months and find no gold. Some people seem to care very little about it, and to old miners the spectacle undoubtedly becomes commonplace, as it has to the natives. Perhaps I was born a little sentimental as to the wonders of Nature, and the celestial wonders in particular.

Some clear, still, cold nights, when the indications favored a brilliant display of northern lights, I have put on my snowshoes and climbed back on the hillside "just to drink them in." It may be vain to attempt to describe such a scene, for one must see it for himself; must stand on one of those hills in a country mantled with snow, among the trees which bend under their spotless burden, every twig a cluster of feathery whiteness. It is night, and yet not darkness, only a soft, subduing absence of the sun's rays.

Over the hills and valleys silence broods in all its cold per-
fection.   Overhead the stars glitter as they do only in these
still, cold nights in the far north.

Then one becomes aware of a sort of weird and formless
presence in the sky, and the stars seem to be dancing on
silvery billows.   A queer electric crackle breaks upon the
stillness, and in an instant the sky is painted with quivering
bands of yellow, changing into every color of the rainbow,
darting with the rapidity of lightning, and changing every
second.

> " Glowing wide and bright, then narrow,
>   And then flashing broad and golden,
>   Sending long bright crimson fingers
>   Far across the cloudless ether.
>   Rosy lights grow clear and vivid,
>   Pale to tints of faintest blushes,
>   Then burst out in glorious shading
>   Close beside the soft, blue azure
>   Where the sharp, clear edges mingle
>   In the softest shades of purple.
>
> " Pale-green shafts shoot out and quiver
>   In the glorious brightness !
>   Flaming pencils touch the hilltops,
>   Sending slender rainbow arches
>   Down their glinting shimmering mantles.
>   Bushes, trees, and shining grass blades
>   Catch the gleam of gold and crimson,
>   And throw out swift, starry flashes
>   Toward the gay, auroral brightness.
>
> " In the north a glorious archway
>   Casts its glancing rays and shafting,
>   And uplifts a glittering halo
>   Far across the dark-blue zenith.
>   Downward flings its mingled shading —
>   Gold and blue, and green and crimson,
>   Yellow, tender pink, and purple,
>   Shrinking from the icy contact,
>   And then sweeping through the cloud paths."

CHAPTER XXII

PREPARING FOR SLUICING — THE SPRING "CLEAN-UP" —
ASTONISHING RESULTS WHEN DIRT WAS WASHED
OUT — SOME LUCKY STRIKES — THE ROMANCE OF
FORTUNE.

Joe and I Have Poor Luck — Trying to Locate the Pay-Streak — Big
Pans in March and April — Pay-Dirt — How the Value of the Dirt
is Reckoned — Old Miners Begin to Speculate — Expense of Getting
Sluice Boxes — Some of the Fortunes — Berry and His Wonderful
Strike — Very Blue when He Heard of the Klondike — Takes Out
$130,000 — A Bird in the Hand *vs.* a Bird in the Bush — A Wiscon-
sin Schoolmaster's Experience — Worth a Million — Better than
Trading — Sudden Rise in the Value of Claims — Computing the
Value of a Bonanza Claim — Wonderful Results — The Aggregate
Amount of the Spring Work — Some of the Lucky Ones on El-
dorado Creek — Fortunes on the Bonanza — Lucky Days — "What
Will I Do With All That Money ?"

HARDLY more than a score of the claims on Bonanza
and Eldorado creeks were thoroughly worked during that long winter of 1896-97. As already mentioned, labor was scarce, and the newcomers who had acquired the rich territory were unable to do much except in
a small way. Joe and I had poor luck in finding the pay-
streak, and it was well towards spring before our pans began
to make any unusual yields. Those who had secured help
and worked their property more extensively were generally
unaware of what would develop in the spring clean-up,
though the richness of some of the better known claims was

fairly well known, for at times the gold fairly stuck out of the dirt. The tests that had been made had given an astonishingly high average, and as bed-rock was reached the results were simply staggering. About the middle of March two boys, one from Juneau and another from Stuck Valley, Wash., began to take out wonderful pans from the bottom of their shaft. They were not quite sure of the evidence of their own eyes, and invited another man to go down and pick out a pan of dirt in the pay-streak. He did so, and was surprised to find two hundred and eighty-two dollars and fifty cents in it. In fourteen pans of dirt from the bottom of the shaft they took out one thousand five hundred and sixty-five dollars. March 20th, Clarence Berry took out over three hundred dollars to the pan, James MacLanie over two hundred dollars, and Frank Phiscater over one hundred and thirty dollars. There were four men working one claim which began to yield about one hundred and twenty-five dollars to the pan. Then we began to hear of big pans from the shafts which had reached bed-rock all along the creeks, and one-hundred and two-hundred-dollar pans became common in April. On April 13th Berry took out a pan of thirty-nine ounces — four hundred and ninety-five dollars — and in two days took out one thousand two hundred dollars by his tests. On the 20th it was reported that some miners working a lay on No. 30 Eldorado had found a pan containing eight hundred dollars.

When some of these men reckoned up the value of the dirt they had been dumping out, they had bright dreams of wealth. The method of computing the value of a dump is very simple. The miners' assays consist of panning out a number of pans of gravel at stated intervals during his shift. An average of the whole is easily arrived at: the bucket in his shaft contains so many pans, and the worth of a bucket becomes a simple matter of calculation. Each shift keeps tally of the number of buckets thrown upon the dump, and the daily average value, and after one, two, or even six months' work at drifting an apparently accurate conclusion of the amount of gold in sight can be reached.

Of course, pans varied in such placers, and the lucky owners scarcely dared to reckon into the average yielded by the large pans which they washed for testing, but the value of claims jumped immensely and speculation was rife. Old miners who had turned up their noses at the Klondike at first, and had afterwards come back and spent the winter in looking for more creeks, saw at once the value of the new claims and calculated what they could pay for them. They offered large sums for some of the claims after seeing the tests and inspecting the dumps, and a number of the tenderfeet, dazed by the sight of such sudden riches thrust in their faces, sold out. They thought a bird in hand was worth two in the bush, but they did not understand so well as the old miners what was in the bush. When a mine was bought, the season's work, that is, the dumps, went with it, and the old miner calculated that he could clean out of the sluice boxes, when they could be started, enough to pay the large sums they had offered. Of course, they had to run in debt heavily for a time, and it was something of a gamble, for the dumps might not pan out as well as anticipated, and the rate of interest was high — generally five per cent. a month.

It was not an easy or inexpensive matter to arrange the sluice boxes for the spring work. The sawmill at Dawson had been kept busy beyond its capacity in providing for the growth of the place, and many could not secure the necessary lumber for the construction of their sluice boxes without paying an enormous sum, while if they whip-sawed it on claims it would cost about three hundred dollars a thousand, figuring in the cost of labor and the logs. But when sluicing once began people who had debts quickly paid them off, and those who had lived from hand to mouth all their lives suddenly had all their old baking-powder cans and old jars and kettles in their camp full of gold dust.

There were plenty of cases bordering on the romantic in that lonely valley then. One of the most conspicuous was that of Clarence J. Berry. Not very successful as the owner of a fruit farm in Fresno, Cal., he determined to try his luck on the Yukon. He reached Juneau with only sixty dollars in his pocket, but made his way undaunted over the Chilkoot Pass, and finally down to Circle City, where all the excitement then was. He lived along as best he could, and looked about for a location, but without much success. In the fall of 1895 he returned to California almost as poor as he had started. But he had faith in the richness of the country. In February he married Miss Ethel Bush of Selma, Cal., it being understood that they were to make a venture into the Great Northwest to carve out their fortunes. They had the usual run of hardships in making their way to the Yukon. Stopping at Forty Mile, Berry found absolutely nothing to do for a long time, but finally secured a chance on a claim and made a little gold, but scarcely enough to keep him going. When the news of the strike on Bonanza Creek reached Forty Mile, Berry was one of the bluest of the blue, and had scarcely enough ambition left to go with the rush. But his wife prevailed upon him to go, and he struck it rich within a short time. He was soon able to build a comfortable home for his wife at

Dawson, but she remained much of the time at the mines, where she poked around the dumps, and, during the time she was there, picked up about ten thousand dollars' worth of nuggets.

In a few months Berry took out one hundred and thirty thousand dollars, from which he paid twenty-two thousand dollars to miners. He paid the experience men fifteen dollars a day and settled with them every evening by washing out a few panfuls of dirt with melted snow. Three men, named Flack, Sloan, and Wilkinson, worked a claim on Eldorado, and when they had sunk a shaft eighteen feet Sloan and Wilkinson sold out their interests for fifty thousand dollars each, but Flack refused to sell. He preferred to take his chances with the bird in the bush. The three owners when they came to clean up the dump obtained over fifty thousand dollars each out of the dirt thrown out before the pay-streak was reached. A miner by the name of Alex. MacDonald took out ninety-four thousand dollars from a forty-foot patch of ground only two feet thick. He employed four men to do the work and consumed but twenty-eight days. His claim was No. 30 Eldorado.

There was one man who a year before had been a country schoolteacher in Wisconsin. In the spring of 1896 he started on a pleasure trip to Juneau. His funds gave out and he was compelled to go to work, but later on he joined a party of tenderfeet and started up the Stikine River for Lake Teslin. Before the lake was reached eleven of the party gave up in disgust, and the schoolmaster and one other were left alone with less than a year's provisions. They pushed on to the lake, built a raft, and started down the river. Along in October they came floating down to the mouth of the Klondike, as green a pair as ever found their way into the country. They heard about the discovery, but found all the good claims staked. Finally, they secured a chance to work a claim on shares, which gave them each one-fourth interest in the claim. They took out eighty thousand dollars in thirty days from one claim on Eldorado, and twenty-two thousand dollars in twenty days from another, and by the time they washed out their dumps they were interested in a half dozen other claims of value. The schoolmaster calculated that he was worth at least three hundred thousand dollars, and that his chances were good for a million by the time his interests were worked out.

Something like a realization of the force and completeness of the awakening may be had from a simple observation of the experience of a Seattle boy who had arrived at the Klondike too late to stake a claim, but still while the majority had little faith in the permanent value of the new discovery. He found a fellow who was willing to sell his Eldorado claim for eighty-five dollars, and he purchased it, but was unable to work it. In April, or in less than four months after his purchase, not having put a pick into the dirt of the claim, he sold it for thirty-one thousand dollars in Canadian money, which in dust at seventeen dollars an ounce would be equivalent to about thirty-five thousand dollars. There were many similar cases where claims were sold in November for as many dollars as they were valued in thousands in the spring.

Sometime in the winter a French Canadian, while intoxicated, sold his claim on Eldorado for five hundred dollars. When he became sober he regretted exceedingly what he had done. Some of his friends told him that a contract made with a man when intoxicated would not hold, and he threatened proceedings to have it declared void.

The fact was that all the parties were more or less intoxicated when the sale was made. It was one of those saloon incidents quite common when the tired and lonesome miners meet at Dawson to break the hard monotony of their lives. Rather than hazard a lawsuit, the purchaser of the claim offered to the French Canadian what was, in effect, about one-tenth of the original claim, to surrender all right and title, real or imaginary, that he might have. It was about the middle of March when he accepted this settlement, and in April he sold his interest in this small part of the claim for fifteen thousand dollars, and went home to spend it.

Frank Dinsmore, a poor prospector, in 1896 took out of a claim on Bonanza Creek ninety pounds of gold in a single day, netting him twenty-four thousand four hundred and eighty dollars. A man working on Alec McDonald's Eldorado claim shoveled in twenty thousand dollars in twelve hours. McDonald is a great big, raw-boned, rough, good-hearted working man. One day he paid over to the Alaska Trading and Transportation Company at Dawson one hundred and fifty thousand dollars in one payment. Among the mass of gold was twelve thousand dollars in nuggets in a granite bowl. They weighed about forty-five pounds. Alice Henderson, a newspaper correspondent, happened to be present at the time the payment was made. Alec turned to her and said, in an off-hand way:

"Help yourself to the nuggets. Take some of the bigger ones."

She hesitated, and he said: "Oh, they are nothing to me. Take as many as you please. There are lots more."

She finally took a nugget which represented about two hundred dollars in gold. Frank Phiscator was another prospector from Michigan. In the fall of 1896 he was a pauper prospector. In the spring of 1897 he was a millionaire.

One June day, when the dumps had been pretty well washed out, the Canadian surveyor went up to Eldorado Creek to gain an idea of the output of the twenty-four claims that had been at all worked there. He calculated that at the rate of seventeen dollars an ounce it aggregated about eight hundred and twenty-six thousand dollars, and this was the result of little more than a scratching of the pay-streak of the claims. One claim on the creek had been sold in April for forty-five thousand dollars, and five thousand dollars had been paid down. The other provisions of the sale were that fifteen thousand dollars should be paid on May 15th, or about a month after the sale, the purchaser, if failing to make the payment, forfeiting the claim, and the balance to be paid by July 1st, failing which the claim and all money paid should be forfeited. This was considered by some a very hazardous deal. It required immense faith in the dirt; but the purchaser seemed to know his business, and when the papers were completed he said he never felt surer of a homestake in his life, although he had been mining for over twenty years. After the purchase, as sluicing could not yet be done, he set to work with two rockers, and made his payment on May 11th, or four days before it was due, and the balance was ready about the 20th of June. The claim had been sold for an amount which was practically equivalent to but two months' working of a space about twenty-four feet square, and with a rocker at that.

If Bonanza Creek did not develop such remarkable results at first it was still rich past the comprehension of the owners. About the middle of April, George Cormack, acting for Tagish Charlie, his associate, sold one-half of Claim No. 2 below for five thousand dollars, five hundred dollars down, and the balance to be paid by July 1, or forfeit the money and the claim. On July 1, while passing the claim, the Canadian surveyor witnessed the payment of the four thousand five hundred dollars by the purchaser, and when the business was completed he asked him how he had succeeded.

" Oh," he said, " pretty well."

" Have you any objections to telling me what you have done? "

" No," he replied. " I drifted about twenty-four feet long by fourteen feet wide, and cleaned up eight thousand dollars."

" I know the area of your claim," said the surveyor, " and assuming that your claim is all equally rich, we will see how much you will take out of it."

Some of these miners were not good at figures, and more of them had been too busy and excited taking out the gold to drop into mathematical calculations. But it was a simple problem. Given the length and width of the claim, the product gave the area in square feet. Dividing this by the result of multiplying 24 by 14, and multiplying the quotient by eight thousand dollars, would give the value of the dirt in the whole claim. The surveyor went through the process.

" It's two million four hundred thousand dollars," he said.

" My God! " said the man, " what will I do with all that money? "

" Oh, I wouldn't worry," said the surveyor, " for you are not likely to be troubled to that extent. It is hardly possible that your claim will average anything like that in richness. But assuming that it will average one-quarter as rich, you will still have six hundred thousand dollars. Or, assuming that there is a narrow strip in your claim only fourteen feet wide which you have just happened to strike on, and that it continues through the length of your claim, which is two hundred and fifty feet, you will still have eighty-three thousand dollars, which is enough to kill you."

CHAPTER XXIII

STORIES OF GREAT HARDSHIPS AND SCANTY REWARDS
— A ROMANCE OF THE KLONDIKE — CLAIM JUMPERS —
AN OLD SLAVE'S LUCKY STRIKE.

IT is impossible to adequately describe the effect upon
Dawson of these revelations of the rich character of
the mines which came when the sluices were cleaned
up in the months of May and June. Gold was brought
in from the creeks by the ton, and, as one man expressed it,
was " stacked up by the cord " with the trading companies
for safe keeping. Men who had stumbled over the rough
trail in September, poor and disheartened, disgusted with
their condition and sick of the country, came down in the
spring as millionaires and threw their gold dust about like
so much grass seed. But it must not be thought be-

(328)

cause so much gold dust was in evidence that every one was rich. The fortunate ones always become famous, but little is heard of those who work as hard and gain but little.

These Alaskan and Northwest Territory gold fields constitute as odd a prize drawing proposition as ever was conceived of. It can be likened to nothing that admits of a better comparison than a lottery. Old miners have looked along the creeks for years, and their practiced eyes have detected colors in many places. Selecting spots, they have worked, sometimes half frozen, oftener half starved. The season has closed, the water has run, and it has been found, time and time again, that expenses have barely been paid. Only a little distance away men rushed in, staked off any part of a creek's bed they could get, and took sacks of gold from the most uninviting bit of earth any one ever saw. The lucky one did not strike the pocket because of his ability as a miner. Chance favored him, that was all. In nineteen cases out of twenty the miners had missed it and waited another year for a new trial. Finally came the Klondike.

The placers are the most deceiving I have ever seen. Imagine a man working on good " color " and finding the ground worth only a few dollars per day, and then turning to a waste of mud and moss with no surface indications and unearthing a bonanza! This seems to be the situation all over Alaska. The man who goes there to mine does so at the expense of health and happiness, and it is with him a question of making a fortune quickly, or taking chances with death.

About Dawson were scores of men who could weigh their gold by the bucketful and who valued their claims at millions. Four hundred valuable diggings were stretched along the creeks, and every digging was a fabulous mine of gold. Yet there were weary men who had come to Dawson after searching the country throughout, and never a nugget could they show for their toil and their long tramp over broken ground into a country whose natural disadvantages are exceeded by those of no other place on earth.

One old miner there was, a Glasgow Scotchman, noted for his steady, upright, moral life. He was sixty-four years old.

"How long have you been mining?" he was asked, one day.

"Forty-two years," he replied.

"Where?"

"Everywhere in North America where mining has been done."

"And you never made a homestake?"

"I never made more than a living, and very often a scant one at that," he replied, somewhat mournfully.

The miners of the Yukon speak of a "homestake," meaning the accumulation of enough gold to enable them to return to "God's country," as they call the United States, and live the rest of their days comfortably. This old Scotchman had been searching through the Yukon valley for ten years and had at last come to look forward to the possibility of dying and being buried there. He had thought — and it must have been a bitter thought, too — that in his last days he might have to be assisted by his friends as he had often helped others.

But he was at last fortunate enough to locate a good claim in the Klondike district with another old Scotchman who had had a similar experience. They could not afford to work it much, but when March came and the prices of mines rose to such fabulous figures, they sold out for twenty thousand dollars — ten thousand dollars each, after over forty years of hardships, much of the time cut off from all associations, and deprived of home and family life, and the pleasures of existence amid civilized surroundings.

But even this tardy favor from fortune carried with it an element of that poor luck which had followed them for so many years. Had they waited twenty days longer they could have sold their claim for forty thousand dollars just as easily as they had sold it for half that sum. Still, they were glad to acquire even their little fortune, and they embraced the first opportunity to leave the country and return to a civilized land to end their days. They had at last made their homestake.

Others were far from being as fortunate as that. There were men who had been knocking around the mountains for years, and who came too late to secure claims, working about Dawson for anything they could get, and though they make good wages in such a booming place, it was little more than enough to keep soul and body together at the prices they were compelled to pay for the stalest kind of provisions.

Scores of practiced miners came into the camps that first winter who could not even secure a lay on any of the rich placers. They were glad to have the opportunity to work for some of the lucky tenderfeet who had stumbled into the golden valley. Their feelings during that long winter, as, exposed to the fierce blasts of Arctic weather, they toiled in the frozen shafts or turned the crude windlasses, and knew that the lucky fellow whose claim they were working was enabled to pay them by washing out every evening a few buckets of the rich earth they were thawing, may be imagined. They had searched, some of them for years, along the Yukon for such places as this, and when it was found they could get only fifteen dollars a day while a lucky tenderfoot was taking out thousands.

But they did not grumble at fate. None knew so well as they that mining is a gamble anyway, and those who had had the good fortune to find the prize were entitled to it. It was a little too much for their hardened resignation to this blind fate, however, when they were asked to work for less than fifteen dollars a day in the new placers. To be sure, they had often worked in diggings where they had earned more than their employers, but when these tenderfeet, who needed the experienced men to work their rich properties, asked them to labor for less than fifteen dollars in dirt that frequently ran over a hundred dollars to the pan, it was a little too much. The difficulty was finally adjusted so that the experienced miners received the high rate of wages while the inexperienced received about ten dollars a day.

I knew one young man who had been a sailor and had roughed it in about every way possible, finally bringing up on the Yukon, where, he said, he had the hardest experience he had ever met in his life.

" I've known what it is to go hungry for a month at a time," he said, as he was taking the steamboat to go home for a visit, having made a little money for the first time since he came into the valley. " I know what the chance for getting rich in this country is," he continued, " and although I have got enough at last to enable me to go home for a little visit after all these years, I wouldn't again go through what I have endured here for the best mine in the Klondike. Two years ago I landed at Forty Mile with my partner, and we worked hard and often went terribly hungry. When we heard of the strike on Bonanza, I wanted to go, but in the eight months we had been working we had taken out not more than thirty dollars of clean money. Ill luck seemed to follow us wherever we went. Finally we got up to Dawson and were fortunate enough to secure a lay on an Eldorado claim. After working a while my partner became disgusted and left, for none of the big strikes had been made then. It was the hardest mining we had ever struck. After a time we found some good indications, and by the end of the season we were able to take out enough so that I had six thousand dollars for my share. That is the first piece of good luck I have had in my two years in Alaska, and it does not begin to pay me for what I have suffered."

Jack McQuesten, who is called the " father of the country," has comparatively very little to show for his long life and many hardships on the Yukon. He has done fairly well as a trader, and by his generosity has helped many of the old miners of the country in their desperate straits. McQuesten went to Dawson, but not till the choice ground had been taken up. His claim panned out so well, however, that for the first time in twenty-six years he paid a visit to the states, carrying with him about ten thousand dollars. Neal McArthur was one of the old miners in the country. In recounting his experiences to a party of friends, he said:

" I have been mining for more than thirty years, but not until I struck Alaska over nine years ago did I begin to know what suffering was. It would be impossible for me to tell all I have gone through and the many times that death has been near me. I recall one instance that may serve to illustrate what the people are to expect if they rush unprepared into the Yukon country. It was in the fall of

1881.   Winter had come on earlier than usual, and, in consequence, only a few boats were able to reach the points
along the river.   In the dead of winter our provisions gave
out, and it seemed as though we must all die.   Finally it was
agreed that we must go to St. Michael, one thousand seven
hundred miles away, if we hoped to escape with our lives.
I cannot begin to recount the horrors of that journey.   It
was bitter cold, and to make matters worse we did not have
the proper clothing.   We were weeks in reaching our
destination, and we were more dead than alive when we
got there.   I have worked all through the diggings of
Alaska, but I hardly made a living.   Some seasons we took
out next to nothing, and then next year we would strike a
pocket carrying enough gold to keep us going for a time.
Last fall, when the news reached us of the strike on the
Klondike, all who could packed up their effects and hastened
to the new fields.   It was like a drowning man catching at a
straw.   We were ready to do anything that promised a return.   I was fortunate enough to locate a good claim and
came away with enough to last me the rest my days.

  " There are men in this country who are poor, and who
will remain so.   It has not been their ' luck,' as they call it,
to strike it rich, but I may say that the country offers to
men of great fortitude, steadiness, and some intelligence an
opportunity to make more money in a given time than they
could possibly make anywhere else.   You have, of course,
a good deal to contend with; your patience will be sorely
tried, for the conditions are so unique that they have surprised many who have gone in hopefully and have left in
disgust.   There are many obstacles and disagreeable conditions in prospecting."

  Troubles are not certain to cease when gold in rich quantities is found and all that remains is to get it out. In Alaska and the Northwest Territory now, as has generally been the case in valuable gold regions, there are men who are desperate and unscrupulous, and who, under some pretext, may seek to deprive a weak man of his rights. In the rush and excitement attending the development of the Klondike district such cases were too commonly overlooked, even by the justice-loving miners who were too hard at work and too busy to mind the troubles of others. There was some genuine heroism displayed in defending claims.

Along in April there came into one of the camps an elderly man accompanied by a boy, as we thought, about fifteen years old. We thought him one of the nicest boys we ever saw. He and his father staked out a claim on one of the new streams. The old man said he came from Massachusetts. He was a quiet, peaceable man, minded his own business and paid no attention to anybody. But a few days after he commenced work on his claim it got around that he had struck three-dollar dirt.

Some of the mean characters knocking about the place thought they might run the old fellow off his claim. So one night two or three of them went to the tent, shoved their guns in the faces of the man and his boy, and told them if they didn't get off that claim within twenty-four hours they would be shot. The old man said nothing to them, so one of them owned up afterward, but just lay there, and the boy kept quiet, too.

The old man, whose name was Henry Williams, talked it over with his boy, and between them they agreed that they would stick it out. So they took turns lying awake and watching for the claim-jumpers. Three or four nights afterwards the jumpers came. The boy was asleep and the old man was on watch. Before the old man knew what had happened they had shot him in the shoulder. The boy heard the shot, and out he jumped with a gun in each hand, dropped two of the fellows, and wounded another. The fourth man ran away without firing a shot. Then the boy fixed the old man up a little and came down into the town and told what had happened.

The men assembled right away and went out to the old man's camp and brought him back to town, fixed him up the best they could, and found that he was not very badly hurt. After they had found this out and told the boy that his father was all right, he dropped to the floor as if he was shot. They picked him up and laid him in a bunk.

And then they found out that he wasn't a boy at all, but a girl, and a pretty girl, too.

As I heard the story, the man had been very unfortunate in the East, and determined to go to Alaska. His wife was dead, and he had only one child, this girl, and did not know what to do with her. But she was determined to come with him as a boy, and she made her father agree to it. There was nothing in Dawson too good for them after that, and that girl could have married any unmarried man in town had she chosen to, and there was some talk of her doing so. There are plenty of opportunities for such romances in the Klondike.

And many queer people were to be found. It seemed as if nearly every nation of the earth was represented and everybody was as good as everybody else. It made no difference as to color, or previous condition. There was one old fellow who had once been a slave, and his wool was as gray as a sheep's pelt. He had come into the Yukon valley with a freighting outfit and had no idea of trying for gold.

But when he reached the neighborhood of Dawson, old as he was, he contracted the fever and staked out a claim.

"You know that old black fellow down the creek," said Joe one day when he had returned from witnessing some of the spring sluicing.

"Yes," I said. "What about him?"

"Well, you may believe it or not, but the old rascal has cleaned up thirty thousand dollars in gold dust. You ought to hear him talk about what he is going to do with it. His name, he says, is St. John Atherton, and he comes from down in Georgia, 'just a piece out of Atlanta.' The daughter of the man who owned him during the war is living there yet, he says, on the old plantation, but very poor. The old fellow says he is going back to buy that plantation, and then he is going to have that woman do nothing but live like a lady all the rest of her days. I believe he means just what he says. He's a queer old darky, but he seems to have a good heart."

CHAPTER XXIV

INCIDENTS OF THE TRAIL — DEATH AND BURIAL OF A BABY — A WOMAN'S THRILLING EXPERIENCES.

News of the Outside World — When the Ice Goes Out of the River — It "Marks Time" — An Unpleasant Sight for a Hungry Man — Grub at Last — Happy Incident of a Yukon Honeymoon — Mrs. McKay's Story — Death of a Baby — The Little Casket and the Grave by Lake Lindeman — Misfortunes of John Matthews — His Troubles Over — Impression of the Trail — Strong Men Dismayed at the Outlook — Trying to Look Cheerful — Learning of the Klondike Discoveries — Taken for a Man — Over the Summit — Ravenous Appetites of the Men — Through the Cañon and the Rapids — A Woman's Experience — Clinging to the Boat in Terror — In the Presence of Death — Quick Decisions of Gold-Seekers — Many Unfit for Work in Alaska — The Situation Facing the Tenderfoot — Where Shall He Find Gold ? — "Did You Take This for a Picnic ? "

ONE of the blessings of the influx of people during the summer and fall of 1897 lay in the opportunity it afforded us of learning what was transpiring in the outside world. Up to the first of July we knew just as much about current events in the United States as the people of the United States knew about the Klondike. There were a few stories which leaked through, nobody knew how. One does not need to go far away from the river to acquire a full measure of that bliss which comes from ignorance. I have heard of a cultivated German, a scientific hermit who has long lived among a colony of Indians in the northern part of Alaska, who did not hear of the Franco-Prussian war until three years ago. It is not strange. It is the best country in the world for a hermit to whom seclusion is the principal thing in life.

It is a great event on the Yukon when the ice really begins to go out. It means that in a few days a little steamer will come puffing up the river. The old " Yukoner," as a usual thing, does not await this event with any impatience for the news of the outside world, but with an eagerness for something to eat. By the first of June he has ceased to look forward with delight to the day when he shall roll in wealth, and has begun to anticipate with mingled emotions the time when he can get a square meal. Having secured that he can afford to be social to new arrivals.

But the ice in the Yukon generally has an exasperating way of moving out. As the river rises some six hundred miles south of the Arctic Circle and flows northwest till it meets that frigid geographical device, and as the mouth of the river usually remains frozen till the first of June or later, the ice in the upper part does little for a month but " mark time." This it does by breaking into cakes which, on account of the dam of solid ice below, slide one over the other, and the force of the swift current and ice above finally results in such pressure that the cakes stand up almost perpendicularly, sometimes ten feet high. The great mass will move along gradually, like people coming out of a crowded theater, and like them will finally get out — all except a few straggling cakes which for some reason were belated. This glacial aspect of the river makes a very pretty sight, but it would be pleasanter to watch when less hungry. The people on the river generally rush to the banks when they hear that the ice has ceased marking time and is really going, and they will stand for hours and watch it, though I know in my case the thought uppermost in mind was something more than that of the piece of moose ham which tasted as if it might have been cured during the late War of the Rebellion.

"Grub" came at last. We rarely spoke of edibles or provisions on the Yukon. It was grub. Being an essential of which we often stand in dire need, a short, crisp, forceful word was required — something which could be pronounced quickly even if the thing itself came slowly and in small lots. Dawson gave itself up to square meals for a time, though the gold excitement was at its height, and soon it began to be visited by new arrivals from over the pass. There were some old acquaintances, of course. Some of the first were those who had been on the Yukon, but had gone out for the winter, and there were some peculiar and interesting incidents, of course, following such a rich season.

James McNamee and Charles M. Lamb had been partners in Alaskan prospecting operations. They had explored several creeks in the far north, but fortune had not smiled upon them, and in the summer of 1896 Lamb decided to return to California and get married. He did so, returning with his wife the next June. When he and his bride stepped from their little boat at Dawson, he was greeted by his partner:

"Lamb, you're worth a fortune. Up in the cabin is thirty-seven thousand dollars, which represents your interest in the amount of money that we have taken out of the claims since you went after a wife."

It was a very happy incident of a honeymoon in the Yukon.

Of course there were always interesting stories of ex-

periences on the trail to be told by the newcomers.   Among
those who arrived about the first of July was Mr. McKay,
one of Alaska's pioneer traders, and his wife.   She said it
was the grandest trip she had ever made in her life.   Still it
had its sad incidents.   One morning about the first of June,
while she was at Lake Lindeman, a Mr. Card, who, with his
wife and child, was making the trip in, and camping at that
place, came to her tent and said that their boy was dead.
They were young people and this was their first child, a
baby of seven months.

" We all showed our sympathy," said Mrs. McKay, " by
helping all we could in their distress.   We made a little
casket of rough wood, padded it with a soft blanket, and
covered it with some black cloth, lining it with white muslin.
I laid the baby in it, and then went to one of my trunks, and
from my best hat took some French violets, which I arranged about the baby, putting some in his little clasped
hand.   We put up a small tent near the bereaved parents,
and there the body lay till the next day, when we buried it.
The little grave was made by tender hands, and a wooden
tablet at the head tells the traveler who lies there.   We also
built a little picket fence to protect the resting-place, and
every one who goes over the trail will see it marking the
close of a brief career."

This gives a little glimpse of the incidents of that hard
trail amid the most wonderful scenery in America, and is a
suggestion of what may happen — of what disheartening
events did happen when the great rush of two months later
was inaugurated.

On June 13th, at Lake Bennett, there was another sad
occurrence.   A man named John Matthews, who, with his
father, had packed his outfit over the mountain passes, ex-

periencing all the slavish drudgery of the task, had at last reached the lakes. He could see the watery way to the goal stretched out before him. The sun was shining. It seemed that all the hardships had been endured, and that the latter part of the journey would be easy, floating down the river, turbulent in places, of course, but the water was to be his servant. He built his boat, loaded it with his outfit, and started. All went well till the boat struck the whirl of the rapids and was swamped. His outfit was at the bottom of the river as ours had been. Where the accident occured, however, the water was shallow and they managed to recover most of the goods, though nearly all of them were spoiled. Matthews and his father went into their tent and were cleaning up their guns. While the latter's back was turned a shot was heard. Blue smoke came curling from the tent flaps, and the distressed father saw his son lying on the ground, his head torn by the accidental discharge of his gun. His troubles were over. A meeting was called and the poor boy was buried there amid the silent and dreary hills.

A woman who arrived early in the summer with her husband and her son told an interesting story of her experiences and impressions, and it gives a true picture of some of the trials of the trail, even before the great rush.

" Our troubles began," she said, " when we reached Dyea. The air rang with noise and confusion. There was no wharf there. The steamship lay at anchor two miles from shore — that is, from low-water mark. Beyond this point up to dry land there was a sea of mud — a dismal stretch of mud flats wide away. Everything had to be taken ashore in small boats and landed in the mud or on the rocks. They had to take out freight as fast as it was landed

CAUGHT ON THE TRAIL

A party of gold-seekers who failed to get over the summit in the fall. Their provisions are cached in the little hut at the right. The party wintered here until spring enabled them to continue their journey.

from the boats and carry it above high tide.   Seventy-five or one hundred men were ashore engaged in this kind of work.   There were a lot of lazy fellows among them, men who wouldn't work, who were born tired, and what on earth they ever came up there for, where there is nothing but the hardest kind of work to do, I can't imagine.   I don't know how they ever expect to reach the Yukon, or what they expect to do when they get here.   The horses and cows had to swim ashore.   It seemed cruel to plunge them into the icy water and compel them to swim such a distance.

"How dismal appeared the outlook!   Our surroundings seemed to mirror our feelings.   The wild coast scenery presented no trace of beauty.   The dreary ocean, the awful mountains piled on mountains, the rock-ribbed shores with their mantle of snow and ice, and the dismal mud flats, all conspired to make us feel blue.   If I had been faint-hearted, I should have felt like giving up then and there. Strong men were dismayed at the outlook.   Many gave up, sold their outfits, and went back.   One steerage passenger offered his outfit for his passage back.   Such pigeon-hearted men — men who haven't the courage to say boo to a goose — are not cut out for miners.   But I just thought to myself, ' I will never say die.'

" Such a time as we had unloading our goods!   A part were put on the tide flats, and the rest on the rocks, nearly five miles from shore.   Some of our packages were washed off the rocks.   Some people lost a lot of things.   One man had two thousand gallons of whisky aboard the ship.   He found many of the kegs floating on the water, also a lot of cigars.   We had to go on shore before they were through unloading.   The goods were not checked off, as they should have been, but were thrown out of the boats into the mud and on the rocks in utter confusion. The men had to work two nights and two days to segregate their freight and to save it from being washed away by the tide. We lost a sack of hardware, three sacks of feed for the horses, and several bales of hay. We also lost one hundred pounds of bacon. However, we fared better than we expected.

" I felt pretty blue, though I tried to look cheerful. I could never have imagined a country to be so desolate, cheerless, and dismal. Nature, sad, melancholy, and woful, seemed even to have stamped her seal upon the Indians and their dogs, which latter, as an accompaniment to the death song of the winds, were incessantly howling. And such lugubrious howls I never heard before. But it just made my heart ache to see how cruelly they were treated. Men seemed to become heartless up there. The environment, perhaps, makes them so.

" Well, we started out in a snow storm, but under foot it was nothing but slush and water and bare ground. We did not arrive a day too soon. We were afraid the summit would be bad, although on account of the elevation the snow might be harder. I felt quite at home in our cosy little tent, and baked bread and cookies in our little sheet-iron 'Yukon stove' for the first time. It was a perfect little jewel. I kept a pot of baked pork and beans on hand all the time, but for the first two days ashore all we had was tea, bacon, and biscuits. We would not have had even that limited fare had I not taken it from home.

" ' Homesick any yet?' asked my husband one evening.

" ' Not I,' I replied, but I had a hard struggle.

" We had not gone far before we met some people coming out and received the first news of the Klondike. Then we were elated beyond measure over the prospect. Every

burden seemed lighter now; every hardship less severe.
Hope lightened up the gloom of our surroundings and
thrilled every nerve with joy. Nothing fatigued us, nothing tired us then. I really felt very glad we had come, and
the tent even became quite pleasant.

"There were five women on the trail going over to the
Yukon, including myself. We all wore men's suits. You
ought to have seen us. One day I was working at the stove
when two men came to the entrance of the tent. One man
said, ' Mister, can you give me a drink of water?' I said,
' Yes, sir,' and handed him a dipper of water. While I was
getting the water the other man made a remark to him not
audible to me. When he took the water he seemed so dis-
concerted that I could not refrain from laughing, and he
said, ' Excuse me, Madam, I thought you were a man.' I
wore a man's mackinaw suit and cap. We had a lot of fun.
They all told me that I looked fine in my man's suit. I
felt like a fish out of water when I first put it on, but soon I
grew accustomed to it and I liked it better than our regular
costume. It seemed so funny when I went down hill or
through wet places, I would instinctively reach around to
hold up my skirts. Then how they laughed.

" I got along very nicely, and was all the time very busy,
and industry, you know, always begets happiness. So I
was both busy and happy. One day I lined the horse
blankets, and every day and every hour and every minute
there was a plenty to do, and how the time flew!

" When we started to move through the cañon I made
up my mind to walk, and did for a short distance, but my
husband insisted on my riding, so they fixed a place for me
on top of several bales of hay on the sled my son was drawing. I did not want to ride on his sled as he was always

letting it tip over, but my husband said he would be more careful if he had me for a passenger. We had two other sleds heavily loaded, and my husband had to stay behind and watch to keep them from capsizing. We had proceeded about four miles when over went the sled, but I jumped off in time, and was not even frightened. Afterward several bales more of hay were added to the load, and we started off with myself perched on top. Presently over it went. My son was admiring the grand mountain scenery at the moment and paying little attention to his sled. I uttered a scream and tumbled over backward, turning a complete somersault. I was so frightened that I had a terrible headache the rest of the day.

" We worked along and finally pitched our tent at Camp Pleasant, with tall cliffs on either side of us lifting their awful forms skyward until they reached the very clouds. The awful, solemn grandeur of that mighty mountain fastness beggars description. The trail to the summit led up the cañon directly in front of our tent. The snow had become so soft that we could not use the horses beyond this point, and we had to haul our goods by hand. We had five men helping us. Until then the horses had been of great assistance. There were tents in every direction about us and no conventionality. Anybody was as good as anybody else. Everybody spoke to everybody and got acquainted.

" At last we got over that terrible summit, but it was not half so bad as I expected to find it. It took me about an hour to climb to the top. I had two staffs to assist me in climbing. The day was so beautiful and the scenery so sublimely grand that I really enjoyed the adventure much. The weather was good all the time, in fact. Then we went into camp to build our boat. I was so glad to take up my

abode at one place, if only for a little while. This thing of
packing up and moving every few days was something terrible. I was sick for nearly two weeks, but managed to do
the cooking for the men.

"Cook? I had to cook all the time. I never saw men
eat so. They would come in wet through and as hungry as
bears. They would want something to eat every time they
came into the tent. The night we camped I promised the
boys some pancakes for supper, and they ate so many it kept
me frying for a long time. I made some syrup of sugar. I
don't make them often. I cooked some evaporated onions,
and they were very nice. We had very good soup also. I
made it from beef extract and put in some evaporated vegetables and a little bread.

"The day we came over from Lindeman, I walked from
the mouth of the cañon. They call it nine miles. My! I
was tired, and I was very lame for several days. It was the
first time I had walked so far. They always insisted on my
riding; but we had sold the horses and I had to walk. I did
not want to sell the horses to the man who bought them.
This man had worked one span of horses to death. I told
him he could not have our poor horses to kill by overwork.
He just laughed. While he was at the tent he heard me
say I wished that we had some tomatoes, and, notwithstanding the fact that I had talked so harshly to him, he sent me
two cans.

"Oh! yes, those turbulent waters terrified and appalled
me. I rode through all those awful torrents that the men
did, and we went through all the rapids excepting White
Horse. Everybody made a portage there. My husband
said these rapids were much worse than last year, and he
deemed it unsafe to go through. The day we crossed Lake

Bennett the wind blew very hard, and the lake was exceedingly rough. How the great waves rolled and tossed our boat about like a feather, though it contained six tons of freight besides ourselves! You can imagine how terrified I was. From Lake Bennett we entered Three Mile River. We had no sooner entered it than our boat got stuck on a sand bar. The men had to get into the cold, icy water, waist deep, to get the boat off. We got stuck on sand bars several times after that. One time we were delayed for three hours.

"Lake Lebarge was terribly rough, and we 'were exceeding tossed with a tempest' for fifteen long miles. I cried nearly all the way. Finally we reached the cañon — that terrible, awful, appalling cañon, a roaring, seething mass of water rushing from both sides and forming a cone in the center. Nearly every one landed above it and looked it over, but we went right through. We got about half way through when a big swell struck the boat, causing the right oarsman to fall just as my husband called for a stroke on that side. The result was that the boat struck the rocks, turned around, and went backward. In trying to turn the boat my husband's oar broke like a pipe stem, and they had to jerk one of the oars out and give it to him. When the boat swung around I surely thought my time had come. I did not scream nor utter an audible sound. They say I clasped my hands together and did bravely. For the moment I was overcome with terror and palsied with fright. I hope I may never experience such feelings of horror again. I felt as if I were in the presence of death, and my thoughts traveled fast. There were dozens of people up on the cliff looking down on us, but no one could have saved us had the boat swamped. We were just three minutes going through.

The distance is three-quarters of a mile. It seemed an age to me. One corner of the boat struck against the wall of rock and was smashed in. The boat was soon repaired and we proceeded on our journey.

"The next bad place was Five-Finger Rapids. We went through to the right, through a passage among the rocks, not much wider than our boat. This is another roaring, seething torrent of water. I was again terribly frightened. Just below Five Fingers is the Rink Rapids. Here we had to keep to the right shore, a wall of rock, just as close as we could to avoid the great boulders over which the water madly plunges in a white, seething foam. The men had to bend to the oars, and they had all they could do to keep our craft off the rocks. Oh, how the water roared! Do you wonder that I was frightened? Thank heaven, it is all over! I would not take the trip again for all the gold in Alaska. But now we're here I'm going to make some gold dust, if I have to run a bakery."

Two things strongly impressed the observer of those who flocked in during the summer rush. First the suddenness with which the decisions to seek fortunes in the gold fields had been made. Hardly a man had decided to come a week before he started, and a number decided, made their preparations, and left all, inside of twenty-four hours, to come to a country where a man must carry with him what he wants for a year. Second, the exceedingly small number of miners there were among them. There were a few, but they could be counted on the fingers, and the rest of them had never even seen a gold pan, much less wielded a pick in the diggings. It was a green crowd, but then, in the Klondike, the tenderfoot flourishes and often makes the strike the practical miner misses. All, to a man, were hopeful, and not one seemed to regret the step, though as the situation gradually dawned upon them, their pensive faces began to tell of the subduing character of their thoughts.

Many were unfit for the work of mining as it has been conducted in Alaska, and a still larger number had no idea of what was required.

The tenderfoot found himself in a city of log houses and tents, facing a situation something like this: He could live at a tavern for about twelve dollars per day or build himself a log house. As, perhaps, he never drove a nail in his life, he had to hire carpenters at fifteen dollars a day, and, as they were not in the country for their health, they made a long job of it unless others are waiting. Finally, with pockets sadly depleted, he moved in.

When this innocent gold-hunter looked about him he found that the only way to get a claim on the Klondike was to buy it, and by that time the cheapest one cost perhaps fifty thousand dollars. He might have five hundred dollars left, perhaps but one hundred dollars, possibly little or nothing. The plentiful gold he had been hearing about, if above ground at all, belonged to some one else and was guarded. If he wanted nuggets he must find them for himself. Where? The old settler would point vaguely to the frozen hills and say:

" Go along and find a creek. Everything is taken up for fifty miles around, but you may get something further away. ' What shall you do when you find it? ' First, pay the government location tax. Then just move a hundred tons of ice to one side. Below that you will find something like twenty feet of frozen mud. Just thaw it and toss it out. Near bed-rock you will see gravel. Perhaps there will be gold in it, and perhaps not. That's a chance you take. Just pile the gravel up and in the spring you can wash it out. You can't do so before, because all the water will be ice. ' What if there is no gold in it, or not enough to pay?' Oh, then you won't be any worse off than hundreds of others. You can hire out to other people, perhaps, and work around till another freeze comes, which won't be very long. What's that? You say your provisions won't outlast another winter? Why, man! why didn't you bring more, then? Did you take this for a picnic? These are the frozen facts, young man, about gold-hunting here. If they are not sufficiently frozen, you will be if you disregard them when the mercury gets well on the downward path to sixty degrees below."

It is easy to see what a deplorable condition a man is in when he faces the necessity of work like this with an insufficient supply of provisions. A mine-owner, no matter how rich he may be in gold, has no food except such as he has laid aside for himself, if he has had the foresight or the fortune to do so, and only those men can be of use to him who have the provisions. To endure work of this kind successfully, one needs plenty of substantial food.

CHAPTER XXV

THE OPPORTUNITIES FOR MONEY–MAKING IN ALASKA —
THE COSTLY EXPERIENCE OF TWO TENDERFEET —
APPALLING PRICE OF A SUPPER — A HORSE MISSING
WITH $49,000 IN GOLD.

A City Laid out on a Bog — Natural Floral Displays — Lousetown —
A Cold Place in Winter — Fabulous Rise in the Price of Building
Lots — Expense of Log Cabins — Making Money Quickly — Expe-
rience of a Cigar Drummer — Clearing $20,000 in Twenty Days in
Real Estate Options — Better than Mining — Spring Water at Twen-
ty-five cents a Pail — Money Brought in by New Comers — Bonanza
Kings and Millionaires — Alec McDonald and His Investments —
"Satin Bags," the Italian Bonanza King — Indulging in a Square
Meal at a Dawson Restaurant — "Your Bill is $52" — How it was
Itemized — Pack Horses with Gold Dust — One of the Horses
Missing — An Exciting Mystery — A Vision of Highway Robbers —
The Lost Horse Returns Safely — Just Stopped to Graze — Found
Dead with $30,000 — The Strain of Too Hard Work.

D AWSON is laid out with the most approved mathematical precision on a bog. It is rectangular in
shape, the streets are sixty-five feet wide, and, in
summer, about a foot deep in mud. At the bottom is the
everlasting frost, hard as adamant. As people who have
become accustomed to the country are used to wading, little
thought is given to this inconvenience, and the summer season, if unpleasant underfoot, has some delights, at least,
overhead and about the hills. The flowers carpet the hillsides, run riot in the valleys, and everywhere clothe the
country in glowing beauty. The soft purple haze as seen

(354)

from Dawson on the neighboring hills seems almost like a mist, but it is only an embankment of wild heliotrope. Wild roses, beautiful and fragrant, wild poppies, and scores of delicate small blossoms vary the color. In winter the streets are more agreeable in their mantle of snow, which covers everything. But the hills are dreary then, very dreary.

Dawson is situated on the northeast side of the Yukon, forty miles in a direct line from the Alaska boundary, and twice that distance from where the river crosses the line. The Klondike River comes down on the east side and cuts the town site in two. That portion of the town on the south side of where the Klondike joins the Yukon is called " Lousetown," and, in fact, was the original site used in years past as an available camping point, and occasionally roving bands of Indians stopped there. At present, a store and two or three saloons comprise the business portion of the place. Some forty or fifty tents house two hundred or three hundred people, and the mountain trail to the mines leads past this place. The ground is much higher and dryer than on the north side, but owing to the proximity of the mountain the site is not large enough for much of a town.

On the north side of Dawson proper the mountains open out and curve around a low marshy piece of land of about one hundred acres. There is hardly a spot on the town site where the moss and earth cannot be cleared away to a depth of twelve or fifteen inches and a cake of frozen ground or ice be found. There would seem to be no question as to the locality being unhealthy and subject to malarial ailments. In other than warm months a strong wind usually blows up the Yukon from the north, except when the weather is colder than fifty degrees below zero, and then a dead calm usually prevails.   Dawson is situated on a bend of the river so as to receive the full benefit of the chilling blasts.   Back on the gulches where the mines are located, the weather is considerably more moderate and there is less wind.   The Yukon in front of Dawson is one-third of a mile wide and the addition of the Klondike waters forms a large eddy directly in front of the town, and into it the drainage and sewage of the city empties.   Consequently, the water is impregnated with foreign elements and has occasioned much sickness to those using it.   At the lower end of the town near the foot of the mountain is a fine spring of good water which an enterprising man has monopolized, and water-carriers earn as high as forty dollars a day in carrying water. A charge of twenty-five cents a bucket is generally exacted.

As the demand for building lots grew and the evidences of the unsanitary condition of the soil became more apparent, people began to pitch their tents and to build cabins on the hillside.   Such locations are some distance away from the business center, but none too far for such as desire to live quietly.   The view from these hill residences, overlooking Dawson and the river, is fine and in time it will become, doubtless, a coveted residential quarter.

September 1, 1896, Dawson City consisted of two log cabins, one small warehouse, a sawmill, and a few tents, with a population of about twenty-five men and one woman. Joe Ladue, the founder, was then selling his best lots at from five dollars to twenty dollars each, and the prices were considered none too low.   These same lots in July, 1897, were selling at from eight hundred dollars to eight thousand dollars each, and with every prospect of going still higher.

In July, Dawson's population had grown to five thousand, and every day people were pouring in.   Log cabins, sixteen by eighteen feet, were renting from forty dollars to seventy-five dollars per month, and few were to be had at these prices. On every hand cabins and tents were being set up. It cost a small fortune to build cabins at Dawson. One of average size costs in the neighborhood of one thousand dollars. Building timber is scarce in the neighborhood of the town, logs being brought down the Yukon from ten to fifteen miles.

Never before, I believe, was there such a place to make money quickly as in Dawson in 1897; those who took fortune at its tide saw the money fairly roll up in their hands. Naturally, there were the usual number who seemed to fail to seize the right opportunity, and so worked along making but little. But the opportunities were there for those who had the business shrewdness to see them. A single example will illustrate. Early in the spring a cigar agent or drummer from Harrisburg, Pa., found himself at Dyea when the first news of the Klondike came over the passes. He quit his job, sent word to his firm that he was going to the Klondike, took what cigars he had, and set out; arrived before the great influx began, and quickly sold his ten-cent cigars for one dollar and fifty cents each. He was only twenty-two years of age, but a born business man; he was all business. He paid no attention to the mines; indeed, he said he didn't care whether he ever saw one or not. There was money to be made easier right in Dawson. The speculation in town lots was daily becoming livelier, and he knew that it would be livelier still when the people began to arrive, so he took written sixty-day options on a dozen lots, paid five hundred dollars down, and in less than twenty days sold out and made twenty thousand dollars cash.

" That's better than thawing out frozen muck for gold,"

he said. " These mines in Dawson can be worked winter and summer."

Then he took options on more lots at greatly advanced prices, for by that time we had heard at Dawson of the excitement in the States over the new discovery, and we knew that soon an army of gold-seekers would be pouring in. When the people came, he made several thousands more. But his business activity was by no means confined to this form of speculation. Observing the poor quality and taste of the water from the Yukon, he preëmpted the springs back on the hill for a comparatively small sum, and soon had a lot of Indians peddling this at twenty-five cents a pail. He hired a few women and went into the bread business.

Money, that is, gold dust, was flying about in all directions, and he just put his business instincts to work to catch what he could of it. By the end of the year he had two hundred pounds of gold ready for shipment to the States when the river opened, and altogether he was probably worth one hundred thousand dollars, all made in six months without going near a gold mine. He had every prospect of doubling it in the next six months, for in the summer season there will be no limit to the demand for his spring water at twenty-five cents a pail. He had a fund of Irish wit and was very popular. The last I heard he was proposing to open a bank, and the chances were that he would in two years have more gold than two-thirds of those toiling in the rich pockets far away on the creeks.

Enterprising men who started business ventures of this kind naturally stood in the way to secure not simply some of the gold that came out of the mines, but much of the money which was brought in by newcomers. The latter fund was greater than one might suppose. While some came in with little money, the majority had realized the advantages of bringing all they could, and it seems safe to say that at least two millions were brought in during 1897. Much of this went for town lots and cabins. Those who brought in large supplies of provisions were tempted by the fancy prices they commanded to sell out all they could afford to, sometimes making enough to enable them to secure valuable claims or interests.

Naturally, the wonderful riches developed in the spring's clean-up resulted in a sudden creation of bonanza kings and millionaires who threw their dust around with lavish hands. Alex. McDonald was conceded to be the richest, at least in claims. Before the summer was over he owned interests in twenty-eight claims, and he kept buying as fast as he could take the money out of the ground to pay for them; indeed, faster.

"I have invested my whole fortune," he said, "and have run in debt one hundred and fifty thousand dollars besides, but I can dig out the one hundred and fifty thousand dollars any time I need it."

From his general appearance and demeanor one would not suppose that he had owned mines which had made him rich beyond the dreams of avarice, and all in a single year. He is a quiet, unassuming man, and takes his good fortune philosophically. He walks about in his rough miner's clothes, and is cordial, in his way, to everybody, for no one is better than anybody else in Dawson. Lippy and Berry were reckoned as second and third in riches, but when strikes were being made every day there was always an uncertainty as to who could really count up the most wealth. An Italian named Antonia, owning some claims on Eldorado, gave many evidences of being one of the most conspicuous bonanza kings. It was said that he had given a written agreement to pay his housekeeper five hundred dollars a week, and he actually " cleaned the town " out of silks and satins, so that he obtained the local soubriquet of " Satin Bags." But he could evidently afford to indulge his tastes, for all he had to do was to dig up the gold when he wanted it.

Tastes were, however, a very expensive thing to indulge in Dawson, and some of the newcomers were slow in appreciating it. The little experience of two young men from the Pacific coast will illustrate the difficulty which some had in accommodating themselves at once to the condition of affairs. They arrived one evening after a rather quick and fortunate voyage down the river. Congratulating themselves on their good luck and having tired of camp cooking, one proposed going to the restaurant and having a good supper. The proposition was accepted, and, entering the first restaurant which had white tablecloths and napkins, they ordered a full course and a small bottle of wine. The menu consisted of eastern oysters, roast duck, moose steaks, and the usual assortment of side dishes. There is no doubt but that they greatly enjoyed the supper, particularly after having lived on bacon, flapjacks, and black coffee for a month. Arising and going to the counter, one of them threw down a twenty-dollar gold piece, and taking a toothpick, said:

" Take out for two."

" You'll have to come again," said the proprietor.

" Oh, isn't that enough; well, here's another twenty; you will have to excuse me, as we've just arrived and are not yet familiar with frontier prices."

" That's not enough yet, my friend. Your bill is fifty-two dollars."

"WHITE PASS HOTEL" ON THE SKAGWAY TRAIL

Contrast size of the sign with that of the "Hotel." The latter consists of only a small log hut.

" W-h-a-t, you don't mean to say you're going to charge us f-i-f-t-y-t-w-o d-o-l-l-a-r-s for our supper? Why, in Tacoma it wouldn't cost over seven or eight dollars."

"Yes, but you're not in Tacoma, and besides, fifty-two dollars is what it'd cost you in any other restaurant in Dawson."

" Will you please make out a statement of the expense?" meekly asked the young gold-hunter, as he and his partner emptied their purses and between them could only produce forty-eight dollars and sixty-five cents. The restaurant-keeper made out a slip, which read:

1 can Eastern oysters for two,	$15.00
1 roast duck for two,	4.00
2 porterhouse moose steaks,	3.00
1 pint bottle of champagne,	30.00
Total,	$52.00

Observing the depressed condition of their finances, and tenderly appreciating their embarrassed condition in the presence of a dozen miners who were amused at the predicament of the newcomers, the restaurant-keeper said:

" Oh, never mind, boys, that's near enough. Here, keep this odd change; we've no use for it up here," and he handed them back one dollar and fifteen cents in dimes and nickels.

The next morning they were observed in their tent as they were getting ready for breakfast. The meal consisted of fried bacon, beans, pancakes, and coffee. Their countenances bore a serious expression, and after a few preliminary remarks incidental to the character of the country and chilly condition of the weather, a visitor remarked that most of the new arrivals preferred to board a few days at the restaurants after having been subjected to a bacon and black coffee diet for a month.

" It's different with us," said one, with a sickly attempt to smile and a sly glance at his comrade.   " We took supper at a restaurant last night and the bill was over fifty dollars, and it broke the two of us to pay it."

The sight of gold dust had become an old story to the people who had wintered at Dawson, but it was a revelation which nearly drove the newcomers frantic with impatience to acquire some of their own.   Nearly every day a little train of pack horses would come in from the mines having on their backs those precious bags which were more of a load than they seemed.

One day in the early part of September a party with seven pack horses loaded with gold came into town from Eldorado.   The gold was in sacks of one hundred and fifty to two hundred pounds, and, of course, the arrival was one of the events of the day in a far-away shut-off town where everything of that character is an object of interest.   When the party brought in their horses ready to have the gold weighed, the leaders of the train were struck with surprise and consternation.

One of the horses was missing!

They had started with eight, and upon investigation they found that one loaded with one hundred and eighty pounds of gold, valued at about forty-nine thousand dollars, was not with the others.   It was a mystery which no one could explain.   No one had seen the animal when it dropped out.   They had worked their way over the rough trail, and supposed that the horses were keeping in line all the way. The minutes of consternation grew into hours, and then into days.

No time was lost in getting back over the trail, making inquiries all along the route if a stray horse with one hundred and eighty pounds of gold on his back had been seen. The hunt lasted all night, and the next day, and the night following, and no trace of the animal could be found.

The matter ceased to be humorous and assumed a serious aspect. A vision of highway robbers began to haunt the honest miners who were sending in their gold. The police were called into requisition, but not the faintest clue could they get as to the whereabouts of either the animal or the gold, though the most diligent search was made in all directions.

The news spread from camp to camp, and the miners began to be of the opinion that a bold highway robbery had been committed somehow. The searchers were puzzled because the animal wore a clear-toned bell which could be heard for some distance, and, though they strained their ears to catch the faintest suggestion of the tinkling of that bell through the wild country of that trail, not a tinkle could they hear. Horse, bell, and forty-nine thousand dollars of gold belonging to the Berry brothers seemed to have dropped completely out of existence.

Towards the end of the second day, when the affair was assuming an alarming aspect, the lost horse came jogging along over the top of the mountain and down into town, jingling the bell as though nothing had happened, and with the sack of gold still securely strapped on his back!

The horse had strayed from the train during the darkness and had wandered off into a meadow to graze. This he had done while carrying about his precious burden, and when content he had slowly made his way towards the town.

The prevailing ideas as to distance in Alaska and the difficulties of moving small distances sometimes are very inadequate. For example, some seem to think that a man can step out of a dance hall or saloon and in a few moments be on his claim; or if he is on his claim and wishes to drop into a store, he can throw down his pick and step over. But these mines extend for a hundred miles around Dawson in a region almost inaccessible in places. It costs twenty-five cents a pound to have things packed from Dawson up to some of the mines. This makes a sack of flour that cost twelve dollars at Dawson worth nearer thirty-five dollars at camps up the stream.

About the first thing the new arrivals of the summer and fall did was to start for " the gulch," a term which was used to designate the diggings on Bonanza and Eldorado creeks and their tributaries. Whether they were experienced miners or not they generally had their eyes opened to the resources of the creeks and to the curious mode of mining. By that time the gulch was almost a city in itself, there being more people there than in Dawson, and the center of the population and the meeting-place was at the junction of Eldorado and Bonanza. Here, gradually, a new city, with all its accessories, was springing up, which threatened to rival Dawson itself. It was the center of industrial activity, and it tended to keep the miners away from Dawson. The miners gave it the name of Eldorado City.

Both Protestants and Catholics early established mission churches at Dawson and did good work under the greatest difficulties. Rev. V. C. Gambell and wife started the first church, the Presbyterian mission, but they had many discouragements. They rented the first floor of a log cabin and held Sunday services there which were fairly well attended, though some of your city ministers would have winced at the surroundings. The top floor of the building was used as a lodging house, and the missionaries had hardly become settled when a drunken lodger upstairs overturned a candle and the building was burned to the ground. Nothing was saved, and the outfits of ten men were destroyed. Fire from a similar cause broke out on Thanksgiving evening and destroyed the opera house and two saloons. Only the snow on the roofs saved the rest of the buildings on the street.

The sanitary condition of the place was better than could have been expected from its situation. Many of the instances of sickness and death were more or less traceable to carelessness, neglect, overwork, and excitement, the relaxation of the mental and physical strain being too much for some to endure. Some men had lived on barely nothing, and that half-cooked. The excitement of washing and accumulating the gold was so great that many men devoted their entire time to it when they should have devoted some to cooking, cleanliness, and rest. One man, after he had washed out thirty thousand dollars of gold, began to have the idea that he was going to be robbed. The mental strain was too great for him, for he was found one morning dead in his tent with his thirty thousand dollars under his head.

In the early fall symptoms of typhoid began to manifest themselves and there were several cases in the hospital. There had been a continual dread of this disease on account of the filthy condition of the streets of the town, but during the summer the general health appeared to be good. It takes a little time, however, for the germs to work in the system, and in the fall months those who had become enfeebled by hardships or improper food began to show the effects.

Two brothers, Robert and Charles Carlson, rich owners of claims on Bonanza Creek, succumbed to the disease in July. They had just sold their claims for fifty thousand dollars and were preparing to leave the country for the winter, when they were stricken down. They had been among the fortunate ones who arrived early when Bonanza was discovered. They worked hard during the winter to prepare for the spring sluicing. Success attended their efforts, but, weakened by them, they fell an easy prey.

Dawson has been growing right along during the past winter. An occasional dip of the mercury to forty-five degrees or fifty degrees below zero has had no effect on the building operations there. All winter long Front street — practically the only one in Dawson — has resounded with the sound of chopping and hammering on new houses and stores. Some of the more recent building improvements of the town comprise about one hundred and fifteen log cabins, three log churches — Catholic, Episcopal, and Methodist — and six hundred tents, that had been boarded up about the bottom to make them more agreeable to the occupants. The business part of the town consists of log and rough pine board buildings arranged in a straight line and close beside one another. In these structures are fifteen saloons, two barber shops, several butcher shops, and half a dozen restaurants, two real estate offices, and one hardware store.

The largest buildings in that region are two substantial storehouses built by the Alaska Commercial Company and the North American Transportation Company. Each is two stories high, and covers about eight thousand square feet. To show how it costs to build up there, I have only to say that one of these storehouses, with a good concrete foundation, cost exactly ninety-three thousand five hundred dollars in September, 1897. The same structure could be built in the Middle States for about four thousand dollars, and on the Pacific coast for four thousand five hundred dollars. Log cabins twenty by twenty-four feet now cost from three thousand dollars to four thousand five hundred dollars. The logs are hewn on three sides and the chinks are plugged with mud and moss. The roofs are constructed of three layers of pine boards, upon which moss and earth are packed to the depth of a foot.

Some of the recent quotations at Dawson will give a fair idea of the ratio of demand to supply: Pine logs, two dollars and fifty cents and three dollars each; window glass, fifty cents a pound; tenpenny nails, sixty cents a pound; meat, seventy-five cents a pound. Carpenters who can do fairly good work get eighteen to twenty dollars a day; common laborers get three-quarters of an ounce of gold a day — about twelve dollars.

CHAPTER XXVI

DAWSON AND ITS INIQUITIES — GAMBLING PLACES, THEIR DEVICES AND THEIR WAYS — NIGHT SCENES IN THE DANCE HALLS — REAL LIFE IN NEW MINING CAMPS.

Saloons and Gambling the Natural Products of New Mining Camps — Strange Sights and Sounds — Gold Dust as Free as Water — Saloons and Their "Brace Games" — Who Pay the Fiddlers — Expensive Society — "Stud-Horse Poker" and High Stakes — Methods at the Faro Table — Gold Bags in Pigeon Holes — Settling Up — "Shorty's" Fatal Forgetfulness — Few Instances of Shooting Now — Ruling Prices in Saloons — The "Rake Off" — When "Swiftwater Bill" Breaks Loose — Losing $7,500 in an Hour — Appearance of Gambling Places — The Dance Halls and the Women — Gallant Partners in Spiked Boots — An Occasional Free Fight — Tobacco-Laden Atmosphere — Tired and Dishevelled Women — More Orderly than Mining Camps in the Rockies — Not a Hard, Reckless, Wide-Open Town — Harvard, Yale, and Vassar Graduates.

I N the matter of iniquity, such as prevails in mushroom towns in mining districts, Dawson was not slow in eclipsing all rivals on the Yukon. Never before had such a crowd of people poured into the Yukon valley, and a rough floating element, which had quickly perceived the possibilities of operation in a place over which everybody on the Pacific coast was going wild, were soon plying their occupations in the city. Still, there were no scenes of disorder, or what are reckoned as such in a place like this. Saloons and gambling were the natural products of such

(370)

a population in a far away mining camp, and no mining camp was ever so far away as these on the Yukon. Circle City had emptied itself, and so had Forty Mile. In those once thriving places the saloons were deserted and the dance halls silent.

Early in the first season, or soon after the discovery, one of the Circle City dance hall proprietors had come up the river, got together enough logs for the sides and ends of a house, put a tent roof over it, and then on one of the boats came the first piano in Dawson and a lot of girls. A dance house was in immediate operation. Others followed quickly, and in the summer of 1897 it was the liveliest town imaginable, a city of many strange sights and sounds. With the sound of the hammer and the axe mingled the howling of the dogs, the squeaking of the violin, the jingling notes of the piano, and the harsh voice of the prompter — "balance all," "ladies' change," "swing yer pards." During the summer, when it was light all the time, the public resorts were wide open every hour in the day. The saloons never closed, and gambling went on without cessation.

Many queer incidents occurred, showing how cheaply the gold dust was esteemed by some of the miners. One boy, who had been working hard all day on his claim, said, when he had finished:

"Now, I'll just pan out one pan for the boys."

As a result he came to town, entered one of the saloons, treated everybody there several times, lost thirteen dollars at faro, and still had thirty dollars left.

Every saloon was, of course, provided with a number of gambling devices, and it was perfectly natural to suppose that they were of that character called "brace games," that is, so arranged as to make it extremely difficult for an out-

sider to win a dollar.   Even faro boxes and cases worked
double, and the dealer generally knew what to do when it
was necessary to make a certain card win.   He who sat
down to a promiscuous poker table was either reckless or
ignorant.   Of course, these things were intended to catch
the tenderfoot, or the old miner who had come in from a
season of hardship and had consoled himself with about the
worst stuff that ever went by the name of whisky.   The professional gamblers reaped the harvest, and the tenderfeet
and the hardworking miners paid the fiddlers.   But gold
was cheap.   Miners did not hesitate a minute to drop it for
a little fun.   And they seldom grumbled at the cost.

It was difficult for an economical man to get around " in
society " for less than fifty dollars a day.   I heard of people
who spent five hundred dollars a day just in killing time
while waiting for the steamer to go out with their gold.
The games were exceedingly stiff, and it was not an uncommon thing to see a miner throw down his sack and bet from
a hundred up on the highest card.   " Stud-horse poker "
was the popular game, and it would often cost from fifty
dollars up to draw a card.

A gambler, winning or losing from five hundred dollars
to three thousand dollars at a single sitting, was not worthy
of passing comment.   In fact, games involving five thousand dollars or ten thousand dollars were running night and
day.   Professional dealers of " banking games " received
twenty dollars a day.

The manner of hazarding money is unique even in a
mining camp.   The player takes his seat at a faro table,
passes over his sack of gold dust to the dealer, who drops it
into a small pigeon-hole.   The chance of " overplaying his
sack " devolves upon the player's honor.   He is given full

credit and can call for as many chips from the check rack as he desires.   As the checks are passed out a tab is dropped on his sack.   At the conclusion of the play the chips on hand are credited to the account of the sack.   The dealer hands the player a slip of paper showing the condition of the account, and the latter takes it and his sack of gold to the bar.   If he has lost he weighs out his gold dust, or, in the event of winning, the barkeeper does the paying.   At first glance it would seem that such a system would afford considerable temptation for dishonest men to walk out with their sack of gold without settling their accounts.   Only one or two instances of the kind have occurred and the condemnation of the community has inflicted such punishment as to warrant the non-repetition of the offence.

About four o'clock one morning a miner known as " Shorty " left his seat at the table where he had been playing all night, saying that he had gone broke.   The dealer handed him his bag of dust and his slips, the latter corresponding almost to a grain with the value of the gold. " Shorty " walked over to the bar and invited a couple of other miners to have a drink.   Then he was seized with a fatal fit of forgetfulness.

He edged toward the door and was about to push it open when the bartender called to him: " Say, Shorty, haven't you forgot something? "

The door swung out.   When it rebounded it stopped half way, and a draught of icy air came in.   There had been a sudden flash of flame, a ringing report in that low-ceiled, smoke-darkened room, and the door as it swung inward was obstructed by the body of a dying man. " Shorty " was buried the next day.   But this was in the early days of Dawson.   It was not long before it became an offense to carry firearms about and a better order was enforced.   Dawson, for such a lively and mixed settlement, has afforded few instances of " shooting."

Saloons, of course, were " wide open " and did not pay a license.   As a rule they sold a fair class of beverages. Drinks and cigars retailed, as at Circle City, at fifty cents, and the two breweries that are located near by could not supply the demand for beer at one hundred and twenty-five dollars a keg.   A poor quality of champagne was retailed at thirty dollars a pint, and a better quality at ten dollars higher.   As at Circle City, in liquidating indebtedness at the bar, the individual doing the honors passed his sack over to the barkeeper, who poured out enough gold dust to settle the account.   It is unnecessary to add that the barkeepers were never charged with neglecting to take enough dust, and particularly when the patrons are somewhat under the influence of copious libations.   Saloon men admitted privately that the " rake-off," as they term overweighing, amounts to about thirty or forty cents on each two dollars and fifty cents spent over the bar.   The receipts for sixty days last summer in one saloon amounted to one hundred and twenty-four thousand five hundred dollars, and the day the successful miners were taking their departure on the first steamer of the season the receipts amounted to six thousand five hundred dollars.   Hardly a saloon in town was receiving less than three hundred dollars a day, besides winning large sums of money at the gambling games.   Barkeepers were paid from twelve dollars and fifty cents to twenty dollars a day, and even the porters, where such luxuries were deemed necessary, were paid from seven dollars and fifty cents to ten dollars.

" Swiftwater Bill " owned some of the richest claims on

Eldorado Creek, and when he broke loose the dust was sure to fly. Bill took a seat at the faro table one night, and in just one hour he had lost seven thousand five hundred dollars in gold nuggets.

" Things don't seem to be coming my way to-night," he remarked as he rose from his seat and stretched himself. " Let the house have a drink at my expense."

There was a rush for the bar, and waiters carried drinks to the various tables where games were in progress. That round cost Bill one hundred and twelve dollars. Then he lighted a dollar and a half cigar and strolled out.

The gambling saloons, in external appearance, are very much like all the other buildings in Dawson, except that they are larger. They are built of logs hewn on three sides and solidly chinked with heavy moss. The roofs are made of poles, on which a layer of moss fully ten inches thick is laid, and then a layer of dirt about twelve inches deep serves to keep out the cold. Heavy embankments of earth piled up against the huts on the outside serve as additional protection against the chilling blasts of the Arctic winter gales. A few saloons are built of lumber, with double walls, between which sawdust and moss are tightly packed, but old Yukoners are of the opinion that buildings so constructed are inadequate against the severe cold weather.

Dance halls are constructed in the same manner and are generally the largest buildings in town, except the storehouses. They are opened at about seven or eight o'clock in the evening, and the band plays on till late in the morning. The amusement continues night after night. The halls are crowded with gallant beaux, the most of them having heavy spiked-bottom shoes, broad-brimmed hats, costumed in the regulation mining suits, and, with cigars between their

teeth, they present an odd appearance. They sit around
the hall on the benches, smoking and talking and immensely
enjoying the relaxation from the hard monotony of the
mines. Each dance costs one dollar, and I have heard of
one man in three nights spending seven ounces of gold, or
one hundred and nineteen dollars, for the luxury. In some
of the halls a free fight sometimes concludes the festivities
along toward morning. Occasionally, men will come to
blows in attempting to win the hand of some woman for the
succeeding dance. " Fair play " is the watchword, and the
best skilled pugilistic gladiator goes to the head of the set
and his rival goes home.

Even if one is not a dancer and has rather strict ideas of
what proper female society should be, he will miss a good
deal of fun if, when he goes to town from his dreary camp,
he does not look in and watch the miners enjoying a little
relaxation. One scene is much like another. You enter a
large building with a smooth floor sometimes overlaid with
heavy drill. You could almost cut the tobacco-laden atmosphere with a knife. Through the blue haze the figures of a
couple of musicians can be faintly distinguished, fiddling
away for dear life, and calling out, " Sashay all! " " Ladies'
through! " as the occasion demands. They receive twenty
dollars a night or more for doing this, and they earn every
penny of it.

At one side, extending the entire length of the room,
is the bar, and the three dispensers of drinks are kept quite
as busy as the fiddlers. Beer, whisky, and cigars are retailed
at fifty cents. A poor quality of champagne sells for thirty
dollars a pint, and a somewhat better brand brought forty
dollars.

Of course, the men greatly outnumber the women.

There are probably a dozen of the latter, some of them young and quite pretty. They have little or no time to rest between the dances, and when the morning sun peeps over the eastern mountains he finds them a tired and somewhat dishevelled lot. But some of the belles of the " dancing set " have been known to make as much as a hundred dollars a night tripping the light fantastic toe for the delight of miners at once lavish and well-stocked with dust.

But while the money that is spent in saloons and dance halls, and the money that is lost continually over the various gambling devices, may seem to be enormous, it must be remembered that these hardworking miners in their dreary camps become at times fairly desperate for a little relaxation from the severe hardships of their existence. If they are lucky, gold dust becomes to them a cheap commodity. It means very little to them when at any time they can dig out all they want. Making all allowances for men of bad character, certain to drift into such places, my observations convince me that Dawson is now a less vicious and more orderly place than the new mining camps of the Rockies were. The severity of life on the Yukon has kept out many desperate characters, and the Klondike has now been largely filled up with people who, while they may not have been experts in mining, have a taste for an orderly life, and are too solicitous to make their fortunes and leave the country to squander money recklessly.

The population of Dawson and the camps that line the creeks that twist away south, east, and southeast from the Klondike and Yukon is as intelligent as any I have ever known in any mining camp in the West. Indeed, it is the most moral and ambitious mining population I have ever seen. A number of old professional miners are up there, who have seen the gilded gambling palaces of Virginia City, and have lived in the hot days of Bodie, Tombstone, Anaconda, and Creede, and they have remarked many times that the miners of the Klondike are another race of men from those they used to know in the States. To be sure, there is gambling and liberal drinking of the hardest of hard whisky, but they say the scenes are never comparable with what they used to witness every night when the Bonanzas were pouring out their golden wealth and Tombstone was making a dozen new millionaires.

The present Klondike miners are not the typical, picturesque miners the world has been hearing about for half a century. It is my private opinion that the awful hardships one endures to get rich up there, the dangers that must be braved, and the privations suffered in getting to the new gold fields by any route, make men there sober and provident. Where men have these characteristics they take fewer chances in gambling. Then, too, the expense of getting to Klondike and the necessary expenditure of several hundred dollars for an outfit keep out of the Alaskan mining region a horde of hard-up, desperate characters similar to those that have made all the western mining camps so notoriously bad. I doubt if Dawson ever will be a hard, reckless, wide-open town in the sense that Virginia City and Cripple Creek have been. It has had during the winter of 1897-98 a population of about two thousand men and one hundred and twenty women, with about four thousand five hundred more miners in the cabins along the creeks, and there have been few more orderly and earnest communities anywhere in the Union. I never knew so many well-educated, thoughtful, and promising men in any camp as there are at Dawson to-day. Some are Harvard and

A Mid-winter Camp at the Mouth of Skagway Cañon

Tents afford the only shelter from heavy snows and bitter cold of an Arctic winter.

Yale graduates. Two young women, wives of ambitious young miners, are from Vassar College, and a physician, who lives there in a log cabin, plastered with mud, was educated at Columbia College and at the University of Paris. I think he is contented. Anyhow, he ought to be for a year or two. He gets half an ounce of gold for each visit, and for simple surgical work his bill runs into ounces of gold very quickly. It seems to me that he ought to clear up two or three pounds of gold every week in the year.

The wealth is earned by such hard work and exposure that the better class of miners do not like to throw their earnings over the bar with the recklessness that characterized the miners in the flash mining days of the West. Moreover, one may readily see that a climate where the wind blows and moans twenty hours out of every twenty-four, and where the mercury fluctuates between two degrees above zero and forty below for five months in the year, is not conducive to conviviality and hilarity as the warm, balmy climate of Tombstone and Virginia City were.

CHAPTER XXVII

A REFUGE FOR CRIMINALS — THE MINES MORE PROFITA-
BLE THAN SPORTING DEVICES — PURSUING A FUGI-
TIVE — A CHASE OF 25,000 MILES FOR AN ESCAPED
MURDERER.

IT was natural, and to be expected, that the Klondike
should prove a tempting refuge for those who had
some penalty to escape in the States. It is in the
Northwest Territory, and so criminals escaping from the
officers of the law in the United States must be extradited.
Moreover, it is so far removed that it seems impossible for
the law to reach them after they arrive at Dawson, where
there is no thought given to the antecedents of the inhabitants or of those who enter too rapidly to be observed.
Besides all this, Dawson and the mines offer opportunities
for making money which have attracted thousands who had
nothing to run from. Many sporting men and gamblers
hastened to the new field, but the supply of gambling de-

vices rather exceeded the demand, and in time these men found more commendable means of earning a livelihood.

The truth is that the richness of the mines has attracted even men of a sporting turn into paths of industry. Several well-known Pacific coast sporting men have to a certain extent abandoned the green cloth and taken up the profession of mining. Nearly all those who cling to the gambling profession have acquired claims and have been hiring men to work them. Frank P. Slavin as a mining man is realizing more dollars than he ever did in the prize-ring. He is one of the best workers in the country, and by hard rustling has acquired interests in twelve or fifteen placer claims and one quartz lode. A Portland, Ore., sport, who has the reputation of "never having turned a crooked card," has retired from the green cloth, donned a miner's suit, and with pick and shovel is digging gold out of claim 62 below on Hunker Creek. Another Seattle sport is now the owner of four promising claims which are being worked this winter. There is hardly a sporting man in the Klondike who does not own valuable mines. Late in the autumn of 1897, between forty and sixty sports arrived without provisions, and they were compelled to pass on down the river to Fort Yukon to spend the winter.

Those who came to Dawson to escape the penalty of crime found that they were not entirely safe. One of the most notable cases occurring in the summer of 1897 was that of the arrest of Frank Novak, after a chase which reads like a romance, full enough of adventure, danger, and hardship to satisfy the most morbid novel reader.

Frank Alfred Novak, familiarly known as Frank Novak among his acquaintances, was, in 1896, conducting a mercantile and banking business at the little town of Walford,

in Benton county, Ia.   He had for his partners in business
a widowed sister and a brother-in-law, and to the outside
world was apparently doing a prosperous mercantile business, besides a sort of accommodation and loan business in
the way of a private bank, where the farmers and residents
of the town did their banking transactions.   The apparent
prosperity of the firm was, however, purely superficial, as
Novak had contracted a gambling mania and was quietly
but surely robbing the firm of its assets by playing the grain
market in Chicago.   In three or four years he had squandered his own substance, and robbed his immediate relatives
and friends of more than twenty thousand dollars, which
had been entrusted to him as business manager in the store
and banker for the village.   The day of reckoning was fast
approaching, and Novak, realizing that the denouement
would blast the confident hopes of those about him, proceeded to take out thirty thousand dollars of life and accident insurance, and then deliberately set about to procure a
victim to be used in his own stead as a cremated corpse upon
which his beneficiaries could draw the insurance.   He also
had the stock of goods and the store building in which he
was doing business insured for about their full value, and
took into his confidence a near relative, who was designed to
collect the insurance after the disappearance of Frank
Novak.

A pretext of danger to the stock of goods through expected burglars or incendiaries was invented, and Novak
began sleeping in his store, ostensibly to guard against such
calamity.   He also began assiduously plying his acquaintances, who chanced to be about the same age, build,
and weight as himself, with invitations to sleep with him in
the store.   These invitations, fortunately, were declined

by each person approached, until the night of February 2, 1897, when a reputable young Irish farmer by the name of Edward Murray acceded to Novak's solicitations and remained with him in the store up to the hour of retiring. They were seen together at 11:30 P. M., and at 1:30 A. M. of February 3d the building was discovered on fire, and was soon a mass of ruins, with the conviction forced upon every spectator that Novak and Murray had been consumed in the conflagration. Upon searching the cooling embers, however, it was found that only one partly charred corpse was in the remains of the building, and, while a number of ineffectual attempts were made by interested parties to establish the identity of this corpse as that of Frank Novak, the anatomical differences were so great and the dental distinctions so peculiar that a coroner's jury found no great difficulty on considering the evidence laid before them in arriving at a verdict that the remains were those of Edward Murray, and that no trace of Frank Novak was left in the building.

Steps were at once taken by the authorities of the State of Iowa and the county of Benton to search out and apprehend Frank Novak, and other persons took a hand in the matter, securing Thiel's detective service to prosecute the search for the murderer. Detective C. C. Perrin was detailed to handle the case. He was peculiarly fitted for it. Tall, of medium weight, he has the figure and muscles of an athlete. His square-cut chin and mouth show the grit and force that finally brought Novak to bay.

A trail was struck, and, although the offense was several weeks old when the detective started upon the case, Novak was followed across the country on foot over several counties in Iowa, and then by conveyance an equal distance, being landed in Iowa City, which was believed to be a happy rendezvous for him, as he was known to have friends living at that place.   Some time elapsed before any further clue was obtained to the movements of the murderer, and he was believed to be in hiding in that city or vicinity until the description of a man tallying with that of Novak was picked up from the appearance of a passenger on a train bound for an eastern port, and, in following up this clue, it developed that this man was a Bohemian, and as Novak was a Bohemian-American, he was believed to be the same person.

The trail was followed to Baltimore, Md., where shipping agents and others recognized the photograph and description of Novak as answering to that of a man who had arrived at that port and shipped for Bohemia on the 18th of February.   A cablegram was immediately sent to Mr. Keenan, American consul in Germany, who had the passenger described apprehended on the arrival of the steamer *Halle* at Bremen on March 1st, and after several days' cabling and comparisons of descriptions it was decided that a case of mistaken identity had led to the arrest of the wrong man, and this clue had to be dropped.

The detective again returned to Iowa City, and, after a prolonged search in and about this place, a clue was finally struck on the 11th day of March in the shape of a description of a passenger who bought a ticket at midnight on February 3d to Omaha, Neb., over the Chicago, Rock Island & Pacific Railroad.   By a diligent inquiry among railway and sleeping-car employes who had been in charge of the cars and train on the date named, the representative of Thiel's service was satisfied that he was on the right track, and immediately went to Omaha, where an active search was taken up, and by the aid of the local police department in the course of a couple of days the fleeing man's identity was once more established by description and photograph in the person of a passenger who bought a ticket over the Union Pacific system from Omaha to Vancouver, B. C.

The detective was now five weeks behind the fleeing murderer, but, nothing daunted, took the next train for Portland, Ore., where a stop was made and search instituted to see if the ticket had been used through to Vancouver, or if the passenger had stopped off at Portland, as is frequently done by persons seeking to get a cut rate to the Pacific coast. The detective's knowledge of this phase of railroad travel proved most fortunate, for, after a quiet inquiry at Portland, running over a couple of days, it was discovered that Novak, using the name of Frank Alfred on his ticket, had stopped at Portland and cashed the portion reading to Vancouver with a broker at the former place.

Being at sea once more as to the probable course taken by the fugitive, still five weeks ahead of the detective, the latter began a quiet search of all the hotels, lodging houses, mercantile establishments, employment agencies, steamship and railroad ticket offices, and other points where information might be obtained touching a transient stranger, and for a while it looked as though every trace of Novak had vanished.

Portland and its suburbs were submitted to this exhaustive kind of inquiry for a number of days, without discovering any trace whatever of Novak's presence or movements, and inquiry was finally extended to San Francisco and other seaport towns on the Pacific coast with a view to picking up a clue at some remote point, on the belief that Novak had eluded notice in passing through Portland. All returning steamers from ocean voyages as they landed at Pacific coast points were met on their arrival, and the several crews and any returning passengers who had been on the outgoing trips were carefully questioned touching any one answering Novak's description having gotten aboard at any other coast point on any of the recent trips of the steamers since February 7th, which was the known date of his arrival at Portland.

On March 31st, at the end of a couple of weeks' search of this character, the steamer *Al-Ki*, returning from Sitka, was met at Seattle, and upon being interrogated all of the officers and crew and one returning passenger at once recognized Novak's photograph, and were capable of giving an accurate description of him in the person of a passenger who embarked on the *Al-Ki* at Port Townsend February 23d, ticketed for Juneau. They also added the information that he had been seen in Juneau a week or ten days previous, associating with a prospector who was going with other gold-hunters into the mining district up the Yukon. This information was promptly wired to headquarters of the Thiel detective service, where steps were at once taken to procure requisition papers for Novak. By the prompt action of the State officers, the requisition was at once obtained on the governor of Alaska for Novak, though, as it transpired, Novak had not been indicted in Benton County, Ia., on the date previously reported, as the grand jury had been so pressed with business that it could not take up this case.

While these proceedings were being had in Iowa, Perrin, who was following Novak, embarked on the first steamer for Alaska, which proved to be the *Al-Ki*, leaving Seattle April 4th, and the requisition papers were forwarded to him at Juneau by mail from Des Moines, Ia., on April

7th, to reach him by the next steamer sailing for the gold country.

After the requisition papers on the governor of Alaska had been procured, it was ascertained that Novak had left Juneau for the gold fields of the Yukon River in Canada, when it became necessary to procure extradition papers on the governor of Canada. A detective went to Iowa to secure the necessary papers; from thence he went to Washington, D. C., to secure the signature of the President and Secretary of State to same. He then went to Ottawa, all of the officials concerned giving the matter the utmost expedition, so that he was enabled to reach the Pacific coast on May 20th, three months and a half behind the fugitive Novak, sailing from Victoria on the steamer *Mexico* May 24th for Juneau. Here he outfitted for the trip into the Yukon country, going in by way of the Chilkoot Pass at Dyea. Another detective was sent to St. Michael, about three thousand miles away, to watch all steamers arriving there from the Yukon gold fields, to see that Novak did not escape on some of the sailing vessels leaving that port for different parts of the world.

June 8th Perrin left Juneau with a year's outfit for Dyea, going over the Chilkoot Pass to Lake Lindeman, where he built a boat.

At the same time Novak and his party were completing a boat on Lake Bennett, but a few miles further on. They had taken in a big lot of supplies, and in getting them over the pass and in making ready for the trip down the river had consumed over a month of time.

One morning Perrin and his Indian guides set sail in their boat on their journey. At the same time Novak's party started on Lake Bennett in a rude scow. Early in the afternoon Perrin saw the scow ahead of him on Lake Bennett, and rapidly overhauled it in his light sailboat. He went within a hundred feet of the boat and exchanged good-natured, joking salutations with its occupants as he swept past, never dreaming that one of the number was the man he sought.

"That scow wasn't built for a racer, was she?" shouted the detective.

"She's slow, but sure," was the reply.

"Well, good-bye," said the detective as his boat drew ahead.

"So long," returned Novak. "Save a little of the gold for us."

"Of course."

From there on down the river for a thousand miles into the diggings the pursuer was followed by the pursued. Perrin reached Dawson ten days ahead of his man, and at once began a sharp search for him, quickly coming to the conclusion that he was not in Dawson. No one remembered having seen a man answering the description. Then the detective went over the trails to the camp and searched in vain along the creeks. He returned to Dawson very much puzzled. Finally, he concluded that Novak must have gone up the Stewart River, without coming to Dawson. There were reports of several miners prospecting on that stream with good results, and many tenderfeet were making preparations to go up there. The detective concluded that he would go, too, and this meant that he would have to winter there. He was about ready to start when the scow which he had passed on the way in was pushed up to the beach at Dawson. Perrin walked over towards the men to exchange greetings.

"Jingo!" he exclaimed under his breath as he came closer to the scow. He remembered his photograph and was pretty sure he had his man, but he talked good-naturedly with Novak, and then laid the matter before Captain C. Constantine of the Canadian mounted police. In a few hours Novak was arrested by Captain Constantine and turned over to Perrin.

Perrin placed his prisoner in a boat and that night started down the river during a heavy storm for Fort Cudahy, where three days later, he took the steamer *P. J. Healey* for St. Michael. The two thousand miles down the river were made in eleven days, and then came a two-weeks wait for the *Portland*. From St. Michael to Seattle, and at all times during the entire trip, a continuous watch was kept over Novak by Perrin and two assistants. Then he started east with his man, and when he delivered him safe in the Iowa jail he had been over six months constantly on the go, during which time he had traveled nearly twenty-five thousand miles and endured many of the hardships of the Yukon.

CHAPTER XXVIII

WOMEN IN THE KLONDIKE—SOME ROMANTIC STORIES— EXPERIENCE OF A WOMAN ON THE TRAIL—HOW WOMEN HAVE MADE FORTUNES.

A Little Home Life — Two White Women in Camp the First Winter — Mrs. Lippy the Pioneer — Mrs. Berry's Story of Her Journey — Beginning to Despair — Starting for the Klondike — A Cabin Unfit to Live In — Picking Up Nuggets of Gold — Wading in Mud Waist Deep — Housekeeping No Joke — Arrival of a Plucky Little Wife — Makes Her Home on a Scow — On Terra Firma at Last — An Eye to Business — One Hundred Dollars a Month for Caring for Two Children — In Doubt as to the Day of the Week — Dogs and Mosquitoes, "but the Gold's all Right" — Romantic Career of a Woman — Joins the Stampede from Circle City — Cooking for $15 a Day — Facing Claim-Jumpers — Making $12,000 in a Few Weeks — Opportunities to Marry Rich Husbands — Gallantry of the Men — What a Woman Should Wear — A Queer Trousseau.

T HERE is a better side to the life in Dawson City and in the camps along the creeks, such a thing as home life amid the rough surroundings, and there are brave women there, women who have shared with their husbands or fathers the hardships of the journey and who preside over their cabins in the town or at the mines with touches of that womanly grace and skill all the more noticeable under such harsh conditions. At first women of this variety were rare, but after the rush from outside was fairly under way there was a marked enlargement in home life, while many respectable women became engaged in self-supporting pursuits, greatly increasing the comforts of the settlement. During the first winter in the camps along the creeks there were but two white women, and their experiences were certainly romantic.

When Mrs. Lippy arrived at the camp on Eldorado Creek, there were no other women there except a few squaws, and these Yukon Indians, male or female, are not worth counting. Her husband put up the first log cabin on the creek, and while it was being erected they lived in a tent. All the furniture they had was made out of boxes and slabs by Mr. Lippy, and all the food they had at first was canned. Mrs. Lippy did no mining herself, but attended to the domestic duties, which are certainly arduous enough in such a place, and she made her husband so comfortable and enabled him to rest so thoroughly that he was enabled to accomplish more than most of the miners during the cold weather.

After a time Mrs. Berry came into the camp, and Mrs. Lippy had some association with her own sex. Mrs. Berry's advent into the Klondike regions was quite romantic, as it was in the nature of a bridal trip, Mr. Berry having married her, as already related, in the spring of 1896, before setting out for the gold country.

" The journey over the ice and snow is one that I am not likely to forget," said Mrs. Berry, in telling the story of her experiences. " The accommodations for a woman were very poor, the transportation was slow, the dog teams we had were not accustomed to the climate, and altogether we appeared to be in a bad fix much of the time. We carried with us our stove and tent, and the latter we pitched every night on some spot where the snow was hard. Our beds were made of boughs. My husband was careful to provide every

comfort possible.   Just before leaving Juneau I was given a
large bear-skin robe, which greatly added to my comfort.   I
rode nearly all the way.   During the journey I was strapped
to the sled or boat, as the case might be, and while it was
considerably better than walking, there was always an uncertainty about my position which made it very uncomfortable.   At first it was very, very cold, but after that I
became used to it.   I want to say just here, that the trip
over the Juneau route, when the lakes and rivers are broken
up and filled with floating ice, is particularly hazardous to
women.   They are not nearly so well able as men to stand
the hardships and dangers incident to such a journey.   I do
not think I would be willing to make the same trip again,
though if my husband goes back next spring I shall probably accompany him.

" When we arrived at Forty Mile we found that there
was absolutely nothing to do.   My husband struck a claim
and made some money in that way, but it was hardly enough
to keep us going.   In anticipation of just such luck, however, we had brought ample supplies with us, and also some
money, and so did not suffer.   Just as we were beginning to
despair there came the news of the wonderful find on the
Klondike.   I told my husband the best thing we could do
would be to go to that section immediately.   He objected
at first, but finally yielded to my persuasion and started for
the diggings.   I was left behind, by my own request, to fix
up the camp and to take all the provisions we had to the new
discovery.   I cannot begin to tell you of the hardships I
encountered.   The river was already beginning to show
signs of floating ice, and I knew it would be only a short time
before it would be completely frozen over.   Finally, however, I got everything in order and started on the *Arctic*

for the new Eldorado. About half way up I came across my husband and his party, and they joined me on the *Arctic.*

" The roughest experience I had during my entire stay in Alaska was at the mining camp fifteen miles from Dawson City. When, having waded and stumbled over the trail, I reached the house where I was to spend the winter, I found it utterly unfit for any woman to live in. There was neither floor nor windows, and Mr. Berry had to cut a hole in the wall in order to get the stove in. Finally all of these difficulties were overcome, and I was fairly comfortable. It was December 6th when we struck the first gold, and it was a happy day for me as well as for my husband, who had worked so hard to gain an independence. Of course, at the time we did not know just what we were making, but it was not long before the truth dawned upon us that we were in a fair way to win a fortune. All last winter I visited the mines, and, as the great chunks of frozen earth were dumped on the ground, I busied myself in picking out the nuggets.

" I think that during the season I picked up something like ten thousand dollars. I used to turn the clods over, and then, with a sharp stick, dig into them as far as I could until I came across something that looked like gold. The largest nugget I found was worth two hundred and thirty-one dollars, and it turned out to be one of the best individual prizes found in the diggings. I enjoyed good health in spite of the hardships, and actually gained twenty-two pounds while in Alaska. I attribute this to my taking good care of myself, never unnecessarily exposing myself to the weather, though I was nearly always around the camp. I liked to be there because it was lonesome at the cabin, and then again there was always the possibility of finding that which we had come so far to secure.

" I did not mind the hardships very much. Mr. Berry's claim was nineteen miles from Dawson, and I walked all the way over the ice. It took us two days to get there, and I was nearly dead when we arrived. When we came out it was spring, and the mud was so deep that I frequently went in to my waist, and over my knees at every step. I wore rubber boots and short skirts all the time I was there. In the winter I wore short skirts, bloomers, fur-lined moccasins to the knee, a fur coat, hood, and mittens. I kept house, and I tell you it's no joke."

After a housewife has gone over the Chilkoot Pass and has shot the rapids, it may be declared a certainty that she is made of sterling material, and it was indeed interesting to watch the women who were among the new arrivals and to hear them tell of their experiences. One July day a man and his wife came drifting down the river in a scow and landed at Dawson. She was a small body, but there was a fire in her black eyes that showed grit and determination, and it was pleasing to notice how quickly she accommodated herself to circumstances. Lots were then selling at enormous prices back in the swamp on which Dawson is located, and she told her husband they couldn't afford to pay those prices yet for such ground.

Their scow was a large one, and in no time she had their goods piled up on one end and the tent set up on the other.

" None of your fancy prices for that house and lot," she said as she began to make things comfortable for living. It certainly was quite as pleasant as living on one of the swamp lost in the summer. They lived there on the bank of the river some little time till the husband finally found a location and started to erect a cabin. In about a month she was bustling around in her new home putting things to rights.

"Yes, sir, I can tell you I am pretty glad to get on terra firma again," she said, "that is, if you can call this sort of ground terra firma. It's an improvement, however. I've been living on a boat ever since last March, nearly five months. To tell the truth, I'm a little tired of gypsy life, though I've stood it pretty well. Yes, our house is larger than most of them here — twenty-three feet by sixteen. But we have two stoves, and I think we will be able to keep it warm next winter. As to furnishing — well, I don't know. This is a queer town, isn't it? But the gold's all right."

She had an eye to business, and it had been her intention to secure a lot near the center or business portion and start a bakery. "Just think of it," she said to her husband, " bread is worth fifty cents a loaf, one-pound pies one dollar each, just such as I used to make at home. They say I could sell a scowload every day. I talked with one woman who bakes, and she said the men came in and threw down their sacks of gold, and when she took out what she thought about the right amount and weighed it, if it went over the requisite weight, they would say, ' Never mind, madam, let it go.' Many times she gets from seventy-five cents to one dollar for a loaf of bread. A sack of flour costs six dollars here, and it makes forty-five loaves of bread."

They paid two hundred and fifty dollars for their lot, which was some distance back near the banks of the Klondike. Before they had owned it many days they sold one-quarter of it, off the rear, for seventy-five dollars, and then one-half of the front for one hundred and seventy-five dollars.　As she was too far from the center to make a bakery profitable, she thought she would turn her attention to other matters, and finally secured a chance to take care of a couple of children.　In telling about them she said:

"One of them is ten years old and the other is six. They are regular little terrors.　I wash them both six times a day, and bathe them all over in a tub of water twice a week, and then they are always smutty.　They are girls and as ugly as sin.　Their mother is a woman from Juneau. Robert says, ' Why don't you whale them?'　He says I am altogether too easy with them.　I have not whipped them yet, and I won't.　I don't expect to have them long.　There is a Catholic church, a school, and a hospital building just below where we are living, and when they are completed I expect the little ones will stay with the Sisters.　The Sisters are expected here on the next boat from St. Michael, which, if there is water enough for it to get up the river, will be here in about a month.　The girls say they don't want to live with the Sisters; that they want to live with me and to go to school from here.　They lived with the Sisters in Juneau, and they say the Sisters are not so good to them as I am; that they make them work, and that they whip them. The little ones appear to like me very much.　I get one hundred dollars a month for taking care of the little terrors, and I guess I earn every cent of it, but their mother furnishes the bedding and a tent for them to sleep in."

I had found out that this woman made wonderfully fine bread, and had purchased some occasionally.　A little real bread is a great delicacy on the Yukon, and while I had looked upon myself as quite an expert I could recognize the superiority of her light loaves.　One day when I went to the cabin she had just finished baking.

" I've baked seven loaves of bread, four pies, and a batch of ginger-snaps to-day," she said. " By the way, what day is it? "

" Saturday, I believe, but I'm not sure."

" I can never tell in this region without looking it up. This perpetual daylight, when there is so much to do, gets one all mixed up. Never saw such a place to live in in all my life. Still, we get along nicely. There are some advantages in the country besides the gold. We have been having a lot of the most delicious fish — king salmon. There are two fishermen who live on the river bank just below here, and I guess they must have taken a fancy to me, as they send us fish every day. They sell their fish for fifty cents a pound, but they don't charge me anything for them. Yesterday they gave me ten or twelve pounds, five or six dollars' worth, and to-day they gave me another large piece. I give them a loaf of bread and a pie once in a while. To-day I took them a loaf of bread, a pie, and a lot of ginger-snaps. My, but they appear so grateful! I love to give to them, for they appear so grateful for such trifles. There are two of them — a father and a son. They have a lot of dogs, eight large ones and seven small ones. There are more dogs to the square yard here, I guess, than in any place on earth. We have dog concerts every night. Such lugubrious howls as these native dogs give utterance to; and the exotics soon strike the key and become initiated. It is something fearful. I am starving for vegetables and fruit. And the mosquitoes — oh! they are terrible. They make life a burden. But the gold's all right."

One of the most remarkable cases of fortune-making by a woman was that of Mrs. Wills, whom I had met at Circle City in 1896, where she was baking bread on a

Yukon stove, with the results told in a previous chapter. As the Circle City miners congregated at Mrs. Wills's bakery for their daily bread, it became one of the news centers of the place, and to this is due the fact that she was among the first to hear of the rich strike on the Klondike. Although she was making money at the rate of twenty-five dollars a day, it only whetted her appetite for gold, and she no sooner heard of the Klondike than she was ready to start.

It was three hundred long, dreary miles over snow and ice to Dawson. Securing a mate for her dog, she closed her bakery, and started alone. Two days later she was joined by a party of cattlemen, who had heard the wonderful stories of Klondike gold, and they, too, had caught the gold fever. Mrs. Wills would be relieved of the burden of her sleds and her dogs cared for if she would act as cook for the party. This was a bargain, and it is said that she stood the hardships of the journey "like a man."

She made her location on the Klondike, and filed thereon, and at once set a man at work, while she returned to Dawson and accepted a position with the Alaska Commercial Company as head cook at fifteen dollars a day. She paid the same amount to the men who worked her claim. Thus she was able to work the claim and yet employ herself in the more congenial occupation. Later she secured a stove, this time one with an oven that held four bakepans, and again went into the bakery business, and inside of two weeks had customers enough at one dollar a loaf to keep the oven going twelve hours a day.

As soon as all the good claims were taken up near Dawson City, then the claim-jumpers began to get in their work. Several attempts were made to get possession of Mrs. Wills's claim, which promised to pan out exceedingly rich, but she

TOO LATE. A DISAPPOINTED PAIR OF GOLD-SEEKERS

They failed to reach their destination before winter set in. Here they cached their outfit and food before returning to civilization to wait until spring. The trunk of a tree was erected as a landmark to guide them to the spot on their return.

fought the case and held down her claim against all comers. Finding that she could not be scared off it, offers to purchase were tendered, but Mrs. Wills was mining for what she could make, and the sum of two hundred and fifty thousand dollars did not swerve her from her purpose. She expects that her claim will pan out twice that amount. Meantime she is making a net profit of more than fifty dollars a day in her bakery and laundry, notwithstanding the high price of flour and the fact that starch costs two hundred and fifty dollars a box. She pays an Indian squaw who works for her four dollars a day, and for the little log cabin in which the work was done she has to pay thirty-five dollars a month. Her fuel costs her over five hundred dollars a year, but she made money rapidly at this, while those she hired to work her mines found the gold rapidly. She made twelve thousand dollars from them in a few weeks, and she struck the richest gravel of any in May, and was making more money than ever. She is a brave, enterprising woman, who has battled with poverty all her life, and we were glad she was so fortunate at last. People in a mining camp like this are not generally so envious of each other's prosperity as they sometimes are in ordinary society.

It has been said that the Klondike offers a great opportunity for respectable unmarried women, and it is doubtless true. A good woman is at a high premium in that region, and so long as mines are rich, and millionaires are turned out every season, women who have the courage to brave such hardships as a journey to Alaska entails, and are not too particular about the culture of the eligible men, may marry a fortune. The fact is, however, that most good women are particular about the men they marry. But there are in the Klondike some as true specimens of manhood as can be found anywhere. They may not appear so in their rough surroundings, but there is value in their rugged natures. A respectable woman has nothing to fear in the way of insult in these mining regions. It may seem at times on the trail that all spirit of gallantry has been left behind. Men, as a matter of course, have too much serious work on hand in such ordeals to waste much time in helping women over boulders and asking if they may have the honor of carrying their packages just over the next hill, but they never take any mean advantage of their weaker fellow-workers, and they allow full value for the work women are better fitted to do than men. The field for cooking alone is one of immense opportunity for women, and they are not slow to see it. Even though a man is willing to get his own meals after a day's hard work, few of them understand how to prepare food in a wholesome, palatable way. Good nourishing food is what they must have.

Aside from this there are lodging houses, and the actual prospecting and mining, and washing and mending clothes, and nursing, and undoubtedly women stand a good chance for success.

There will be plenty of miners who will see that a woman is protected. An illustration of this, one of the thousands of dramatic incidents of Klondike life, stands out significant of the real character of American men, as a race. Dissension arose in a party of men and women, after which a division occurred, and some of them decided to return to their homes. A man and his wife who could not agree upon this point parted, and the wife suddenly found herself the only woman in a camp with four hundred men, without provisions of any sort, and no money. Some one suggested that she cook for them, so she started bravely in, and those men, recognizing this as an isolated case where they could go out of their way a little, made her feel their care and protection. Its just as natural for men to want to be helpful to a woman as it is to breathe, but during the first weeks of the Klondike excitement men felt hindered very often trying to help women along. They have all they can manage to look out for themselves, and when they found women going up there to work independently, and that they did not want men to help them, the situation presented itself in its true light.

As the number of women in the city increased, several began to turn their attention to dressmaking, which was quite a profitable business. Five dollars was charged for making a common calico wrapper such as could be put together in about three hours. The price for making a plain woolen dress was thirty dollars, and the dressmakers had to pay nothing for fashion-plates. Anything that looked well passed muster.

Wading is an essential part of a trip in the Klondike, especially in the vicinity of the mines, and women should, for their own comfort, provide accordingly. The head-wear affected by women there consists of close-fitting hats or caps, made necessary by the high winds. All clothing is worn loosely to facilitate moving about. No corsets are worn; instead, a canvas waist has come into general use. To this waist are buttoned the skirts (if worn) and the undergarments. In winter women generally wear fur hoods and parkas. On the feet are worn " muck lucks," a sort of boot the foot of which is made of hair seal-skin.

A woman who had some experience in the Klondike says that the venture means " an extra and heroic effort for a big prize, and the harvest depends, as all harvests do, on the amount of strength and energy put into it.   Therefore, if she has the courage to make the great plunge with a possible fortune at the end, in preference to smaller returns over a greater space of time without extreme demands upon her health, she will undoubtedly want to equip herself intelligently.

" First, then, the clothing is to be considered.   Starting in the early spring, the following articles will be absolutely indispensable:

" Four combination suits, heaviest quality; three pairs bloomers; three thick sweaters; three short skirts (waterproof cloth); one fur-lined jacket; two pair wristlets; four pair woolen gloves; four pairs heaviest woolen blankets; six pair woolen stockings; two pairs rubber boots, one pair snow shoes; several yards netting (against the impertinent mosquito later on); two woolen night dresses, and don't forget dark-blue glasses, vaseline, and glycerine, for exposure to the cold winds and all the roughness of outdoor life will play such havoc with hands and faces that much suffering can be avoided by applying the last two when retiring into blankets.   There won't be any downy pillows, because weary heads soon learn to sleep on bundles.

" It is much better to carry wearing-apparel in waterproof bags, as they are easier to handle, and boxes are heavier and take up too much space.   You won't have a bit good time — but if all your belongings are not capsized — and you are not drowned or otherwise killed, and you get to any real where — my! won't you feel it has paid for the attempt — that is, if you're a genuine new woman and not a mere new lady."

CHAPTER XXIX

A SEASON OF WILD STAMPEDES — THE CURIOUS CON-
DITIONS ON SKOOKUM GULCH — NEW WONDERS IN
ALASKA DISTRICT — MY NARROW ESCAPE FROM
DEATH.

Spreading Out Over the Wild Country — Stampedes a Daily Occur-
rence — How they were Started — Enterprise of an Exhausted
Party — Returning from One Rush Only to Fall in with Another —
The Astounding Results on Hunker Creek — Sudden Rise of Skoo-
kum Gulch — How it was Discovered — Kicking Over Boulders
and Finding Gold — Bench Claims — Strike on Dominion Creek —
An Old German's Good Luck on Sulphur Creek — Endeavoring to
Keep it Quiet — The News Leaks Out — Another Great Stampede —
Joe and I Conclude to See for Ourselves — A Misstep and a Drench-
ing in Ice Water — Injured and Exhausted — A Blinding Storm —
"Oh, for a Little Meat" — Joe Starts to Hunt for a Moose — Re-
turns and Finds Me Helpless — "I Guess I'm Done For" — A
Long Night and Day — Walking in a Circle — I Revive on Moose
Broth — Staking a Claim Anywhere — My Last Prospecting Trip.

WHEN summer came there were nearly three thousand people in and about Dawson, the great
majority of whom had come in during the winter and spring, and who were eagerly waiting to make a
fortune. The class was increased when work became slack
in the mines, owing to the running water, and also began to
be increased by those from adjoining settlements who had
been unable to reach the district the season before, and by
the vanguard of that great crowd which was soon to pour
in over the passes. It is a fact significant of the remote-

(407)

ness of the country and scarcity of facilities for communication and transportation, that while all these scenes of newly-discovered millions were being enacted at Dawson, the outside world was pursuing its peaceful way in utter innocence of Dawson and its mines. A few letters had found their way out, and there were rumors along the Pacific coast of the new discoveries, but they were treated in the papers as highly-colored tales, and stuck into inconspicuous places in mining intelligence. Juneau miners had heard a good deal, however, and were soon on their way down the river.

But, of course, the two creeks that were known had long been completely staked. The floating population, impatiently waiting to grasp a fortune, was therefore in a state of stampede all summer. The old miners, observing the lay of the land and seeing that the Bonanza had other " pups " which, while not very inviting to the gold-prospector, looked fully as much so as the Eldorado had appeared at first, and seeing also that the Klondike and the Indian River just above had numerous small tributaries, whose headwaters seemed to center curiously around a ridge of hills, in the center of which was a peak called the Dome, had early begun to spread out over the country and to probe the ground under the tundra of the banks. When they found something that looked promising, they returned to Dawson and applied for a discovery claim. This was happening all summer. No one knew the value of the discovery, for it was impossible to fully know till the winter had again frozen up the streams, but it made no difference to the ever-increasing crowd of feverish fortune-hunters. Stampedes were of daily occurrence, and the bulk of the population was therefore kept in a state bordering on physical exhaustion.

Generally, a stampede would start about in this way: A man looking in the recorder's book would see that a claim had been filed on some new and unheard-of creek. He would give the tip to a friend and they would start off, but the friend would first whisper it to another friend, and in a few hours the whole town would know something was happening. A crowd would be quickly clambering over rocks and struggling through places where there was not even a trail.

Or, perhaps, some fellow would drift into a saloon with a sack of gold, and in the garrulousness of intoxication would confide to some one that he had found it on such a creek or pup, and away the men would rush. There were many curious experiences. One day a party left to go sixty miles up the river, but after going about fifty miles they became exhausted and turned back. On the way back they killed a couple of moose, and each man's share of the proceeds was sixty-one dollars and fifty cents. While they were gone another stampede took place at about ten o'clock at night. Several went up the river and staked claims, knowing nothing as to their value, and came back with no gold, only to fall in with the next rush.

But the result of all these stampedes was to open up a much larger gold-bearing territory, which will be heard from in the future. One of the first and most promising of these discoveries was made by a man by the name of Hunker, who gave his name to the creek which flows into the Klondike about ten miles above the mouth of the Bonanza, and the principal tributaries of which are Gold Bottom and Last Chance creeks. Hunker made his discovery late in the spring, and on account of the abundance of water and the marshy character of the soil little could be done at once in drifting, but the rich results simply astounded those who had become used to that sort of thing.   The pay-streak was measured and found to be two hundred feet wide.   Many believed that the creek would surpass Eldorado.   A half interest in one claim was sold for thirty thousand dollars. On Gold Bottom and Last Chance, pans of from twenty-five cents to twenty dollars were reported near the surface. Bear Creek, which flows into the Klondike between Hunker and Bonanza creeks, was also early prospected and staked out, yielding some fine returns near the surface.   Nuggets the size of peas were brought down to Dawson from its banks and served to increase the excitement of the new-comers.

The sudden rise of Skookum Gulch was one of the queer incidents of the unfolding of this marvelous territory.   It enters Bonanza near Cormack's discovery claim, but in the first rush it was passed by as worthy of no attention.   A man who had for several years been working a claim on American Creek started for the Klondike as soon as the news reached him, traveling on the ice with a dog team, the thermometer ranging about sixty below.   Bonanza and El-dorado were all staked then, and in March, after bringing up his outfit, he formed a partnership and secured a lay on Cormack's claim.   While working there they located claims Nos. 1 and 2 on Skookum Gulch, near by, and at odd times worked the ground.   About the middle of April they struck a pay-streak at a depth of about four feet, and gave up their lay at Cormack's, where they had cleaned up about seven thousand dollars, and went to work on their Skookum claims.   After drifting four days they washed out two thousand eight hundred dollars of some of the coarsest gold that had been found anywhere in the district.   Of course, there was another stampede. The two discoverers worked away till July, cleaning up about forty thousand dollars in the four months. Then they sold out for a big figure and went home.

But there were creek claims, that is, claims staked along the creek from rim-rock to rim-rock. The creek was all located by July, and some of the claims had been deserted, as the surface indications were not extra, and because of the constant rush for other new creeks, particularly on other Klondike streams. No one had thought of bench claims, that is, claims up on the side of the hills.

Conditions in Alaska and the Northwest Territory are so very different from those prevailing in the placer mining regions of California and other countries, that the experience and knowledge of the average old miner, gained after years of toil and hardship, sometimes only mislead him.

This was illustrated in the discovery of bench claims on Skookum Gulch, when a tenderfoot kicked over a boulder and found gold nuggets sticking up under the sod. The wildest excitement prevailed.

It was found that while many of the old prospectors had searched long and faithfully for the nuggets in the creek bed and near the center of the stream, they had entirely overlooked the bench claims, which were found to be very rich. Some of the claims on the creek bed were carefully gone over, but did not prove very good. Miners sunk shafts to bed-rock and toiled night and day for the yellow metal, which lay so plentifully a few rods further up the hill away from the stream. But the saying that gold is where you find it was again exemplified. Thousands of people in the last year had walked over the location and never thought of

looking for gold there.   Experienced miners would have
laughed at a man as a fool for thinking that gold might be
there.   Yet in a few weeks about four hundred bench
claims were staked out.

Boulders were turned over, and there, lying exposed
on the gravel, was coarse gold.   The moss was about twelve
inches thick, and beneath it in one day two men picked up
eight hundred dollars in nuggets.   It was difficult to offer
a theory of how the gold got there.   It was worn but little,
and just below in the gulch some rich specimens of float were
found.   Some good miners thought it might be only the
edge of a wonderful pay-streak of quartz, as some quartz
was found adhering to the gold.   When one old miner saw
what was being picked up under the moss, he said:

" Who'd ever thought of finding gold on the surface of
such a looking mountain as that.   If science went for anything, there wouldn't be an ounce of gold in the whole
mountain.   No, sir, I'm ready to confess that I don't know
anything about placer mining, and I've been at it, off and on,
for years.   These discoveries have been too much for me."

The excitement was intense.   Hundreds of ounces were
taken out of the rockers by the dazed miners.   In half a
day two men picked out with a rocker five hundred and
eighty-five dollars in coarse gold.

Attention was early directed to the creeks of the Indian
River district whose headwaters lay in the same range of
hills in which the rich streams of the Klondike took their
rise.   Various stampedes to Sulphur, Dominion, and Quartz
creeks took place, and by September there was not a claim
to be had, except at large prices, on any of these streams.
The strike on Dominion Creek was made on June 10th by a
man who had been on the Yukon for years, and the result

was one of the wildest stampedes of the year.   The miners brought back many favorable reports and some gold dust. Pans running as high as two dollars and fifty cents were found long before bed-rock was reached.   The discovery claim was located about three miles from the head of the creek, which was soon staked for its entire length of twenty miles.

Some of those who arrived too late to secure claims here started to return to Dawson, and instead of returning by the Indian River went over the hills towards the Yukon.   On the 20th one of the party came to what is now known as Sulphur Creek, at a point about seven miles from the hill that separates it from Hunker Creek, which flows into the Klondike.   They found good prospects, and, going into a partnership arrangement, sunk a shaft.   They worked quietly without letting any one know, but had not proceeded far before they found pans running as high as five dollars.   Then they staked out claims for themselves and went to Dawson to record them.   They endeavored to keep it quiet, but in August it leaked out, and there was another stampede, over five hundred men crossing the rough mountain between Eldorado and Dominion creeks.

They had not been working long before pans running over thirty dollars were found not far below the surface. Two men took out three hundred dollars one day in simply prospecting their claims.   The formation seemed to be much like that of Eldorado Creek, which bears the same relation to Bonanza that Sulphur does to Dominion, and the process which brought gold into one must have brought it into the other.   As these streams flowed into the Indian River they were in another mining district, and so those having claims on the Klondike streams were at liberty to stake on Dominion and Sulphur. The excitement was intense and continued for some time, as new strikes were constantly reported. The old German who located the discovery took out thirty dollars to the pan, and in most places the water on the creek was not deep, so that the claims could be worked easier than those on the Klondike.

But many of the locators either did not have energy to sink their prospect holes, or were too restless on account of the daily stampedes to other creeks to remain, and so it began to be rumored about that Sulphur Creek was of no value. A few of the first locators, however, staid by it, and they were richly rewarded. When the large pans began to be taken out, another stampede occurred. Claims that had been abandoned were staked by other parties and soon could hardly be bought at any price.

About forty men rushed out on this forty-mile tramp, and many of the newcomers were so excited and in such haste to find a hole from which they could take gold that they rushed off without taking their blankets or enough to eat. Indeed, this was a feature of all these stampedes, and many came near losing their lives, and, doubtless, would have done so but for the kindness of more provident prospectors.

Indeed, the dangers incurred in these wild scrambles over the mountains could not be altogether avoided by those who were careful enough to make ample provisions for their trip. Joe and I had a rather narrow escape ourselves during the fall excitement over the tributaries of Dominion Creek. We had not, as a rule, indulged in the stampedes, for we were well aware of their dangers and uncertainties, and aware also that claims were being staked constantly by those who immediately rushed off to another locality, so that if at any time actual prospects should reveal any surpassing richness in the new discoveries it would be time enough to rush in and secure some of the deserted claims.   But when the fall excitement over Sulphur Creek occurred we concluded to go over the hills and prospect a little thereabout for ourselves.   We were at the camp at that time, and during the rush men had dropped their picks and run from windlasses to hurry over to the Indian River district.   Joe and I took our time and put in our packs a good supply of beans and blankets.

I had not been feeling well for several days, having been weak and sometimes a little feverish.   I had attributed it to drinking poor water and to the everlasting monotony of diet at the camp, but I felt better when we started, and thought little of it while we plodded along over the rough hillsides through the snow.   All this country is so rugged that the eye is startled at surveying it from some commanding peak.   Hill crowding hill, mountain jostling mountain, on and on they sweep to the uttermost reach of the vision.

Reaching what we took to be the upper part of Sulphur Creek, we prospected through that region and then started to work our way up a gulch which looked as promising as anything could in that locality.   I was struggling along over a high bluff of rocks along by the bed of the stream, when I made a misstep and rolled, pack and all, over the edge of the rocks, striking on a bit of thin ice at the bottom. It gave way and let me into the ice-cold water.   Joe was ahead and did not miss me till I shouted.   But before he could make his way to the bed of the stream I had pulled myself out, dripping and shivering.   My ankle was slightly sprained, but I minded that less than the cold.   We finally worked our way up to a little clump of spruces, where I dropped down exhausted and half frozen.

Joe had a fire going in a short time and made me a cup of strong tea, but it did little good, and I grew worse and worse. I was terribly weak, but abhorred the sight of beans, which Joe placed over the fire in the hopes of reviving my strength. Oh, for a little meat! I thought.

The day before we had seen several moose tracks and had even caught a glimpse of two or three too far away on the hills to shoot, and, encumbered as we were, we did not take the trouble to follow them. As I lay there on a blanket on the snow I felt as if I would give all the Klondike soil I possessed for a bit of moose steak.

" Joe," I said, " I will watch the beans. Take the rifle and see if you cannot find a moose. I am dying for meat."

He left me, working his way off up the gulch, and I lay there watching the fire play about the kettle of beans. The wind shifted and blew the smoke straight towards me, but I was too weak to move or to mind such a trifle. Then it grew dark and began to snow, and I rapidly grew weaker and sicker. The fire began to work into fantastic shapes and seemed to dance about in the snow, then grow dim, then blaze up in flaming fierceness,— then all was dark.

The next I knew I felt a queer sensation in one of my hands; then I recognized Joe's voice. He was slapping my right hand and shouting in my ears. Finally I opened my eyes. It was dark. The fire was out. The beans were burnt up. It was snowing frightfully and the wind was sweeping through the gulch with a dreadful roar, which fell on my benumbed ears like a wail of despair.

" Come, come, this'll never do," I heard Joe say. " We must get out of this."

I tried to raise myself, but fell back helpless. My ankle began to pain me terribly, and then everything began to swim before my dull eyes again.

"No use, Joe," I said, feebly, "I guess I'm done for."

Having started another fire, he soon brought me a big cup of hot strong tea and held it while I drank it slowly off. I fell back and thought I felt better. Then he arranged some boughs over my head and threw a blanket over them to protect me from the wind. Dragging more poles down the hill, he heaped them on the fire, which roared and hissed almost at my feet. The snow was flying so thick that it was impossible to see but a little way before us.

"I must find a sled somewhere," said Joe, when he had made these preparations, and soon I saw him disappear again in the blinding snow. Then I fell into a sort of stupor.

How like a dreadful panorama my short career passed before me as I lay there during those long dark hours. Was this the end? There was a comfortable little fortune stacked away in our tent over in the camp, and here I was dying, as I thought, just because of a little misstep. On and on dragged the hours, and Joe did not return. The daylight broke, and still he did not come. I had become very faint and was almost too weak to move a muscle. The fire was dying into embers, and it grew very cold, though it had ceased to snow with so much fury.

After a long time, how long I could not tell, I heard shouting, and, making a great effort, raised my head out of the snow and feebly responded. In a few minutes I saw a dark form coming through the snow, and then I recognized Joe running rapidly towards me and pulling a sled.

"Now you'll be all right, my boy," he said. "I'm mighty glad to find you alive."

Then he told me the story of his search.   It seems he had started out in the storm for the purpose of making his way down to Sulphur Creek far enough to find some miners with a sled.   He set off, as he thought, in the right direction and had a hard tramp over the hills in the dark and in the face of the blinding storm.   After walking till about three o'clock in the morning he saw a light and hastened forward in the hope of finding a camp of miners.   What was his surprise upon coming up to the fire to find it the same one he had built a few hours before!   I was unconscious.

He threw some more wood on and started out again. At last he came to a sled track, and, after following it for nearly six miles, came upon two men who had half a moose on a sled.   In my extremity Joe had forgotten to eat anything and was nearly famished when he came upon the miners.   They hurriedly cooked him some meat, and he told them of my danger.   They told him to take the sled, and, cutting off a piece of moose meat, strapped it on, and Joe started back for me, running much of the way.   He had experienced a little difficulty in finding me, and about given me up for dead, when he heard my feeble response to one of his cries.

He told me this while he hurriedly built another fire, and put the moose in a kettle for a stew.   That stew braced me up at once.   Nothing will ever taste so good again as did that steaming moose broth.   During the day I began to regain my strength, and we started down the creek to find the two benefactors.   At first Joe insisted upon my riding, and he tugged away like a hero over the rough places, but I began to feel better, and the last part of the way hobbled along fairly well, resting occasionally.

" We ought to stake a claim somewhere after going through all this," I said to Joe while we were taking our first rest near the mouth of the gulch, which had not yet been staked. We had built a fire and were about to take a little lunch.

" Well, we might as well stake here as anywhere," he replied. " Never mind the indications. They don't count in this country. The only thing to do is to stake anywhere and trust to luck. It certainly looks better here than on Bonanza."

But we finally worked our way down the creek and took the first available claim, and after a few days went back to our camp. That was the last prospecting trip we made in the Klondike.

CHAPTER XXX

STAMPEDERS WHO NEGLECTED TO RECORD CLAIMS —
CREEKS TOO NUMEROUS TO REMEMBER — POSSI-
BILITIES OF OTHER DISTRICTS — NEW GOLD FIELDS.

Midnight Rush to Montana Creek — Staking by Torchlight — A Pugil-
ist on Hand — Locaters Rested after Their Journey — Their Stakes
Stealthily Removed and Others Substituted — The First to Record
Takes the Claim — Great Stampede to All Gold Creek — The
Rush for Bryant Creek—Intended to be Named for William J. Bryan
— Result of the Slip of the Pen — Neglecting to Record for Fear
Something Better Would be Found — Tenderfeet Frozen Out —
Waiting Three Days to Reach the Gold Commissioner — The
Country Staked for a Hundred Miles Around — Frauds Perpe-
trated — Impossibility for the Officers to Measure Claims during
the Wild Stampedes — Wild Race down the Frozen Yukon to
Buy a Claim — Old Miners' Belief in Stewart River — Gold Found
Everywhere — Difficulties of Prospecting on the Stewart — Some
of the Gold-Bearing Creeks Which May Be Heard From — In the
Same Belt as the Klondike.

N
O sooner had the exhausted gold-seekers returned
to Dawson from the rush to Sulphur Creek than
another took place to Montana Creek, a little
stream eighteen miles long entering the Yukon on the east
side about eight miles south of Dawson and heading up
towards Eldorado. It was a dark and stormy night, the
air was filled with a light snow, but there was the greatest
excitement, especially among the new arrivals. About two
hundred and fifty men joined in the rush, many of them

(420)

going at two o'clock in the morning. Some tumbled into boats and poled up the river against the strong current, and others clambered over the mountain and gulches. Those first on the creek built fires, and by torchlight measured off their claims and planted their stakes. A pugilist from the Pacific coast was the second man to locate. By midnight seven claims were staked off, and then the rush kept pouring in till the whole creek was staked and some were left without places to stake. When the men had finished their sprint over the trail or their difficult trip up the river, they were cold and hungry, and so they camped as well as they could somewhere on the creek before taking their way back. Some of the late arrivals, noticing this delay, stealthily removed stakes and put up their own. Then they rushed back to the recording office in Dawson, and, of course, were there long before the original claimants. When the latter arrived there was naturally considerable loud talk and some threats. There was nothing to do, however, but to accept the situation, for the first man who records takes the ground, unless there is a long litigation, which might bring no satisfaction. It is as important to be the first to reach the recorder's office as it is to be the first to locate a claim.

The rush to All Gold Creek was the largest of the season. At least five hundred men participated in that and endured the greatest hardships. The stampede to Bryant Creek, which is about nine miles up the Yukon from Dawson, took place early in September. The stream is about twenty-five miles in length, and rises within a few rods of one of the gulches which opens into Eldorado, whose waters flow in a different direction. Many of the claims were located at midnight. J. H. Howell of Seattle was the original discoverer of gold on this creek, and, desiring to honor an old schoolmate and friend, William J. Bryan, the late Democratic candidate for President, he named it Bryan Creek, but the Canadian recording officer, having apparently never heard of the Nebraska orator, with an upward stroke of the pen added the letter " t " to the word, and thus Mr. Bryan was deprived of another honor.

There were many instances of the shifting tide of fortune in the Klondike creeks. All Gold Creek had been located early in the summer, and there was the usual stampede and failure on the part of the indolent or restless to find the gold. Later, it was more thoroughly prospected, and gave evidences of being as rich as some of the more famous streams.

Late in October news was brought to Dawson that a prospecting party had made a rich strike on a little creek flowing into the Yukon about two miles above. It was named Dion Creek, from one of the leaders of the party, and many of the late newcomers managed to secure claims on it. The gold was found about two and a half miles up, and it was reported that the pay-streak was about five feet thick on top of bed-rock. Being close to Dawson, and on the Yukon, it was especially attractive, as it could be worked cheaper. Very little prospecting was done on it, however, as most of those who staked left to attend to other matters, so that it was an impossibility to judge of its richness with any degree of accuracy. Single pans of dirt worth as high as fifteen dollars were found, and the creek was soon staked for its whole length.

In the latter part of December great excitement was again aroused by new strikes on Dominion Creek. Those who were at work there were slowly thawing out the ground, and it was reported that on No. 19 below Discovery the owners had sampled gravel at a depth of six feet, or about two feet from bed-rock, and had taken out pans averaging five dollars each. As this was better than had been found on Bonanza and Eldorado at that depth, the claims of the Dominion Creek district at once jumped to an enormous price. It was said that seventeen thousand dollars was refused for one claim on Sulphur creek, where, two months before, claims could have been bought for two thousand five hundred dollars. The gold was of good quality, even better than that of Bonanza and Eldorado.

Calder Creek, which heads up just across the divide from Eldorado, and runs into Quartz Creek in the Indian River district, was discovered in the latter part of October, and promised well. In November not less than fifteen claims were being worked on it, the miners having sledded across from Eldorado.

During these stampedes some very queer cases happened. Some miners would participate in every rush and stake out claims on the new creeks, but they delayed in recording them because they could have but one in the district, and every one was living in the constant expectation that something even better would turn up. In this way some had staked a dozen different locations without recording any of them. The result was that often a prospector came along one of the creeks with enterprise to sink a hole, and would find good pay-dirt. He would at once record the claim, and the original staker would be " left."

During the last week in August a mad rush was made to Moosehide Creek, about eight miles north of Dawson, where a prospect of seventy-five cents to the pan was reported. A number of tenderfeet were fortunate enough to secure good locations, but they forgot, after staking their claims, to have them recorded. Their neglect soon became known in Dawson, and another rush took place, resulting in the freezing out of the original tenderfeet.

The difficulty in determining the richness of any new district lies in the fact that it is impossible to go to bed-rock in the summer. The banks along the creeks are marshy, and in many places it seems necessary to sink the shaft in the very bed of the creek, so that no prospecting for real values can be done till winter sets in.

Some idea of the uncertain character of prospecting may be gained from the fact that Victoria Creek, a tributary of the Bonanza, located in the fall of 1896 when the first rush was made, and practically deserted, was again prospected, and in June came reports of big strikes on it. In a short time claims were selling at good figures, but no one seemed to know whether they were as rich as reported. The danger that those who had claims on creeks which did not promise well would organize stampedes so as to sell off their claims to hungry newcomers, of course, always existed.

As a natural result of all these stampedes and strikes, the office of the gold commissioner was besieged continually by men wishing to file claims. At some of the busiest times men were compelled to keep their places in line for three days before they could get to the commissioner's desk. Sometimes the thermometer stood forty below.

When the people began to pour into Dawson in the spring of 1897 the furtherest claim staked was not more than twenty miles away. But by the end of the year the country was staked for a hundred miles about, and prospectors were wandering in the mountains further away than that. The tenderfeet kept on locating dozens of creeks further and further away, till finally we gave up trying to keep track of them, or even to remember their names. The gold commissioner has had a difficult undertaking with so many new men, for there seemed to be a lot who came for the purpose of locating all the claims they could, and after winter set in again they carried out their purpose, though with many hardships and privations.

The distance to these new creeks was always great, the weather intensely cold, and the stampeders in nearly every case were forced to break trail through two feet of snow. Under these conditions it was impossible for the gold commissioner to prevent stampeders from staking an unlimited number of claims for friends and acquaintances, who afterwards recorded them in Dawson, after first swearing that they personally staked the claims and found gold prospects upon them. On Rosebud Creek, the scene of one of the winter excitements, two men staked twenty claims each. A man was arrested for staking two claims on Hunker Creek, and a jeweler in Dawson forfeited his mining rights, together with the titles to four claims, for recording a claim that had been staked for him by a stampeder.

The gold commissioner received information that many stampeders had staked and recorded more than one claim in each district. Under the existing laws, each individual can record but one claim in a district. Owing to the pressure of business at the commissioner's office it was impossible to thoroughly identify each applicant for a mining claim, and this made frauds possible.

Early in December there started from Dawson an exciting race for a fortune, perhaps the longest and most unique that was ever recorded in the history of any mining camp in the world. Two dog teams hurriedly left Dawson and went flying down the river over an unbroken trail of ice to Circle City, a distance of over three hundred miles to the rim of the Arctic Circle.

Fred Trump owned a half interest in claim No. 46 below discovery on Hunker Creek. Like many others, when provisions were scarce, he was compelled to leave for Fort Yukon, but he got only as far as Circle City. There was practically no grub to be had, and he was without funds, and repeatedly tried to sell the property for two thousand dollars. Shortly after his departure from Dawson, pay-gravel running five dollars to the pan was struck on the claim in which he was interested. An offer of fifty thousand dollars for the claim was declined, and other properties adjoining became almost equally valuable.

Captain Guiger came up from Circle City on December 4th and said that Trump was vainly trying to sell his half interest in the claim for two thousand dollars. That night at ten o'clock a well-equipped dog team started out over the ribbon of broken ice to Circle City with orders and gold dust to purchase the claim at any price under twenty-five thousand dollars. At four o'clock the next morning a second team followed in hot pursuit, and Dawson was left to wonder what the result of the race would be. When the ice goes out the world may know.

It was the opinion of many old miners late in 1897 that in a few years the headquarters of the gold-mining on the upper Yukon would be on the Stewart River. During the latter part of the season many had worked their way up the river and its tributaries, and from time to time came reports of wonderfully rich finds. It was, of course, too far away to be verified, and too great a distance for a large stampede, but several small parties left Dawson for the river, and as they did not return disgusted, as the stampeders so often did, the fact was generally regarded as conclusive that they were finding gold in large quantities.   It was calculated that as many as two hundred and fifty were wintering on the streams and its creeks, and there is certainly room there for many thousand.

Although the bars of the Stewart River had been successfully worked for ten years, there had been no real prospecting done on the many important tributaries till last year.   Everywhere that the explorers and scattering prospectors have gone on the Stewart and its branches gold has been found.   On many creeks the prospects were extra good.   Several things have conspired to leave this field practically untouched.   The question of getting supplies in is a very serious one.   At the same time, the few hundred men who have been on the Yukon for several years have found sufficiently attractive diggings nearer to the older district and closer to the supply bases.   The Indians also have a fear of the natives of the headwaters, and cannot be prevailed to go up the river a great distance.   From the mouth of Stewart River to Mount Jesus on the north fork the distance is estimated at four hundred and fifty miles, and to the head of this fork in the vicinity of five hundred miles in all.   The south fork is practically unexplored, only one or two parties having been on it, and then not for a sufficient distance to determine its character or length. The prospectors and those who have been on the river say that it carries a larger body of water than Pelly River, and is beyond doubt the second largest feeder of the Yukon.

The first gold discoveries there were made in 1885 on bars within about one hundred miles from the mouth. These were rich.   During the fall, in less than fifty days

time, as high as six thousand dollars to the man was rocked
out.   In 1886 fully a hundred men were working on the
river bars with good success.   Some went up the north fork
nearly to its head.   Each succeeding season the bars have
been worked until they failed to pay the high wages.

The Stewart empties into the Yukon about seventy
miles above the mouth of the Klondike.   From its mouth to
the forks is about two hundred and seventy miles, and the
north fork extends some two hundred and fifty miles further
on.   A trifle over two hundred miles from its mouth the
Frazer Falls make an insurmountable bar to possible steamboat navigation.   They make a fall of thirty feet in a distance of one hundred and fifty feet, and are not over
seventy-five feet in width.   Here a portage of about half a
mile must be made.   From there on rapids are encountered
for about six miles.   But these can be poled and lined over
without great difficulty.

Among the tributaries upon which gold has now been
found is Rosebud Creek, about forty miles up on the south
bank.   No prospecting has been done to any extent.   Lake
Creek, about sixty-five miles up, has shown gold on its bars,
but no work has been done.   McQuesten River is much
larger than any of these creeks, and several good bars have
been worked on it, some of them paying as high as fifty dollars per day with rockers.   Some work has been done on the
side creeks emptying into the McQuesten.   The McQuesten
is supposed to head close to Beaver River, which is the
largest branch of the north fork of the Stewart.   Forty
miles further up on the south side is Crooked Creek, upon
which gold has been found in small quantities, but only surface work has been done on it.   Mayo Creek comes in on
the northern bank about forty miles above Crooked Creek.

About six miles up there is a cañon which extends for six miles, and through which it is impossible to take a boat. Two boats were carried around it in 1894, and the stream was traversed for about seventy-five miles. More or less gold was found on the bars all along. In the cañon coarse gold was found in several places. As high as ten cents a pan was found on the surface.

Much of the Stewart River lies in the same belt as the gold-bearing regions of the Klondike, and that there is gold there cannot be doubted. The difficulty is in getting to it. It is necessary to take a full year's outfit to prospect on the upper waters. Owing to the distance prospectors have had to spend the best part of their time in bringing up their outfits. By the time a man has poled from Forty Mile or Dawson up to the mouth of the river, and from there a hundred miles to the McQuesten, the summer season is past, and he must have winter provisions or hurry back. Miners have not felt that they could afford to do this so long as there were good paying mines near Forty Mile on the Klondike, and the recent prospects on the stream come from those who have been led by the wonderful Klondike placers to look more carefully into all this region. To the old miner, acquainted with the general rules of indications of gold, the Stewart would look much more promising than the Klondike, but it is unsafe to apply to Alaska any rules that hold elsewhere in the world. It is a queer country, and when the thousands who have now rushed in have poked around in the hills for a time we shall know a great many new things — that is, if the people who are doing the poking do not die in the attempt.

These gold fields can be developed but slowly. Ten thousand men can come here and be lost in the great territory when they scatter to prospect. A few of them will strike a mine and become rich. When they do strike pay-dirt their fortunes will be made. In years to come, after an awful sacrifice of human life and energy, when the treasures of this great land are located, its wealth will be something beyond our present comprehension.

CHAPTER XXXI

THE GOVERNMENT OF THE KLONDIKE — CHARACTER-
ISTICS OF THE CANADIAN MOUNTED POLICE —
CANADIAN REGULATIONS — THE MAILS THROWN
AWAY ON THE TRAIL — A QUESTION OF LIFE OR
DEATH.

Attention Paid the Yukon District by Canadian Government after
Gold Discoveries — Concerned Over Loss of Revenue — Detach-
ment of Police Sent In — When the Organization was Formed —
Its Principal Features — Officers and Constables — The Yukon
Territory — Powers of the Gold Commissioner — His Word Final
in All Cases as to Claims — Experience of a Seattle Man — How a
Double Sale was Quickly Untangled — Government Rights over
the Yukon Region — The Proposed Royalty — Indignation of the
Miners — A Meeting and a Protest — Possibilities of Trouble —
Uncertainty of the Mails — Difficulties of a Carrier — Mail Matter
Taken by Returning Miners and Thrown Away on the Trail — A
Matter of Life or Death.

THE Klondike region, being in the Northwest Territory, is subject to the laws of Canada, but it was
not till after pioneers from the United States began
to find gold about the boundary line that the Ottawa government paid much attention to the country. The hardy
miners who first prospected up and down the streams, suffering great hardships, had secured their supplies from trading companies navigating the Yukon, and when, by 1894,
it began to appear that considerable gold was being found,
and that much merchandise was being taken into the North-

west Territory free of duty, the Ottawa government thought
" that the time had arrived to make more efficient provision
for the maintenance of order, the enforcement of the laws,
and the administration of justice in the Yukon country,
especially in that section of it in which placer-mining for
gold is being prosecuted upon such an extensive scale."

It was evident that the Dominion government viewed
with considerable concern the loss of revenue or duty upon
the provisions which were taken to the pioneers with so
much difficulty and expense.   Accordingly, a detachment
of twenty members of the mounted police force was detailed
for service along the upper Yukon.   The officer in command, Inspector Constantine, in addition to the magisterial
duties which he was required to perform, was authorized
to represent, when necessary, all the departments of the
Canadian government having interests in that region.   His
instructions particularly authorized him to perform the
duties of Dominion land agent, collector of customs, and
collector of inland revenue.   Later, Mr. Thomas Fawcett
was appointed gold commissioner, surveyor, and general
agent of the Minister of the Interior for the district.   It
was thus, after Americans in the course of their difficult
and generally unremunerative prospecting throughout the
region had found gold, that the Canadian officials awoke
to the necessity of sending in the machinery of the government.

Whatever may have been the motive of the Canadian
government in sending in agents to the new district, it must
be said to her credit that she has sent good ones, and that
the supervision of the mounted police has given the people
of the Klondike a sense of security which is not usually enjoyed in new mining camps, especially when so far removed

from the centers of civilization.   Their scarlet uniform is
the symbol of law and order in the Northwest.

The force was organized when Alexander Mackenzie
was Premier, and was one of Sir John Macdonald's inspira-
tions.   After his return to power in 1878 it always remained under his own eye.   The nucleus of the force was
got together at Manitoba in 1873.   It originally numbered
only three hundred, but by its coolness and pluck at critical
periods it accomplished much by reducing the Indians and
lawless whisky traders to a state of order.   The police built
posts and protected white settlers, and the surveyors who
had already began parcelling out the country and exploring
the route of the Canadian Pacific Railway.   In 1877
nearly the whole of the little force was concentrated on the
southwestern frontier to watch and check the six thousand
Sioux who sought refuge in Canada after their defeat and
massacre of Custer and his command on the Little Big
Horn.

It was through the efforts of the mounted police that
the Sioux were finally induced to surrender peacefully to
the United States authorities in 1880 to 1881.   After the
outbreak of the half-breeds under Louis Riel in 1885, the
force was increased to one thousand men, their present
number.

Like the Royal Irish Constabulary, on which it was
modelled, the mounted police is, in the eye of the law, a
purely civil body.   Its officers are magistrates, the men are
constables.   But so far as circumstances will allow, its organization, internal economy, and drill are those of a cavalry
regiment, and when on active service in a military capacity
the officers have army rank.   The affairs of the force are
managed by a distinct department of the Canadian govern-

ment, under the supervision of a cabinet minister. The executive command is held by an officer styled the commissioner and ranking as lieutenant-colonel. The assistant commissioner ranks as a major, and, after three years service, as a lieutenant-colonel. Ten superintendents with captain's rank command the divisions, with about thirty-five inspectors as subalterns who correspond to lieutenants. The medical staff consists of a surgeon, five assistant surgeons, and two veterinary surgeons. The non-commissioned officers are as in our army, while the troopers are called constables.

The rank and file are not excelled by any picked corps in any service. A recruit must be between twenty-two and forty-five years old, of good character, able to read and to write English or French, active, well built, and of sound constitution. Their physique is very fine, the average of the whole thousand being five feet nine and a half inches in height, and thirty-eight and a half inches around the chest.

There has always been an unusual proportion of men of good family and of education in the service. Lots of young Englishmen who came out to try their hand at farming in the far west have drifted into the police, as have also well-connected Canadians. Waifs and strays from everywhere, and of every calling, are to be found in the ranks. The roll-call would show defaulters if no man answered to any name but his own. There is at least one lord in the force, and many university graduates. As a rule they are men who get along well with the miners. They experience much the same hardships in winter, and they like to see fair play, but they are stern in carrying out the law of the land.

The Yukon Territory, so designated by Canada for the purpose of government, is about one-half as large as Alaska,

A Scene on the Border

Canadian mounted police collecting customs duty from Klondikers at the point where the Canadian Government has established a boundary line at White Pass. The huge pile of boxes, bags, and goods of all kinds belong to gold-seekers *en route* to the Gold Fields.

and extends from British Columbia on the south to the Arctic Ocean on the north, and from the one hundred and sixty-first meridian on the west to the mountains eastward separating the watershed of the Mackenzie from that of the Yukon. The chief official is known as the Commissioner of the Territory, and all the officials, with the exception of the judge of the court, may be suspended by him for cause. The police is under his orders, and he is given ample authority to meet any emergency that may arise without waiting to hear from Ottawa. The judge is sent to administer the ordinary laws of the territory. Besides the gold commissioner there is a registrar of the land district, a lawyer, whose duties combine the clerkship of the court and the registration of titles, four land surveyors acting under the gold commissioner, and a number of custom officers stationed at various points along the line of entry into the district. The mounted police force on the Yukon was but a hundred at first, but has been increased to two hundred and fifty, stationed along the trails and at Yukon centers.

But a small part of the machinery of government was on hand during the first year of the Klondike excitement. Some of the higher officials did not start until late in 1897, and during the winter were tied up at the mouth of the Big Salmon River, unable to proceed to Dawson. Meanwhile authority was vested in the inspector of police and the gold commissioner. The power of the latter to settle all disputes as to claims is absolute. He listens to cases involving ownership to gold claims, and renders his decisions promptly. If there has not been some mistake in reports, his decision is final. And the adjustment that he announces becomes the law by which all interested parties must abide.

A single case will illustrate. Michael Kelly, a well-known pioneer, went to the Klondike with his son. Father and son located several claims on different creeks with the understanding that they would share the proceeds equally. The elder Kelly decided to return to Seattle early in 1897, and left his son on the claim last located. At that time the Klondike was not known to be a bed of glittering gold.

Kelly was anxious to return to the gold fields, but desired to raise money in order to leave his family in comfortable circumstances. He met a man by the name of Crawford and proposed to sell him a half interest in his claim for one thousand dollars. Crawford mortgaged his property, disposed of his jewelry, and, by taking some friends in with him, secured enough money to pay Kelly the one thousand dollars. Crawford went to the Klondike in the spring, and, to his dismay, found that young Kelly, not knowing what his father had done, had sold the Bonanza claim to an English syndicate for ten thousand dollars.

When the elder Kelly learned what had taken place, he said that Crawford had made his purchase in good faith and that his rights must be protected. The affair was referred to the gold commissioner, who decided that Crawford and his associates were to have half of the claim, but that they must pay to the English syndicate one thousand five hundred dollars out of the first clean-up, while the Kellys should return to the English syndicate five thousand dollars, or half the original purchase price.

This decision was accepted by all parties without a murmur, and a tangle was settled in a day that in the United States would have been a source of endless litigation. Miners said that Crawford's claim was worth between one hundred thousand and three hundred thousand dollars.

It should be understood that all the territory in these regions constitute what are known as crown lands, the government having the right to reserve it all from pre-emption for any purpose. The reservation of gold-bearing lands is simply a partial exercise of the right of the crown to exclusive domain, and the British government has always claimed that gold and silver were royal metals, and has claimed the right to draw royalty from such metals. As soon, therefore, as the government heard of the rich discoveries on the Klondike, steps were taken to reduce the length of the claims to one hundred feet, and to exact a heavy royalty. At first it was proposed to make this royalty twenty per cent. and to reserve every alternate claim for the government to dispose of in any way it saw fit. It would have the right to work them for the crown if it chose, and the government would be in a position thus to draw rich revenue as a result of the long searches and many hardships of the pioneers of the country.

When the intention of the Dominion government became known in Dawson, there was great indignation among the miners, Canadians as well as Americans. A meeting was held on the street, and it was evident that any attempt to enforce such a law would either amount to nothing or else the development of the mines would stop.

" What inducement is there for us," said one miner, " to endure all the hardships and expense of mining in this country, if, after we have found gold, the government steps up and takes a fifth of what we dig, and, above that, takes one-half of the claims? Many of us have been enduring hardships here for years, and until now have scarcely made more than enough to provide ourselves with provisions. Now, when we have found something worth developing in this frozen region, Canada talks of keeping the best half for herself while we do the work. I guess not."

The Canadian officials on the spot seemed to sympathize with the sentiments of the miners, but they said they should strictly enforce whatever became the law. A protest was drawn up and a committee appointed to proceed to Ottawa and present the case of the miners. In their protest, which was a long document worded with skill and force, they claimed that the value of the placers had been exaggerated, and many claims would not be profitable if such a tax were imposed, the rate of wages and the cost of provisions being so necessarily high.

" This," they said, " is a land of tremendous solitudes and marvelous wildness. It appears to be a land of immense promise to the prospector, but the appearance may be deceptive. It is outside the range of language to picture the trials that encompass the explorer who goes forth here with pick, shovel, and gold-pan to search for gold. Only strong men are equal to the task, and only men of great courage and perseverance can press far. If the government place a heavy hand on the prospectors, already almost frenzied with toil and privation, prospecting in this district will be abandoned by the majority, and prospectors will turn toward other gold fields. This is not a threat; it is a condition."

It was pointed out that if the government reserved every alternate claim of one hundred feet it would be impossible to co-operate along the creeks for building dams for sluicing without trespassing on government claims, and if the government should sell its claims it would simply mean that the old miners who had found the mines and suffered all manner of privations would be crowded out by capital, which would reap the profit without having been forced to undergo the hardships.

But the temptation to reap a large revenue was too great for the Ottawa government.   Besides, it was a source of no little chagrin to many Canadians to see the gold worked out of British soil by Americans to be carried down the coast and into the mints of the United States instead of those of Canada.   This was natural.   Doubtless the people of the United States would have felt in much the same way had the conditions been reversed, although no restrictions whatever had ever been placed on Canadians mining on Birch Creek and in other portions of Alaska.   The Canadian government did not wish to impose so heavy a tax as to put an end to the development of the country, but it evidently intended to impose all that seemed possible of endurance. So during the early part of 1898 the laws were modified to some extent.   The length of claims to be thereafter allowed was to be two hundred and fifty feet, a royalty of ten per cent. should be levied and collected on the gross output of each claim, and every alternate ten claims should be reserved for the Canadian government.   These are the main features of the restrictions which the government propose to begin enforcing with the spring of 1898.   How successful it will be remains to be seen.

It will be observed that these regulations add greatly to the expense of mining on Canadian territory.   In the first place, in order to prospect at all, a man must secure a free miner's certificate, which costs him ten dollars a year, and if for any reason he fails to renew it promptly he shall forfeit all rights to whatever claims he has.   When he stakes off a claim of two hundred and fifty feet along a creek he must at once have it recorded, and that costs him fifteen dollars. To work it during the winter he must pay something like a thousand dollars for provisions by the time they have reached the camp. His fuel will cost him at least five hundred dollars, and timber and appliances for sluicing as much more. To work his claim successfully he must pay at least ten dollars a day for all help. If he hires two men his expenses under this head are not likely to be less than four thousand dollars. Supposing in the spring he is so fortunate as to clean up ten thousand dollars. The Canadian government takes a thousand of it, and his expenses have used up at least six thousand. He might, therefore, be so fortunate as to save three thousand for himself, a sum which would not much more than provide for his necessities for another year. It is evident, therefore, that placers must be very rich, and must be worked on a large and economical scale to meet such restrictions and expenditures.

The natural result will be to stimulate the search for gold placers on American soil, and if any at all comparable with those in the Klondike are found, the Klondike will be deserted in a twinkling, by Canadians as well as Americans. If paying mines are not found elsewhere, and the Klondike region continues to disclose new riches, the restrictions which Canada has imposed may lead to difficulties. Of one thing we may be sure; the laws, whatever they are, will be enforced. If a royalty is demanded it will have to be paid, and whatever customs duties are levied upon supplies brought into the country will have to be paid. The police will see that the law is carried out, even though they consider it unjust.

One might think that a handful of police could do very little with the thousands of miners who within a year will be scattered all through the hills about Dawson, and that if these people took it into their heads to regulate mining there to suit themselves, Canada could do little to prevent it. But while there may be dangers in such a possibility, they are not great.   The country is of such a nature that a few police can hold all the points at which gold must pass in going out of the country.   But what is of more importance, the people who are there recognize the advantages of police protection in maintaining their rights against each other.

If any one is looking for a strong illustration of the uncertainties of existence in this world, he can find nothing better than the mail service on the Yukon.   Some realization of its efficiency can be derived from the fact that gold was discovered on the Klondike creeks in August, 1896, and that it was not till the middle of July, 1897, that the world knew about it.   It did not learn of it then through the mails, but because a dozen or more men who had meanwhile become millionaires, or something approaching millionaires, walked off a ship just in from St. Michael with several hundred pounds of gold dust.   Yet there was supposed to have been a mail service.

In 1896 the United States made a contract for carrying the mails between Juneau and Circle City, and in writing to the postmaster-general in the fall of that year concerning his first round trip, one contractor said that he had started from Juneau on June 10th.   He took along lumber for building a boat, but after the Indians had packed it to the foot of the summit and taken nearly seventy dollars for it, they refused to carry it further, and so he had to leave it there and build a raft at Lake Lindeman.   Reaching Lake Bennett, he built a boat, and finally reached Circle City. But he found he could not undertake to pole up the river alone on a return trip, and so he came out by the way of St.

Michael. It cost something like six hundred dollars to make the trip, and some of the contractors threw up their contracts.

When Dawson was established there was no way to receive or send mail except by those who happened to be going in or out. Whoever wished to send a letter would pay from one to two dollars to one starting out over the passes, but who gave no guarantee that the letters would be delivered or mailed in the United States. Indeed, it was always understood that if emergency came, the letters would have to be thrown away. Any one who goes over the trail will find in many places bits of paper, evidently the fragments of letters which had been sent out in the hands of some one who could carry them no further, and so tore them up.

Of course, there are many miners around Dawson who never expect to hear from home, and these men will never know whether their friends or relatives ever received letters sent them. The missives are started in good faith, and the man going out agrees to put them in the post-office, but when he is struggling on the trail nearly dead from exposure and fatigue, hurt by accident, or anything like that, the situation resolves itself into a question of life or death for many a traveler. In an emergency he goes into his pack and throws away everything he can possibly throw away — probably leaving nothing but a few provisions and his outfit. Going over the passes and lakes, with their attendant perils and difficulties, is too much for eighty out of one hundred. They simply give up. It is a crucial test of strength and grit. The few that pull through know what it means.

Couriers have left Dawson with great packages of letters, fully intending to carry them through. On the way they gave it up in despair, and so, to prevent the letters being found and read, they are torn up or burned.

The experience of two partners who started to make the trip out shows clearly why a little mail matter may be a serious addition to the burden. They had dogs and sleds. One of the men fell into a crack in the ice, and went in over his head. By a miracle his head came up at the right place, and his partner pulled him out of a very dangerous position. By the time he was on the ice again his clothes were frozen stiff and he was nearly done for. As the sled had remained on the ice, his partner quickly lighted a fire in the stove — materials for a fire always being " laid " beforehand — and cut and tore off the wet garments on the spot. The fellow was nearly stripped in an air where the thermometer registered about twenty-five degrees below zero. Part of their outfit was lost. If the stove had gone in, it would have been a serious matter. After that they lightened their packs.

The destruction of letters was not unusual. In fact, that possibility was understood by all parties. The guides who agreed to try to carry a package of letters accepted the money for the service, but said that if it came to a pinch they would throw them away. On this basis of chance did the Yukoners conduct their correspondence with the outside world. Recently the mounted police have undertaken to forward the mails from station to station along the trail between the coast and Dawson.

CHAPTER XXXII

THE SUDDEN RISE AND MAGICAL EXPANSION OF SKAG-
WAY — CURIOUS SIGNS FOR THRIVING ENTER-
PRISES — THE DEBATING SOCIETY IN MRS.
MALONEY'S BOARDING TENT — ONE HUNDRED
DAYS' GROWTH.

Seeking an Easier Pass than the Chilkoot — Why Gold-Seekers Began
to Stop at Skagway — A Peaceful Scene in July — The Original
Promoters Quickly Overwhelmed — A Thousand Tents and a
Thousand Pack Animals — Organizing the Town — Marvelous
Real Estate Business — How a Hotel Keeper Announced His
Facilities — A More Modest Announcement — "Any Old Thing
Bought and Sold" — Tons of Provisions Scattered on the Beach —
Saloons and Dance Halls — An Opening Night — The Symbol of
Law and Order — Herds of Gambling Men — "An Easy Graft" —
Greenhorns at Packing — Runaway Animals — Many Ludicrous
Scenes — The Serious Side — A Clergyman's Observations — The
Part the Women Played — Widow Maloney's Debating Society —
Respect for the Chair — Debating the Merits of Armies of the
World — Some Race Feeling — Mrs. Maloney Does Not Permit
Abuse of "Ould Ireland" — A Hundred Days of Growth —
"Biggest" Town in Alaska.

PERHAPS no feature of the rush for the Klondike in
1897 is more significant of the conditions affecting
travel in these northern lands than the stories of the
efforts to enter by the Skagway trail, as told by the few who
managed to work their way through and reach Dawson
early in the winter.   It is an instructive chapter, not simply
in the story of the Klondike, but in the annals of human
nature.   It is doubtful if there is anything in history to
compare with the sudden rise of the city of Skagway, and

(446)

the trials of the thousands of people who endeavored to make their way from it over the White Pass to the head-waters of the Yukon.

Parties from the Pacific coast had for some time been seeking an easier way to pass into the Northwest Terri-tory than that afforded by the Chilkoot heights, and one Captain William Moore, who had been a pioneer in that region, and had acquired much experience in steamboating, persuaded these parties to take hold of the White Pass. Moore's son had meanwhile located a hundred and sixty acres where the Skagway harbor would necessarily be, and work was begun to put the pass in shape.

The company proceeded to build a sawmill and a wharf, and was intending to open a trail when the first news of the richness of the Klondike awakened the people of the west coast. One day, when one of the earlier steamers heavily laden with the first of the gold-seekers was steaming up Taiya Inlet, the captain of the steamer remarked: " I understand that there is a good trail over the mountains here, and a better pass than the Chilkoot. It is easier to land cargoes, too. Suppose I put you all ashore here."

The gold-seekers consulted, and the result was that they were put ashore. This was on the 26th of July, and at that time Skagway presented as peaceful a scene as any one could wish. There was one log building and a tent. In less than a month, and long before the forerunners had made their way over the pass, Skagway was a place of two thousand people, while twice as many more were scattered along on the trail. It had become a place of a thousand tents and buildings, mostly the former, and a thousand pack animals. Saloons and dance halls had sprung up like magic buildings, and were in full blast, and many of those who had arrived with the intention of going over quickly settled down, either in despair of getting over at all, or simply to fleece those who bravely persisted and those who were constantly arriving.

The sudden inpouring of people completely overwhelmed the original promoters of the enterprise; they had been dreaming of rich results from the monopoly control of this trail after being put in shape, but they soon found that they had nothing to say, not even concerning the site of the town and harbor to which they supposed they were entitled.

On August 12th the people held a meeting and organized a town government by electing A. J. McKinney mayor, and a committee was chosen to lay out the town in regular form with streets sixty feet wide and lots fifty by one hundred feet. A law was passed forbidding any man to hold more than one lot, and he must do fifty dollars' worth of work on it within thirty days. Within a few days real estate business was flourishing; lots were being transferred for from one hundred dollars to two hundred and fifty dollars for such rights as the squatter had. Lots in what appeared to be the business portion were held at high figures, and few were sold, while more squatters settled back in the woods, and even down on the tide flats, in ignorance of the tides that sometimes run up. Some of the business enterprises which sprung up in those few days were indeed picturesque. There were restaurants in tents, of course, but some of the signs were very pretentious.

A Seattle man, who started for the gold fields in August, and who was, like so many others, caught at Skagway, devoted his energies to running an improvised hotel, the announcement of which was conspicuously posted as follows on the " outer gates ":

Holley House, Holleywood.

Skagway, Alaska.

Hotel and cottages, The Most Delightful Health Resort on the Coast of North America.

Cusine and Accommodations First-Class.

Six Cottages in Connection With the Hotel.

Barber, Billiards, Bath, Private Supper Rooms, Music in the palm garden adjoining the dining room.

Charges from $2 up according to the location of the rooms.

Meals á la carte.   Private Suites.   Extra charges for meals served in rooms.

Note — Anybody kicking about looking-glasses or pillows will be " trun."

Some were more modest, however, as, for instance, one man who had pitched his tent in a rough spot in the midst of trees.   On a line stretched from his tent to one of the trees hung a pair of old light-colored trousers, and painted on them in large letters was the word:

" MEALS."

On a large sign on the outside of one tent was a legend announcing to the passers-by that they could there buy or sell " boats, horses, provisions, outfits, or any old thing." Horse-shoeing was a great industry, and there were too few who understood it.   In one shop four men were kept busy, so busy that they had no time to straighten up their aching backs.   But they received large prices, five dollars for putting on an old shoe.   All prices for services were " up in the air."   Men charged two dollars and fifty cents for swimming a horse ashore, two dollars for landing a boat, four dollars a ton for lightering freight.   Camping sites were ruling at ten dollars a week.

In less than two months more than one thousand one hundred locations were being made, and the town of tents began to give way to the town of frame houses.   The trail was not open, and not even the correct distance was known, before the eager throng was crowding with horses, goats, oxen, and mules hitched to carts, wagons, and drags, and carrying pack saddles loaded with flour, bacon, beans, dried apples, and hay. Already the saloons and dance halls were up and ready for patrons. Tons of stuff were scattered over the beach, and shiploads strung along the trail. Lumber was in great demand, and lots selling as high as one thousand five hundred dollars.

The first dance hall was opened a few hours after the arrival of one of the steamers laden with people bound for Klondike, about the middle of August. A Juneau man had put a piano aboard, and, having secured quarters, he had a great opening, taking in one hundred and thirty-four dollars the first hour from drinks alone. On the outside of the dance house was a tree to which was hung several significant notices, and from one of the limbs dangled a one-inch rope with a noose, put there as a warning or symbol of law and order by the Vigilance Committee, and it was quite effective against high crime. Three of the notices read:

" Free Dance To-night."

" Packers Wanted on the Trail. Apply to Mack & Company."

" Saddle Horses Wanted — No Cheap Hatracks."

Of course herds of gambling men hurried from the Pacific coast to set up at Skagway, and, for a time, every kind of a game was running in the most open manner. As one of them expressed it, it was the " easiest graft " on earth. But as the place grew the citizens regulated these enterprises and order was fairly well maintained.

" Skagway," said one man, " reminded me a good deal of a circus town, there were so many tents. It looked a

A RESTAURANT AND ITS PROPRIETOR ON THE DYEA TRAIL
The sign "Meals" is painted on the remains of a pair of old trousers.

good deal as Cheyenne did in the early days. Eating
booths were scattered all about.   The saloons were made of
boards loosely thrown together.   You could almost throw a
cat through the cracks.   There are some very curious and
interesting signs painted on boards and stuck up outside the
tents to announce the business of the occupants.   One that
particularly attracted my attention read: ' Hot bread and
stamps for sale.'

" On arriving, people made reconnoitering trips over a
portion of the pass, returning full of exuberance at the easy
time they would have in getting over.   They were right in
this at that time, but they reckoned without their host.
They did not know of the trouble in store for them in getting their stores and belongings off the boat.   It took nearly
a week to get things sorted, and then there was the greatest
jumbled-up mess one ever looked at.   Many of the goods
were damaged much by water.   It would have taken a
Philadelphia lawyer to straighten things.   When the individual outfits were finally distributed, new troubles happened, caused chiefly by the inexperience of the people
themselves.   Men attempted to pack horses who had never
before in their lives seen a pack; the horses were new to the
business, and more than once I have witnessed sights that
convulsed me with laughter, and at the same time caused a
feeling of sadness for the poor chaps whose troubles would
almost drive them to desperation.   A greenhorn (we were
nearly all greenhorns) would pack his horse down with
flour, beans, and other things too numerous to mention,
and tie them on any way, when all of a sudden there
would be a kick, a buck, and the next instant a maddened
horse would be running over tents and through the little

city, scattering beans and flour in all directions. Sometimes it would take a whole day to capture the horse. It was such things as these that caused many a fellow to sell his outfit for anything he could get and return to civilization.

"This, though, was the ludicrous side, many things occurring on the trail, when the mud in the meadows was knee-deep, that would drive the stoutest-hearted man to despair."

A clergyman who came in over the trail said that when the history of the present excitement should be written up, woman's part in it would form a chapter of special interest. "Along the Skagway trail," he said, "I was attracted by the sound of an axe in the wood, and, going in its direction, I found there, all alone, a slim woman about twenty years old, felling trees and building a cabin. I took a snap-shot picture of her before she knew of my presence. She told me that she and her husband started for the Klondike, but, not being able to proceed, her husband opened a saloon till spring, and wished her to serve in it. This she positively refused to do, but, being willing to take her part in the struggle, she determined to build a log cabin and sell it when the rush was on. I gave her a lift with a few logs she had ready for the wall, and left, feeling that she was a noble woman and a true wife.

"There were hundreds of idle men, grudging every day the food they ate, and impatient to reach the diggings. Many of them were quarrelsome and given terribly to profanity. Therefore, I suggested that we might get together and form a debating society. It would at least take our minds off our monotonous surroundings and help pass away the idle hours. This was agreed to, and Widow Maloney's restaurant was selected, being the largest tent in the camps. The time for discussion was to be anywhere from 4 to 10 P. M. The chairman was to take his seat when the boarders got through supper, about an hour after sundown, and preserve order as the disputants came and went at pleasure. The audience, too, was free to come and go as the spirit moved, and no objections were to be raised by the chairman if in the heat of passion any one went a-scattering lead from his revolver, for it was conceded by all that the only two governments which in any event could interfere were those of the United States and Canada, and as these bodies themselves did not know which had jurisdiction over Lindeman, it was evident that moral suasion alone could be appealed to. The question then came up, Who had enough of this commodity on hand to preside over the turbulent crowd? Several were suggested, but they were objectionable, because on the least provocation they might open a blazing battery from the seat of authority. Finally, I was made supreme spokesman in Mrs. Maloney's restaurant, presumably because of a meek and lowly appearance. On taking my seat, however, at the first meeting, I presented a rope, and, holding it before the astonished audience, assured them that while I might be living in a place without political rule, I would hang by the neck, on the pine tree outside, every mother's son of them who did not respect the chair. This had a soothing effect, and the lion, the lamb, the kid, and the calf huddled together for a while in sweetest harmony.

" One evening the subject of debate was, 'Is Prosperity Coming or Going in the United States?' The discussion at times was very animated, as all the political parties of the country were represented, and each claimed that his, and his alone, could give the people the horn of plenty. The cut-down in the New England factories was freely talked over, and it was generally agreed that cotton operatives in the States are only befooled by the politicians when they promise them anything. Their only hope lies in themselves. When they agree, North and South, to work only for living wages and uniform hours of labor, they may think as little of politics as they do in other countries. Not pauper labor in Europe, nor political parties in America, are at the root of the present troubles.

" Another evening was given up to the discussion of the merits and demerits of the several armies of the world. This was the liveliest night of all. Men from all nations were present, and, of course, each reckoned his own best and bravest. The Englishmen thought there was nothing on earth that could stand up before the redcoats, and the Irishmen present declared that that was so because there were no Saxons inside. The Celtic race alone made the British army respected. An Englishman pertinently asked ' If Irishmen were such fools as to fight for the greatness and glory of old England?' 'They have to, or starve,' cried a dozen voices. Paddy Sheehan, however, got into hot water when he attempted to prove that it was the Irish that fought and conquered in the late War of the Rebellion.

" A Rhode Islander present was so cruel as to charge against poor Paddy's race in reply, that the only time it distinguished itself was at the first battle of Bull Run, when they made the quickest time on record to the other side of the Potomac. This led to pulling of revolvers, and for a time there was a threatening war-cloud over the head-waters of the Yukon. It capped the climax, however, when a Canadian boastingly declared that there was a fragrant smell to the English rose and a piercing sting to the Scotch thistle; but nothing but a butterfly would either love or fear the shamrock.

"Up to this point Widow Maloney took no part in the discussion; but to sit still and hear a 'hathen furn'r' speak disparagingly of the emblem of her dear land was more than she could stand, and, taking up a stick that lay by the stove, she made for him, shouting, 'An' is it ould Ireland ye're abusin', ye blackguard?'

"To pull his gun on a woman would have been sure death to the Canadian, and he knew it. He also knew that to stand up or sit down was dangerous, and therefore he put himself outside of Widow Maloney's tent quicker than I can tell. Everyone who had said anything slightingly of the Irish race, or of Ireland, was now profuse in his apologies to Mrs. Maloney. But Jack Rogers, from Chicago, went beyond all others in exalting Ireland, in that he declared there was a woman in the moon, and that he believed her to be an Irish maiden, for she had a shamrock on her breast. The idea of a woman being seen in the moon was such a novelty that the meeting adjourned to see her. Every one who witnessed the new and strange sight that night will never forget it, and, as for Mrs. Maloney, her anger was charmed away by the thought that perhaps in the moon there were Irish maidens who bore the shamrock, and her wounded feelings were healed by the assurance of all present that the woman in the moon was not either Canadian or British, and most likely was a daughter of one of the kings who reigned of old in Tara's halls."

It will be difficult for people of staid eastern towns of slow growth, or no growth at all, to realize the extent of the mushroom expansion of Skagway. As I have said, in the last week in July, it was a quiet nook in the dreary hills with a log hut and a tent near the flat beach.

In one hundred days there was a substantial town of five hundred frame and one hundred log buildings, besides tents scattered all through the woods. Many of the buildings were of two stories and some of them of three. Among the enterprises which were flourishing were:

A wide-awake six-page weekly newspaper — the *Skagway News*.

A church and schoolhouse combined, seating capacity three hundred persons, built by contributions from all denominations.

A private post-office.

Three wharves for heavy-draft vessels, costing twenty thousand dollars each.

An electric light system was being introduced, and a city water system, consisting of a simple board flume, brought an ample supply of good water from a lake on the mountain side.

A jail was built, and sundry United States government officials, including a United States commissioner, with a number of doctors, lawyers, etc., were among the citizens.

Skagway could accommodate one thousand eight hundred people at the hotels and lodging-houses. A three-story hotel, fifty by one hundred feet, was in course of construction, capable of accommodating four hundred people.

In three months it had become the " biggest " town in Alaska.

CHAPTER XXXIII

DIFFICULTIES AND HORRORS OF THE SKAGWAY TRAIL — PRECIPICES OVER WHICH HORSES TUMBLED — A LIFE FOR A SACK OF FLOUR AND A LITTLE BACON.

An Impassable Trail — The Blockade — Stories Brought to Dawson — Principal Features of the White Pass Route — Slippery Places for Horses — Over Precipices into the River — Porcupine Hill — Where Most of the Horses Were Lost — The Sight of a Life Time — Death on Summit Lake — Efforts to Open the Trail — All Kinds of Pack Animals — Scarcity of Fodder — Selling Hay and Throwing in the Horses — The Big Marsh — Floundering in the Mud — Thieving on the Trail — Looking for Pierre, the Frenchman — Discovered with Stolen Goods — Appealing to Hearts of Stone — Six Shots Sounding as One — The Limp Form of a Thief Hanging by the Wayside — A Heap of Stones Cast on the Body — Chances to Make Money on the Trail.

THE immediate cause for the rise of Skagway was the apparently reasonable assertion that the White Pass was much easier to go over than the Chilkoot Pass, the latter being about a thousand feet higher than the former. But the secondary and main cause for the growth of Skagway was the fact that, from the first, the White Pass route was well-nigh impassable. In the first place, the people had rushed in before the trail was ready. Several thousand people set out to take Nature as they found her in Alaska, and then discovered that she was utterly unmanageable. The pass might have afforded a comfortable route for the few who were acquainted with the conditions of trails, and familiar with the requirements of packing, but when several thousand people endeavored to pass over in midsummer, with all sorts of rigs, with horses, mules, and oxen, they found it an impossibility. The result was a blockade. Only a small number of those who started reached even the summit of White Pass. The great majority simply settled back, and made Skagway a booming town for no better reason than that its inhabitants could not get out of it. I do not believe that history can show a grimmer joke than that town. It had not the slightest reason for existence in that desolate region, except as a gateway to an entrance which could not be forced.

The stories which were brought into Dawson of sufferings on the trail were vivid and stirring, though, to tell the truth, we had very little sympathy for the eager crowd that was endeavoring to come in. Most of us had been in Alaska long enough to know that it is very difficult to secure a sufficiency of food when only a few are in the country, and we realized that, if the crowd at Skagway got through, there would be an enormous number of mouths to fill with comparatively few provisions in sight for the purpose. By the time we began to hear the stories of the Skagway trail it had become sufficiently evident that the only salvation of Dawson for the winter was in the White Pass proving impassable. We regarded the stories of the difficulties of that trail, therefore, with a sort of selfish satisfaction.

Unlike the Chilkoot Pass route, which is a constant ascent, ending with a steep climb to the summit, the White Pass route is a succession of hills, so that a great deal of waste climbing is done, probably enough to make up for the difference in altitude, which, apparently, is in favor of the

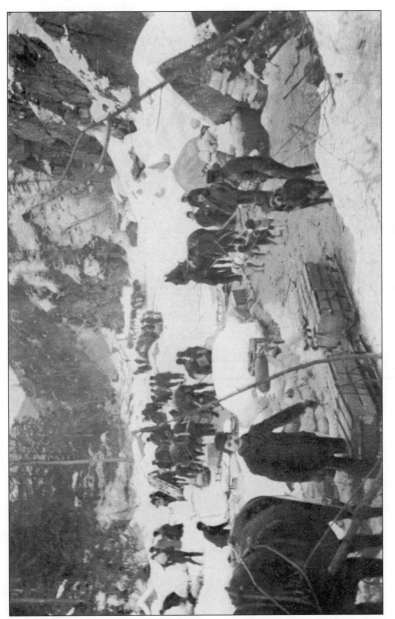

A Blockade on the Skagway Trail

White Pass. The trail was constructed something on the principle of a huge trap. For the first three or four miles it looked very easy and attractive. For this distance there was a wagon road over which horses and wagons would meet with little difficulty. Then the Skagway, which is a shallow stream, though very swift, had to be crossed. Some of the first pilgrims had constructed a rude bridge of logs over which but one horse could pass at a time. Wagons had to be unloaded, horses led carefully over, then the wagons drawn over and reloaded. From this bridge wagons could be used three miles further, when what was quite appropriately dubbed Devil's Hill was encountered. Here the trouble began. The trail was not over two feet wide, and at the top of the hill horses were compelled to make a jump of two feet high and alight on a slippery rock. At one place there was a path up a steep incline on which logs had been laid, forming a sort of ladder.

" When you get to the top of it you are five hundred feet above sea level," said one of the few who came through safely. " The hill is very rocky, but I was careful to make notes of its condition, and there is no reason why a mountain climber should not put his horse over there with comparative ease. Notwithstanding that fact, I found a dead horse on the pass. I examined it and found that it had broken one of its legs. The owner had no more use for it and killed it. After leaving the first hill you descend, entering a cañon, when another hill is encountered with a rise of eight hundred feet.

" The path over it, or, rather, around it, should not be dignified by the name of trail. It is less than two feet wide at many places, and the walking, especially for horses, is the worst imaginable. The formation on the surface is a soft, slippery, slate rock.   The path winds its crooked way around the mountain, while below it drops off sheer five hundred feet to the river.   This is the place where so many horses and packs have been lost.

" One pack train of seventeen horses lost eight of them down this slide on the first trip over.   The footing is all that a clear-minded, strong-nerved man would care to encounter, and it is practically impossible for such horses as are there to pack any considerable amount of supplies around this bluff.

" On the farther side of Porcupine Hill is a place where one must be very cautious.   Boulders from four to ten feet square are met with.   One must work around the corners of these boulders to get down in safety.   It took me about one hour and a half.   I went slowly, picking my way, as one accustomed to mountain climbing will do, and had no difficulty in reaching the foot of the hill.   I was careful to note the dangers that a horse would encounter, and I say that a horse can go over Porcupine Hill all right if the person handling the animal knows his business.   Inquiry satisfied me that the death of many horses was due solely to the inexperience of those in charge.   The packs are put on the backs of the horses with gross carelessness, and what is the result?   It is up hill and down hill, and around boulders, and before the journey is accomplished the packs begin to slide, and the horse's burden is thus increased threefold.   A slip is made, the pack gives way, and the animal goes down to its death, or breaks a leg and is killed by the owner, who curses his luck and starts back for another horse.

" Following this place is what is known as First Bridge Hill, which covers a distance of three miles.   Then comes the hill called Summit Hill, four miles of as tough climbing as one ever saw. It was on this hill that the great loss of horses occurred. The trail runs along the side of a rocky mountain, where a misstep will send an animal from five hundred to one thousand feet below. On the side of nearly all these hills the liquid mud was two feet deep, and in some places it ran like a stream. There were sharp rocks and round rocks, and great slabs of granite down which the horses slid into mud holes.

"Half the people are greenhorns and don't know how to pack a horse. They pile on the load, and when the horse gets to a bad place, the pack hits against the rocks, and, of course, makes the horse step out to keep his balance. Down go his feet, and over goes the horse. I saw one mule turn three complete somersaults, and the owner never went after either the mule or the packs. You can see dead horses and lost packs all along down the precipice, and all mixed up together. 'Why don't they go after them?' Well, it would take them a week to go down there and bring up a pack. It's two thousand feet down there in some places. Some men, after packing heavy outfits over seventeen miles of this trail, sold out for enough to pay their fare back to the United States.

"It was a sight such as one would not care to see more than once in a lifetime. Horses, tents, feed, supplies, and men were piled together is an apparently hopeless tangle. A drizzling rain was falling most of the time. Stubborn fires were smouldering and sputtering, and men were standing or wandering about as though they were dazed by the obstacles ahead. I couldn't help noticing the tired, haggard look on almost every face that I saw, as though the load of anxiety and care was more than they could endure."

Summit Lake is about a mile wide and six miles long, and near the middle is a tall, rocky inlet which, in rough weather, is noted for the breakers which dash upon its shores. One foggy morning, shortly after a party had started on its journey, a squall sprang up, and not being able to make out their bearings in the fog, their little boat was driven straight upon the rocks. She capsized and threw the three men into the icy water. One of them immediately sank and was never seen again. The other two struck out for the shore and finally reached it, though one was so exhausted that he had to be dragged out of the water.

There were any number struggling along the trail who would have turned back had it not been for their pride. All those poor fellows worked as they had never worked before, and when they finished were wet through with perspiration or rain, or both. When night came, they lay down on the damp ground. By morning they were too stiff to move at first, but, when they got around to it, another hard day's work followed. All along was strung a line of struggling horses and cursing men, picking their way over and around rocks, logs, and dead animals.

Completely balked by this impassable mountain barrier, with the prospect of spending a long Alaskan winter on an inhospitable sea coast, where blizzards and storms have free play for over four months of the year, the six thousand or more gold-seekers at Skagway finally combined to close the trail and assail it with dynamite which had been brought up from Juneau. So an army of about two hundred men started in to open it for all. Notices were posted all along the trail warning miners to get out of the way under penalty of punishment. Up to this time but five parties had succeeded in getting over the summit, and the other thousands were strung all the way along from the coast for fourteen miles into the mountains of the interior. From time to time steamers arrived loaded down with other gold-seekers. When in a few days the trail was reopened it soon became as bad as ever.

After a time the stench from dead horses became so offensive in Skagway that a mass-meeting was held to plan for the abatement of the nuisance. As a result a great number of bodies were gathered together and cremated.

One passenger said that up to October not more than twenty complete outfits had reached the lakes over the Skagway trail. "A majority of those who got through," he said, "had not more than two hundred or five hundred pounds of outfit. I knew one man with only one hundred and seventy-five pounds. On the summit snow is now fully six feet deep and the fall continues quite heavy. There are some of the miners who will make an attempt to get in with sleds and dog trains, when snows have covered the trails, and the lakes are frozen. No one has been getting in of late, and, in fact, very few have attempted to do so, for the trail is in such a bad condition that it is absurd to think of doing so."

Every description of pack animals could be seen on the trail, from the family driving horse and the trick mule, down to the smallest Mexican burro. It was impossible to hire any packing done, and only an option on a horse after the owner was through with him could be obtained, and these sold for ten times as much as the animals were worth anywhere else. Two people who had an option on four little cayuses for four hundred dollars, to be delivered in one week, dead or alive, were shortly afterwards offered six hundred dollars for them.

When this sort of thing had been going on for a little time, horse feed became scarce and horses were at a discount. Early in September a man could pick up a good horse for ten dollars. A party which, during the season of high prices had rushed back to the United States and secured a few horses, found, when they returned, that they could not be sold. So they loaded their horses with fodder, which was at a great premium, and started for the summit. Reaching there they sold the feed for eighteen dollars a sack and threw the horses in, so they got out of the dilemma very well. But by the time the hay was brought up to the hungry animals waiting for it, the other animals met on the trail, by each taking a passing nip, had reduced the quantity by about fifty per cent. The horses are fond of birch leaves, but they soon contracted mud fever, and, as they were insufficiently fed and not sheltered at all, they soon became worthless. They really died from lack of care. Horses were a good deal better on the Skagway trail than burros, although the best thing of all was an ox, which was very good for muddy traveling, and could carry a big load. The burros taken up were almost a failure. They were good over rocks, but no good at all in the swamp, which forms about two-thirds of the entire distance.

Those who succeeded in working their way past these obstacles found themselves finally at the big marsh. Of this no adequate description is possible. It is a terror for packers. A horse flounders and rolls in the mud, until he either gives up from exhaustion, or else tears his pack loose, or breaks a leg. Many of the miners were camped on this bog, which is a mile and a half long, waiting till the freeze of winter covers the ground so that they could get across. The ground was soft and springy, and very muddy even be-

A PACK TRAIN CROSSING THE SKAGWAY TRAIL IN WINTER

fore it was trampled up. A man went to his knees in the mud, and a horse wallowed to his belly. After crossing the marsh the trail is much the same as in the earlier stages, up and down over a continuous chain of hills and mountains.

At times the gold-seekers were encouraged to believe that there was a betterment, owing to the men's efforts to corduroy the bad places, and the occasional glimpse of sun, but a night's rain would undo it all, and the morning would show it worse than ever. The horses floundered over the boulders and through the mud, which is nothing more than decomposed vegetation, and broke their legs. Then they were shot or knocked on the head. Lack of animals, and particularly the fact that it is impossible to move supplies, led many to split up their outfits and hurry on with barely enough to last them until they reached the river camps.

People who had flattered themselves that they had sufficient foresight to take in lumber to be put together for boats after crossing the pass, found that the proper thing to do with it at Skagway was to throw it away. One man built his house entirely out of lumber which had been intended for lake boats, and which had cost nearly three hundred dollars in the United States. This Skagway man picked up all he wanted of it for eighteen dollars a thousand, and much of it cost him nothing. Owners were glad to give it away to get it off their hands.

Towards the end of the season, when thousands of men and animals and tons of freight were scattered along the trail, thieving began. Some who had sold their outfits at Skagway, and pushed on light-handed so as to get through, began to appropriate new outfits on the other side.

A party of prospectors had, after great hardships, packed their goods over the worst part of the Skagway trail, had cached them, and were moving them by relays to the lakes. Some of the goods it had cost thirty dollars a hundred to get over.   One day, about the middle of August, they missed from their cache a sack of flour and one hundred pounds of bacon.   They had taken no precaution against theft, believing that under such conditions as exist in Alaska a man's property would be held sacred.

Immediately upon discovering their loss they notified the other miners in the vicinity.   A meeting was called at once.   Each gold-seeker felt that his sack of flour might be the next to go, and it was agreed that a food thief was as dreadful an enemy as a murderer.   Food to these men was life.   A committee of six vigilantes was chosen by lot to search out the criminal and punish him, the penalty to be death.

In a tent near the summit lived a Frenchman known only as " Pierre."   He was low-browed, dark-visaged, and surly.   He had no friends and seemed to desire none, while his doubtful manners and appearance made him an object of suspicion and dislike.   At dusk of the day on which the loss was made known the vigilantes climbed to the summit. They went silently and paused when near the tent for a whispered consultation.   Approaching still nearer, they saw that a dim light was burning within, and upon the canvas was cast the grotesque shadow of the Frenchman. He was stooping close to the ground.

" He's burying the grub," whispered one of the vigilantes.

Leaving two men outside, four entered the tent.   One was the prospector who had been robbed.   Pierre started up at the appearance of his visitors.   His movement for a gun was arrested by a sharp word of warning, and he stood as though petrified, his eyes riveted on the muzzles of four revolvers.

There was no need of searching further. In a rude hole dug in the hard earth in the center of the tent lay the sack of flour and the bacon. The owner recognized the marks and identified them as his property. Without a word the Frenchman was seized, and with stout ropes, brought along for the purpose, was tied hand and foot. He begged piteously for mercy, and his black whiskers stood out on a face pale as that of a corpse. He appealed to hearts of stone. There was no softening light in the eyes of his captors.

They carried him out, and to a pole before his fragile habitation they lashed him fast. All six withdrew a short distance, and, at a word, six shots rang out, sounding as one. Then the vigilantes left.

A life for a sack of flour and one hundred pounds of bacon!

The limp form, bleeding from six wounds, hung there all night, and the next day it was there, and the next. Over the trail, a short distance away, passed many men. When they looked toward the lonely tent and saw its sentinel they averted their faces and hurried by. Even the horses shied, seeming to feel a nameless horror in the atmosphere. Late on the afternoon of the third day two men stayed in their journey to finish the work of the vigilantes. They unbound the body and dragged it further up the hill. They could not wait to dig a grave, but they piled stones high above the body and left it there. The lonely cairn is a warning to others who, like Pierre, hope to reach the Yukon with no other outfit than light fingers.

While this terrible struggle was taking place on the

Skagway trail, the route by the Chilkoot Pass remained open, and hundreds went over. But the prices for packing were enormous. The Indians and professional packers quickly raised the price to thirty and even forty cents a pound, and many threw their outfits away rather than pay such rates. Others who had money were willing to pay almost anything, so great was their haste to get through, while many who had the sense to proceed more moderately took advantage of every opportunity for making money.

A man named Johnson had early in the season managed to get himself and family over the Chilkoot Pass, together with a small knockdown boat. When he reached Crater Lake he determined to cut off part of the distance around it by putting his boat together and ferrying his supplies. While loading his boat a man came along and offered him ten dollars for a lift over the lake. Johnson said he was not in the ferrying business, but, if he had room when his own goods had been loaded, he would do so. He found that he had room, and while loading in the stranger's effects another came along and offered ten dollars for a lift over the lake. The result was that Johnson made forty dollars that afternoon after two o'clock.

Now, when an old Yukon miner strikes a placer capable of yielding about one hundred dollars a day by hard work, he regards himself as one of the lucky men of the earth. The early pioneers had wintered with the blizzards and summered with the mosquitoes, and up to the discovery of the Bonanza had barely made enough to pay for their supplies. And here Johnson with his knockdown boat had a Klondike shoved by Fate right under his nose. He had sense enough to see it, and to take advantage of this golden opportunity. Many were so anxious to get to Dawson and pick gold off the bushes that they wouldn't have seen a chance twice as big.

Johnson just set up his tent and established his family, and announced that he was the only ferryman on Crater Lake. In thirty-one days he made three thousand dollars, and meanwhile his wife had broken open some of their supplies and was making pies that sold like hot cakes for a dollar each. Later in the season Johnson sold his little boat for three hundred dollars, and bought a larger one and a new stock of supplies from those who were anxious to drop a part of theirs, and made his way to the Yukon, where he was in plenty of time to get a good claim in one of the paying districts. Some of those who had rushed by him had spent a lot of money, more than they would earn in a long time working at fifteen dollars a day, and working hard, and they had allowed their provisions to be reduced. Then, caught in the ever-shifting eddies of the stampedes, they rushed here and there staking claims, some of them doubtless securing good ones, but it was as yet unknown, and their claims were no better because they had hurried. Those who came later had the same opportunities, and meanwhile had been picking up the money which the others had dropped.

CHAPTER XXXIV

THREATENED FAMINE — STORES OF THE TRADING COM-
PANIES CLOSED — STEAMBOATS STUCK ON THE
YUKON FLATS — THE PERILOUS SITUATION REAL-
IZED.

Miners Hasten to Secure Provisions — Companies Fear Speculation in
Food — Eggs at $4 a Dozen — Good Mining Claims Traded for
Provisions — Candles at a Dollar Apiece — Waiting Three Hours to
File an Order — The Trading Companies Confer — Doling Out
Provisions — The Steamboats near Fort Yukon — Fruitless Efforts
to Get over the Bar — Captain Hansen's Efforts — Returning to
Dawson — Watching the River for the Steamboats — The Situation
Realized — Plenty of Whisky, but Little to Eat — Police without
Supplies — The Warehouses Threatened — Police Contemplate the
Necessity of Seizing Provisions — Fancy Prices for Dogs — Mine
Owners Threatened by Failure to Pay Debts.

A S soon as the old miners became aware of the great
rush from the States which was threatened, they
hastened to the storehouses of the different companies to secure their supplies for the next winter. This
began as soon as the first provisions arrived, and the result
was that the greater part of the cargoes were sold as fast
as the boats came to Dawson. A little later the companies,
instead of turning over the provisions, took orders and the
gold dust for them and kept tabs on the buyers, something
as rations are distributed in army camps. Prices were not
raised by the companies, but it was evident that the threatened scarcity would greatly enhance the price of such pro-

visions as found their way into the hands of the people, and
there were evidences that many who had plenty of money
were calculating to buy from the companies all they could
and hold for speculation. It was largely to shut off speculation of this kind that the companies adopted the system of
doling out provisions in small lots, carefully noting how
each man was taking.

Curious instances of the value of food came to light
every day. Two men arriving early in June brought in four
hundred dozen eggs, which they had collected on the way.
Within eight hours they sold nearly all of them at four dollars a dozen in gold dust, and they had a fair working capital
right away. Bacon was then selling at sixty-five cents per
pound, but flour held at twelve dollars per hundred; indeed,
flour seemed to be the cheapest article, except gold, on the
market.

When the question of supplies began to assume a very
serious character many bright men who had brought in large
outfits saw a chance to dispose of a part of them for interest
in claims. Old miners who could not secure provisions
enough for the winter, and who realized that it would be
cheaper and better for them to dispose of a part of their
rights for food rather than leave their claims and endure
the dangers of a journey up or down the river, made such
arrangements, and it was a very fortunate thing for some of
the newcomers.

Some of those who had thrown away their provisions
on the passes, or had disposed of them earlier on the trail
in order to get through, then saw men who had arrived
somewhat later pick up choice claims that their money
would not have bought. One fellow had six boxes of
candles, which were very scarce. He sold off a lot of them

at a dollar each, and obtained besides some good interests in claims on Quartz and Hunker creeks.

Too many on their arrival at Dawson made no preparations for the winter, and it was difficult to make them realize the kind of weather that was before them. There was plenty of work, and money in abundance, so everything looked rosy to many who were so constituted that they would have difficulty in taking care of themselves anywhere.

When the stampede " for grub " really began it had about the same effect on the stores which a run has on a bank. They closed their doors, and but one was open for sales in small quantities. When the last two steamers up arrived from St. Michael bringing about a thousand tons of provisions, extra offices were opened to receive winter orders, and the rush to get them in resembled the opening of a box-office sale for some great theatrical attraction. Hundreds stood in the long lines. One man told me he waited for three hours before he could get his order in, and then he did not receive the goods, though he had to pay cash in advance. The orders, however, were guaranteed. All this time men were coming in daily, many of whom, in the rush and the difficulty of getting over the passes, had thrown away their provisions or sold them at Dyea or Skagway, expecting to stock up at Dawson.

The day before the steamer left Dawson, the North American Transportation and Trading Company closed its doors. A notice was posted announcing that nothing would pass over its counters until the arrival of another steamer with supplies.

But the days passed and no steamer came. The people eagerly watched the river, hoping to hear the familiar sound of the whistle announcing one of the little steamers, and to see it come around the bend of the stream, but they waited in vain.

About the middle of August the two companies had a conference and they estimated that there were about five thousand five hundred people then in the Klondike district, a large number of whom were wholly without outfits and unprepared for the winter. The North American Company had four hundred paid orders unfilled, and no provisions there with which to fill them. The Commercial Company had about five hundred paid orders, one-third of which had been filled, and there was enough on hand to fill about fifty more. Plenty of provisions, they said, were down the river, but the water was very low. They did not know then that the boats were stuck below Fort Yukon, and could not possibly get up. At the Alaska Commercial Company's office a crowd sometimes numbering fifty was daily lined up in front of the doors, begging for an opportunity to purchase sustinence for themselves and their partners at the mines. As fast as one man was waited on, the doors were unlocked and another admitted. Then the click of the locks would be heard, bolts would slide to place to prevent a raid from the desperate men, and a sack of flour with a few pounds of bacon would be doled out. No one could secure much more than enough to sustain life for a few weeks. To those who were preparing to leave, food enough was given to last them over the trail to salt water, if everything went well. Everything possible was being done to get people to leave.

During the first two weeks in September several attempts were made by no less than four steamers to cross the bars above Fort Yukon. They failed simply because it is impossible to get a three-foot steamer over a twenty-two-inch bar, that being the depth as measured. Even had they gotten over the bar the situation would not have been greatly improved, for they were carrying in men who would need most of the provisions they had aboard.

Captain Hanson went down from Dawson on a steam barge expecting to pick up the barge of another steamer, and on his arrival at Fort Yukon he loaded his own barge with a cargo. He made the most persistent attempts to get over the bar so as to return, but failed. Half the cargo was removed for a second attempt, but that failed. Then he started with no load at all, but that time also failed, so uncertain are these bars in the bed of the Yukon. His steamer drew but twenty-four inches.

Having thus failed to return with an empty boat, the captain deemed it his duty to return to Dawson and inform the people of the situation. He left the fort in a patched bark canoe, and the next night was obliged to send Indians back with the following message:

" The bottom dropped out of canoe and only my shoulders are dry. I am at the cache twenty-eight miles above Fort Yukon. Get another squaw canoe and send it up as soon as you can."

There was no other canoe to be had, so an arrangement was made with two fellows who were going up the Yukon to pick Hanson up.

Day after day the people at Dawson watched the river for the steamers which they thought must surely come. The toot of a steamboat whistle would have brought the whole population to the river bank, eager to welcome the arrival of the much-needed supplies. The river, which had frozen over a little once, opened again, and many wondered what was the trouble.

On September 26th Captain Hanson arrived in his Indian canoe, and told the people that it would be an impossibility for the boats to get up before the river closed for good.   Then the situation dawned upon them in all its appalling reality.

Men who had been exulting in their success, and were counting upon returning in the spring with sacks of gold, suddenly realized that to remain till then they must run the risk of starvation.   In the saloons, which were the public resorts, men congregated and talked over the situation. There was whisky enough.   Large as was the consumption, there was the fact that a full winter's supply of liquor had been brought in somehow, but not half enough food.

Among the more industrious miners who wished to stay and work their claims the disadvantage of having so many non-producers in the place was very apparent, and there was a feeling that such should go, if any.   Three or four hundred gamblers and sporting men had come in during the summer, and some advocated driving them out and dividing the provisions equally among the workers.   The thirty mounted police at Dawson, who were practically without food for the winter, were said to be openly in favor of such a step.

Up to the first of September the new arrivals had averaged from three to twenty per day, and there seemed to be every prospect that this rate would be continued far into the winter.   The old miners, and those used to the Yukon winters, began to appreciate the dangers of the coming situation.   When the river rose a little, winter was settling down, and doubts were entertained as to the possibility of more boats reaching Dawson.   There were at least three hundred men working in the gulches, and in the hills were several prospectors who knew nothing of the situation, and would not till they came in for provisions. They were depending on the company stores for supplies.

The situation became the great subject of discussion in the city of cabins and tents. It was evident that a large number, even a thousand, could winter safely at Circle City, four hundred miles below, for to that place they could draw their supplies from Fort Yukon by dog teams. There were at least five hundred people who intended going down the river to St. Michael, and from there home, but when that avenue was closed earlier than expected by the freezing of the river, some other steps had to be taken, for some of these had already sold off their stock of provisions and could not buy them back.

There was considerable complaint that the trading companies had allowed whisky to take too large a place in the cargoes of their Yukon boats, and there was no doubt as to the large quantity brought in, but there would have been serious complaints in various quarters had this failed to arrive. Had the river permitted the boats to come up there would have been provisions enough for the people to have worked through the winter somehow.

It was estimated that during the summer there had been brought to Dawson about eighteen hundred tons of food, clothing, and other merchandise. Meanwhile, nearly every one on Circle City, Forty Mile, and Fort Cudahy had come to Dawson. It was estimated that there were something like six thousand people in the city and about the adjacent country who expected to depend upon Dawson for supplies. Boats were arriving at the rate of five a day, and each averaged about three passengers. Not more than one in ten of these parties carried provisions enough to keep them through the winter.

At Fort Yukon, about three hundred and twenty-five miles from Dawson, there was about six hundred tons of provisions. The question was a very simple one. As "grub" could not be brought to Dawson for everybody, some of us must go down to Fort Yukon for it, or go out by the coast and winter in the United States.

Captain Hanson gathered the miners together and made a short speech to the effect that it would be vain to hope for the arrival of the river vessels, and that his company had done the best it could to supply the increased number of mine-owners, but that there were still more than two hundred and fifty unfilled orders on their books. All he could do was to advise people to go to Fort Yukon, where there was plenty of food, and live through the winter. He told them they could find employment there cutting cord wood for the use of the steamers next year. He had, he said, done all he could to relieve the situation, and had it not been for the thousand people who had rushed in without sufficient supplies all would have been well.

The situation as regards the other company was as bad, or worse. Indeed, the company, in anticipation of the arrival of the boats, had taken a lot of orders, and with them the miners' money, and when the time came they could not be filled. There was much grumbling. Some spread the idea that the company had a good stock of provisions, but were holding off for speculation, and the warehouse was threatened for a time. Only the fear of the Canadian police prevented an attack upon it. But it became evident that the companies had no stores to speak of. The only thing that could possibly be bought was sugar, baking-powder, spices, and a little dried fruit.

Major Davis, in command of the police, said: "Instances have occurred in this territory before when supplies ran short, and it was necessary to form police and civic communities to seize all provisions in camp and issue weekly rations. It was done at Forty Mile post two years ago. The necessity for similar action is beginning to be apparent in this case, and I would not be surprised to see an uprising, and the non-producers ordered to leave the camp and go down the river to Fort Yukon, where there is plenty of grub, and the provisions in this camp seized and distributed. My force is destitute of winter supplies."

Apparently, it would have required only an uprising of this sort to have secured the co-operation of the police. Another unpleasant phase of the situation consisted in the lack of dogs, and provisions for them. Any one would have said, to have seen the swarms of dogs which were always a feature of Dawson, that there were altogether too many for a camp facing starvation, but these dogs were kept busy most of the time going to and from the mines, dragging slabs for the fires to thaw the frozen ground, and logs to build miners' cabins. And when it became evident that there would have to be an exodus on account of the food situation, dogs were worth their weight in gold.

To add to the complications, a good many of the mine-owners were deeply in debt for claims they had purchased, the obligations, which bore an enormous rate of interest, falling due the next May or June. They had leased some of their claims on lays, and they were quietly falling back and waiting for the lessees to dig the gold out to liquidate their indebtedness by the time it became due. The men on lays, unless they had been so fortunate as to provide a sufficient stock of provisions, were in time compelled to throw up their profitable contracts and run with others for food. This left some mine-owners in a very threatening position, for they might have to turn the property back to the mortgagees.

September 13th a large number of the owners held a secret meeting at the junction of Eldorado and Bonanza creeks, and promulgated a notice to the effect that after October 1st, and to June 1st, the wages for miners would be one dollar an hour, instead of one dollar and fifty cents. But in less than twenty-four hours the situation changed, for the men who had food could almost dictate their wages and the owners were glad to get them at fifteen dollars a day. There was the possibility that they might have to pay more.

CHAPTER XXXV

THE GREAT EXODUS FROM DAWSON—DOWN THE RIVER
TO CIRCLE CITY AND FORT YUKON—SAD FATE OF
SOME OF THE EXILES—A BURIAL UNDER THE
ARCTIC SKY.

A Great Day in Dawson—Drawing Lots to Determine Who Should
Go—The Restaurants All Closed—Effort to Go Up the River
Thirty-five Miles in Seven Days—The Party Finally Returns—
People Pouring in While Others Were Pouring out—Arriving
With Worthless Outfits or None at All—Swept By Dawson in the
Running Ice—Petty Larceny Becomes Frequent—Food Scarce at
Circle City—Men Arrive from Circle City Badly Frozen—Suffer-
ing on the River—Exiles Badly Frozen—Sad Fate of Young
Anderson—Wounded, His Friends Dragged Him on a Rude
Sled—Dying within Sight of Circle City—Thawing an Arctic
Grave—The Funeral—Extracts from His Diary—Strong Miners
Weep—The Scarcity of Supplies—A Restaurant Price List—A
Fresh Supply of Caribou Meat—Curtailing the Work on the
Mines—Those Left Pull Through.

THAT was a great day at Dawson when the miners
fully realized the situation and immediately began
to make their calculations for the winter. After
the government officials had posted their bulletin warning
the miners to get out of the country if they valued their
lives, many of the men pooled what provisions they had and
drew lots to decide who were to remain for the winter and
who were to attempt the trip to Fort Yukon or the coast.

It was a question which were taking the greatest risks,
those who remained prepared to spend several months on

short rations, or those who faced the hard thirty-days trip with just enough provisions to last them if not delayed, for those to whose lot it fell to leave the country were grub-staked for the trip. In this way the population was thinned out. Some who had to go started for Fort Yukon, and others for the coast. Later, others started out for Fort Yukon, hoping to get back to Dawson with supplies.

The exodus was stimulated by two facts, the first being that there might be a famine if all stayed, and the second, that those who had provisions, and at the same time had claims, could sell their provisions at greatly advanced prices to those who wished to stay and work. Thus they were insured a profit on what they could bring in on their return, and a profit from the working of their claims while they were out.

The restaurants all closed in the fall, though one ran on for several days on a supply of beefsteak which sold at two dollars and fifty cents a meal, and the meals were not large. A man with a truck load of potatoes, flour, and bacon could have bought a good interest in any of the rich claims of the richest streams. A little steamer named *Kiukuk*, which was to run up to the Pelly River where the Dalton trail begins, was called into service by men who offered as high as two hundred and fifty dollars to be taken aboard for her journey of one hundred and seventy-five miles. She was as crazy a craft as there was on the Yukon, about fifty feet long, and of thirty horse-power only. She was old, rickety, and pretty much broken down. She had just before made two trips up to the Pelly, taking over eight days at each trip. Ordinarily, one would not have cared to make a short trip on her in smooth water, yet there were several men who actually wanted to pay a big price for her to take her down

the Yukon to St. Michael.   They were persuaded from this
foolhardy undertaking, and so they obtained her for the trip
up the river to Selkirk, expecting to take the trail there.

She left with about fifteen passengers, and in a few days
back they came to Dawson.   They had spent seven days on
the steamer and had gone only thirty-five miles.   Her
machinery broke down from one to three times a day, and
she had a faculty, strong in any Yukon steamer, for constantly running aground.

On one occasion, but apparently through mismanage-
ment, she was driven head-on to a rocky shore where her
bow was violently torn away and her frame severely shaken.
But for the double protection in her bows she surely would
have sunk.   At the end of the seventh day, surrounded by
an ice pack, the trip was given up and they returned.   The
only thing left was to drift down the river, or, if wanting to
get out of the country entirely, to pole up the stream with
its freezing waters and floating ice.   Many who had had experience on the stream, and had a few provisions, preferred
to wait and make the trip after the river was thoroughly
frozen and the snow, which now was falling, had grown
hard.

It would have been an amusing scene, had it not savored
so much of the pathetic, to watch the people who were pouring into Dawson from the trail, while others were pouring out the same way.   These people had suffered all manner of hardships on the journey, and many of them, in their
haste to get over, had disposed of their outfits.   Their impression seemed to be that so long as wages were fifteen dollars a day, they could not want for anything.   It was some
time before they could be made to understand the peculiar
difficulties of the situation.   They could not get over the

impression that where there was so much gold there must be enough to eat.

It is a pitiable situation when men are huddled together in a little place in the Arctic regions, in need of food, offering any amount of money for it, and unable to get it because there is no chance for any to come into the country for six or eight months.

Few of those who came in had packed their outfits correctly. Each month's supplies should be put up separately and labeled, and then if one loses a part of his supplies the variety is not sacrificed. Many lost their flour and saved their baking-powder, or *vice versa*. Provisions should be put in water-tight sacks of not over fifty pounds each. The covering should be made of good ducking, capable of being handled roughly, of standing out in the rain, if necessary, and of not being torn by limbs, snags, and the like. Many a man reached the river only to find his beans damp, flour a pasty mass, and his dried fruit fit only to give to the all-devouring dogs.

Many boats, containing men who had been working for many days and enduring great hardships, came floating down the river in the ice and were unable to make a landing. Once eight boats loaded with provisions, but with no passengers, went floating by. The owners had doubtless left them to go ashore and camp for the night, and meanwhile the ice had broken and taken the boats down the river. It was useless to try to reach the boats at that time.

Matters assumed a very serious aspect by the middle of October. There were over a thousand people, including women and children, living in tents in Dawson, and they were arriving at the rate of seventy-five a day. Many of them had provisions enough to last them only a part of the winter. A heavy snow was falling, and beans, flour, bacon, and other provisions were selling from one dollar and twenty-five cents to one dollar and fifty cents a pound. The few head of cattle which Dalton had brought in over his trail only temporarily relieved the situation.

Petty larceny began to be frequent in a place where but a little before a man could leave anything lying about with safety. But no one stole gold. People were stumbling over that and never thinking about it. They began to steal from caches. One man was detected in stealing from a cache and shot through the leg, but he was not a thief naturally. The food situation had made him desperate.

Altogether about nine hundred people had left Dawson by the first of December, and as nine-tenths of these had hardly more than three months' provisions, the situation at Dawson was considerably relieved. So many went down to Circle City or Fort Yukon that many began to fear that they would need all the provisions at the latter point, and that the spring supply for Dawson would therefore be late in coming up. When the heavy detachment reached Circle City the stock there at once became so short that most of them had to procure sleds and continue their journey, the river being frozen. The hundred or so people at Circle City were calculating to send to Fort Yukon for provisions.

Joaquin Miller, the poet of the Sierras, who had been among the summer arrivals, reached Dawson from Circle City on December 4th, very badly frozen, having lost a part of the great toe of his left foot, his left ear sloughing off, and both cheeks frozen. He had left Circle City with a party thirty-five days before without dogs, as there were none left there. They worked along all right till they reached Forty Mile, where they encountered a blizzard.

Mid-winter on the Trail

Tent of a pair of gold-seekers pitched by the side of a corduroy bridge in Skagway Cañon.

From that place they endured all manner of hardships. Circle City was not a bed of roses for the miners there.

Reports, he said, had reached Circle City of miners being frozen in between Dawson and that place. One miner was brought in so badly frozen that he had to have his feet amputated. Such was the fate of some of those who had left Dawson just before the winter's fury set in.

Among those who had started down the river in boats was a young man named Anderson, who belonged in Brooklyn, N. Y. On the way down, and when seventy miles from the nearest habitation, he accidentally shot himself in the abdomen. He pushed on with grim determination, though suffering great agony, but when thirty miles from Circle City a cold snap came on and froze the river. The party with him saw that it was necessary to abandon the boat, and so they rigged up a rough sled and started to pull the wounded man over the ice. It was terribly cold.

Day by day his strength failed, and dreary were the camps they made on the frozen shores of the river. His two companions toiled bravely on, but he kept sinking lower and lower, and when almost within sight of their destination he passed away. Two hours later they drew the body into Circle City on the rude sled.

Out in the little cemetery was piled a heap of wood, and soon it was blazing fiercely in the Arctic winds; for graves must be dug here — if they are dug at all — as gold is mined, by thawing the ground. As night settled down the glowing coals shone out brightly in the darkness. More wood was heaped on, and little by little the grave was sunk in the icy soil.

Then came the burial. There was no minister, no choir, no melodious anthem, no words that told of the Christian's

hope in a glorious resurrection. Rough miners carried the
body to its last resting place, and as they stood there rev-
erently some extracts from the young man's diary were
read. He had kept it almost to the last moment, and there
were many references to his mother, to his home, and his
hardships, and between the lines could be read a record
of the indomitable courage and the filial love of the man
who had sought his fortune on the Yukon.

Strong miners, muffled in their heavy winter coats, stood
with tears in their eyes while the words were read, and then
the frozen clods were shoveled into the icy grave. There
are other graves on the Yukon — many others. And there
are dead without graves.

There was a party of two or three hundred between
Forty Mile and Circle City when the river suddenly froze,
and they were compelled to abandon their boats and push
on, almost wholly unprepared for the hardships of such a
journey. Some of them suffered severely. Ten or a dozen
women were subjected to the ordeal of losing their boats
and taking the long, wearisome tramp to Circle City in the
biting cold.

The prices of all supplies continued to rise till they were
hardly within the reach of those who had not rich gold
mines to depend upon. Flour was worth from seventy-five
dollars to one hundred dollars for fifty-pound sacks; beans,
one dollar and fifty cents a pound; candles, one dollar and
fifty cents each, and very few of them at that; fresh fish,
one dollar and twenty-five cents a pound, and very scarce.
Cooking utensils, too, were none too plentiful, men satisfy-
ing themselves with pieces of tin for frying pans and old tin
cans were in demand as coffee pots and for other cooking
purposes.

This was the sign hanging over the counter of one of the Dawson restaurants early in December:

Meals, ...	$3.50	Ham and Eggs, . . . 5.00
Coffee, tea, or chocolate, .	.50	Porterhouse steak, . . 5.00
Sandwiches, . . .	.75	Cove oysters fried, and ham
Boston baked beans, . .	1.00	and eggs, . . . 9.00
Pie and cake, . . .	1.00	

In the latter part of November a large band of caribou crossed the Yukon a few miles below Dawson in the migration from the headwaters of the White and Copper rivers, and Dawson hunters went out and killed about fifty head. This supply of meat was a great relief, and it sold at good figures. Of course meat can be kept in prime condition all winter in such a climate. Though game was scarce it could be found in small quantities if hunted for, and men who were hungry would take their guns and start on hunting expeditions, seldom, however, going far from camp.

The inevitable result of the scarcity of food and the exodus of people was to delay work in the mines. It was useless for owners to attempt to work their shafts unless they could secure provisions, and there were many cases where men who had begun to take out of their shafts many hundred dollars a day, on coming down to Dawson and finding that their bags of gold could not buy the ordinary necessities of life, at once departed either for the coast or for points down the river. The newcomers who had reached the city with barely enough provisions to feed a canary bird were, of course, of no use in the mines. But the exodus was so great that those remaining were left with a fair chance of pulling through, which is about all any one can expect to do on the Yukon during the winter. From time to time some little additions in the way of meat were made to the supply.

CHAPTER XXXVI

DISCOVERY OF GOLD ON MUNOOK CREEK—THE SUD-
DEN RISE OF RAMPART CITY—THRILLING EXPERI-
ENCE AND LOSS OF LIFE ON THE MOUNTAIN TRAIL.

A Rival to Dawson and the Klondike—American Territory Preferable
—Old Munook and Little Munook—Taking a Fortune from a
Small Hole—Stream Prospected Before—The First Excitement—
Stampedes from the Arriving Steamboats—Beginnings of Ram-
part City—Arrival of the Hamilton—Crew Stampedes and Takes
the Knives and Forks—A Literary Woman's Rush for a Claim—
Settling in the New Camp—High Prices for Claims—Taking
out $1,500 in Five Days—The Fever of Speculation—Wealth of
a Man with a House and Lot—High Price of Timber—The
Rough Trails—Fatal Experience of Two Yale Graduates—
Spending the First Night on Hoosier Creek—Taking Food for
Only One Day—A Terrible Night—Tucker Falls Exhausted—
Running for Help—Secured at Last—Returning to Find His
Companion Dead—Buried in the Wild Gulch—Situation of
Munook—High Value of Its Gold.

O NE important result of the inability of the river
steamboats to reach Dawson, and the consequent
shortage of provisions there, was to turn the attention of gold-seekers to Munook Creek, on the lower
Yukon. Those who could not reach Dawson from St.
Michael, and those who, having reached it from the coast,
could not stay but went down the river, were naturally attracted to the new region. Now that public attention has
been turned towards the Yukon valley, the sudden rise of
new mining camps and new cities may be expected, for the

(496)

country has a wealth of gold-bearing streams which have never been properly prospected, and many promising ones have never even been explored. While the sudden rise of Dawson was phenomenal, it soon had a dangerous rival, and that on American territory.

It is needless to say that experienced miners will prefer gold-bearing streams on American territory if they can be found of a richness to compare with the Klondike. If the Dominion government insists on the restrictions she has ordained, mines on American territory, which are considerably less rich than those in the Klondike, will prove more attractive, for they will yield larger net returns. In view of these facts, the rise of Rampart City in the vicinity of the Lower Ramparts of the Yukon in the fall of 1897 can occasion no surprise, and it would not be strange if the predictions made as to its rivaling Dawson should be quickly verified.

An old Indian by the name of Munook, a Russian half-breed, found large quantities of gold on the creek which now bears his name some time in August, 1896. According to the story on the river, some Indians had informed Munook that they had seen gold on a branch of the creek, and with his son he started in. In a short time he had taken out three thousand dollars' worth of gold from a hole eight feet square and fifteen feet deep. The stream had been prospected in a superficial way for years, and while gold was always found, it had not been in sufficient quantities, for the conditions were the same here as in other Alaskan fields. A layer of muck covers the gravel from a few inches to two or three feet in thickness; in winter it is like adamant, and in the summer like axle grease that has been exposed to the sun.

Old Munook and his son worked on quietly, taking out considerable gold, but nothing was known about it by experienced miners till the boats began to run on the river in the spring of 1897. The evident advantages of the situation lay in its nearness to the base of supplies, and several miners made their way up the creeks and at once struck good pay-dirt on Little Munook and another tributary which was called Hunter Creek.

The first excitement was when a steamboat loaded with people bound for Dawson reached the mouth of Munook Creek. Miners there were looking for supplies, and when they told what they had found, the excitement was so great that many of the passengers bolted for the mountains at once, also many of the crew. The principal creeks were staked for some distance, for the law which the miners had instituted allowed claims of one thousand feet in length, and from five hundred to a thousand feet in width, according to the nature of the valley.

Observing that as many as a hundred men would winter there, the Alaska Commercial Company made preparations to supply them with food. But when the next steamboat came up there was another stampede, some fresh discoveries having been made, and so many of the crew left the boat, carrying away the knives and forks, that the passengers left were compelled to resort to their fingers in eating. On bed-rock two and four dollars to the pan had been discovered, and nuggets worth ten and twelve dollars had been taken out. The miners were at work clearing up a sightly place high up from the river for a town site, and in hardly any time there was a town of tents there. The Commercial Company began building its log warehouse, and everything promised to thrive. When the steamer *Hamilton*, after continuing on her way up the river, went aground a short distance from the new city, many more of the men came down decided to settle in the new camp. Many claims were staked off quite near the city, but little could be done except at bar diggings before winter came.

By the first of September the discovery claim on Little Munook had sold for five thousand dollars, and Rampart City was a cluster of tents on the hillsides, but the Commercial Company were finishing up their building and the newcomers were busy putting up log cabins. The population was then three hundred and increasing with every boat that came up the river. Ten days later all figures and values had quadrupled. One claim on Little Munook was held at fifty thousand dollars, for the owner of the adjacent claim had taken out one thousand five hundred dollars in five days, and had not reached bed-rock. The news spread, and in a little time the recorder had taken in over two hundred dollars in registering claims, and people were clambering over the hills in every direction. A literary woman from the Pacific coast who had started for the Klondike was infected by the excitement, jumped off the boat when it reached Rampart City, and rushed for a claim, taking the trail like a man, and sleeping on the ground with her blankets wrapped about her.

Gradually the population approached a thousand, and the fever of speculation was rife. Real estate offices were opened and the scenes enacted at Dawson a little earlier were repeated. Had there been no Klondike, which had become a sort of shibboleth on every one's lips, the discoveries on Munook would have been enough to have created a rush from the States, for the creeks and gulches are unmistakably rich. On one claim two thousand dollars were taken

out while sinking to bed-rock.   On another, two men took
out six hundred dollars in six days, and the top gravel
seemed to be full as rich as that in the Klondike district, according to reports of men who had had some experience in
both places.

None of those who left the United States later than the
first of August to go by the water route arrived at Dawson
City, but they were frozen in all along the river.   Those
who reached Munook Creek, however, were fortunate.   By
the last of September, a man who owned a house and lot in
Rampart City counted himself worth two thousand dollars.
Every fresh boatload rushed up the creeks to stake out
claims, and many large transactions took place.   By October the new town had a population of over one thousand
souls, including several women.   Lots were selling for as
high as one thousand two hundred dollars, and any kind of
a cabin for eight hundred dollars.   The Indians were paid
nine dollars a day and board for building cabins, while the
wages of men in the mines ruled at fifteen dollars a day.
The real estate boom rather outstripped that of the previous
year at Dawson.   The value of lots and buildings sometimes
increased tenfold in a very few hours.   The reason for the
excessive price for building is that there is no wood to speak
of nearer than eighty miles.

The trails over the mountains to the creeks were no exception to such routes in other mining regions.   Indeed, if
anything, they were a little worse, for the country had not
been so traversed by Indians.   A mile seemed as long as
five miles in any ordinary country.   It was a wild and precipitous region, and in going from one creek to another it
was necessary to cross great divides, tearing through the
brush or stumbling over niggerheads.   Unfortunately, as

at other places of mining excitement, people rushed in without any adequate idea of what they were to encounter, and without sufficiently providing for such a journey. Only a dozen miles or so over the hills seemed easy.

One September morning three young men started for Hoosier Creek, about twenty miles away, to locate claims. Their names were H. B. Tucker of Troy, N. Y., J. P. Powell of New York city, and George M. Reed of Boston. It was raining when they set out and growing colder, and the trails were getting worse every hour. After traveling about seven miles Reed sprained his leg, and, finding that he would be unable to continue the trip, he left the party and made his way back to town.

Tucker and Powell proceeded on their way and reached a cabin at the mouth of Hoosier Creek, and spent the night there. They were wet through, and as there was no stove in the cabin they dried themselves as best they could before an open fire at the door of the cabin. Friday morning they started for the head of the creek. They left their blankets and all their food, except barely enough for one day, having been told that they could make the trip and get back to the cabin by evening. The cold rain continued all day. The creek became very much swollen, and traveling up the gulch, wading through icy waters, and wandering through the swamps and brush was a terrible undertaking, especially for men without experience in the country and without knowledge of the conditions. The two finally made their way to the headwaters of the creek and staked their claims, but by that time it was night and they knew it would be utterly impossible to make their way back through the darkness.

When they had started in the morning Tucker had put

the day's provisions in his handkerchief, and he lost them while wading the creek. All they had left was four hardtacks and a piece of chocolate to divide between them. Most of this they had eaten during the day.

These two exhausted men had a terrible night to face in that wild gulch with the cold rain pouring steadily down on them, without food, without shelter, without blankets or covering of any kind except their soaked and half-frozen clothes. About two o'clock in the morning the rain turned to snow, and by dawn the ground was white. Tucker slept a little through pure exhaustion, but Powell was awake all night. As soon as light came, the latter urged Tucker to start down the creek before the snow became so deep as to make walking impossible. Tucker made a heroic effort to respond to Powell's appeal, but after proceeding a little way his knees gave out and he fell. Powell put him on his feet and they started once more, but Tucker's strength was all gone and he fell again and again, and finally could go no further. He grew delirious and at last became unconscious.

Powell, after doing everything in his power to get Tucker down the creek to shelter, found that it was impossible, and at about seven o'clock, seeing that the only chance to save Tucker's life was to get assistance, he placed him in as comfortable a position as possible and started down the creek shouting for help and firing his revolver to attract attention. His hope was to find a party of friends who had talked of coming up Hoosier Creek that day. He was finally successful in his quest, but not till some hours had passed, and one of the party immediately started back with Powell to find Tucker, carrying food with them. They reached him about one o'clock, but they were too late. The poor fellow was dead.

Marking the spot, they came down the creek to the
cabin, where Powell rested that night, and made his way
back to Rampart City the next day. A party set out to the
place where Tucker died and he was buried there in the
wild and lonely gulch, as it was impossible to bring his body
in until the trail was in a better condition.

Tucker was a graduate of Yale in 1894, and his father is
editor of the Troy *Press*. Powell was also a Yale graduate.
The trouble in this case was that they miscalculated the distance that they could travel in a day, and went utterly unprepared to spend a night in the mountains.

One may realize something of the dangers of traveling
on Alaskan trails from incidents like these. Considering
the number of people who have rushed in without any
proper understanding of what tramping on these trails requires, it seems a miracle that so few have perished. Yet
the death roll is by no means a short one.

Munook Creek, which promises to be one of the richest
gold fields in Alaska, runs into the Yukon about nine hundred miles below Dawson. It is situated below the bars
which obstruct vessels, and if the rich prospects already
found continue, its chances for development are very much
greater than those of Dawson. There are a number of
small creeks flowing into the Munook, and upon nearly all
of them gold has been found near the surface. Even if
it is less rich than the Klondike it may pay better, and certainly people there will run less risk of starvation.

The Munook gold which has been assayed has been
found to be of much greater fineness than that of the Klondike, which has proved something of a disappointment to
those who have brought large quantities of Klondike gold
to the mints. Munook gold yields about eighteen dollars

to the ounce, while Klondike gold averages about sixteen dollars to the ounce.   The difference on twenty-five pounds would buy a man a winter's outfit in Alaska.   Taking into consideration the Canadian restrictions as to the size of claims, as to royalty, and customs taxes, together with this difference in the intrinsic value of the gold, a man in the Klondike would have to take out at least thirty per cent. more gold in weight than at Munook to net the same return, while living expenses at Munook should be much cheaper.

CHAPTER XXXVII

WE DECIDE TO LEAVE THE COUNTRY — INCIDENTS OF
A HARD JOURNEY IN WINTER TO THE COAST —
THE DEATH OF JOE — MY ESCAPE.

D URING the summer and fall of 1897, or while the
events narrated in the preceding chapters were oc-
curing, Joe and I did what we could on our Klondike claim, much time being spent in preparations for drifting the coming winter. Our spring clean-up, while not
large, because we had been unable to work as extensively
as others, and because we had poor luck in finding the pay-
streak and were compelled to sink several holes before striking rich dirt, was still good enough to provide us with a

comfortable amount of gold dust. While only the large fortunes suddenly amassed by the few who had worked large fractions of their claims attracted attention, we, nevertheless, congratulated ourselves upon our good fortune, knowing that our money was in the ground and could be taken out, if we chose, in the winter. When we returned from our somewhat unpleasant trip to the Indian River district, we at once became aware of the situation as to the food supply at Dawson, and, as we had neglected to lay in provisions early, we realized that our hopes of a prosperous winter might be dashed to the ground. We hurried down to Dawson and found affairs as already described. It was impossible to secure a full stock of provisions for the winter, but any one who would leave the country could get enough for the trip. To those who insisted upon staying a little was being doled out, with the understanding that when enough time had elapsed for its consumption another batch would be sold. The possibilities of speculating in food supplies were carefully guarded against.

Joe and I reflected and consulted. We had experienced a touch of famine the previous winter when but a few people were in the Klondike, and we did not look forward with any degree of satisfaction to the possibility of something worse. It was necessary for us either to stay to hold down our claims, or to find some one who would work them on shares. It was easy enough to find among the eager newcomers men who would make such an arrangement, but as they had no provisions to depend upon, and knew scarcely anything about mining, they would be able to do little work.

It so happened at that time that the excitement over the Indian River district was at a high point, and we had a good offer for our claims there and also the claim on Bonanza.

Joe and I lit our pipes and thought. There were many points in favor of the bird in the hand.

" But there may be millions in those mines," said Joe.

" Possibly," I replied. " We don't know about that, but we do know that there's a lot of frozen muck and gravel and hard work in them. And we know, too, that by next April we might be willing to trade one of them for a hundred of flour."

We smoked and thought a little more, and concluded to take the bird in the hand. We reckoned that when we got the money we should have about twenty-five thousand dollars apiece.

"We can afford to have poor luck for a year or two," I said to Joe. " And I don't feel as if we were selling our birthright, for there is plenty of gold to be found in Alaska; better diggings, I'm thinking, than these British moose pastures, especially if the government concludes to take a large share of the profits."

The next question was whether we should go down or up the river. Joe was inclined to take the former course, but as his claim in the Birch Creek district was being worked, and as we heard rumors that there was little food to be had at Circle City unless it was sledded from Fort Yukon, we decided that we would go out to the coast and in the spring bring in a big outfit. Outfits are always profitable, and we thought there was money in the scheme.

But we were in no hurry, for we wished to wait till the ice had become solid and the trail a little packed. We got together our stove, tent blankets, and other necessities for the trip, and took life easy. So many small parties had been going out that dogs were extremely scarce. The price had started at one hundred and fifty dollars, but had soon risen to two hundred dollars, and when we began to think about them they were worth about two hundred and fifty dollars.   We smoked and thought again.

With good dogs we figured that we could reach the coast in about thirty days; without them it would take about forty under good conditions.   But Alaskan travel is uncertain, with or without dogs.   One thing, however, was certain; the dogs would eat up a good part of what they would draw before they reached the coast unless we made remarkably good time, so we concluded to save our money, even if we lost some time, and draw the sleds ourselves.

So one morning late in November we bade good-bye for a time to Dawson and the Klondike, and started for the coast in a blinding snow storm.   The mercury bottles were frozen solid.   The river was rougher than the rocky road to Dublin.   It had frozen once, then broken up and frozen again so that it was all humps and bumps, and the only way to maintain a tolerably smooth course was to cross back and forth where the way seemed to open out best.   In spite of every precaution the sleds were continually overturning while we were slipping and sprawling.   Parties with dogs fared even worse.   The dogs could go anywhere, but the sleds followed them sometimes right side up, but more often on one side.   Many sleds were broken.   Soon many of the dogs had badly lacerated feet, and in some cases they were frozen, so that we were rather glad we had concluded to depend upon ourselves, though the dog teams quickly got ahead of us and others overtook us.

All the way from Dawson to the mouth of the Pelly River the river was so rough that dogs were hardly able to haul more than enough to last them to the coast, and it was hard, cold drudgery for Joe and me.   In some places the ice was piled fifteen feet high. All the way along we encountered the wrecks of boats which had been abandoned when the river closed, the parties pushing on with only barely enough to keep them alive on the trail.

We worked along slowly, and when we had gone a dozen miles it seemed as if we had gone a hundred. Men with frozen cheeks, noses, fingers, and feet were encountered, and occasionally one in a very bad fix, but we managed to get along very comfortably till we came to the Lewis River.

The current of this stream is so rapid, and the weather up to this time had been so mild, that it was only partly frozen over, and in many places it was full of rushing and crushing ice cakes. When I say mild weather I mean, of course, mild for Alaska. As a matter of fact, the mercury had not thawed for a couple of weeks. We speak of mild weather up there in the winter when it averages about fifty below zero. Wherever the ice jams were, the ice was piled in cakes as high as six-story buildings, sloping up gradually on one side and breaking off in sheer precipices on the other. It made it much easier traveling coming out than going in. The current setting down the river runs the ice in such a way that the slope is toward Dawson. In coming out the slope can be climbed first, and then the precipice can be descended, but in going in these precipices are encountered face to face.

The greatest hardships were endured here on this long stretch of country, both by those going out and by those who had bravely made the effort to reach Dawson. One could hear tales of suffering every day, but every one who was getting along fairly well had no time for the troubles of others, although in severe cases great kindness was shown.

There was one man who had started out early in a boat and had been compelled to return to Dawson, where he finally secured a dog team. At the foot of Lake Lebarge he slipped and fell and sprained his leg. He had plenty of provisions, but his team made poor time, and he was suffering great pain. He offered good money to those who overtook him to pull him out, but they were in too great a hurry to get out of the country themselves.

Another young man had been left at Five Finger Rapids with both feet frozen. His companions were unable to help him along to the coast, and so left him as comfortable as they could, realizing what would be his fate. He sent messages to his friends in the East, and there he was left in a little hut with no one to care for him, except such passers-by as had their sympathy touched. He was finally taken care of by a poor family. In many camps we passed men were sick, and the prospects were that they could not survive the trials of a winter in such a place, sleeping on the snow with the thermometer sometimes as low as seventy degrees below zero.

Joe and I, who, by spending a winter on the Klondike, had learned how to prepare for the cold weather and rough trails, worked our way along very well over the rough river, though in places the ice was so thin that we and others we encountered had narrow escapes from being plunged into the river. We heard of one man who, in crossing, had broken through and slid under the ice. Of course, that was the last of him in such a swift current. At Thirty Mile River it was necessary to make a portage, for the river was running too swift to freeze at all. The trail along the banks was a hard one, and we were constantly in danger of sliding off into the river.

A One-Horse Sledge Team
A pair of gold-seekers on their way to the Gold Fields.

After many trials we reached White Horse Rapids, camping on a hill near by. The traveling on the lakes was very good, but it was a hard climb up that hill. Much of the time we had to crawl on our hands and knees while dragging our sleds, and a careless move would have sent us down into the river.

When we arrived there preparations were being made to take back to Skagway a young woman who was very ill. She had been rescued from almost certain death at a camp near Lake Lebarge. She had been pushing toward Dawson with a party, and, early in November, when going over the last hill at Miles Cañon, she slipped and wrenched her right knee. A stretcher was made for her and the party pushed on to Lake Lebarge, where they finally made camp, but the limb, without medical attendance, grew rapidly worse, and she succumbed to a low rheumatic fever. Her life was despaired of. Finally, she was sent back to a camp at the White Horse Rapids, where a doctor was at last found who put the knee in a plaster cast. After a time she started for Skagway lashed to a sled drawn by five dogs — a ride of one hundred and eighty-five miles, over hills and down valleys, and through blizzards!

A little incident of the trail! A little chapter in the history of gold-seeking in Alaska!

Another true story of the Dyea trail is that of the Indian mother who was found kneeling in the snow, bared almost to the skin and frozen stiff. But in her rigid arms, wrapped in fold upon fold of thick furs, she held a little child, warm and safe. The mother had given her life for her child — only a poor Indian woman, but with as fine an instinct of protective motherhood as that exemplified by any of a superior race.

As we were lying on a pile of boughs in our tent that night, with our wet feet shoved up near the red hot stove, Joe said:

"William, a fellow's life ain't worth much till he gets out of a place like this."

I gave him a quick glance to see if he were looking well, and saw that he was, and, as he was always sober-minded, I thought nothing more about his remark.

"You know what you told me when we arranged in Colorado to come to Alaska," I said.

"Yes, it takes grit, but we have made pretty well for a two years roughing it, and I was just thinking that if I ever got out of here I would not be fool enough to return. Colorado is good enough for me. You too. We've got a snug sum, and what we need now is to get it out with our lives."

He said no more and we were soon asleep. The next day we pushed on toward the cañon. All the way along the rapid river there were open places from which a fine mist came, which quickly settled as frost upon everything. It was the most picturesque spot I ever saw. The rapids were inspiring in their grandness, seething and rushing along between the fantastically shaped ice that had gathered along the banks. Over this ice we made our way carefully, though not without some fear that it would break with us and that we should be whirled off down the boiling stream, but after about three miles of it we came safely to the cañon.

"There's where I sailed out on the bottom of the *Tar Stater*," I said to Joe, as we looked up between the bluffs.

"Well, things did look blue that day, didn't they? But the question now is, which course shall we take here?"

There were two routes which we could take. One led up a hill about a hundred feet high and almost as steep as the side of a barn, and then along the top of the bluff to the other end. The other was through the cañon on the ice which had formed along the edge of the rocks. The first meant packing on our backs most of the stuff we had, and in the condition of the trail it would take all day to do it. By taking the latter course we could go through in a few minutes — if the ice would hold. We saw by the tracks that numerous dog teams had already gone through, and there seemed to be no reason why we should not at least make the attempt.

So we started in. The waters were roaring with that thunder tone which brought vividly back to me my four-minutes trip of a few months before, and along the walls was an uneven shelf of ice which the dashing spray had formed. It seemed sufficiently wide and strong at first, but it gradually narrowed and at times brought us very near the angry water. Joe was ahead and picking his way very carefully. Finally, he came to a place where the shelf of ice was very slanting and he stepped to the outside edge so as to push the sled along and steady it, to prevent it from siiding into the water.

I was preparing to do the same thing when I heard a sharp cry from Joe, and, looking up, I saw him slip, then slide over the edge of the shelf into the raging rapids. His hand clutched the rope of the sled, and, quick as a flash, I sprang forward to catch it. But it was too late. Over went the sled into the misty foam and sank at once, for it was heavily loaded.

As I stood almost rigid with fright I saw Joe struggling bravely in the waters, but being swept rapidly down, and

I knew he was no swimmer. I started and ran, but just then he was drawn under the ice shelf, and that was the last I saw of Joe. The whole thing was over almost in an instant.

Overpowered with horror and grief, I dropped down upon the ice in the midst of that roaring cañon and cried like a child.

Poor Joe! He was a brave, good, generous fellow, with a heart strong, yet tender. How he had worked and suffered to save my life that wild night on Indian River! And now he was taken away from me so quickly that I could not even throw out a helping hand. Fate had marked that cañon as a fatal place for Joe and me. We had for years worked together, suffered together, and helped each other, and always without any real disagreements. And that awful cañon had swallowed him almost in an instant; and I could not even hope to find his poor body to raise over it in that wild region some rude memorial to a noble friend.

Poor Joe! Just as he had with strenuous effort wrested a little fortune from the unfriendly soil, and was hopefully looking forward to a life of happier conditions under a more genial sun, he was snatched away by Death,— dragged down to an icy grave where the wild waters lash themselves in a continual fury and their savage tumult is unceasing. And the precious dust, for which he had risked and endured so much — that, too, had become the prey of that awful, insatiate force that has claimed many a life, and waits to claim yet more.

I sat for a long time bewildered, mourning with all my heart for the poor fellow, and then walked back to my sled, which had kept safely to the shelf. Then for the first time I realized my own serious predicament. I was left with the provisions, but with no tent, no stove, no cooking utensils, and only two blankets. I was tempted to jump into the rapids and follow Joe, for I knew I should freeze unless I could fall in with another party who could give me shelter and warmth. I decided to push on through the cañon, realizing that I should not be much worse off if I also made a misstep and fell in.

That was a sad and lonely journey for me through those mountain gorges. I stopped for nothing, not even lunch, for I had nothing with which to build a fire, as I had no dry splinters. In the afternoon a terrific snow storm came on and fell so rapidly that it soon obliterated the trail. To go on meant certain death; to attempt to camp in that storm with but two blankets to protect me meant, probably, the same thing. But the latter course offered the only chance of safety. So, as I slowly waded along, I looked about for a sheltered spot. Turning the edge of a mountain which came down to the winding river I uttered a cry of joy. There, in a nook, was a little tent half buried in snow. I hurried on, and, when near, shouted loudly, but no one appeared. Opening the tent, a breath of warm air met me. Crouching close to a hot stove was a man who looked weak and sick. On a pile of boughs was another man looking still weaker and sicker.

" Got any grub? " said the man at the stove, in a husky voice, looking up to me with eager eyes.

" Too much," I said. " I want a fire and a tent."

" Wake up, Jim! Wake up! Something to eat! " he said, rousing the other man.

They had lost their provisions a long ways down the river, and had been passed along from camp to camp with just enough food to last them, but one of them had frozen the soles of his feet and for a whole day they had been camped there with nothing to eat.

"I began to think I should have to kill one of the dogs and eat him," said one of the men, after we had feasted.

"Dogs? I saw no dogs about."

"Wait a minute."

We mixed up some flour and bacon and stepped out to where the snow was drifting ever deeper and deeper. Kicking about in some little mounds in the drifted snow we found three dogs, sleeping as peacefully and snugly as possible. But how they ate! And then they lay down and let the snow drift over them again.

The next day we pushed on rapidly, for Jim's feet were better, though still painful. I knew we must make good time if my provisions lasted three men and three dogs over the pass. But we had fair weather till we reached the summit, which we crossed in the teeth of a blizzard.

While we were at Sheep Camp there was a bad accident on the summit which we had just safely crossed. The blizzard was still raging, and as a party of coast-bound miners were coming over, an avalanche came thundering down the mountain side above the narrow defile through which the miners pass. It covered a large section of the new tramway, and several sleds and tons of provisions were a total loss. On the other side a glacier broke away, and rushed down with terrific force, burying two sleds and a part of the outfit of two men.

We reached Dyea without further adventures. It was a sad journey. And as I stood on the deck of the steamer, looking back on those sombre shores and frowning summits, my thoughts were of my lost friend and his tragic death.

CHAPTER XXXVIII

THE GREAT RUSH TO THE KLONDIKE AND ALASKA—EXCITEMENT ALL OVER THE WORLD—PREPARATION FOR A QUARTER OF A MILLION PEOPLE—WHAT IT WILL MEAN IF ALL BECOME RICH.

At Seattle — The Stampede of 1898 — Nothing to Compare with It — The Days of '49 Eclipsed — Transportation Engaged in Advance — Fitting Up Vessels to Accommodate the Trade — " Klondicitis " — The Topic of Conversation Everywhere — Preparing Outfits — Returning Klondikers Besieged — Women and Children Have the Fever — Old Gold-Seekers Aroused — All Sorts of Men Join in the Rush — Great Exodus from California — Associations of Women — Gold Dust on Exhibition — The Craze Reaches Jerusalem — A Quarter of a Million of People — How It Appeared to a Returned Klondiker — All After Gold — Money Spent for Outfits — What It May Mean — Doubling the Gold Production in a Single Year — If All Make Fortunes Gold Will Become Cheap.

B Y the time I had arrived in the harbor of Seattle I had about made up my mind that I had seen all I cared to of the Klondike, and that I should look about for a chance to employ my capital in the States. I had formed no adequate idea, even from the stories which had leaked into the Yukon valley, of the extent of the excitement over the Klondike discoveries, and my surprise upon landing and learning the true situation may be imagined. I do not believe there is a more remarkable incident in the whole drama of human history than the great stampede of 1898, a term which must be given to the exodus of people bound to the frozen regions of the north in search of gold. The stampede of Eastern people to California in 1849 and 1850 cannot be compared with it. That movement was gradual, in a sense. It could take place at any time of the year, and people had more and easier routes than Alaska affords. But all the miners who poured into California in the first three years did not number over one hundred and twenty-five thousand, and many careful historians have put the number at less than a hundred thousand. There were never more than fifty thousand arrivals in the South African gold fields in any one year. Not more than seventy thousand people went to Australia when gold was discovered there. But the number of people leaving the Pacific coast alone for the Klondike or other parts of Alaska in the spring of 1898 was estimated at seventy thousand, and it was calculated that one hundred and fifty thousand more from the Eastern states, Canada, Europe, Australia, and South America were preparing to set out.

By the first of January, 1898, the five transcontinental railroads had contracted to sell to Eastern agents tickets for carrying more than forty-five thousand people going to the Klondike before June, and the demands for tickets were coming in every day. The two principal steam navigation companies, operating between Seattle and San Francisco on the south and the Yukon river on the north, had orders for the transportation of over twenty thousand travelers, while new companies for the trade had been formed by the score and were bringing into use almost every steam craft of any size on the coast. The more conservative estimate of the number of people transported by the railroads to the coast to take north-bound vessels was placed by passenger agents at not less than two hundred and fifteen thousand.

At the shipping towns all winter hundreds of men were employed night and day in fitting up vessels suitable for carrying people and provisions up the Yukon River from the time navigation opened to September. It was said that every vessel on the Pacific coast from Chili to British Columbia that could be bought and made serviceable for a sea voyage was in preparation for the Klondike business. Twenty or more sea-going craft were fitted out in Eastern seaports and went around the Horn to be ready for the grand rush to Alaska. Millions of dollars' worth of capital was put into shipping and transportation companies, and the demand for facilities seemed to have no limit.

The way the fever had taken hold of the people of the coast, especially in California and Washington, was something appalling. The papers called it " Klondicitis." In the larger centers of California the preparations for going to the Klondike were as general and as earnest as they were in Eastern localities for men going to war in the early sixties. Wherever I went I heard little but " Klondike " talked about on the cars, in the hotels, in the saloons, and even on Sundays at church. Whenever you observed a knot of men in the street, in a rural highway, or in any public place in California, you were pretty sure to find that the latest news of new strikes in the Klondike diggings was under discussion. All the letters that had come straggling down from Dawson were passed from hand to hand and read aloud until they fell into tatters. " Yes, I'm going this spring," was a popular button worn. In all the large cities nuggets and bottles of gold dust were on exhibition in show-windows, and groups of men were always about the yellow stuff which at Dawson would not have attracted half as much of a crowd as a nice roast of beef. Wherever I went, railroad billboards were covered with Klondike circulars, and, later, in every depot I entered as I came East were to be found circulars announcing an easy route to the Pacific coast and the Klondike.

The fever affected all lines of enterprise. It was a great thing for business on the Pacific coast. Hundreds of firms and individuals were preparing outfits of fur caps and coats, rubber goods, sleds, stoves, tents, and all sorts of devices, and were selling them like hot cakes.

The Klondike fever seemed to be in the air. Women and children shared in the desire to get rich in the Klondike, and maps of Alaska were pored over by whole families for evenings at a time. When I was visiting an old friend of mine in Los Angeles I was besieged by all the neighbors for information as to the Klondike. One evening I asked his son, a bright lad of ten years, if he knew the length of the sea coast of California, and he said he did not. But I found that he knew the exact length of the Yukon River. Little schoolboys and girls knew the topography of the Yukon and Klondike regions better than they did that of their native State. The fact that several hundred men went from the Pacific coast to the Yukon River mines in 1894, 1895, and 1896, all very poor, and that they came back in 1897 very rich — some of them millionaires and some of them bringing with them sixty thousand dollars, seventy thousand dollars, and eighty thousand dollars in actual gold — set the communities in which these successful Klondikers were personally known well-nigh wild with anxiety to go and do likewise.

The desire on the Pacific coast for information about the possibilities in the marvelous new diggings has amounted almost to hunger. The public libraries all had constant calls for literature relating to Alaska. All the returned Klondikers were run after and appealed to by crowds of men and a few women for Klondike information. The more successful Klondikers were driven to exasperation by uncountable questions from droves of people. William Hewitt, who came back to his Ventura country home with a five-gallon oil can filled with gold dust and nuggets, had more than one hundred callers and talkers every day for weeks, and as many letters from every State in the Union. J. C. Miller was on the verge of nervous prostration and had to leave his Los Angeles home when he got back from the Klondike because he was visited by a swarm of gold-crazy men day after day for a month.

Clarence A. Berry and his wife, who came from Dawson with more than one hundred and ten thousand dollars, were followed by such throngs on the streets of San Francisco that they fled to their quiet ranch home at Selma, where a flood of letters came in upon them with every mail. Jacob Wiseman, a returned Klondiker in Walla Walla, Wash., was bothered so much and so long by Klondike-wild people that he quit the town secretly and went and lived under an assumed name at Tacoma for a few weeks.

The men who were making ready for the Yukon River and Klondike country were of all stations. Naturally, the old-time miners were most mightily moved by the news of the gold find in Alaska, and, possessed by the characteristic restlessness of gold-seekers, many of them had gone to Alaska and had been struggling all winter from Dyea and Skagway over the Chilkoot Pass to Dawson. About every able-bodied and ambitious man in California who had been out of employment for a time was either arranging to start for the Klondike or was just itching for a chance to get

away.   Hundreds of men gave notice to their employers
that they would quit their jobs and sail as soon as possible
for Alaska.   The Santa Fé and Southern Pacific railroad
companies each received applications from scores of men
for relief from duty.   Every police force in the larger cities
up the Pacific coast States had vacancies caused by the resignation of men going to the gold diggings.

Clerks, lawyers, editors, reporters, doctors, merchants,
butchers, cobblers, stablemen, ranchers, and especially
engineers and men who love adventure were getting ready
to start for the Klondike when navigation began.   The men
who had a few thousand dollars saved, and believed they
could soon double their capital by lending it at exorbitant
interest rates, or by trading, were largely in evidence among
those who were soon going north.   More than three-fourths
of the members of the graduating classes of the San Francisco and Los Angeles medical schools were hastening their
studies with a view to getting established in the practice of
their profession somewhere in the Klondike country.

Every community, even the most humble hamlet, had
some citizens who were packing and planning to live a year
at least in the Klondike gold region.   In such towns as
Fresno, Stockton, Riverside, Pomona, and Redlands there
were companies of twenty and thirty men who were going
to dig for Klondike gold.   The greatest rush of people in
any Eastern city in the United States for the Klondike
placer mines was from Chicago.

The number of women going to the Klondike as soon
as navigation opens was increasing as the continuous reports
of richer and more abundant finds came down from the
frozen north.   The allurements of the yellow metal were
almost as potent among the women of California as among

the men, and the exhibits of Klondike nuggets and golden dust in the store and bank windows and public places, and the personal knowledge of men who went to Alaska poor in 1895 and came back rich, all had their effect. The book-sellers said they had hundreds of calls from women for books and maps giving a knowledge of Alaska, and the newspaper accounts of the work and success of the miners on the Klondike were read by as many California women as men. Every community of two thousand or three thou-sand people had a few women residents making ready to go to live in the Klondike region for a year or two. In Los Angeles there were twenty women making Klondike prepa-rations. San Diego had half a dozen, San Francisco more than one hundred, Portland, Ore., a score, and Seattle twice as many more. But few of these women were going with husbands. The greater part of them had no husbands, and they went to the gold regions expecting that where men may get rich either as workers in mines or owners of mining claims they also may do so.

A few women went as mining prospectors. Miss Jennie Hilton, who has made a small fortune in gold-mining in Arizona, contracted with a syndicate of business-like women to spend two years in gold-mining in the Klondike region. The profits were to go to the members of the syndicate, who will pay Miss Hilton a good salary and twenty per cent. of the first year's find of gold. Several associations of women were formed for mining in the Klondike region, and each sent several women to seek gold for them.

The competition among the transcontinental railroad companies for the transportation business, and among the cities of San Francisco, Seattle, and Tacoma for the enor-mous sums spent on the coast for Klondike outfits, was very

keen.   Three of the railroad companies had cars filled with
Klondike exhibits traveling from town to town in the
Eastern States.   The cars were substantially the same.
Each contained glass jars of nuggets and gold dust, literature about Alaska and the new diggings, and a complete and
varied assortment of the articles necessary for living and
successful mining in the Arctic regions.   There were
miners' pans, rockers, picks, hammers, shovels, quicksilver
contrivances for holding particles of gold, besides samples
of fur and wool garments worn in the Arctic regions, fur
hoods and muffs and walrus skin shoes.   There were hundreds of pictures showing how the gravel of the mines is
thawed and dug out, and how it is finally sluiced when the
warmer weather of midsummer comes; pictures of miners'
life in the Yukon cabins, and photographs of Dawson and
the surrounding country.

The rush of people to the Klondike during the five
months of navigation in 1898 was the most wonderful ever
known to any region — gold or otherwise.   White, red,
brown, and black men alike were stirred by the discovery of
a new gold field, and all came over seas from the antipodes
and across continents to join in a grand rush northward up
the Pacific.

One company alone received more, than twenty-five
thousand inquiries from people saying they were making
ready to go to the Klondike.

The letters that the transportation companies received
every day showed that the Klondike fever was by no means
local.   It reached Russia and even staid old Jerusalem,
where one would believe that digging gold within the Arctic
circle would not have a moment's consideration.   A gentle-
man in the Central Pacific offices showed me a letter from a

Greek in Jerusalem who said that he and a company of other Greeks there are going to Dawson with stores of goods to trade. Norwegians and Swedes have been more deeply interested in the newly-found gold mines in Alaska than any people on the continent of Europe. Several of their countrymen were among the Klondikers who came down from Alaska with fortunes. A sloop having on board ninety Norwegians left Christiania in October, going around the Horn and reaching San Francisco in April. Hundreds of letters from Englishmen were received, and there were large concerns doing a thriving business in London in fitting out prospective Klondikers with Arctic raiment and miners' tools. The Canadian Pacific Railroad expected to carry several thousand young Englishmen and Canadians across the continent on their way to the Klondike. Dozens of large expeditions were forming in England and Scotland for digging gold in the Yukon River country.

The Britannia-Columbia Company sold thousands of pounds' worth of stock and sent more than five hundred men to mine and trade in the new gold region. An expedition of three hundred Scotchmen sailed for Montreal in the latter part of January on their way to Alaska. A company of young Italians was in San Francisco, impatiently awaiting the sailing of the first boat for the Yukon. They were, they said, the advance guard of several hundred of their countrymen who have been charmed by the news of the fortunes made on the Klondike.

A fairly conservative estimate of the number of people who were going into the Klondike or to other gold fields in Alaska was two hundred and fifty thousand. I met them all the way on my trip East. Every west-bound express was loaded down with Klondikers.   One day I saw fourteen coaches on a west-bound train.   Nine coaches make an ordinary and a heavy train, but the rush was so great that five additional coaches had been attached to the train. Every day there were from three to six additional coaches to each westward-bound train.   The passenger list of a single day's through train included about two hundred men and one hundred dogs bound for the gold fields.

To one who has just returned from a two-years experience in the gold regions of the Yukon, who has seen death and suffering as an incident of everyday life, who knows what mining in Alaska or in the Klondike means, who has been forced to rush back to the States to make sure of enough to eat, and who has seen his dearest friend swept away under the ice by a raging river which can count its victims by the score, these preparations for rushing for fortunes into those frozen mountains appeared like madness. Yet when we come to study it, it is nothing of the kind.   It is human nature manifesting itself in a certain direction. What had Joe and I gone into Alaska for?   Gold.   What did the ten thousand or more people who sought to go in in 1897 want but gold?   And what were the two hundred and fifty thousand people I found preparing to rush in after but gold?   It is that which society in its growth and economic development has decreed as the standard of all value, that which the old alchemists tried to make, which the miser gloats over, that which when held in abundance gives men standing in society, influence, and power.   That is what all are after, and the stampede would probably not be more remarkable if the only way to save the immortal soul was to winter in Alaska.

But there is money to be made in the United States as

SNOWED IN. WAITING FOR BETTER WEATHER
A gold-seeker clad in his parka, with dog and horse, near his snow-covered tent.

well as in Alaska. One might make as much in a day on the stock exchange as he can find in a year in Alaska or the Klondike. But that is not the point. The impression is that the gold of the Yukon can be obtained easily, that the land is a poor man's country, and that in a year or so one may return rich and take that place in society that wealth can give. But gold does not grow upon the bushes of the Yukon hills; it does not lie to any great extent on the ground; in the whole great valley probably there are few places where boulders can be turned over disclosing shining nuggets underneath. There are acres of gold there, but to secure the precious metal one must be prepared to work as he would not work in the United States. He must run the risk of losing his life or ruining his constitution, and even then he may not find the wealth he sought.

During the winter following the gold discoveries on the Yukon there were at least two thousand people at Dawson and in the mines. The output was reckoned at about six million dollars; that is about three thousand dollars for each person. No man can go into the Klondike and live a year and profitably work a mine for any such amount of money as that. The trip in with a fair outfit can cost no less than five hundred dollars. By the time he has staked a claim, built a hut, and prepared to work the mine, he has spent nearer two thousand dollars, and if he is careful and has good luck he may get out of the country at the end of a year on the balance.

But, it will be said, there were several men who went in with thousands in the summer of 1897 and came out with millions. They certainly came out with thousands. So much the worse, then, for those who did not make thousands, for, as I have said, the output per person was not greater than three thousand. If a hundred or so came out with thousands, how about the other one thousand nine hundred who did not?

It has been said that ten thousand people rushed into the Klondike and to other points on the Yukon in 1897. But the output can hardly be greater than twenty million, that is two thousand per person. If two hundred and fifty thousand people rush into the country, it is not likely that they will spend less than three hundred dollars each in getting into the country. That means seventy-five million dollars. They will probably spend more on the average. Supposing that these people spend a year in Alaska and take out an average of two thousand dollars each — an amount that would not pay their expenses — the aggregate output for 1898-99 would be five hundred million dollars, or *more than twice the gold production in 1897 for the entire world.*

It is plain, therefore, that the great rush of people into the Yukon valley means one of two things; either a great loss of money for those engaged in the rush, or a complete upsetting of the standard on which all values are based.

But they are not after the paltry two thousand dollars! They would not rush in for that. Their hopes are to come out as some of the lucky ones did last year with fortunes of fifty thousand dollars or more apiece, perhaps a million. They do not stop to think what that means. If one-half of them made fortunes of only twenty-five thousand dollars each and the other half made nothing, it would mean an output of over four billion dollars in gold, or more than all the coined gold in a world which has been coining it for fifty centuries.

There must either be a terrible disappointment to the thousands who are going into Alaska and the Klondike or there must be a monetary upheaval. If all become rich in gold, the metal will become cheap, too cheap to be worth the hazards and privations endured by those who sought it.

CHAPTER XXXIX

RESOURCES OF THE YUKON VALLEY — POSSIBILITIES
OF QUARTZ MINING — COOK INLET, UNGA ISLAND
AND COPPER RIVER — THE FUTURE OF ALASKA.

Waiting for More Thorough Prospects — Comparative Smallness of the
Klondike District — Room for a Million to be Lost in — The Klon-
dike all Located — The Government's Gold Map — Traces of Gold
Everywhere — Most of Alaska Unexplored — Some Comparisons
with Early Production in California — Difference in Conditions —
Obstacles to be Overcome — Possibly a Dozen Klondikes — Induce-
ments for Quartz Mining — A Belt of Rich Rock Thousands of
Miles Long — The Quartz Mines of Unga Island — A String of
Islands that May be Rich in Gold — A Test of Klondike Quartz —
Credit for the First Discovery — Cook Inlet and Its Mines — The
Benefit of Waiting a Little Longer — The Copper River Country —
Stories of Rich Diggings — Friendly Indians with Mineral Wealth
—Points of Distribution — Unforeseen Results of Our Purchase of
Alaska — Its Future.

WHILE it may seem that there can be but one
answer to the question as to whether the hopes
of the thousands of people who have gone to the
Yukon valley can be realized, it is certainly impossible for
any man to say what may be the results till the great country
has been more thoroughly explored and prospected. The
general conception of what is required in life in Alaska
or the British Northwest Territory, is quite as inadequate
as the usual idea as to the size of the country, and of the
comparative size of the so-called Klondike district. The

(534)

area of the whole of the Klondike and Indian River districts, upon which any work of importance was done before
the spring of 1898, is not greater than that of the State of
Rhode Island.   But the area of Alaska alone is four hundred and twenty times that of Rhode Island, and the British
Yukon district, in which the Klondike region lies, is at least
two hundred times the size of the State of Rhode Island.
In other words, almost the whole excitement over gold discoveries in the north has centered in a little clump of mountains forming about one six hundred and twenty-fifth part
of the great country whose future has become a matter of
such interest, and upon the development of which results
so largely depend.   It will thus be seen that while there remains little chance for newcomers in the Klondike, it would
be easy for a million people to be so placed in the whole
country that they might feel lonesome.   Those who
stumbled upon the Klondike placers just happened to find
one of the rich pockets under the moss and muck of the
land, and even as a result of nearly two years of excitement
much less of the district has been worked than has been
preëmpted.   Comparatively little ground has been worked
yet.   The claims on the various creeks forming the district have all been located; wherever gold has been found
on the side hills above the creek beds bench claims have
been located, and a few quartz claims have been recorded.
But even so, the Klondike district is a small one compared
with the area of country over which gold has been found.

As a result of the new interest in these gold fields, the
government of the United States has recently prepared a
gold map combining the results of its recent explorations
and the reports of those who have found traces of gold in
various parts of the country.   Wherever such traces have

been found it is indicated by yellow spots, and the most striking thing about it is the extent of the country so dotted. Gold is everywhere, apparently, on all the creeks and rivers, and yet most of the gold that has been taken out has been from a few small creeks and gulches. A large part of Alaska is entirely unexplored, is a real *terra incognita*. The fact that so many have had their attention attracted in its direction constitutes the possibility of startling results.

When we consider that the country in question is five times as large as California, and that gold is found over such a large area, while the placers of California were not large in comparison with the whole State, and, further, that placers of such richness as those of the Yukon have never before been found, it is easy to see that the most astonishing results are possible, when human energy and ingenuity is once centered on the problem of securing the gold.

The gold production of the United States for the first six years of the California discoveries (nearly all of it the result of working the alluvial of that State) is officially given as follows:

1848, . . $10,000,000	1851, . . $55,000,000
1849, . . 40,000,000	1852, . . 60,000,000
1850, . . 50,000,000	1853, . . 65,000,000

From that point it began to decline rapidly, for the placers were exhausted to a large degree. On about a score of mines, which were worked in a crude way during the winter of 1896-7 on two streams in the Klondike, fully five million dollars in gold was produced. The evidence of this fact is that more than that amount was brought down in the summer of 1897 from this region, and there was certainly considerable gold taken out that winter that was not brought down.   While during the succeeding winter more claims were worked, the scarcity of food rendered the labor of many who were in the district inefficient. Nevertheless, the production can hardly be less than twice what it was in California in 1848, and if the people rushing into the country in 1898 accomplish anything like what the Forty-niners did, or what the gold-seekers in 1851 in Australia did, it can not be an exaggeration to say that the gold production of Alaska and the upper Yukon territory may reach a hundred millions annually; and while the rich placers of California were quickly exhausted, those of the North seem inexhaustible.

But the difference in climate and in the conditions as to placer mining between California or Australia and the Yukon must be taken into consideration.   In Australia and California a man with pick, shovel, and pan could, in the days of gulch or creek mining, prospect in all seasons, was nearly always within easy reach of supplies, and could prospect many miles of creek in a few weeks; for there the ground was not frozen and was not covered with muck, and the pay was, in most cases, found along the present streams, something that is not true on the Yukon, where the gold in all creek claims is mined from what is called a pay-channel, or, sometimes, two pay-channels.   The pay-channels do not follow the lines of the present streams at all, though confined by the same walls; and prospectors in endeavoring to locate the pay are in no way guided by the course of the present streams nor assisted by modern erosions, except that in summer they may find evidence that there is a rich pay-channel in the presence of gold in the bed of the stream, washed from such pay-channel; but in order to find the deposit the prospector must wait until the ground is frozen.

But such obstacles will not baffle human ingenuity, and it is safe to say that the discovery on the Klondike is but the beginning of systematic mining on a large scale, for, immense as the riches of the district are, they are merely an object lesson of the opportunities which lie waiting throughout the Yukon basin. Even the crowds who have already gone will hardly make a showing in that vast area. We have yet to hear from creeks like Sulphur, Montana, and Moosehide, which are known to be rich and which were largely discovered and staked by those who first rushed in after the news of the Klondike. It is not extravagant to say that another year may develop a dozen Klondikes, and that the principal scene of operations will be in Alaska, where miners are free from the extortion of royalty and taxes by the Canadian government.

In many respects quartz mining offers greater inducements to those seeking fortunes in Alaska than the working of the frozen placers, but, as yet, little is known of the possibilities in this direction. There is the natural assumption that where such rich deposits are found in the creek beds and on some of the hillsides, gold-bearing rock of great value must exist. It would seem to be a fact that the gold in nuggets found on Bonanza and Eldorado bears no evidence of having traveled any distance — in fact, the majority of the nuggets are as angular and irregular in shape as though just pounded out of the mother lode. This leads to the inference that that mother lode is not very distant from where this gold is now found, and the only debatable question is, is it in lodes of sufficient dimensions to pay for working by stamp mills, or is it a series of widely-disseminated, thin seams that the miners term " stringers," so scattered as to render working them unprofitable? Time alone will reveal this secret.

Gold has been found at the head of Lake Lebarge on a stream flowing into the lake from the east. Prospects, too, are found on the Dalton trail, on the other side of the Yukon River. A man riding across the Alsek on this trail was thrown from his horse, and in clambering ashore caught at a small tree, which pulled out by the roots. Where he landed he saw something shining on the rock. He picked it up and found that it was gold. He showed this gold at Fort Cudahy in July, 1896, the amount being about one dollar and sixty cents. Other prospects have also been found along the same trail, about midway between there and Selkirk.

From these circumstances and discoveries it may be assumed that in all this country there is gold, while in one particular zone it is especially abundant. This zone lies outside of a range of mountains which extends to the westward of the Rockies and has the same general trend. It consists of cretaceous rock, rising into very high peaks in some places, and crosses the Yukon River just below the boundary. The ore-bearing rocks crop out at intervals on the hills, being covered up in between by thousands of feet of sedimentary shales, the peculiar formation being due to a tremendous crumpling up of the whole region in some ancient epoch.

Opposite the mouth of Klondike Creek, and opposite Dawson, a tunnel has been driven into a wide body of ore in the rocks, which is said to assay thirty-six dollars in gold and eighteen dollars in silver to the ton. On the trail from Circle City to Birch Creek is a quartz vein ten feet wide that shows much free gold. On Deadwood Creek, in the neighborhood of Birch Creek, is a wide vein rich in silver.

So far as any tests of importance have been made, there can be little doubt of the existence of a great belt of ore, and some rich specimens have been reported. The Canadian surveyor who made a test of a specimen taken from a claim on Gold Bottom Creek said of it:

" I had no sieve and had to employ a hand mortar, which those who know anything of the work will understand would not give the best results. The poorest result obtained, however, was one hundred dollars to the ton, while the richest was one thousand dollars. Of course, I do not know what the extent of the claim is, but the man who found it said that from the rock exposed the deposit must be considerable in extent."

The credit for the first quartz discovery in the Klondike seems to belong to one W. Oler. On December 15th he found a well-defined ledge of gold-bearing quartz on Hunker Creek, just above Last Chance. It was of pure white, resembling the rose quartz of California, and the ledge averaged seven feet wide on the croppings. Crude assays of the quartz showed free gold, and a half interest in the claim was purchased by Ladue for eight thousand dollars. Oler was regarded as one of the best quartz experts on the Yukon.

Reference has already been made to the large stamp mills on Douglas Island opposite Juneau. Several other mines in that vicinity are being successfully worked by capital. Indeed, it requires capital, for while the ledge of gold-bearing rock stretches for many miles the ore is of low grade. With capital these mines in 1897 produced almost as much gold as the Klondike placers.

Nearly all the mining in western Alaska thus far is at Cook Inlet, Prince William Sound, and Unga Island. At Unga there are a number of quartz mines, one of which, the Apollo Consolidated, has a development of about eight hundred feet, and forty stamps at work. In 1896 it crushed about forty one thousand tons and produced over three hundred thousand dollars' worth of bullion. It is now shipping about thirty thousand dollars a month to San Francisco. The island is but one of that great group which stretches for such a distance into the Pacific, and scarcely any prospecting has been done upon them, though there are many indications that they are nearly all of the same formation. For anything that may be known, all these islands may be rich in gold.

Actual operations have been largely confined to the districts known as Cook's Inlet and Prince William Sound, into which flows the Copper River. The country about Cook Inlet is not developed yet, so that it is impossible to say how rich it may be. So far, while no very rich placer claims have been reported, many are paying well. Mills Creek is reported to be the best. One company located there, working twenty men, averaged one thousand dollars a day for the season of 1897. The season lasts for not more than four months. There were only about forty men wintering at Sunrise City, and thirty at Cook City, and they had provisions for three years, so that they possessed some advantages which were lacking in the Yukon districts.

A man who has been at Sunrise City for two years tells me that the miners have not really commenced on the Cook Inlet district yet. It requires a whole season to fully prospect a claim. Some men work a while without getting anything, and then go away pronouncing the place of no value. But one fellow illustrated the wisdom of staying a little longer. He had five hundred dollars when he arrived at the Inlet, and went to work on Lynx Creek. He took out about one dollar and fifty cents a day to the man, and was drawing on his capital to pay his help at the rate of four dollars a day per man. When his money was nearly all gone the men stopped work and pulled away, saying there was no gold there and that the poor fellow had lost his capital. One day, however, he came to town with a sack of one thousand dollars, which he had taken out in a week, and he took one thousand a week for the remainder of the season.

Only two streams and their tributaries have ever been mined — Six Mile River and Resurrection Creek. The tributaries of the former which are paying are Cañon, Mills, a tributary of Cañon, and Gulch creeks.

Some mining is being done all along the banks of Six Mile River, which is a big stream one hundred and eighty-five feet wide at Sunrise City, with a rapid current. There is gold in its bed, but on account of its size and the current it is not an easy stream to work, so most of the miners keep to the gulches. There are places where Six Mile River might be turned from its course at a small expense, and the exposed bed should furnish rich ground for extensive work. Large companies have organized to develop this district on an extensive scale.

One report states that the best paying property is on Granite Gulch, a tributary of Six Mile, but no one has yet seen bed-rock there. The tributaries of Resurrection Creek which are paying are Bear and Palmer, but the gold on the former is worth only about fourteen dollars and forty cents per ounce, while that on the other is worth about sixteen dollars.

Right across Turnagain Arm is Burt Creek, which was the scene of a rush during the season of 1897. It is not thoroughly prospected, but it is reported that a man took out pans of from eighty cents to one dollar and twenty cents right on the surface.

There is one good thing about the Cook Inlet country — it is a comparatively cheap place in which to live. It costs but about one hundred dollars to build a cabin, and provisions cost very little more than at ports of the United States. Freight rates from Seattle are only about half a cent a pound, which is very different from the rates to the upper Yukon.

On Prince William Sound is what is commonly known as the Copper River country. Some copper ore ledges of great size have been found on Fidalgo Bay and Latouche Island. Some of the ledges are said to be fifty feet wide and to carry copper sulphides assaying from twenty to fifty per cent. of copper, but little gold.

Where there is any placer gold on Copper River remains to be seen. It is a very rough country around the mouth, and the men who have been up the river far are hard to find. Those who have been up a little distance claim that for the first one hundred and twenty miles the gold to be found is too fine to pay for getting out, but that beyond there are placers which will rival the Klondike. This, however, must be partly guesswork, until more prospecting has been done.

From letters received, however, from a party which went on a prospecting trip in the summer of 1897, very rich gold fields are a possibility of the upper river. One

member of the expedition stated that he had discovered
quartz which yielded twenty dollars to the ton, and that
the streak was a very wide one.

In the fall of 1897 there were about two hundred prospectors at Orca and the vicinity of the mouth of the Copper River, awaiting a favorable opportunity to advance
towards the headwaters. One of the men who had been
to a point about fifty miles up the river heard of rich deposits of gold which had been found north of Spirit Mountain, on a tributary of the Chittyna River, about twenty
miles from its confluence with the Copper. It was said
that one of the locators had taken out sixty thousand dollars the season before, and that supplies had been brought
in to the camp by men who had kept the discovery secret.
There were all sorts of stories about these diggings, which,
it was said, would rival those of the Klondike, but time
only will prove the truth of these assertions.

Copper River is not a good place for a tenderfoot.
Forty miles up the river are the rapids. The entrance to
the mouth of the river is very difficult, and can be made
only by those who know the roundabout way of getting
in. Above the rapids the river freezes over towards the
last of October, and the slush and snow make it almost impassable for any but the strongest traveler. By January
the snow is likely to be about twenty feet deep on level
places, and that is the best and most practicable month for
traveling.

People who have made the journey up the river at this
propitious time have reported that the Indians are friendly
and that they have marvelous mineral resources, though
their implements are very crude. Their chief metal is
copper, which they have in abundance, as pure as ever came

from a smelter. They also have gold bracelets and finger ornaments, but when asked where they got this gold they are very reticent and simply point mysteriously towards the northeast.

There are numerous other places in Alaska in which gold has been found, and many more where it is just as likely to be found. The Kuskokwim River is one of the great streams of North America, but probably not half a dozen white men now living have any knowledge of it beyond the Roman Catholic mission at Oknagamut, and certainly no man who has been heard of is qualified to speak with authority of the possibilities of the country it traverses, so far as mining is concerned. All that can truthfully be said is that on two or three of its bars " colors " have been found.

In the coast region above the mouths of the Yukon practically no prospecting has been done save on the shore of Norton Sound, and not much even there. Silver has been discovered on this sound, the ore yielding one hundred and forty-three ounces of the white metal to the ton, and a ten-stamp mill is kept thundering. Gold has recently been found there in the sea-sand. A few years ago Lieutenant Stoney found a few grains of gold on bars of the Burkland and Selawik rivers, and Mr. Miner Bruce, in the summer of 1894, saw in the possession of an Eskimo near Fort Morton an ounce of coarse gold said to have been washed from gravel of the Kowak River. Further than this scarcely anything is known. This district also waits the investigation of prospectors.

I have already spoken of the possibilities of the Tanana and Koyukuk rivers, each having tributaries heading up into the same belt of mountains from the gulches of which gold has been taken. This is the story all over the great country.

So long as the wealth is there it will undoubtedly be secured in time, but it will take a long time unless something is done for transportation. Therein lies the key to the development of such a country. Whoever can successfully solve the problem of cheap transportation and easy communication will not simply do a great thing for the country but will make millions of money. If there is coal in the mountains, and it is asserted that there is, others can become rich in mining and selling that great article of fuel. The sale of merchandise cannot fail to be profitable. Indeed, I have heard of several who, having been in the Klondike regions, have said that, so long as merchandise sold at such high prices on the Yukon, they would be satisfied with the profits upon that business, letting those who sought the gold take their chances. This species of speculation will be of great advantage to the country, for it will, perhaps, insure the workers in various placers the supply of food needed to take them through an Arctic winter.

Another requirement will be suitable points of distribution. For example, Dawson under the present conditions can be used as a distributing point for only a small section — that little section of mining land about the Klondike. If those who are prospecting on the Stewart find another rich region it will be necessary to have another distributing point further up the river. It now takes so long a time to go back and forth to Dawson for provisions that little time is left for work in the creeks.

When these problems have been solved there will be a new era in the world. There will no longer be a complaint of the scarcity of money if gold continues the standard of value and the great means of exchange. The future of Alaska may have a great deal to do with the future of society in general.

When Russia sold that great country to the United States for less than half a cent an acre, it was little dreamed that in a year or two a single industry would pay the bill; there was little thought that the salmon industry would pay it again; no one but a most extravagant dreamer would have dared to declare that in a quarter of a century it might be one of the richest mineral fields in the world. When W. H. Seward, Secretary of State, negotiated the purchase it was almost universally decried by the politicians and other wise people considered it a bad deal. Most Americans thought they were getting what Russia did not want, and were paying a big price for it. The purchase was opprobriously termed "Seward's Folly," "America's Polar Bear Reserve," and "The New National Refrigerator." But now Great Britain is ready to dispute every inch of that small section of the boundary line about which there can be any dispute. Seward and Sumner, who supported the purchase, were doubtless even wiser than they knew, but it shows that the foresight and sagacity of some men may be vindicated long after they are dead

CHAPTER XL

ADVICE TO GOLD-SEEKERS — THE IMPORTANCE OF HAV-
ING A GOOD OUTFIT — POINTS TO BE REMEMBERED
— WHAT TO DO AND WHAT NOT TO DO.

Some Advantages in Not Being in a Hurry — Not a Poor Man's Country
— Good Advice from a United States Government Expert — A
Place for Strong Men and Those Who Can Afford to Lose —
Expenses Which Have to Be Met — The Cost of Cabins and Facili-
ties for Working Mines — One Thousand Dollars for Sluice Boxes
— The Advantage of Having Partners — Unwise to Take Less
Than a Year's Outfit — Suicide Cheaper in Lower Latitudes — It
Takes a Week to Dig a Grave — Times When Every Man Looks
the Picture of Distress — Sail North Only in Good Vessels — How
to Mark Packages — Trunks an Inconvenience — Sugar and Salt as
Hard as Quartz — Tobacco as Good as Money on the Yukon — As
to Furs — Shot Guns Better Than Revolvers — Jack Dalton's Rules
for the Trail — Possibilities of Losing a Toe or a Foot.

NOTWITHSTANDING the richness of Alaska and
the belief that a great future lies before it, no better advice, it seems to me, can be offered any one
in search of a fortune than to stay away from Alaska,
and especially the upper Yukon, for the present. There
will be time enough to secure some of the gold in the
country when better and safer means of communication
and ways of living are provided. That may not be long
hence. Already steps have been taken to greatly miti-
gate the difficulties of the passes, but these passes are
only the beginning of difficulties. At present, a trip to

Alaska with the intention of staying there a year or more is a great risk for any man, and for the poor man who knows nothing about placer mining, and has a family depending upon him, it would be almost criminal to put a large amount of money into an Arctic outfit and make the attempt. Such a man would have about as good a chance to make a fortune by staking all that his outfit cost him on the gambling table at once.

Alaska placers, I have no doubt, offer better opportunities than most other gold-fields. But only prospectors and capitalists who can lose without being badly damaged should go there until more is known. I cordially indorse the advice given by Mr. Samuel C. Dunham, the expert sent into the Yukon country to report for the United States Department of Labor. He said, in Dawson, after studying the Klondike: " The poor man should not be encouraged to come here. No man should think of coming who cannot bring with him at least a ton of food and at least one thousand dollars in cash, and who cannot lose a year of his labor, his ton of food, and his thousand of cash without wrecking his family or imperiling his life scheme. Neither should the weak man be encouraged to come here. Only the strong, healthy man, capable of enduring the utmost hardship and the severest toil, is adapted to this region. For the prospector who is strong, and who has the degree of independence I have suggested, this land affords excellent opportunities; and for capital I know of no place that holds out better chances."

In a previous chapter I have said that no one could afford to go to Alaska or to the Klondike and mine a year for less than three thousand dollars. Yet some seem to think that an outfit costing something like four hundred dollars is about all that is necessary.   Possibly, a little more specific information as to some of the essential expenses of mining would enable intending gold-seekers to advise themselves.   We will assume that a man has gone to the Klondike successfully on about five hundred dollars, that is, that he has taken in a year's outfit without losing it, and has paid the necessary charges in getting it there by any of the routes.   We will assume also that he has located a claim in some district which promises to be paying and that he has paid the charges incident thereto, charges the nature of which have been already explained.   This is assuming that he has made a pretty successful beginning, though he knows nothing as yet about the richness of his claim.   He has simply arrived at the point where he must endeavor to find out how much he can make out of his spot of frozen earth.

The first essential is to built a cabin on his claim.   The cost of a rude hut about ten by fourteen feet will be about six hundred dollars, and this is assuming that he will not go to the extravagance of using sawed lumber.   Having his hut ready and his outfit cached, at the beginning of winter he can set about working his claim.   This requires both labor and wood.   If he reaches bed-rock on one hundred dollars' worth of wood he will be doing well.   If he finds the pay-streak the first time he is doing very well.   If he hires labor to remove the dirt that is thawed out it will cost him about ten dollars a foot for each shaft he sinks.

The cost of handling dirt from shaft-sinking to clean-up (labor bills), winter working, averages twelve dollars a cubic yard.   In other words, by the time he is ready to think about sluicing he has spent on his outfit and his cabin, and for fuel and labor, not less than two thousand five hundred dollars.   Seventy-two sets of longitudinal riffles per claim are used during the summer season, as claims are at present worked in the district, and these cost on an average five dollars a set. The cost of sluice-boxes, riffles not included, averages twenty-five dollars a box. The cost of setting a line of sluice-boxes and keeping the line set through a summer averages two thousand dollars.

The cost of building a rough dam sufficient for the ordinary working of the average five-hundred-foot claim in the Klondike division is about one thousand dollars. The cost of constructing a waste-ditch on claim No. 30, Eldorado Creek, was about one thousand two hundred dollars. It is an average ditch.

The cost of handling the dirt (labor bills), summer working, from the ground-sluicing to the clean-up, averages five dollars a cubic yard on the entire quantity removed. The cost of pumping for drainage of a summer pit four hundred feet long by thirty feet wide, averages seventy-two dollars for twenty-four hours.

Wheelbarrows cost twenty-five dollars apiece, whether bought or made; shovels, three dollars and fifty cents apiece; mattocks, five dollars apiece; blacksmith's portable forges, about two hundred dollars apiece; sluice-forks, six dollars apiece; axes, four dollars and fifty cents apiece; hand-saws, five dollars and fifty cents apiece; nails, forty cents a pound; gold-scales of average capacity, fifty dollars a pair; quick-silver, one dollar and twenty-five cents a pound; black powder, one dollar and twenty-five cents a pound. These prices are for the supplies delivered on the claims. Some of these articles may have been taken in with the original outfit.

These are the main items of expense to be incurred by one who wishes to become the owner of a claim, who works it himself with hired help, and who has taken into the country all he wants to eat. In no other way can he expect to make a fortune unless in pure speculation. He could not become rich by working at days' wages, though his expenses would be less.

If the dirt turns out to be rich he will be all right. If it does not he will wish he had never heard of Alaska. In any case, the dirt must be of exceptional richness to pay him for such an outlay of money. It cost Clarence Berry about twenty-two thousand dollars to take one hundred and thirty thousand dollars out of some of the richest dirt that was ever discovered.

With the knowledge of these facts a man who is intending to go to the Klondike to become rich can advise himself, for he can understand what it means when I say that a person who knows nothing about mining, and has little money, would have as good a chance of making a fortune by putting it at once upon a gambling table.

Still, the gold is there, and millions will be made, and it is probably useless to advise against seeking to become one of the millionaires. The most important advice to be impressed upon those who are going to the Klondike or other points on the Yukon is have a good partner and a year's outfit. Partners are a necessity in Alaskan travel, but parties larger than three or four do not get along well together, and usually split up. A two-years outfit is safer and better than less. It is constructive suicide for one to go to the Klondike with less than one year's supply of food. If the men who are starting out so gaily from comfortable homes could only look ahead and see what fate awaits every one of them in the way of hardships and privations amid those frozen mountains and unspeakably depressing gorges and cañons, they would not leave a thing undone to insure some greater degree of comfort and to protect their lives. Suicide comes cheaper in low latitudes than in the frigid North, and funerals cost less.   Consider that it takes a week to dig a grave at Dawson, and crape sells for twenty-two dollars a yard.

If they could stand where I did not long ago, on the summit of Chilkoot Pass, and look below, down through the bald and frozen gorge, upon the camp fires of several hundred haggard, gold-hungry men on their way to Dawson, they would have some idea of what going to seek a fortune in mining in the Arctic Circle means.   Used as I am to the severities and grim hardships of life, that scene at Chilkoot Pass was very impressive.   I saw companies of men wearily working their way, in the face of a gale that seemed strong enough to topple over the very mountain peaks, up the rocky, tortuous trail to the top of the pass. Every man looked a picture of distress.   I know that I did. They all slept in snowbanks, ate frozen canned food, and risked a thousand mortal ailments from exposure.

Another point to be strongly impressed upon those starting out is that they should sail northward only in a first-class ship.   Some of the best vessels have had narrow escapes from shipwreck, and others have been lost.   The demand for sailing vessels has called into the service many on which it is unsafe to risk life.   There are chances enough for a sudden death after Alaska is reached without incurring any more than are necessary before disembarking.

All packages should be marked clearly with distinctive characters which can be easily and readily recognized in addition to the name and address.   This will be found very serviceable when a ship's entire cargo is dumped on either the Skagway or Dyea beach without any thought of the owners; and when it is essential to have them picked out and placed farther up on the beach in a short time.

Take no trunks. They are about as difficult to get over the passes as six-story buildings. The Indians will not touch them, and they are apt to make a sled unmanageable. No package of more than a hundred pounds should be allowed, and the more that can be packed in bags the better. Flour should be put in fifty-pound sacks and two of these slipped into a strong bag. Oil-skin sacks are a good thing in rainy weather and in shooting the rapids, but in cold weather they often become brittle and break. It will be difficult, if not impossible, to reach the Yukon without having some of the goods damaged or spoiled. Flour will get wet, and the best of it will, very likely, have to be dug out from a surrounding layer of dough. Sugar is even more difficult to handle successfully in wet weather. If a part of it gets damp the whole will have a tendency to turn to syrup, unless the weather is freezing, when it will become as hard as quartz. Salt is likely to be affected in much the same way.

Supplies which can be obtained in compressed form, such as tea, are best to take, for the less bulk the better. I have found canned goods always serviceable, though one gets very tired of them. Bacon and beans can be easily managed, and generally constitute a staple article of diet. If you use tobacco, take along plenty of it. It is as good as money on the Yukon, better than paper money. The Indians will take no money but coin.

As to clothing, the principal difference between Alaska and a milder clime is that the former requires much heavier underclothing. Too heavy outer garments only impede the movements of the limbs and really do not keep out the wind. Fur coats might seem valuable, and some will say that they are. They are most usually worn when people are having their pictures taken to send home to their friends. A good fur blanket or robe is, however, well-nigh indispensable. People in Alaska, as everywhere else, have different tastes, and in these matters you will know better how to suit your own after spending a winter there.

Take needles, thread, buttons, comb, brush, looking-glass, and such other toilet and domestic articles as you need; also a ball of twine, sail-needles, and wax. Make a canvas-case with pockets to hold these things — one that can be rolled up and tied. Take also fishing-tackle and shot-guns. It is a great mistake to take anything except what is absolutely necessary if the trip is made overland. The journey is long and arduous, and a man should not add one pound of baggage to his outfit that can be dispensed with. Men have loaded themselves up with rifles and revolvers, which is entirely unnecessary. Revolvers will get you into trouble, and there is no use of taking them with you, as large game is rarely found on the trip. Persons who have prospected through this region for some years have seen few moose. You will not now see any large game whatever on your trip from Dyea to Dawson. Shot-guns are handy for geese.

When on the trail there are a hundred little essentials which can be neglected only to the greatest discomfort and possible peril. Jack Dalton, who is one of the most expert and experienced of men in following Alaskan trails, once laid down the following set of rules for a small party, and they contain many useful suggestions tersely expressed:

"Establish camp rules, especially regarding the food. Allot rations, those while idle to be less than when at work, and also *pro rata* during heat and cold. Pitch the tent on top of the snow, pushing the poles and pegs down into it. While some are busily engaged in building a fire and making a bed, let the best cook of the party prepare the supper. If you have no stove, build a camp fire, either on an exposed point of rock or in a hole dug in the snow; if you have a stove, arrange it on a " gridiron " inside the tent, the gridiron consisting of three poles some six or eight feet long, and laid on the snow, on which the stove is placed. The heat from the stove will soon melt a hole underneath, but there will be enough firm snow under the ends of the poles to hold it up. For the bed, cut hemlock brush and lay it on the snow to a depth of a foot or more, and cover this with a large square of canvas on which blankets and robes are put. When finished it forms a natural spring bed, which will offer grateful rest after hauling a sled all day. In all except the most sheltered locations the tent is necessary for comfort, and the stove gives better satisfaction than the camp-fire, and, as it needs but little wood, is easier to cook over, and does not poison the eyes with smoke.

" There are fewer cases of snow-blindness among those who use stoves than among those who crowd around a smoking camp-fire for cooking or warmth. Comfort in making a trip of this kind will depend, in a great measure, upon the convenience of camping, suitable clothing and light, warm bedding. Choose your bunk as far from the tent door as possible, and keep a fire hole open near your camp. If by any chance you are traveling across a plain (no trail) and a fog comes up, or a blinding snowstorm, either of which will prevent your taking your bearings, camp, and don't move for any one until all is clear again.

" If it is ever necessary to cache a load of provisions

put all articles next to the ground which will be most affected by heat, providing, at the same time, that dampness
will not affect their food properties to any great extent.
After piling your stuff, load it over carefully with heavy
rocks. Take your compass bearings and also note in your
pocketbook some landmarks near by, and also the direction
in which they lie from your cache — *i. e.*, make your cache,
if possible, come between exactly north and south of two
given prominent marks, so that you can find it.

"Keep your furs in good repair. One little slit may
cause you untold agony during a march in a heavy storm.
You cannot tell when such will be the case. If your furs
get wet, dry them in a medium temperature. Don't hold
them near a fire. Keep your sleeping bag clean. If it
becomes inhabited, freeze the inhabitants out. Keep all
your draw-strings on clothing in good repair. Don't forget
to use your goggles when the sun is bright on snow. A fellow is often tempted to leave them off. Don't you do it.
A little dry grass or hay in the inside of your mittens, next
your hands, will promote great heat, especially when it gets
damp from the moisture of your hands. After the mittens
are removed from the hands, remove the hay and dry it.
Failing that, throw it away. Be sure, during the winter, to
watch your footgear carefully. Change wet stockings before they freeze or you may lose a toe or foot."

Remember that if intending to build a boat for travel
down the Yukon the start should be early enough to reach
the lower lakes when the ice goes out. Usually the lakes
remains frozen until late in May. The Lewis and the upper Yukon open a week to a fortnight earlier. Last year
the ice broke on Lake Lebarge in the last of May, at Dawson on the 17th of May, at Fort Yukon three days after-

wards, three hundred miles further down on the 23d of May, and at the mouth somewhat later. The first steamer for the season reached Dawson on June 2d, having voyaged from winter quarters below Circle City.

Do not beguile yourself with the thought that working down the river in open water is at all easy. The Yukon has as many moods as a woman, and presents problems which few men are capable of solving in a hurry, and some which have to be solved in a hurry or it may be too late.

Finally, I would advise the man on his way to the Klondike to go to some creek on the American side of that region — that is, unless he has special reasons for going to the Klondike to seek golden placers. I mean that if he intends merely to go as a tenderfoot to prospect for gold, he will now stand about as good a chance of finding riches on the American side of the line as on the Canadian, and he will not only avoid the impost duties of Canada, but he will save the rather expensive legal procedure of locating claims under the Canadian mining laws. Besides, most of us who have been in the Klondike region think the richest finds of gold in the near future will be principally on the American side. Several hundred men in Dawson and Circle City who have vainly sought gold in the Klondike for months have begun vigorous prospecting on the American side. Some of them are crack prospectors, and that is why we need not be surprised to hear of rich finds in our own Alaska before long.

THE END.

INDEX

D

gardening, 189–190, 194–195,
228, 399
Gastineau Channel, 63
geology, 213–214, 259–260, 266
Glacier Creek, 52, 147
glaciers, 62, 67, 73, 82–83, 130,
202, 213, 255, 518
gold
associated with glaciers, 213
coarse gold, 50, 200, 289–290,
410–412
dust, 202
use as currency, 163, 300
nuggets, 200, 289–290, 324,
395, 410
promotional display of, 521,
525–526
valuation of, 181, 503–504
See also mining
Gold Bottom, 241–243, 268, 271,
409
productivity of claims, 243, 410,
540
gold commissioner. See Canada
Gold Creek, 64
gold fever, 203–204, 247–248,
255, 296, 364, 367, 400,
499
Klondike stampede, 520–533
government. See Canada; United
States
Granite Gulch, 542
graves, 64, 115, 139, 493–494
See also death and injury
grouse, 107, 253
grub-staking, 42, 271
See also mining
Guiger, Captain, 426
Gulch Creek, 542

H

Hamilton (steamboat), 498–499
Hammer Creek, 148
Hanson, Capt., 480–481 483
hardship, 68, 104, 156, 259, 330,
333–334, 396, 421, 431,
434, 439–440, 444–445,
471, 488, 493, 501–503,
509, 528, 548–558
See also trail life
hardware. See provisions
Harper, Arthur, 49–51, 139, 195
Harris, Richard, 64
Harrisburg, 64
Harris Mining District, 64
Hart, Mr., 49
health and disease, 98, 309–310,
329, 355–356, 367, 395
doctors, 524
medical supplies, 56–57
See also death and injury
Henderson, Alice, 324
Henderson, Robert, 241–242, 268,
271–272
Hewitt, William, 523
Hidden Treasure mine, 270
Hilton, Jennie, 525
Holt, George, 48
Hoochecoo Bluff, 138
Hoosier Creek, 501
Hootalinkwa River, 48, 135
horses, 71, 345
difficulties with, 348–349,
453–454, 460, 463–467
disappearance of, 364–365
horse-shoeing and hostling, 449
tormented by mosquitoes, 157,
229

K

Kamschatka (Kamchatka), 238
Kanselar, Mr., 49
kayaks, 234
Kelly, Michael, 438
Kinkuk (steamboat), 487
Klondike, 266, 268, 352–353, 535
    early discoveries, 240–251,
        271–272, 284, 540
    population, 479
    productivity of claims, 243–244,
        285–289, 328–330, 531–
        533, 539–540
Klondike Creek, 51–52, 148, 243,
    539
"Klondicitis," 521
    See also gold fever; miners'
        stampede
Kobuk River. *See* Kowak River
Kowak River, 545
Koyukuk River, 50, 223, 545
Kuskokwin River, 545
Kutlik, 231, 237

L

Ladue, Joseph, 48–49, 268–272,
    356, 540
Lake Bennett, 97–98, 341,
    349–350, 389–390, 443
Lake Creek, 428
Lake Lebarge, 132–133, 350, 510,
    513, 539, 557
Lake Lindeman, 92–97, 341, 349,
    443
Lake Marsh. *See* Marsh Lake
Lama Passage, 62
Lamb, Charles M., 340
land sales, 275, 499–500
    Circle City, 175

    Dawson, 275, 356–358, 396–
        397
    Skagway, 448
    See also log cabins
Last Chance creek, 409–410, 540
Latouche Island, 543
law
    Canadian mining law, 274–275
    miners' justice, 154
    miners' law, 173–175, 213–214
    miners' meetings, 150–154, 174
    mounted police enforcement of,
        432–433, 437, 442–443
    Skagway Vigilance Committee,
        450
    vigilante justice, 472–473
    See also Canada
Lebarge, Mike, 133
letters, 295–296, 408, 444–445
    See also mails
Lewis River, 48, 135, 137–139,
    509, 557
Lippy, Mrs., 393
Lippy, Prof., 287, 359
Little Munook Creek, 498–499
Little Salmon River, 137
Lobdell, James II, 269
log cabins, 93, 145, 162
    construction of, 149, 175–181,
        275, 352, 368, 396–397
    construction over mining claim,
        296–297
    cost of, 149, 176, 181, 357, 369,
        403, 500, 550
    See also tents
logging, 145, 161–162, 176, 180
    for boat building, 101–102
    with dogs, 166
    See also sawmill operations
Long Lake, 92
Lower Ramparts, 219, 497

timber, 76–79, 87, 93, 93–94, 145,
194, 221, 227, 500
See also firewood; logging;
sawmill
Tlingit Indians, 115
tobacco, 554
cigars, 357, 374, 375–376
Tombstone, 378, 381
totem poles, 64
toys, 303–304
trading posts, 141
Anvik, 227
Dawson, 315
Fort Reliance, 50
Fort Selkirk, 139
Forty Mile Creek, 51
Fort Yukon, 218
role in fur trade, 46
Yukon–Tanana Rivers, 221
See also Alaska Commercial
Company; provisions
trail conditions, 102, 194, 196,
500–501
Birch Creek, 200
Chilkoot Pass, 65–66, 72–73,
76, 79, 85–90, 100, 341–
351
Klondike, 250, 252–258,
263–264, 266, 286, 395
with scanty provisions, 487–495
White Pass, 459–475
trail life
dangers of, 47, 140, 308,
414–418, 503
society on, 73–74, 98, 127, 134
See also camp life; hardship
trails
Alaska definition, 76
haste of prospectors upon, 71,

74, 100, 266, 471, 474–475,
510
transportation needs, 196, 214,
238, 239, 393, 408, 546
for great stampede to Klondike,
520–521
Treadwell mine, 44, 64–65
trees. *See* logging; timber
Troan-Dik (Thron-Diuck) Creek,
147–148, 281. *See also*
Klondike
Trump, Fred, 426
Tucker, H. B., 501
tundra, 232
"niggerhead swamps," 192–194,
257
typhoid, 367
See also health and disease

U

Unalakleet. *See* Unalaklik
Unalaklik, 224–226
Unga Island, 541
United States
authority of in Skagway, 455,
458
immorality in, compared to the
Yukon, 378–381
Pacific Coast routes to Alaska,
58–62
preference of miners for, 497,
558
reference to by miners,
299–300, 330
response in to Klondike strikes,
408, 443, 519–533
See also Canada
Upper Ramparts, 145

V

Vancouver Island, 62, 387
Vermont, 33–35, 255
Victoria, 62
Victoria Creek, 424
Virginia City, 378, 381

W

wages
  of Alaska and U.S., compared,
    183–184
  at Circle City, 175, 181, 183,
    196
  of bartenders, 374
  dance hall girls, 377
  of gamblers, 372
  of Indians, 68–71, 218, 221,
    266, 403, 443, 474, 500
  of log cabin builders, 175, 181,
    183, 275, 352
  of musicians, 165, 376
  in Skagway, 449
  stateside mining work, 270
  for work on claims, 190, 199,
    214, 282, 285, 322,
    331–332, 442, 488, 500
water supplies, 202–203, 210–211,
  232, 253–254, 296, 298,
  356–358, 458
weather
  effect on camp life, 82–84
  effect on travel, 72–73, 89–90,
    102
  extremes of, 305–312
  thunderstorm, 161–162
  See also summer; winter
Western Union Telegraph, 133
Whipple Creek, 267

whip-sawing, 101–105, 321
  See also logging; sawmill
whiskers, 312
White, Jim, 277–278
White Horse Rapids, 125–126,
  128–130, 513
White Pass, 65, 447
  early crossings, 48
  impassibility of, 459–474
  See also Skagway
White River, 142, 145–146
  native copper deposits, 49
wildflowers, 232, 354–355
  See also natural beauty
Williams, Henry, 335–336
Williams, Tom, 51
Wills, Mrs., 185–189, 399–403
Wilson, J. M., 285
winter
  darkness and sunlight in, 134,
    307–308
  mining conditions in, 206–209,
    215, 239, 272, 283,
    292–296, 305–307, 368,
    550–551
  relief from mosquitoes in, 157
  trail conditions in, 72, 89,
    224–225, 308–310, 348,
    468, 544
  See also weather
Wiseman, Jacob, 523
women
  at Chilkoot Pass, 74–75, 80–81,
    88–89
  clothing requirements for, 56,
    75, 347, 396, 405–406
  dance hall girls, 68, 75, 89, 150,
    164, 371
  disguised as men, 336
  and domestic duties, 296–297,
    392–406